SOUTH COUNTY

D0289604

RAGNAROK

Volume 1:
Eve of Apocalypse

By
Myung-Jin Lee

English Version
by
Richard Knaak

Los Angeles • Tokyo

Translator – Lauren Na
Graphic Designer – Anna Kernbaum
Editor – Jake Forbes

Production Manager – Joaquin E Reyes
Art Director – Matt Alford
VP of Production – Ron Klamert
Publisher – Stuart Levy

Email: editor@TOKYOPOP.com
Come visit us online at www.TOKYOPOP.com

A 🐟 TOKYOPOP® Book

TOKYOPOP® is an imprint of Mixx Entertainment, Inc.
5900 Wilshire Blvd., Ste. 2000, Los Angeles, CA 90036

ISBN: 1931514-73-9

First TOKYOPOP® Printing: May 2002

10 9 8 7 6
Manufactured in the USA.

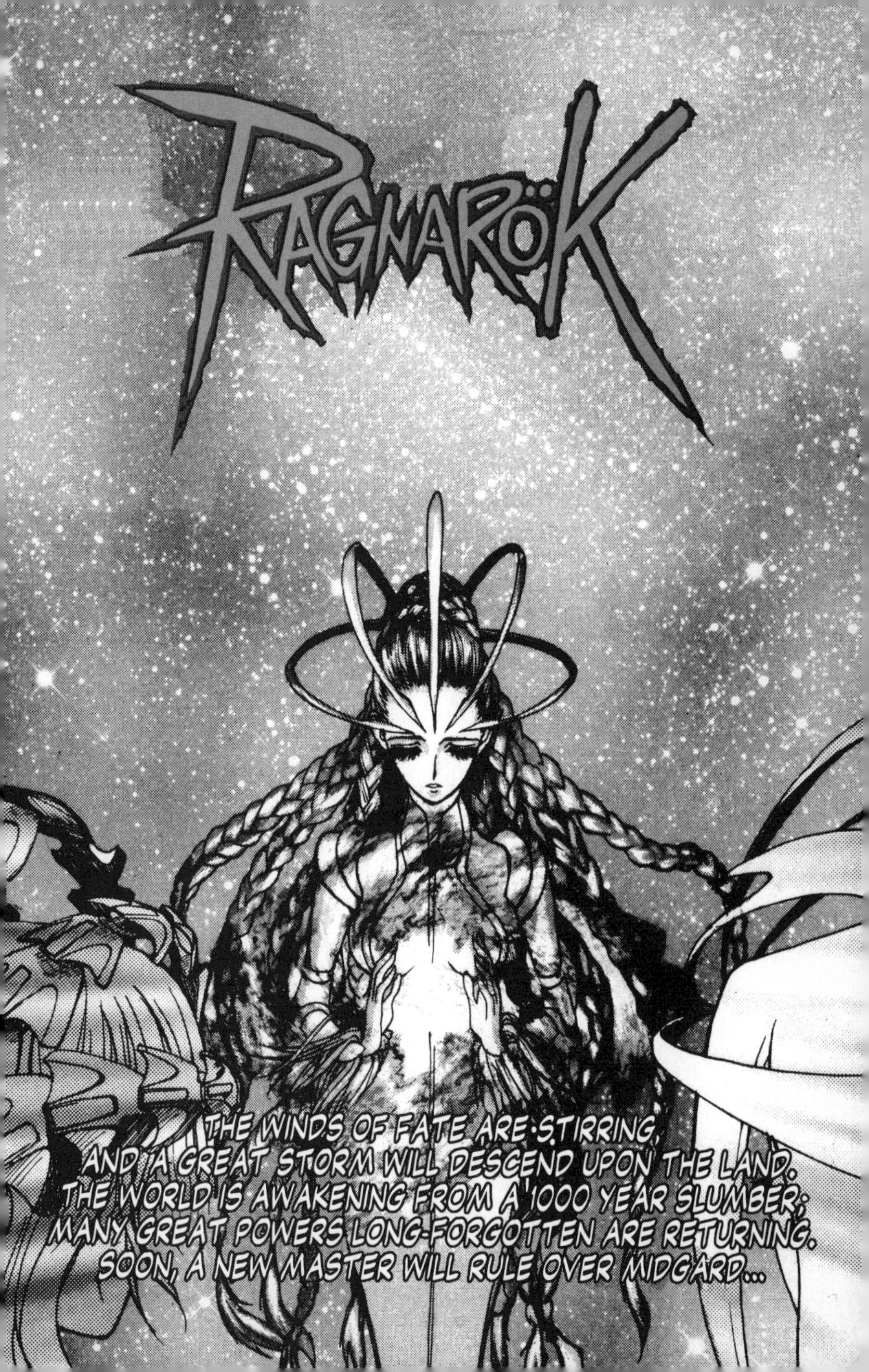
RAGNARÖK
THE WINDS OF FATE ARE STIRRING,
AND A GREAT STORM WILL DESCEND UPON THE LAND.
THE WORLD IS AWAKENING FROM A 1000 YEAR SLUMBER;
MANY GREAT POWERS LONG-FORGOTTEN ARE RETURNING.
SOON, A NEW MASTER WILL RULE OVER MIDGARD...

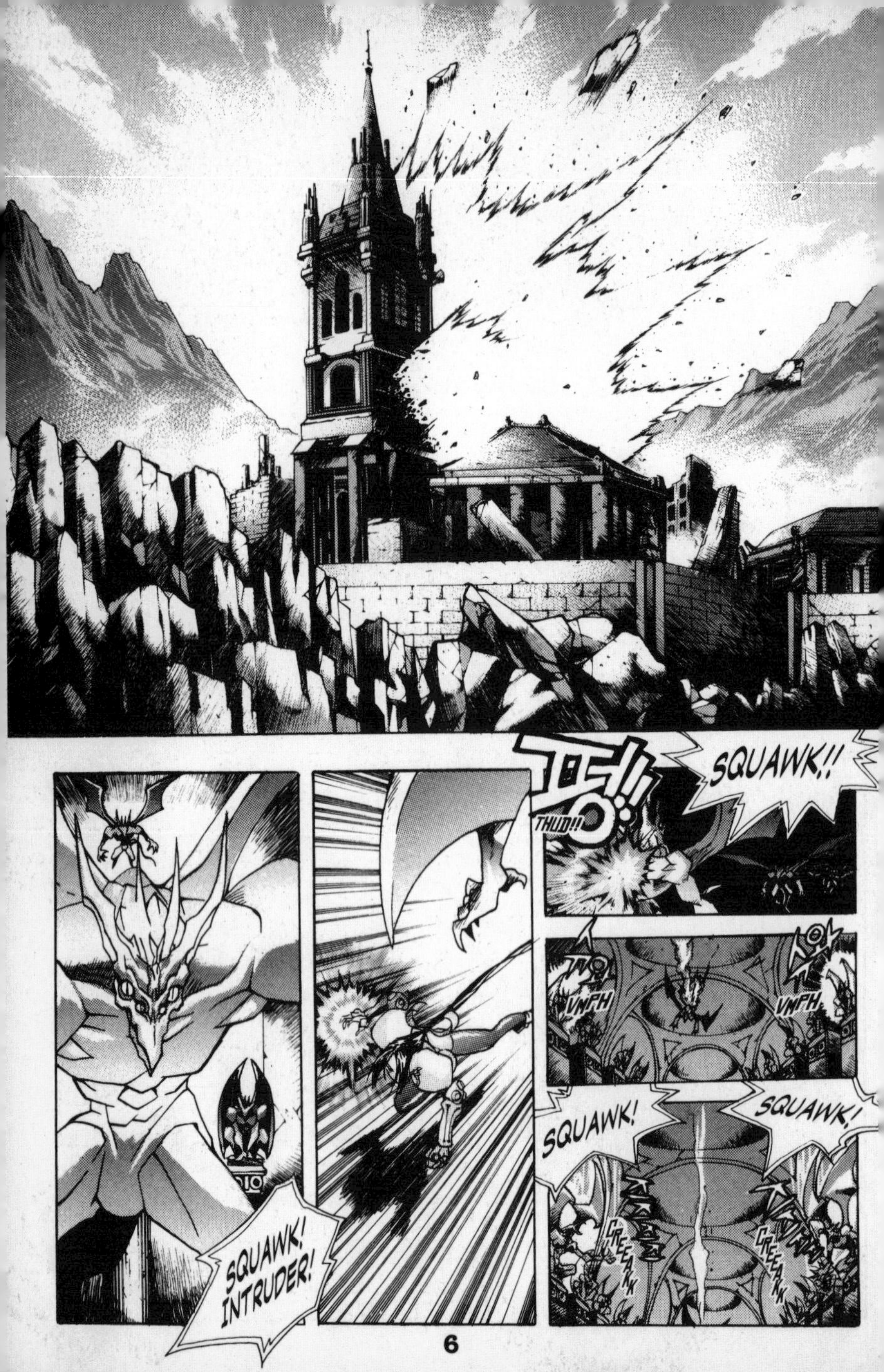
SQUAWK!
INTRUDER!
THUD!!
SQUAWK!!
VNPH
VNPH
SQUAWK!
SQUAWK!
CREEAKK
CREEAKK

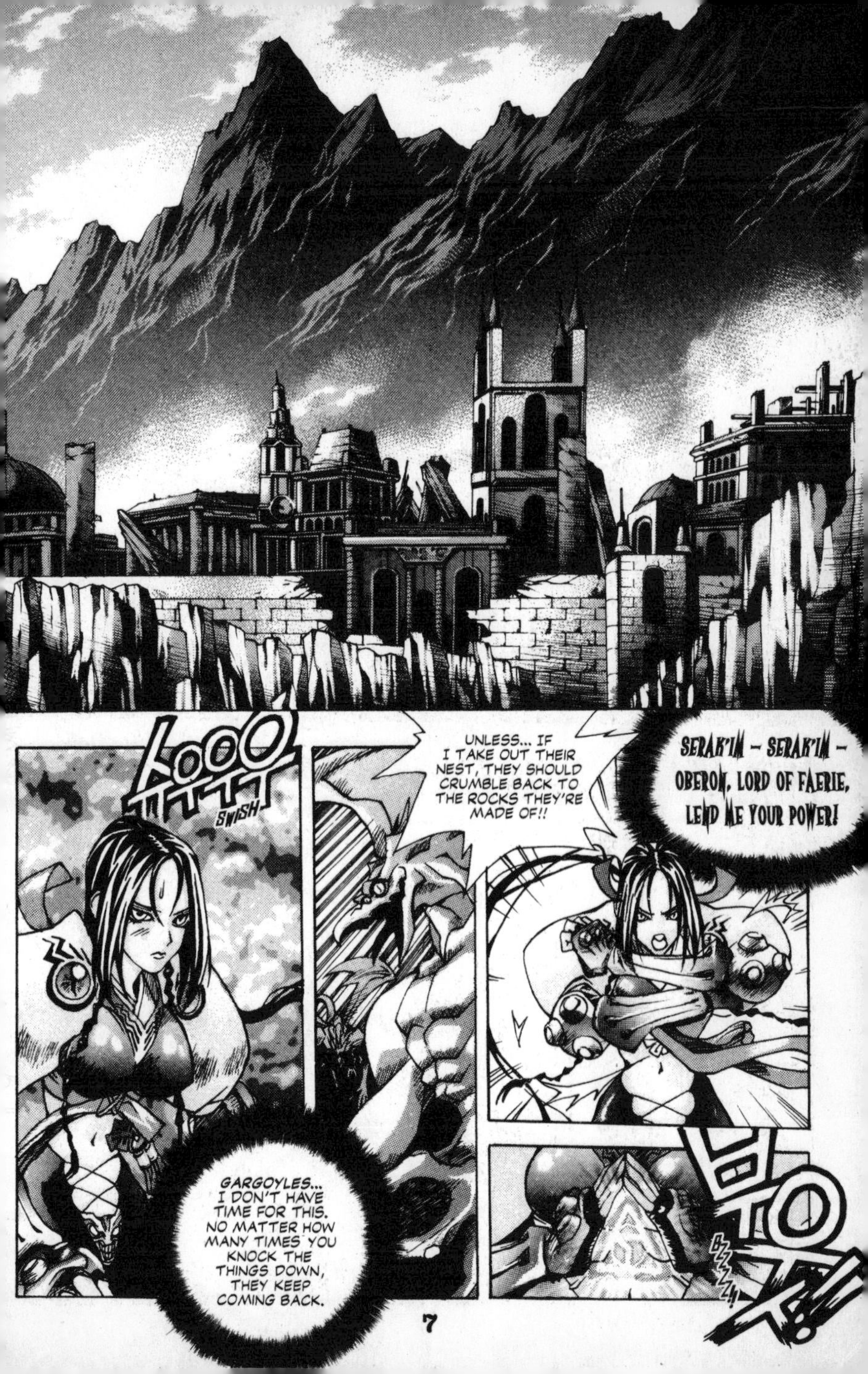
SWISH
GARGOYLES... I DON'T HAVE TIME FOR THIS. NO MATTER HOW MANY TIMES YOU KNOCK THE THINGS DOWN, THEY KEEP COMING BACK.
UNLESS... IF I TAKE OUT THEIR NEST, THEY SHOULD CRUMBLE BACK TO THE ROCKS THEY'RE MADE OF!!
SERAK'IM – SERAK'IM – OBERON, LORD OF FAERIE, LEND ME YOUR POWER!

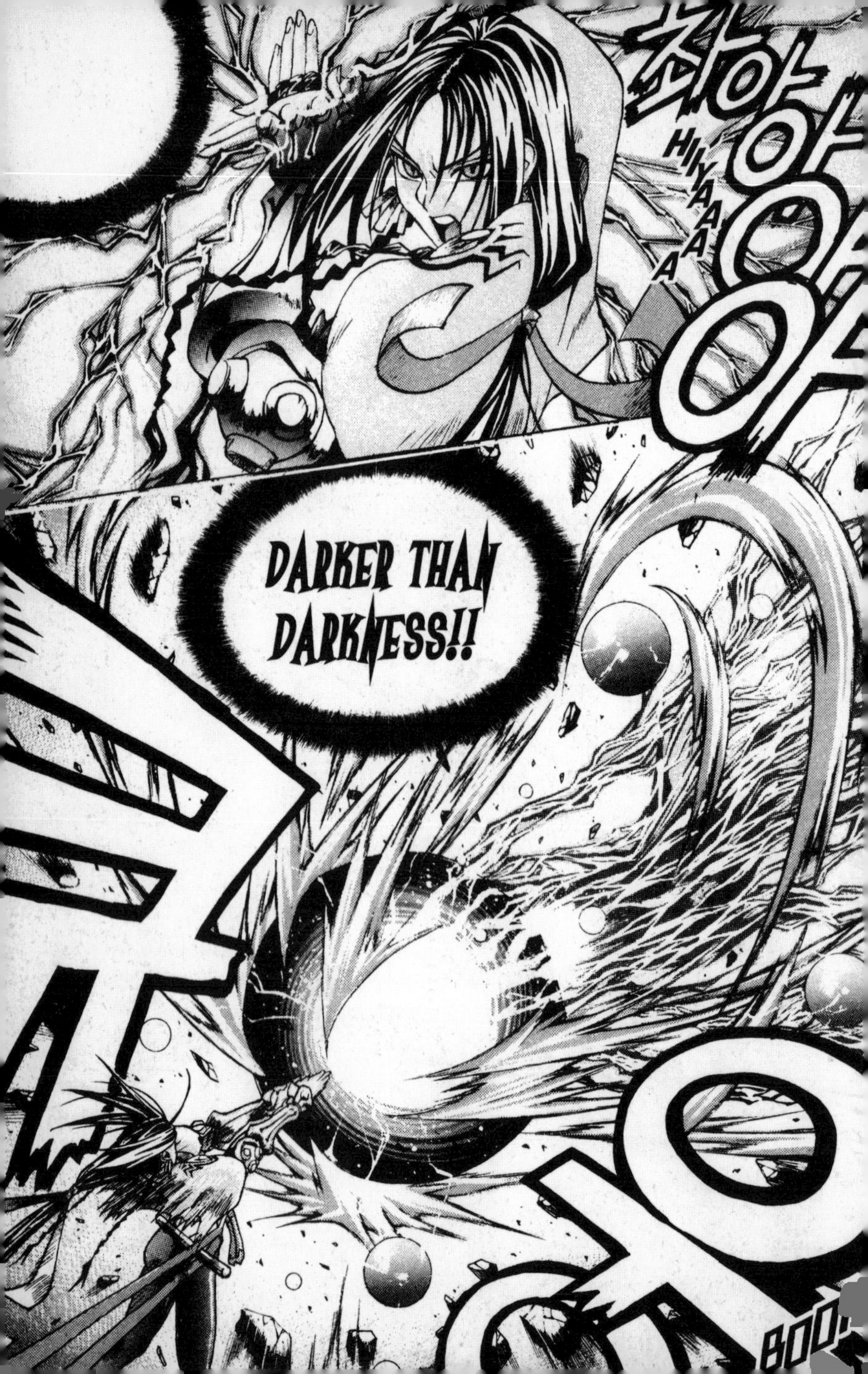
HIYAAAA
DARKER THAN DARKNESS!!
BOO

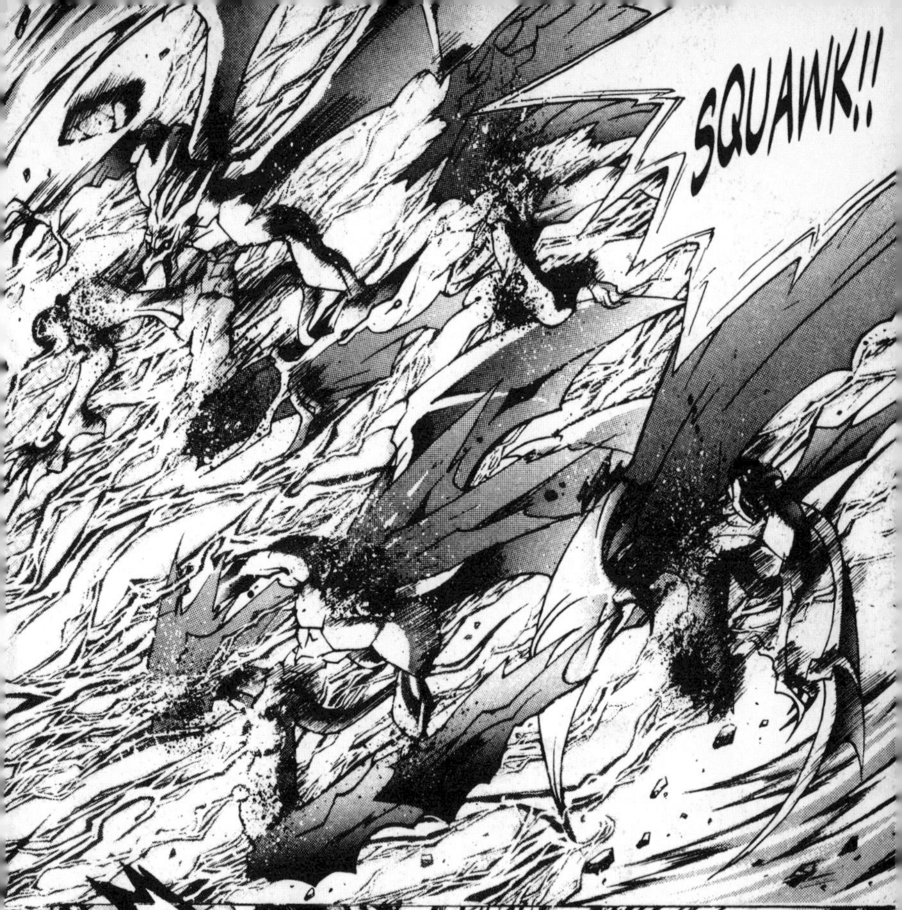
SQUAWK!!
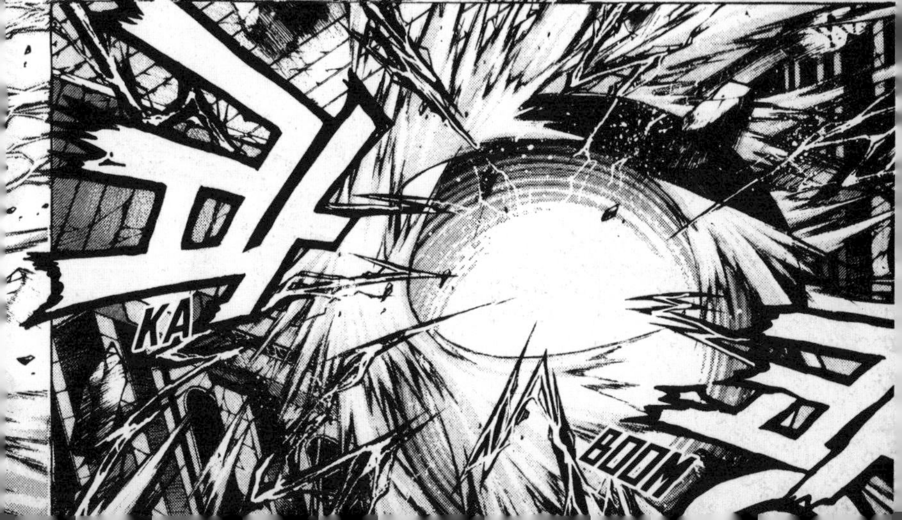
KA
BOOM

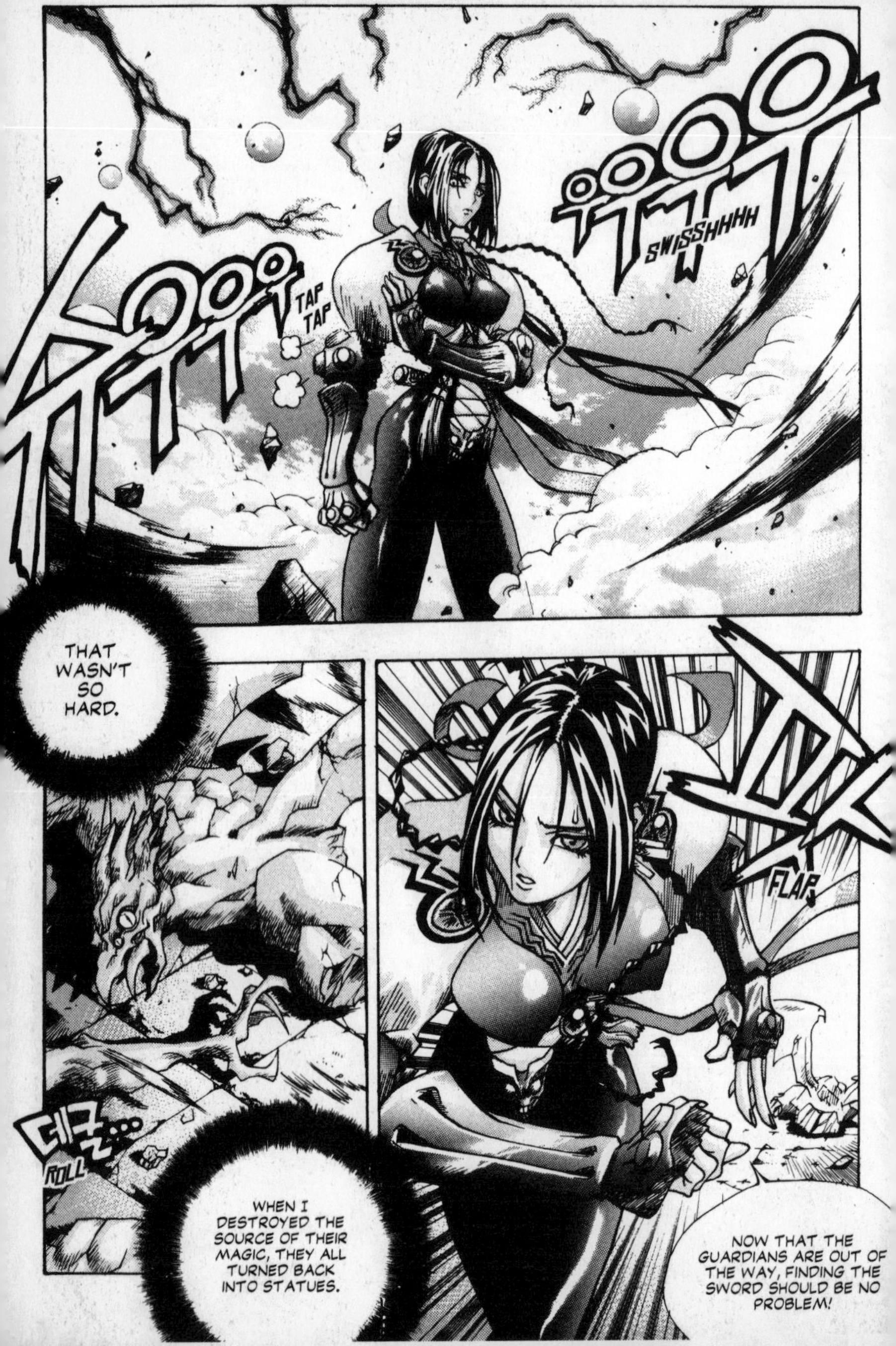

TAP TAP
SWISSHHHH W
THAT WASN'T SO HARD.
데구르...
ROLL
WHEN I DESTROYED THE SOURCE OF THEIR MAGIC, THEY ALL TURNED BACK INTO STATUES.
FLAP
NOW THAT THE GUARDIANS ARE OUT OF THE WAY, FINDING THE SWORD SHOULD BE NO PROBLEM!

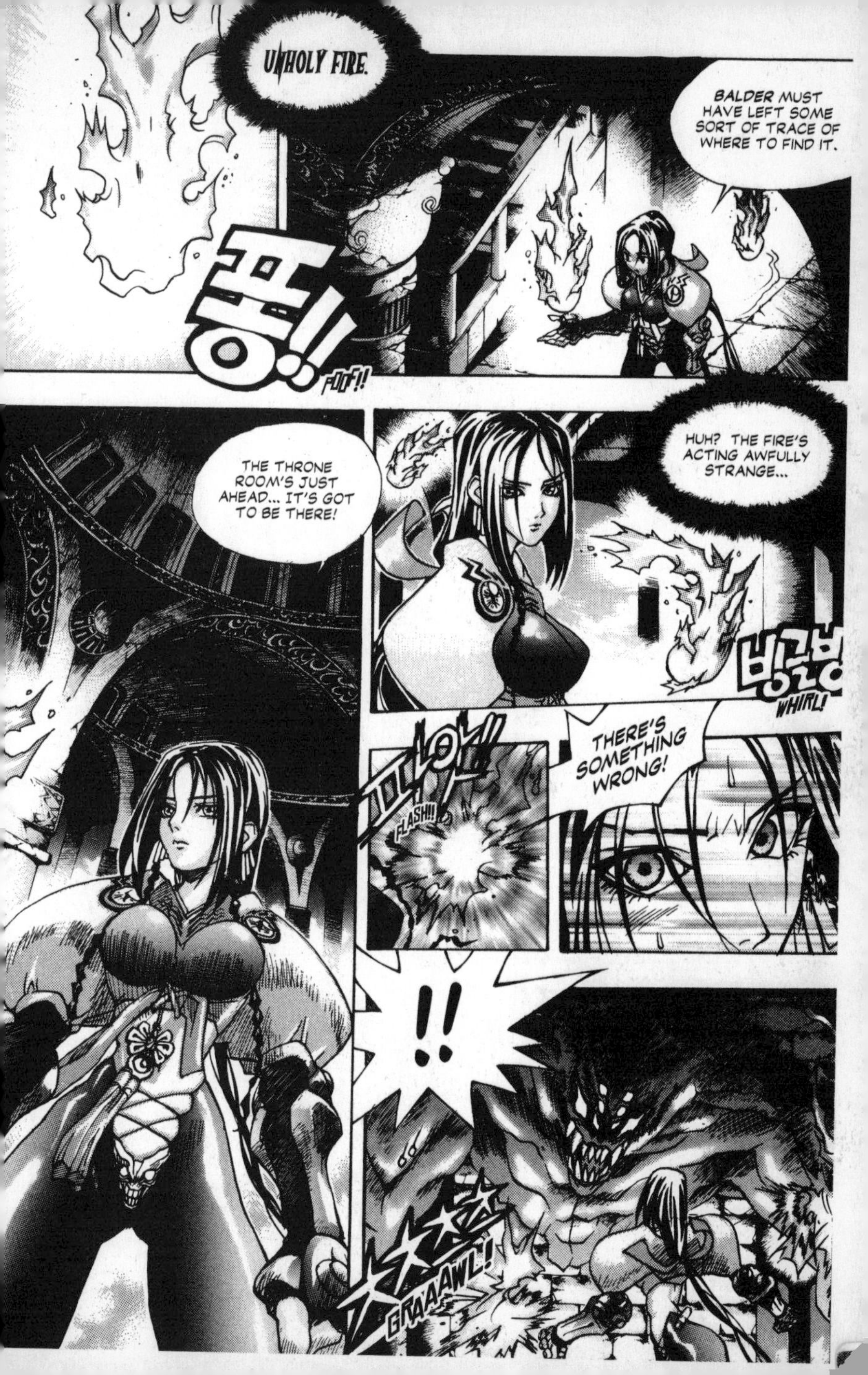
UNHOLY FIRE.
POOF!!
BALDER MUST HAVE LEFT SOME SORT OF TRACE OF WHERE TO FIND IT.
THE THRONE ROOM'S JUST AHEAD... IT'S GOT TO BE THERE!
HUH? THE FIRE'S ACTING AWFULLY STRANGE...
WHIRL!
FLASH!!
THERE'S SOMETHING WRONG!
!!
GRAAAWL!

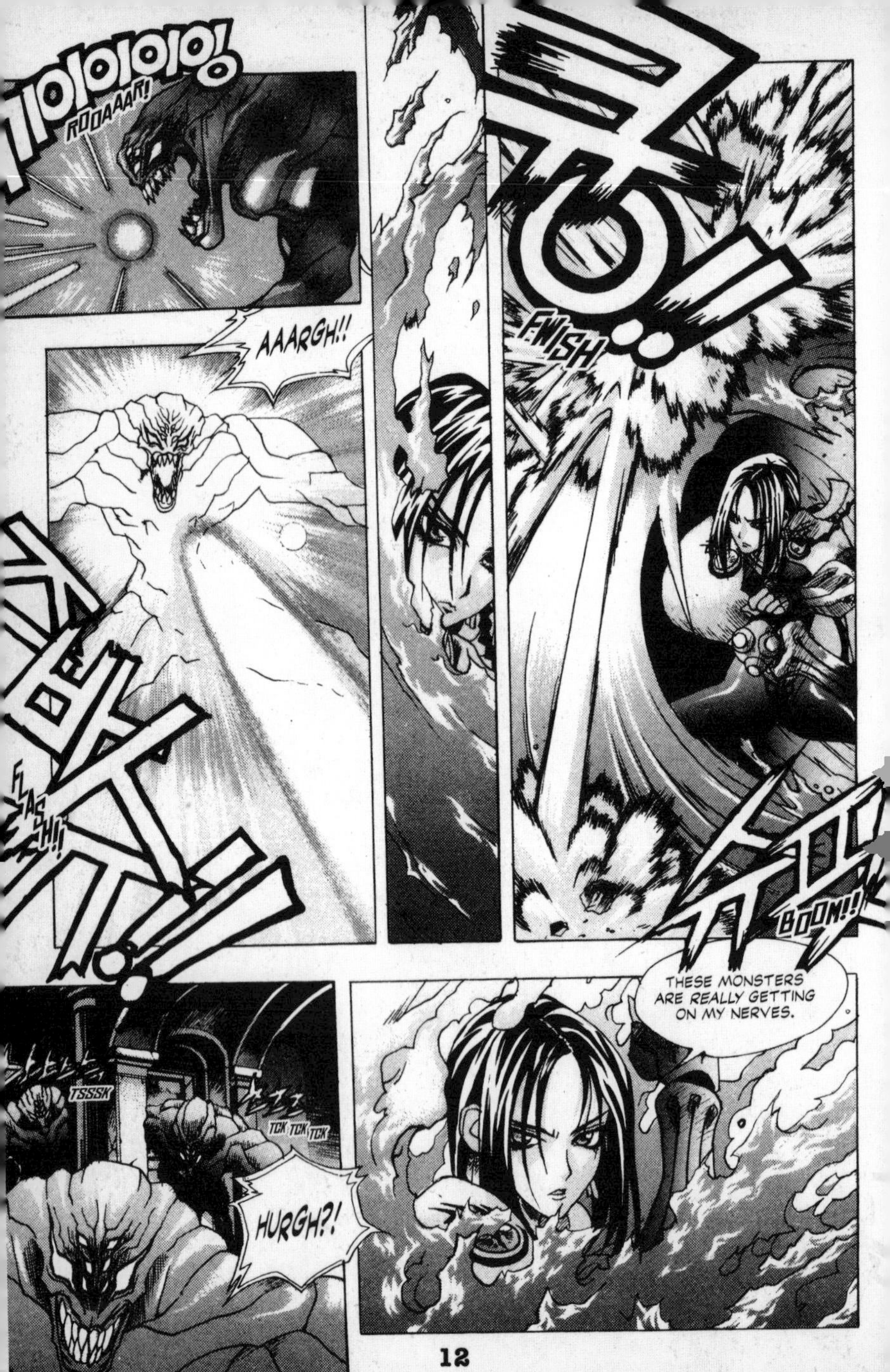

RODAAAR!
AAARGH!!
FLASH!!
FWISH
BOOM!!
TSSSK
TCK TCK TCK
HURGH?!
THESE MONSTERS ARE REALLY GETTING ON MY NERVES.

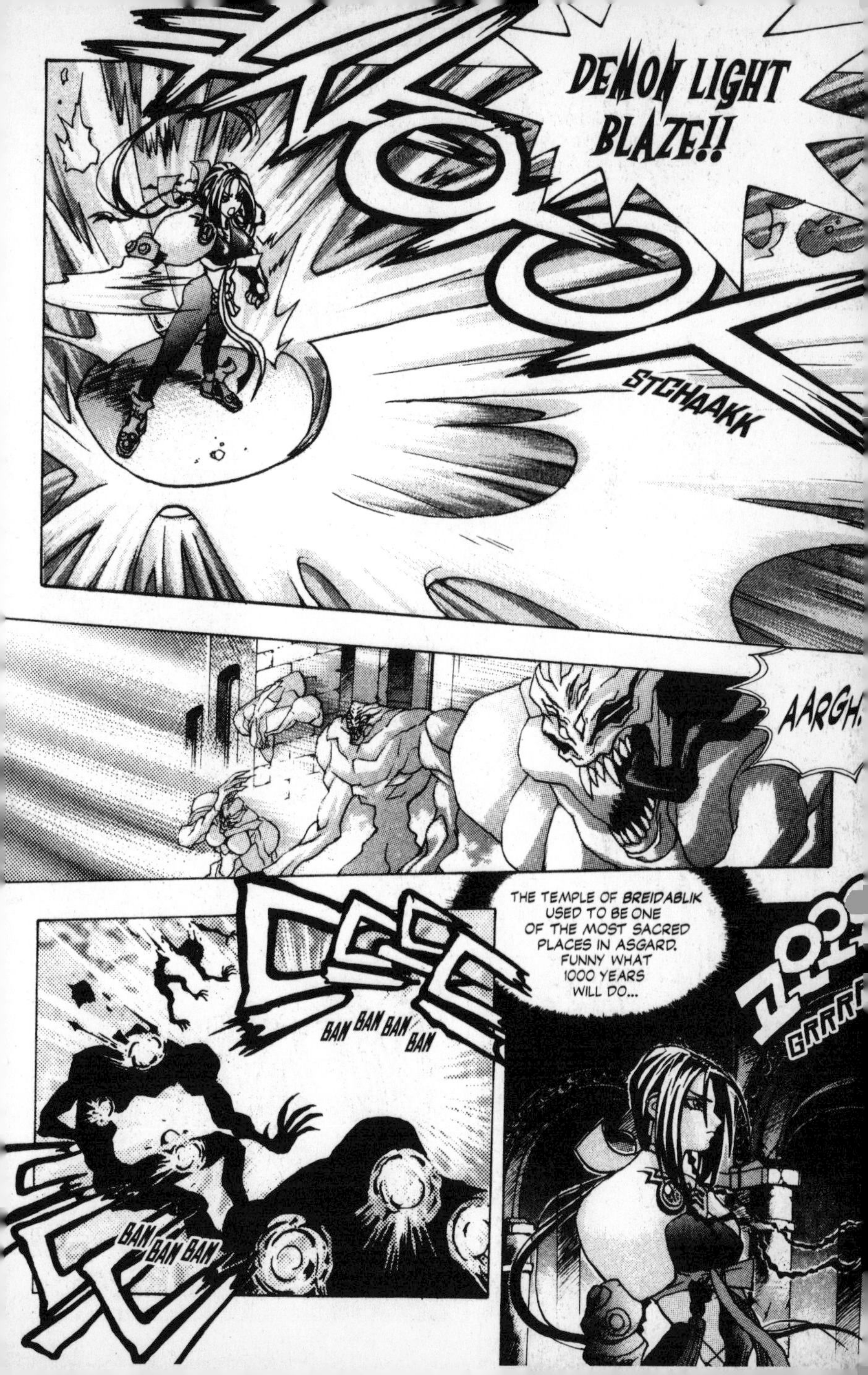
DEMON LIGHT BLAZE!!
STCHAAKK
AARGH.
BAN BAN BAN BAN
BAN BAN BAN
THE TEMPLE OF BREIDABLIK USED TO BE ONE OF THE MOST SACRED PLACES IN ASGARD. FUNNY WHAT 1000 YEARS WILL DO...

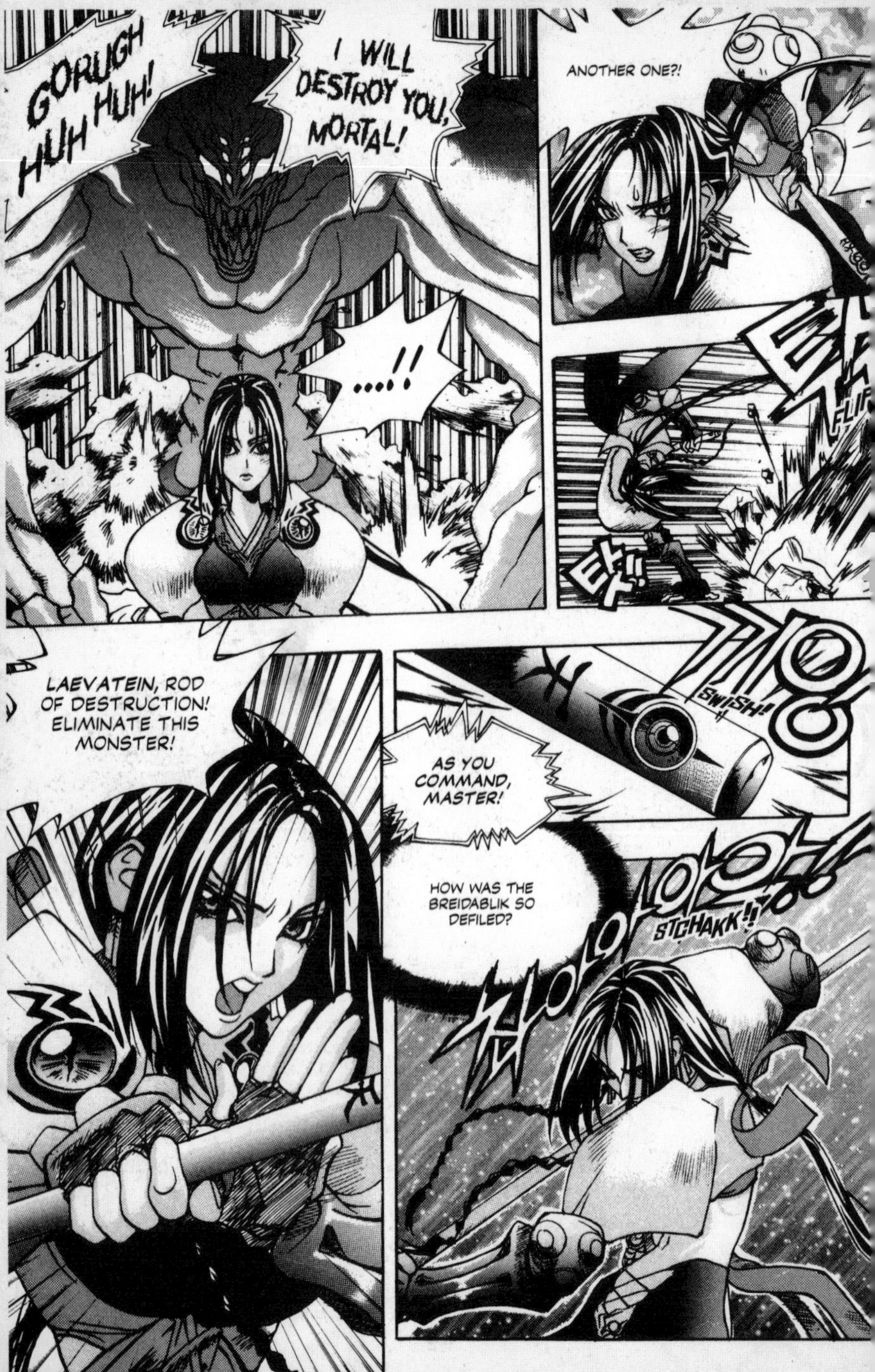
GORUGH HUH HUH!
I WILL DESTROY YOU, MORTAL!
....!!
ANOTHER ONE?!
탁!!
LAEVATEIN, ROD OF DESTRUCTION! ELIMINATE THIS MONSTER!
SWISH!
AS YOU COMMAND, MASTER!
HOW WAS THE BREIDABLIK SO DEFILED?
STCHAKK!!

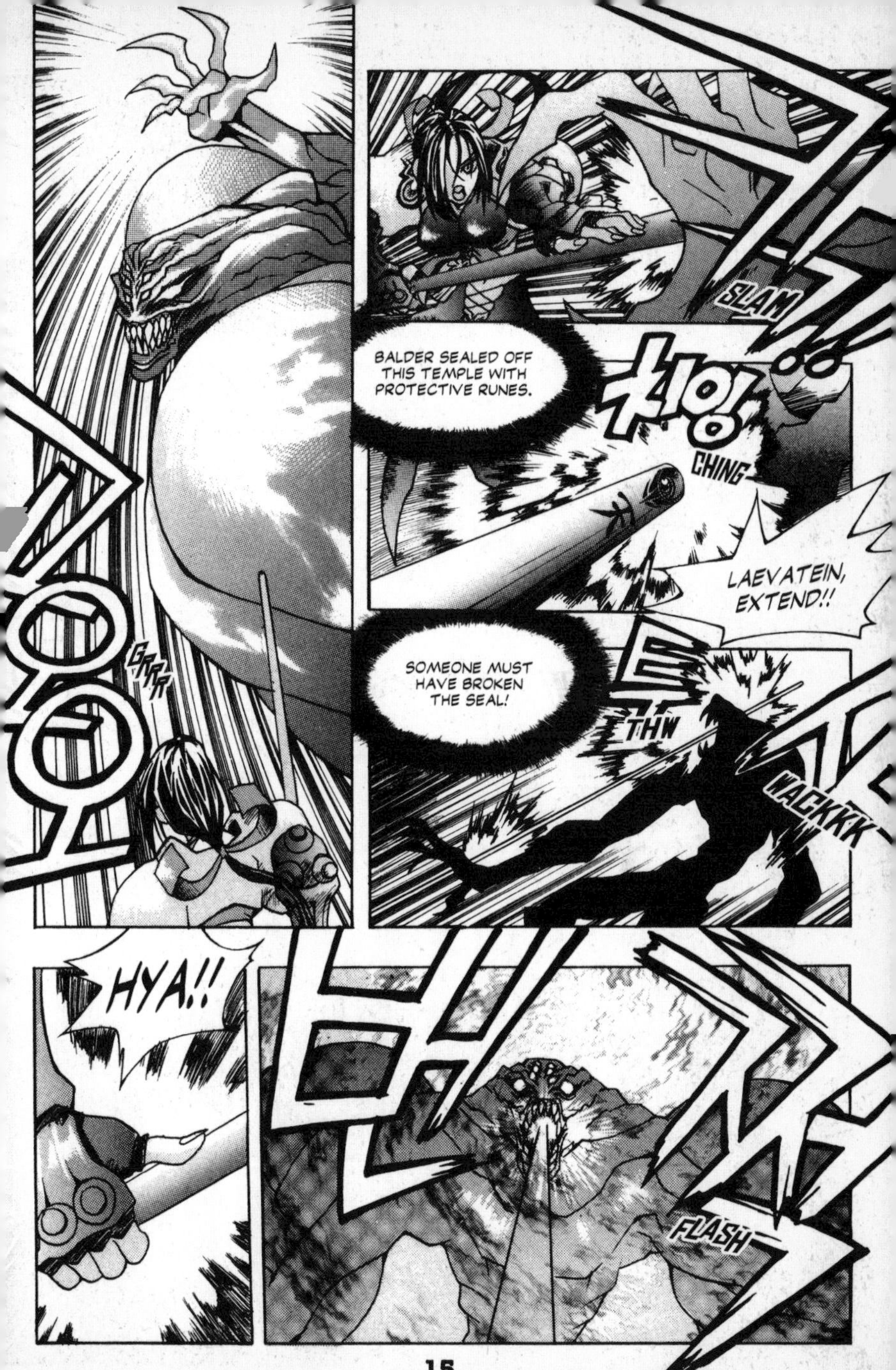
GRRR
SLAM
BALDER SEALED OFF THIS TEMPLE WITH PROTECTIVE RUNES.
CHING
LAEVATEIN, EXTEND!!
SOMEONE MUST HAVE BROKEN THE SEAL!
THW
WACKKK
HYA!!
FLASH

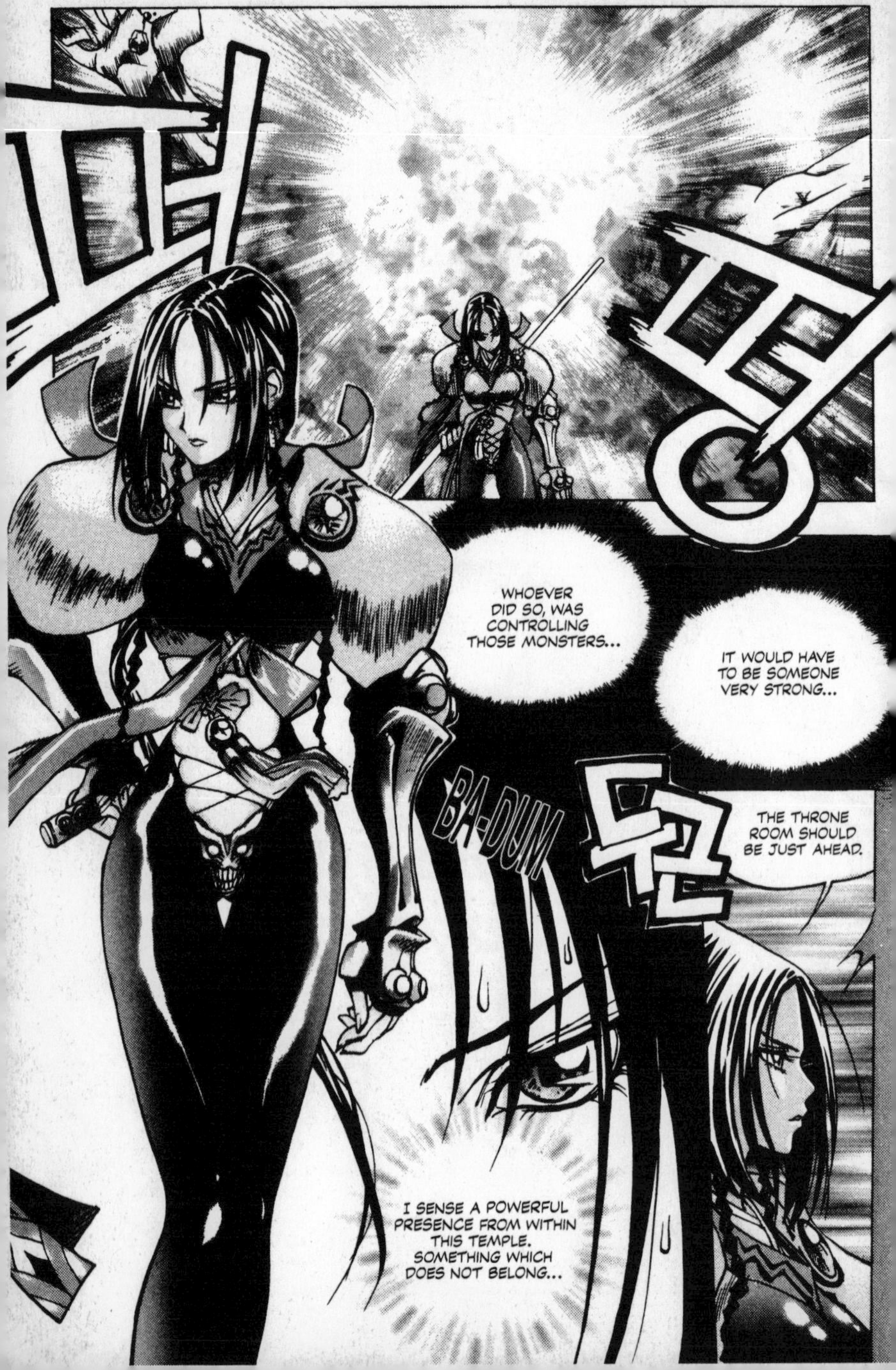
WHOEVER DID SO, WAS CONTROLLING THOSE MONSTERS...
IT WOULD HAVE TO BE SOMEONE VERY STRONG...
BA-DUM
THE THRONE ROOM SHOULD BE JUST AHEAD.
I SENSE A POWERFUL PRESENCE FROM WITHIN THIS TEMPLE. SOMETHING WHICH DOES NOT BELONG...

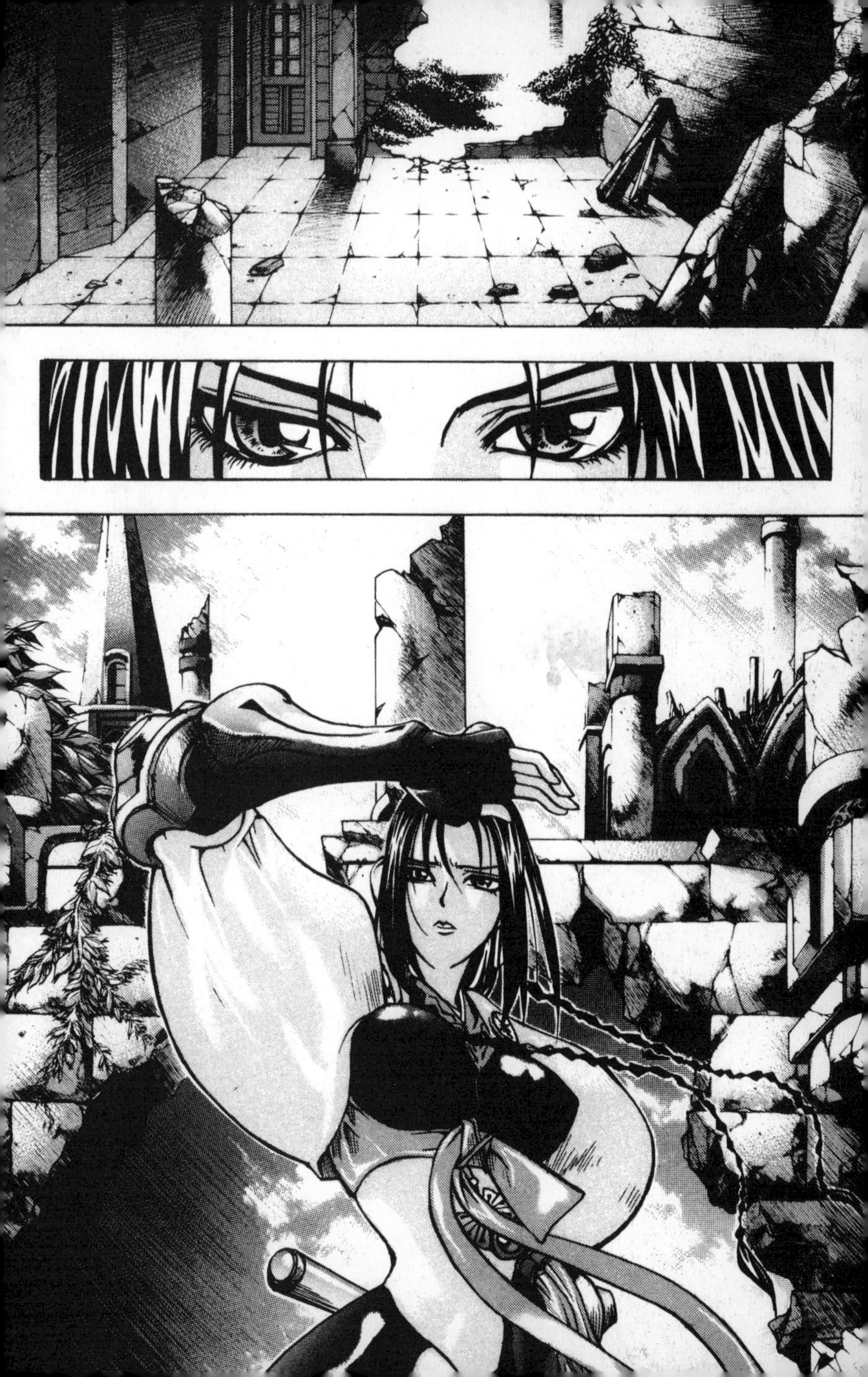

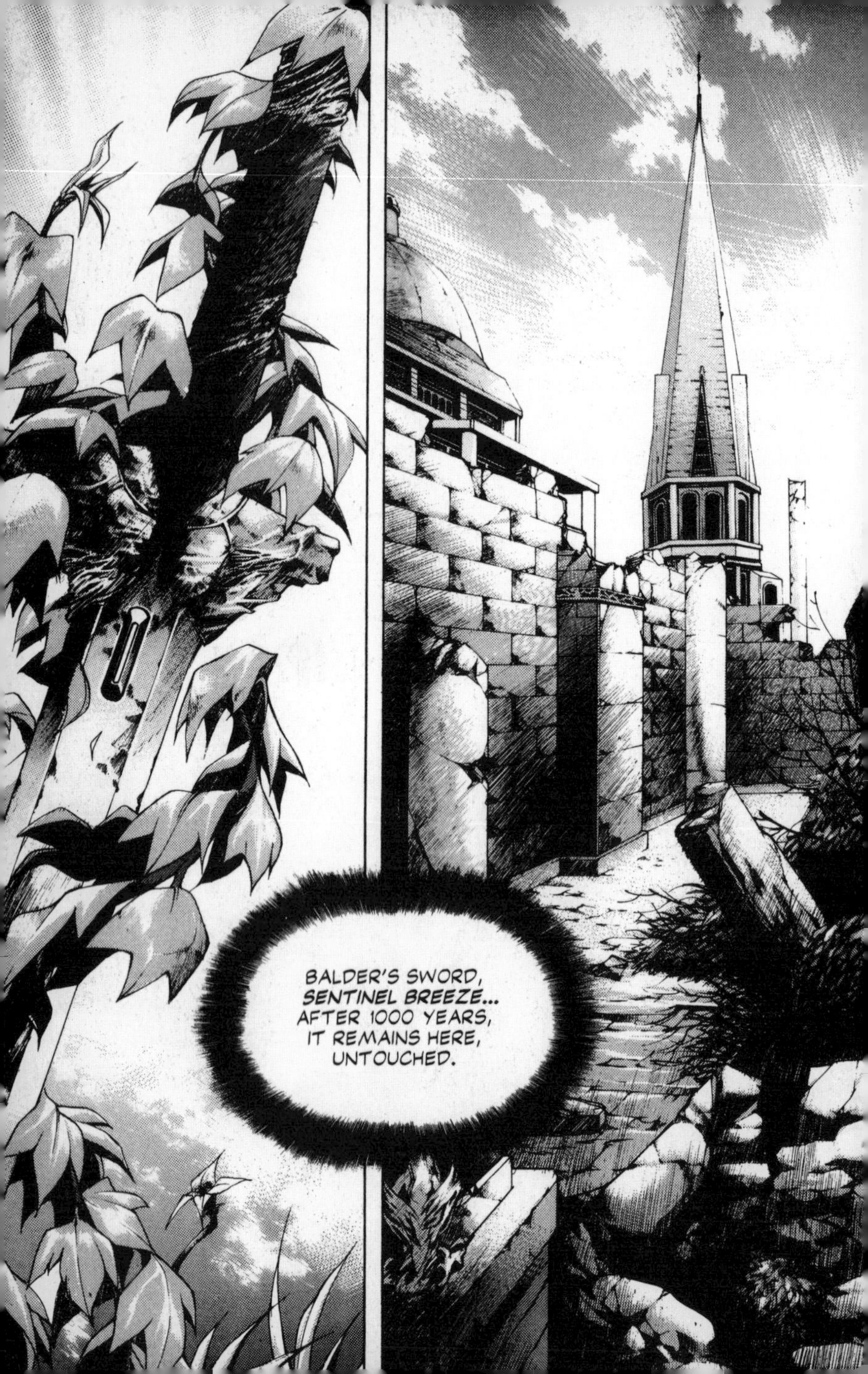
BALDER'S SWORD, SENTINEL BREEZE... AFTER 1000 YEARS, IT REMAINS HERE, UNTOUCHED.

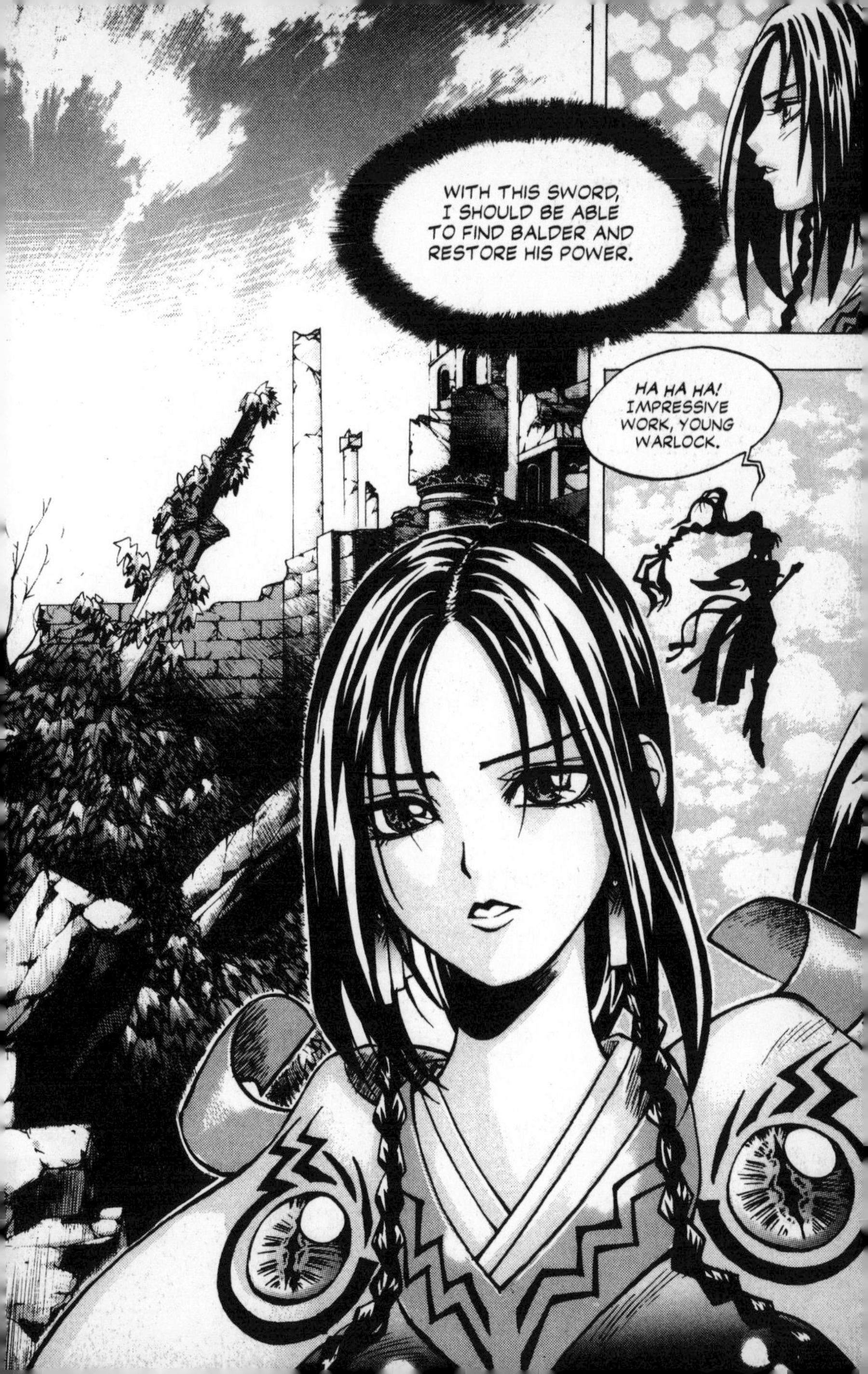
WITH THIS SWORD, I SHOULD BE ABLE TO FIND BALDER AND RESTORE HIS POWER.
HA HA HA! IMPRESSIVE WORK, YOUNG WARLOCK.

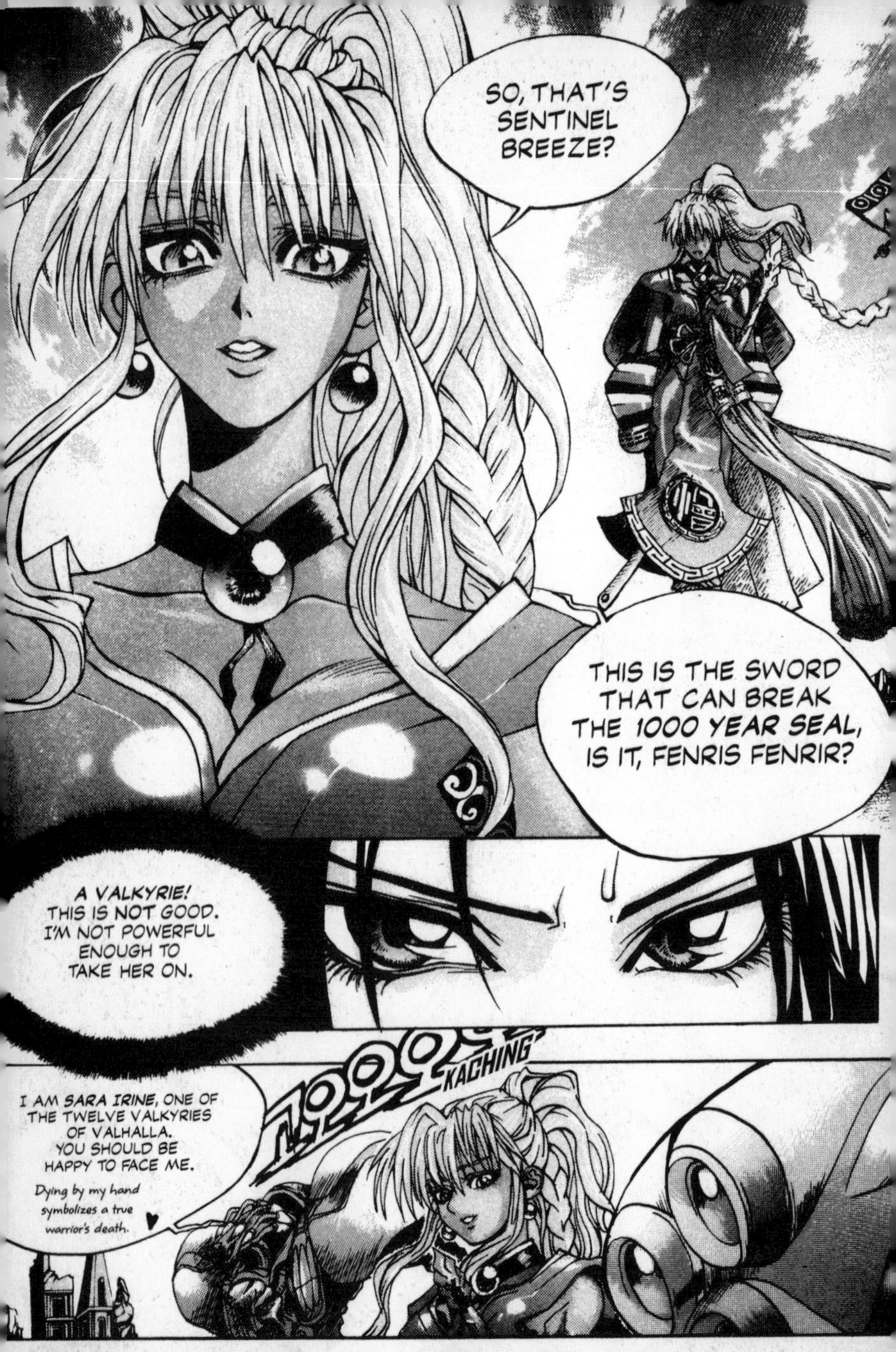
SO, THAT'S SENTINEL BREEZE?
THIS IS THE SWORD THAT CAN BREAK THE *1000 YEAR SEAL*, IS IT, FENRIS FENRIR?
A VALKYRIE! THIS IS NOT GOOD. I'M NOT POWERFUL ENOUGH TO TAKE HER ON.
KACHING
I AM *SARA IRINE*, ONE OF THE TWELVE VALKYRIES OF VALHALLA. YOU SHOULD BE HAPPY TO FACE ME.
Dying by my hand symbolizes a true warrior's death. ♥

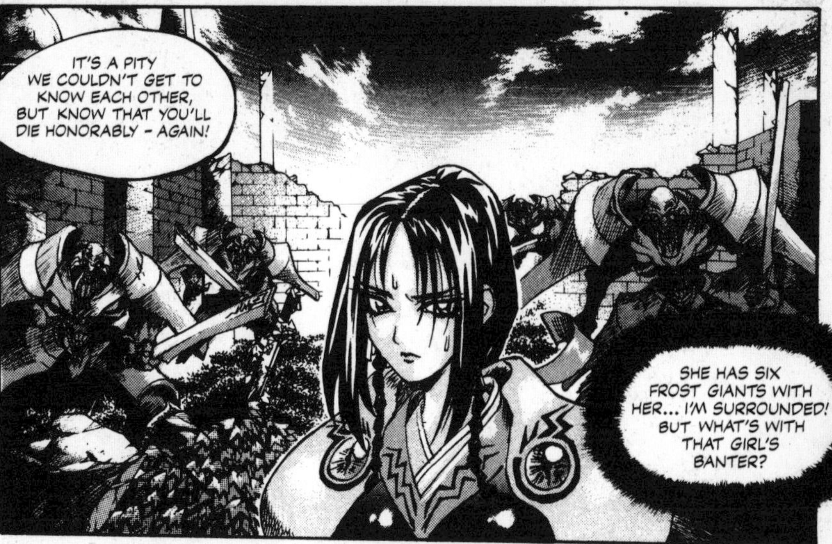
IT'S A PITY WE COULDN'T GET TO KNOW EACH OTHER, BUT KNOW THAT YOU'LL DIE HONORABLY - AGAIN!
SHE HAS SIX FROST GIANTS WITH HER... I'M SURROUNDED! BUT WHAT'S WITH THAT GIRL'S BANTER?

↑ Hasn't been listening!

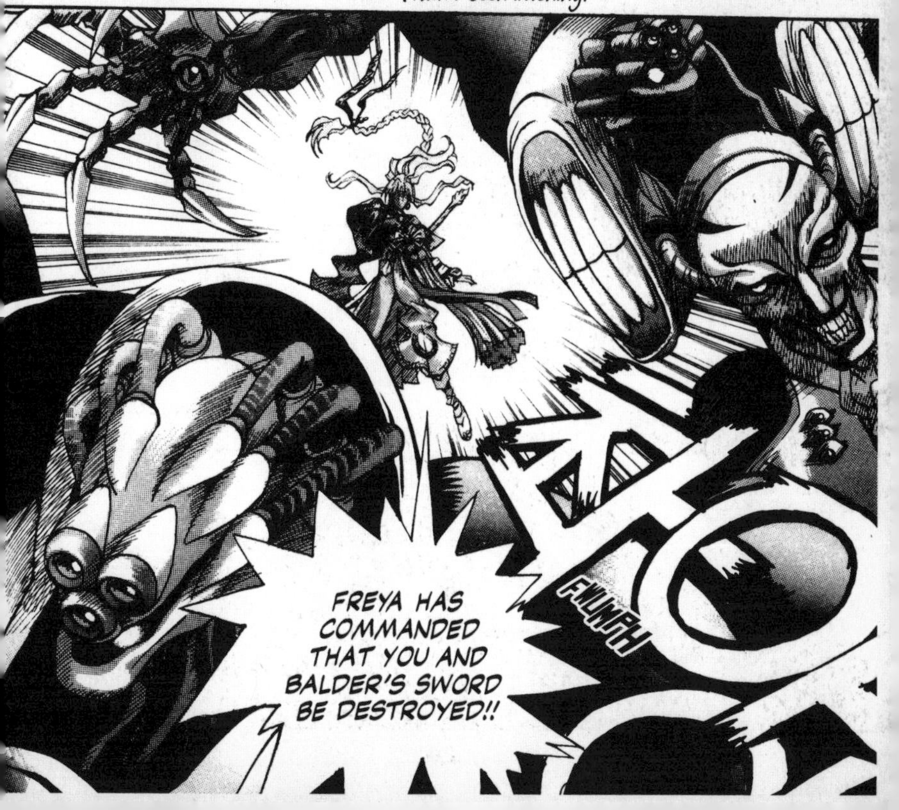
FWUMPH
FREYA HAS COMMANDED THAT YOU AND BALDER'S SWORD BE DESTROYED!!

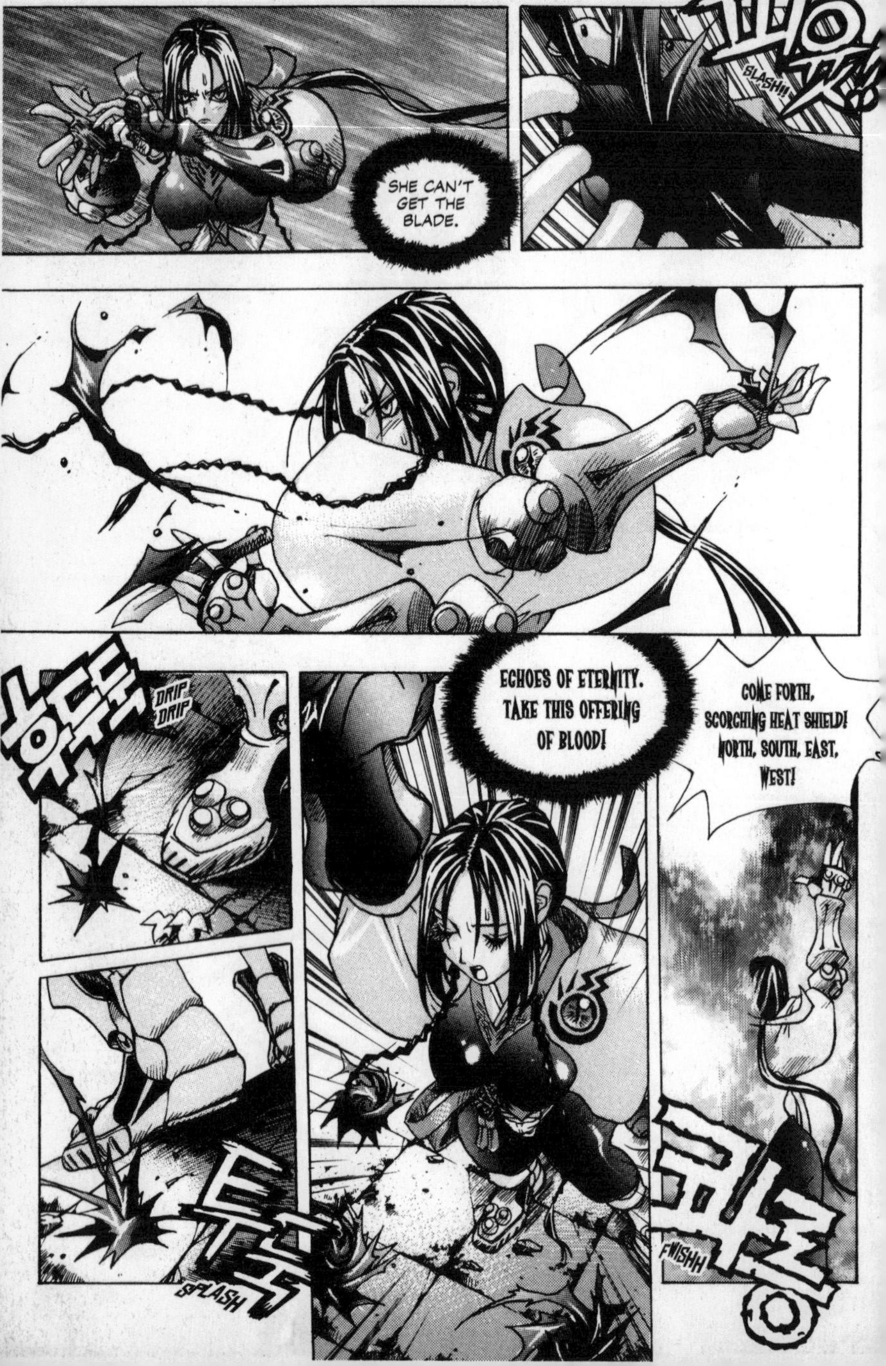
SHE CAN'T GET THE BLADE.
SLASH!!
DRIP DRIP
SPLASH
ECHOES OF ETERNITY. TAKE THIS OFFERING OF BLOOD!
COME FORTH, SCORCHING HEAT SHIELD! NORTH, SOUTH, EAST, WEST!
FWISHH

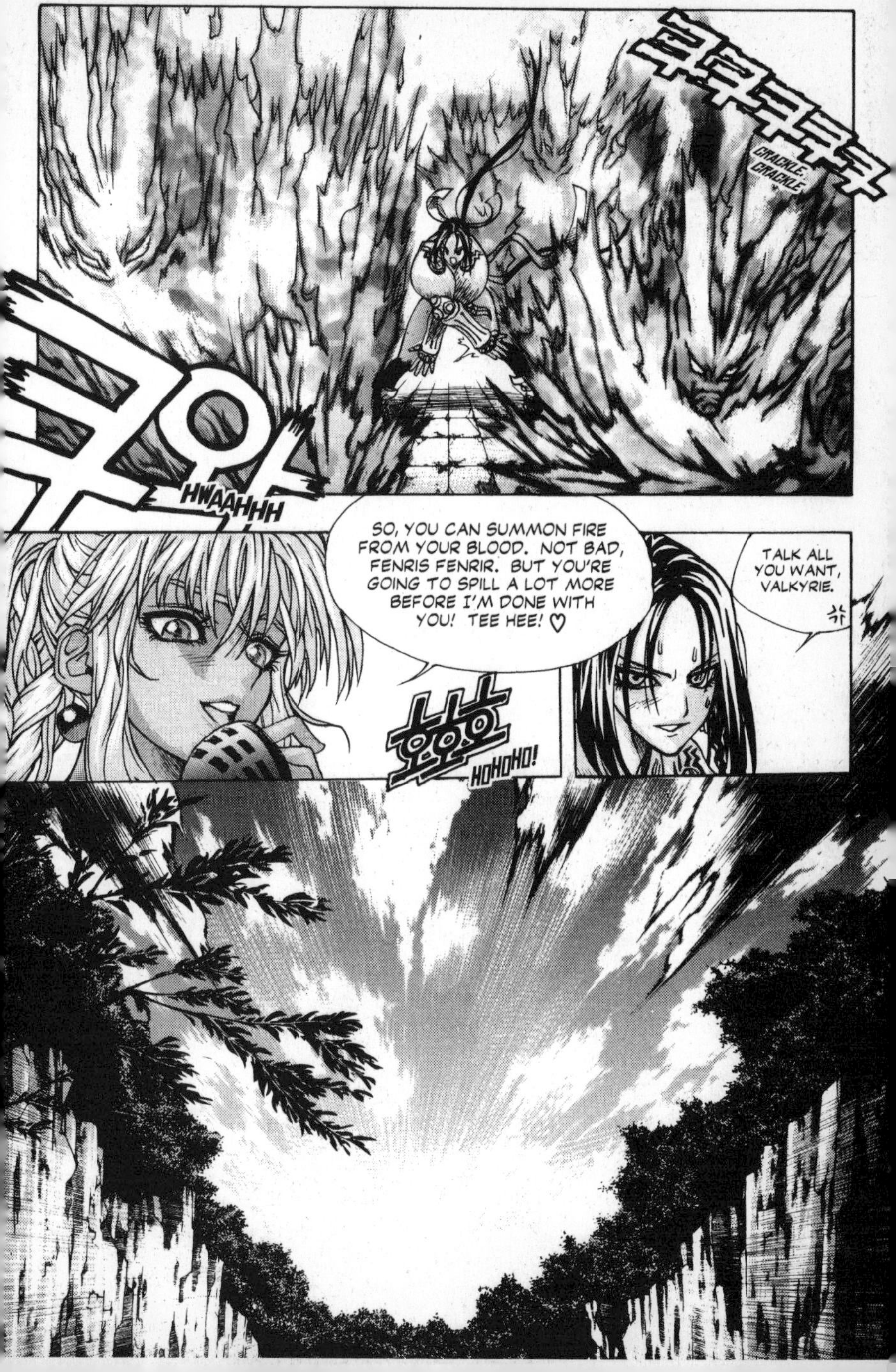
CRACKLE, CRACKLE
HWAAHHH
SO, YOU CAN SUMMON FIRE FROM YOUR BLOOD. NOT BAD, FENRIS FENRIR. BUT YOU'RE GOING TO SPILL A LOT MORE BEFORE I'M DONE WITH YOU! TEE HEE! ♡
HOHOHO!
TALK ALL YOU WANT, VALKYRIE.

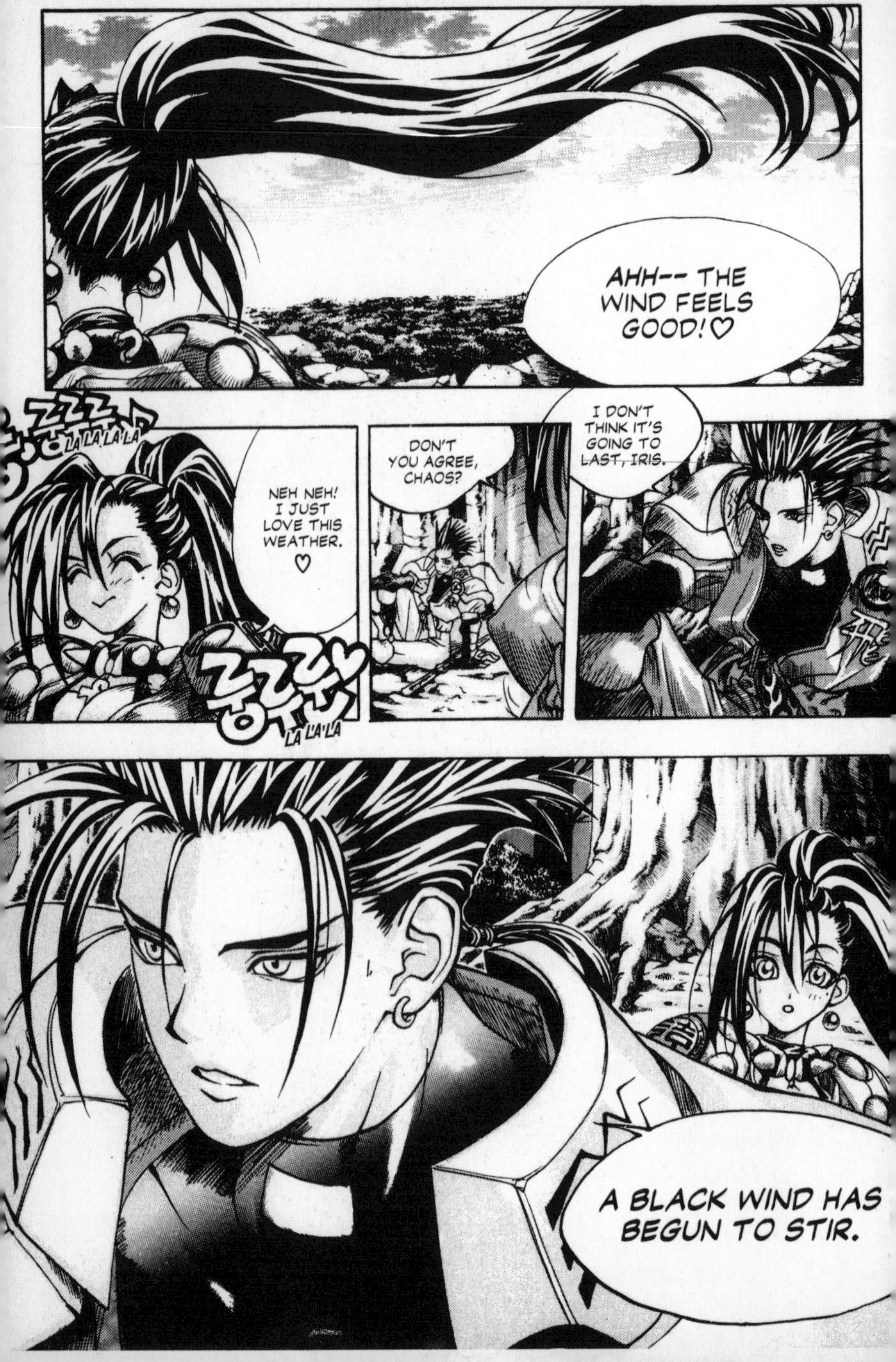
AHH-- THE WIND FEELS GOOD!♡
LA LA LA LA
NEH NEH! I JUST LOVE THIS WEATHER. ♡
LA LA LA
DON'T YOU AGREE, CHAOS?
I DON'T THINK IT'S GOING TO LAST, IRIS.
A BLACK WIND HAS BEGUN TO STIR.

RAGNARÖK

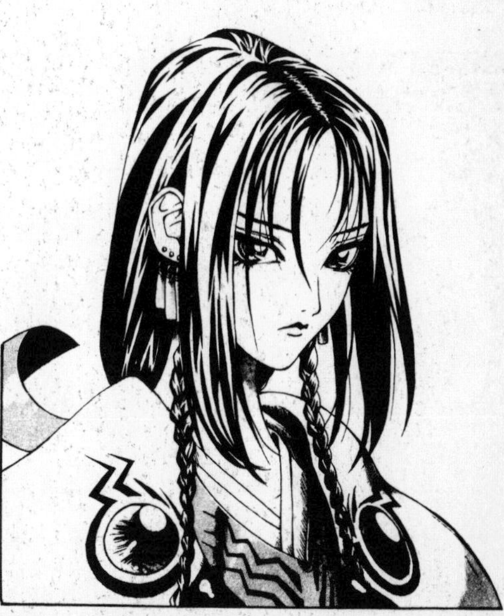

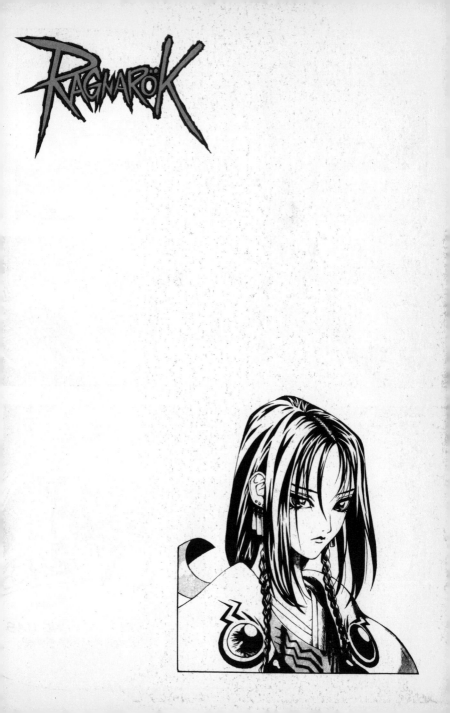

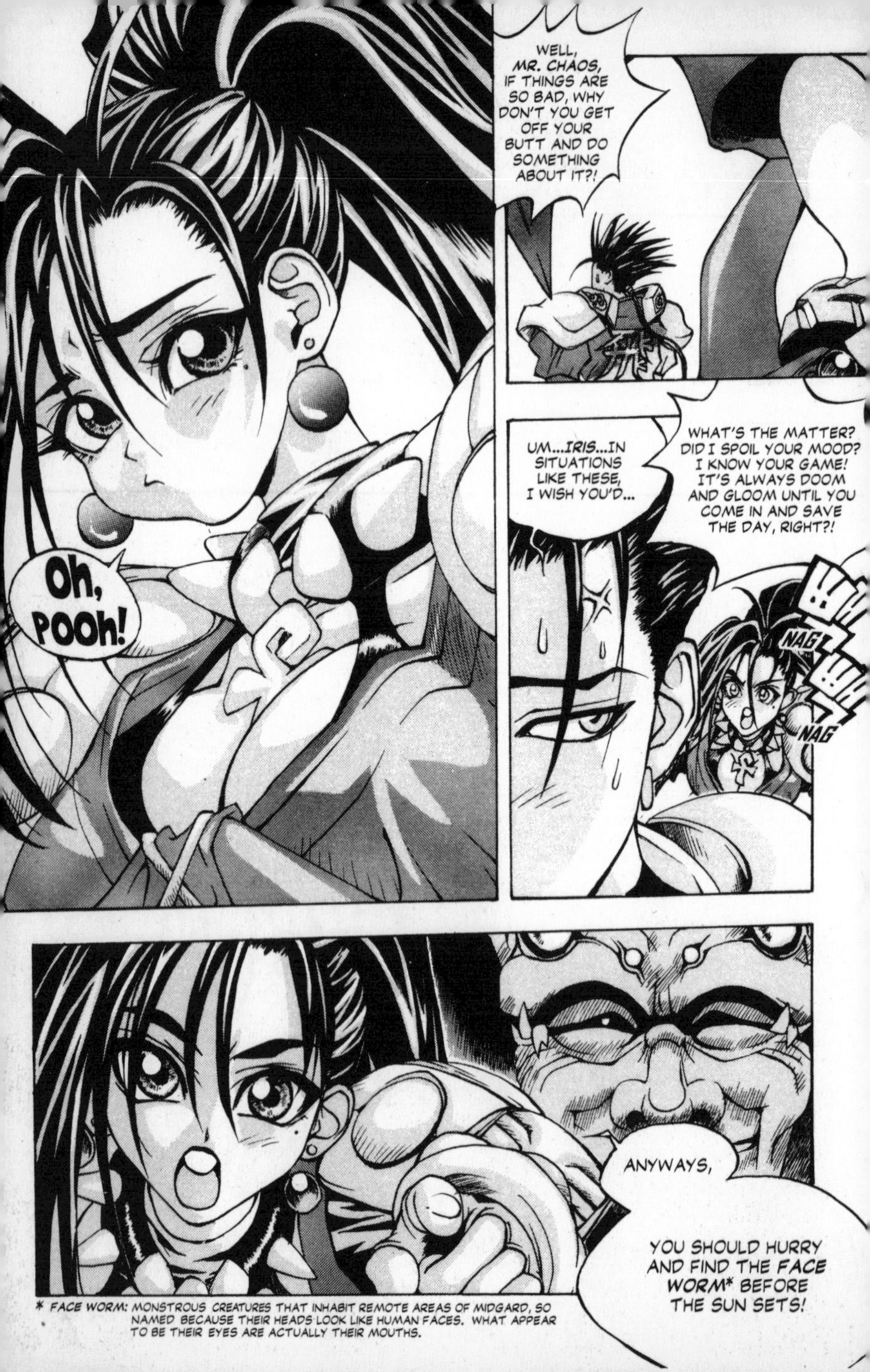
Oh, POOh!
WELL, MR. CHAOS, IF THINGS ARE SO BAD, WHY DON'T YOU GET OFF YOUR BUTT AND DO SOMETHING ABOUT IT?!
UM...IRIS...IN SITUATIONS LIKE THESE, I WISH YOU'D...
WHAT'S THE MATTER? DID I SPOIL YOUR MOOD? I KNOW YOUR GAME! IT'S ALWAYS DOOM AND GLOOM UNTIL YOU COME IN AND SAVE THE DAY, RIGHT?!
!!
NAG
!!
NAG
ANYWAYS,
YOU SHOULD HURRY AND FIND THE FACE WORM* BEFORE THE SUN SETS!

* FACE WORM: MONSTROUS CREATURES THAT INHABIT REMOTE AREAS OF MIDGARD, SO NAMED BECAUSE THEIR HEADS LOOK LIKE HUMAN FACES. WHAT APPEAR TO BE THEIR EYES ARE ACTUALLY THEIR MOUTHS.

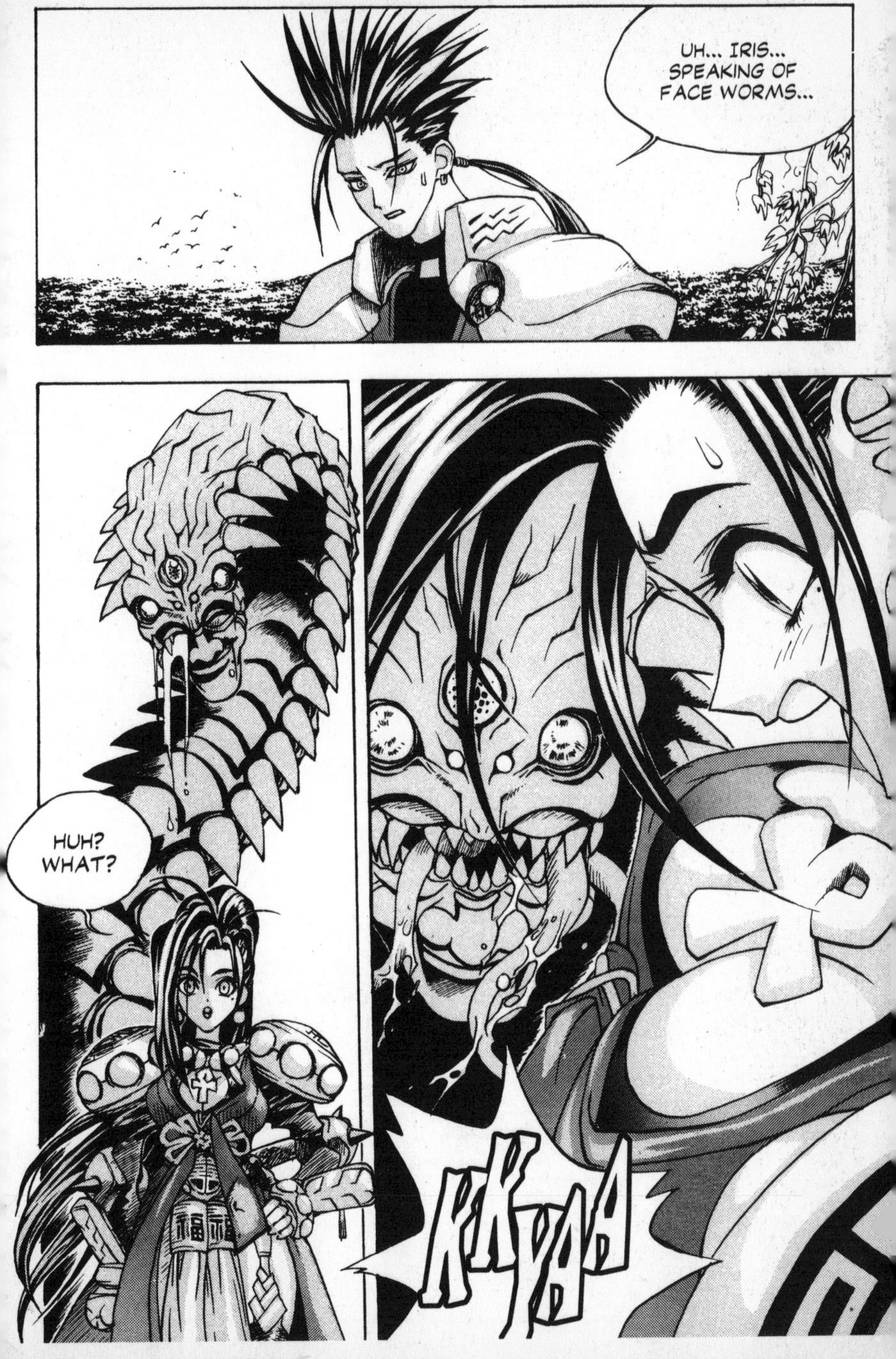
UH... IRIS... SPEAKING OF FACE WORMS...
HUH? WHAT?
KKYAA

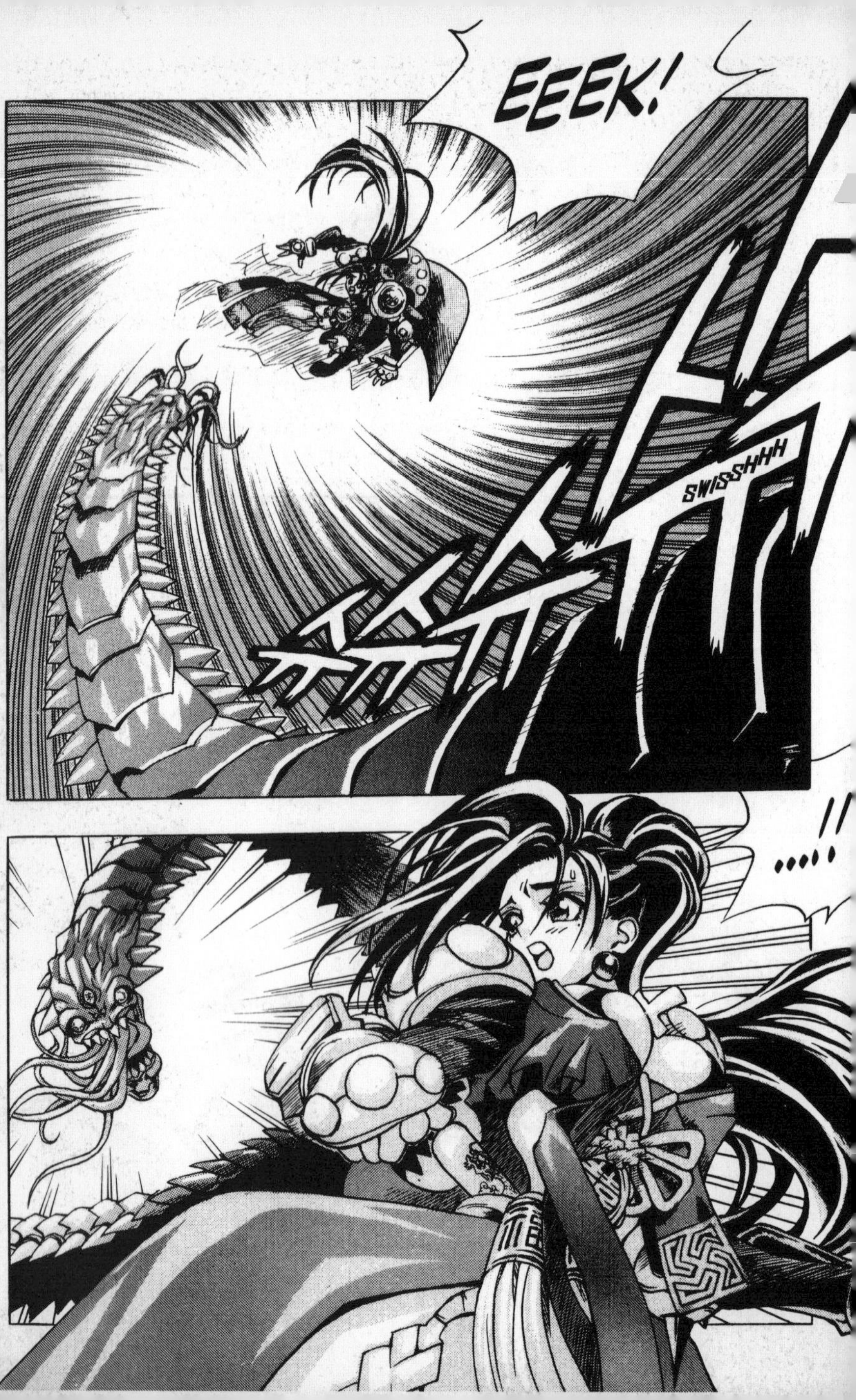
EEEK!
SWISSHHH
....!!

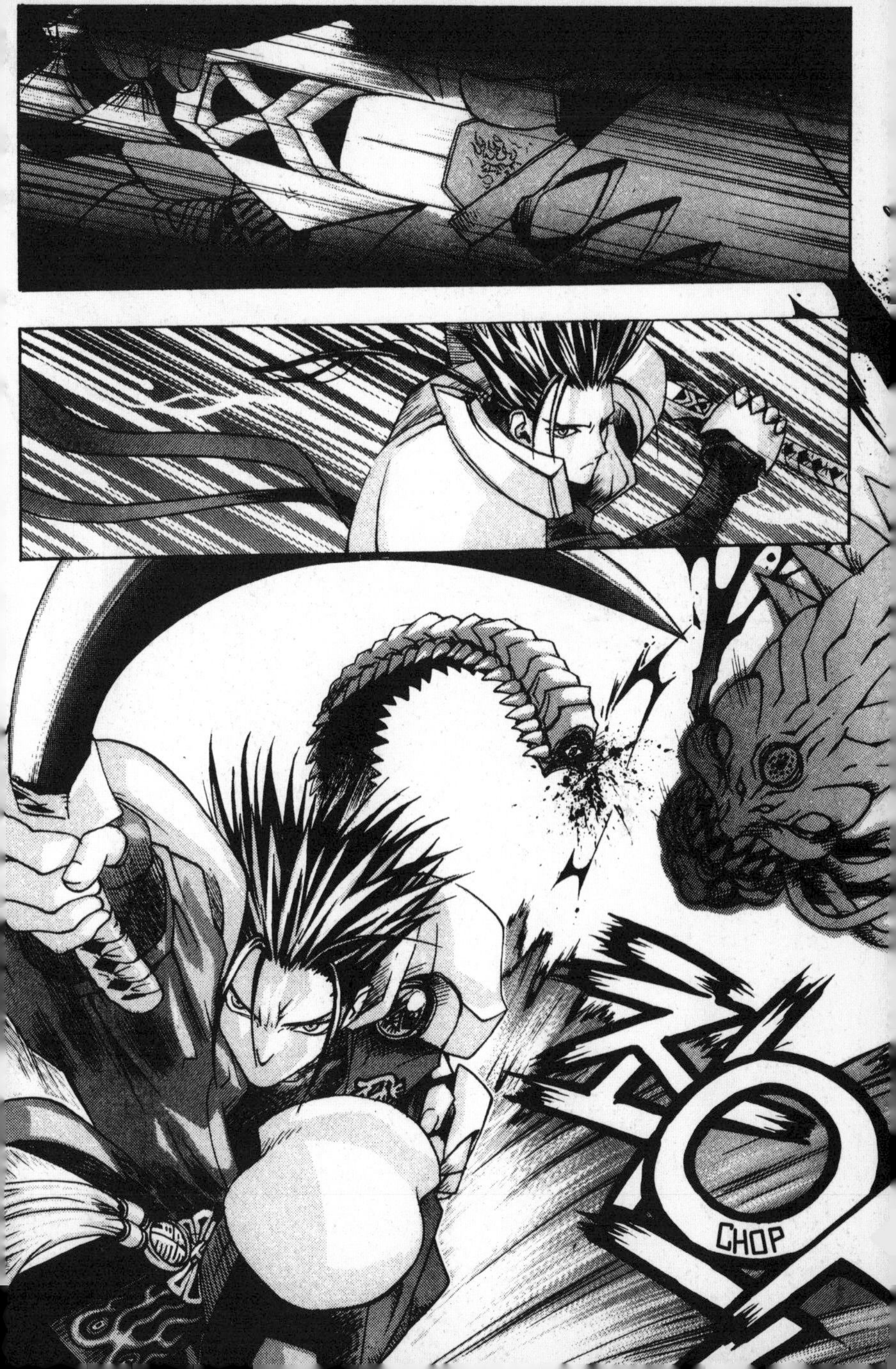
CHOP

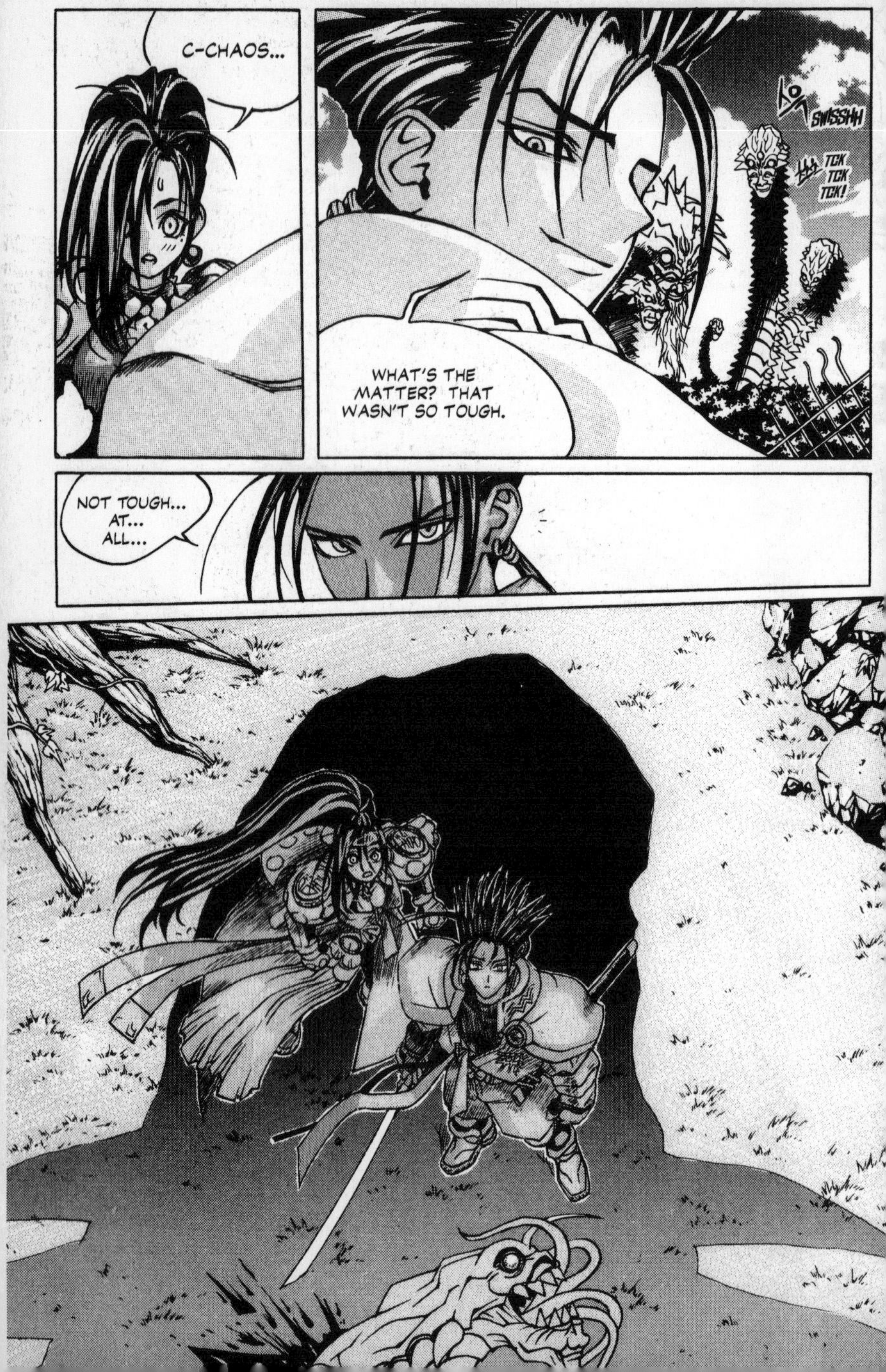
C-CHAOS...
SWISSHH
TCK TCK TCK!
WHAT'S THE MATTER? THAT WASN'T SO TOUGH.
NOT TOUGH... AT... ALL...

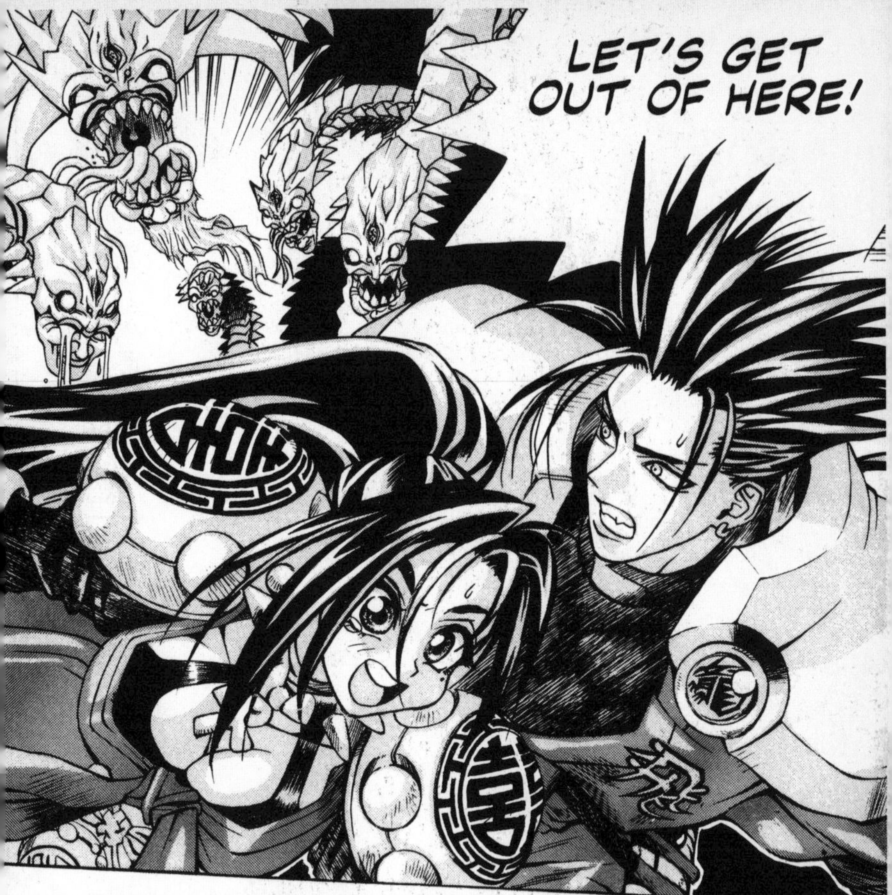
LET'S GET OUT OF HERE!

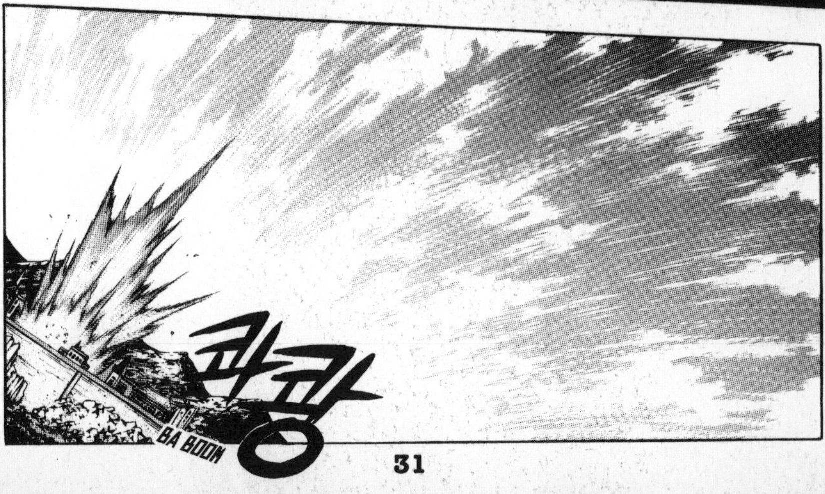
BA BOOM

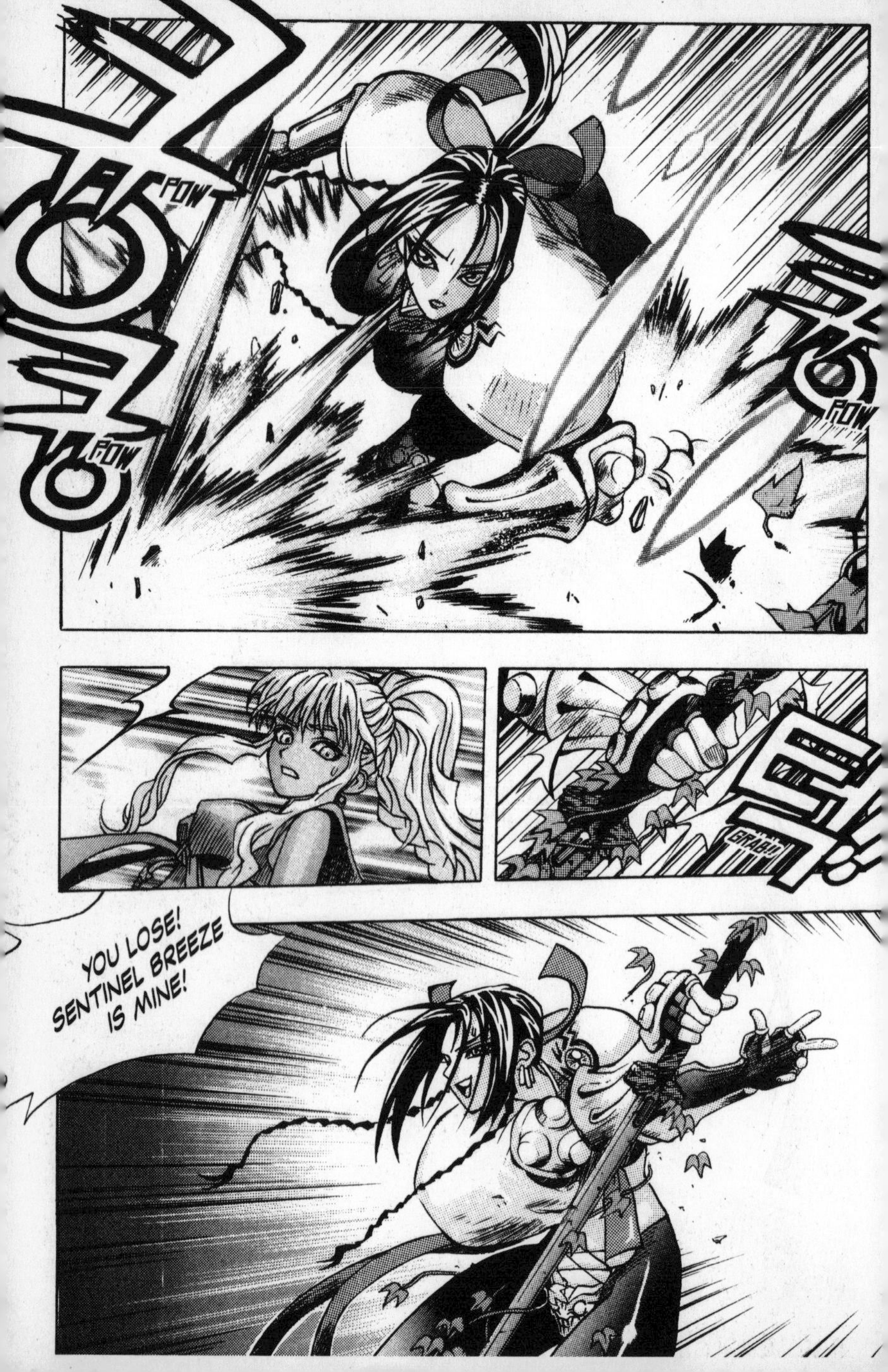
POW
POW
POW
GRAB!!
YOU LOSE! SENTINEL BREEZE IS MINE!

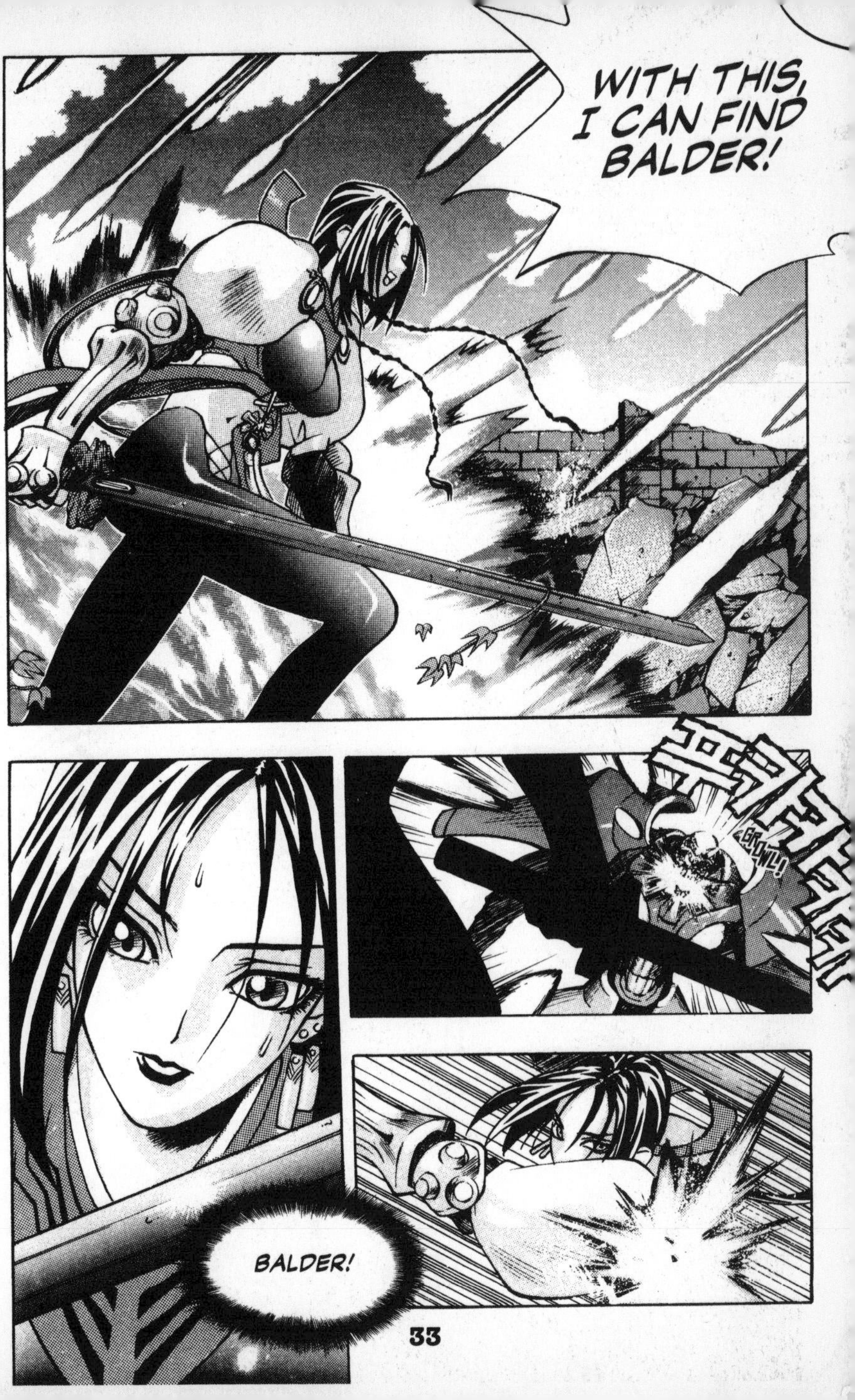
WITH THIS, I CAN FIND BALDER!
GROWL!
BALDER!

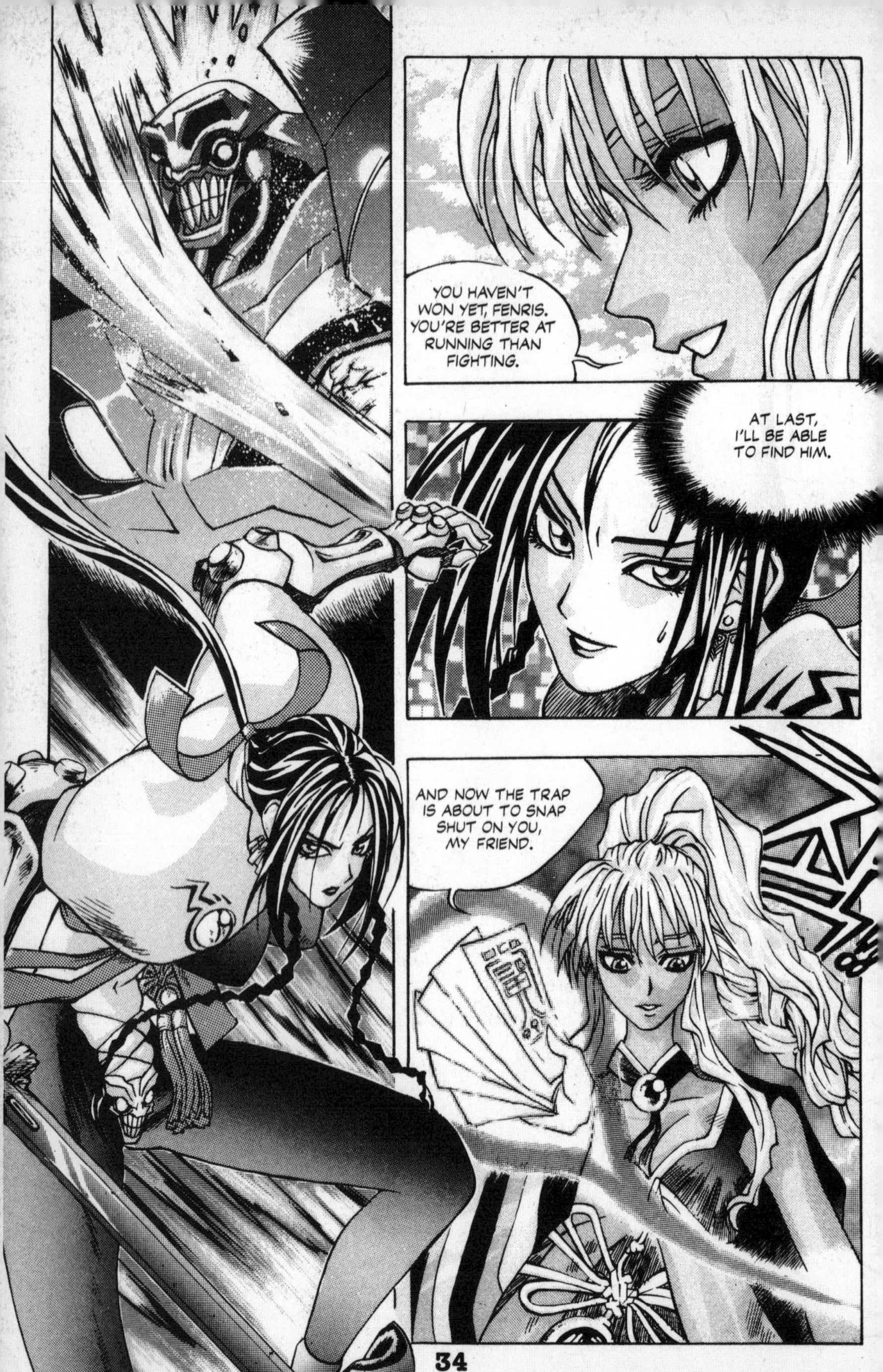
YOU HAVEN'T WON YET, FENRIS. YOU'RE BETTER AT RUNNING THAN FIGHTING.
AT LAST, I'LL BE ABLE TO FIND HIM.
AND NOW THE TRAP IS ABOUT TO SNAP SHUT ON YOU, MY FRIEND.

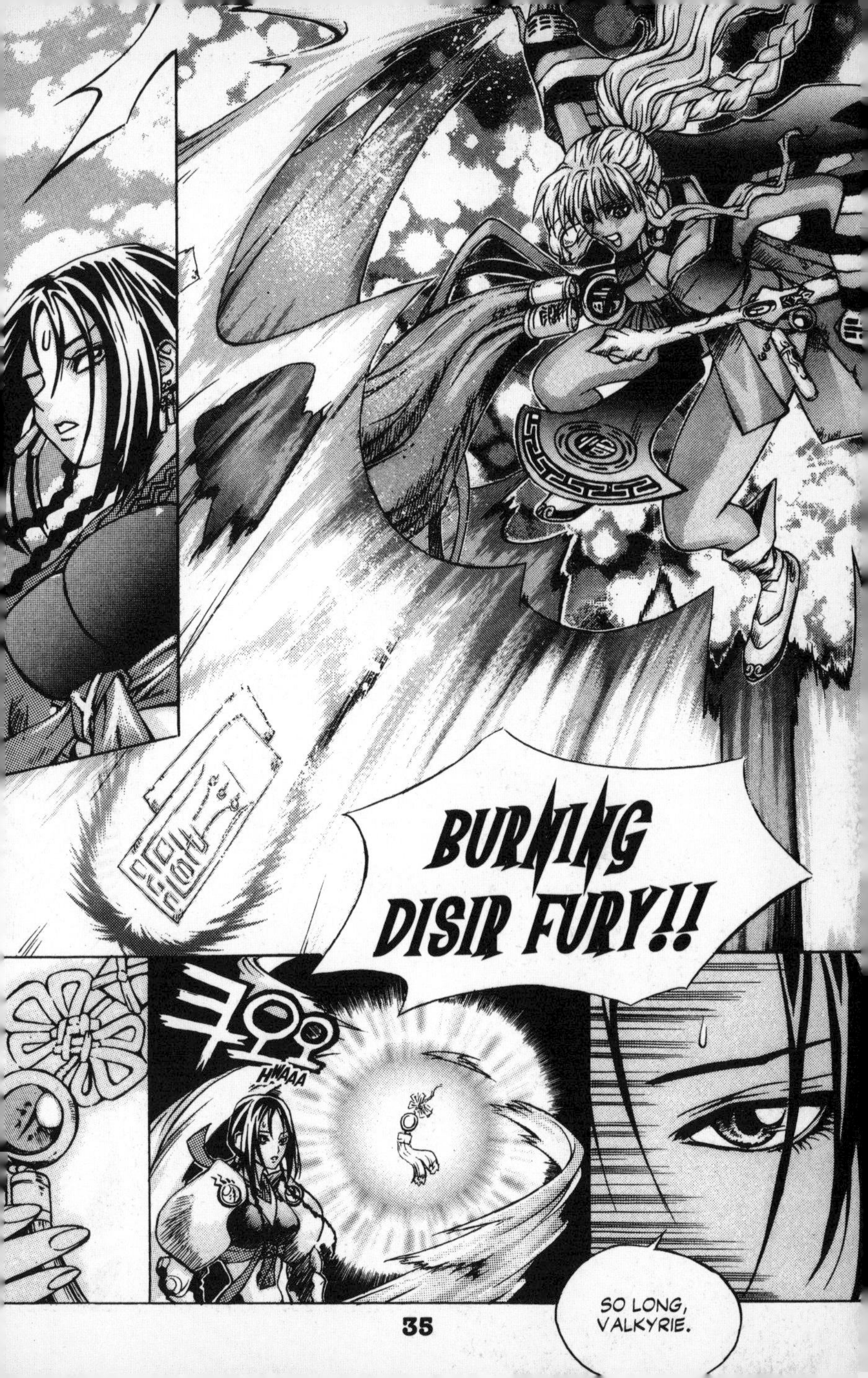
BURNING DISIR FURY!!
크오오
HWAAA
SO LONG, VALKYRIE.

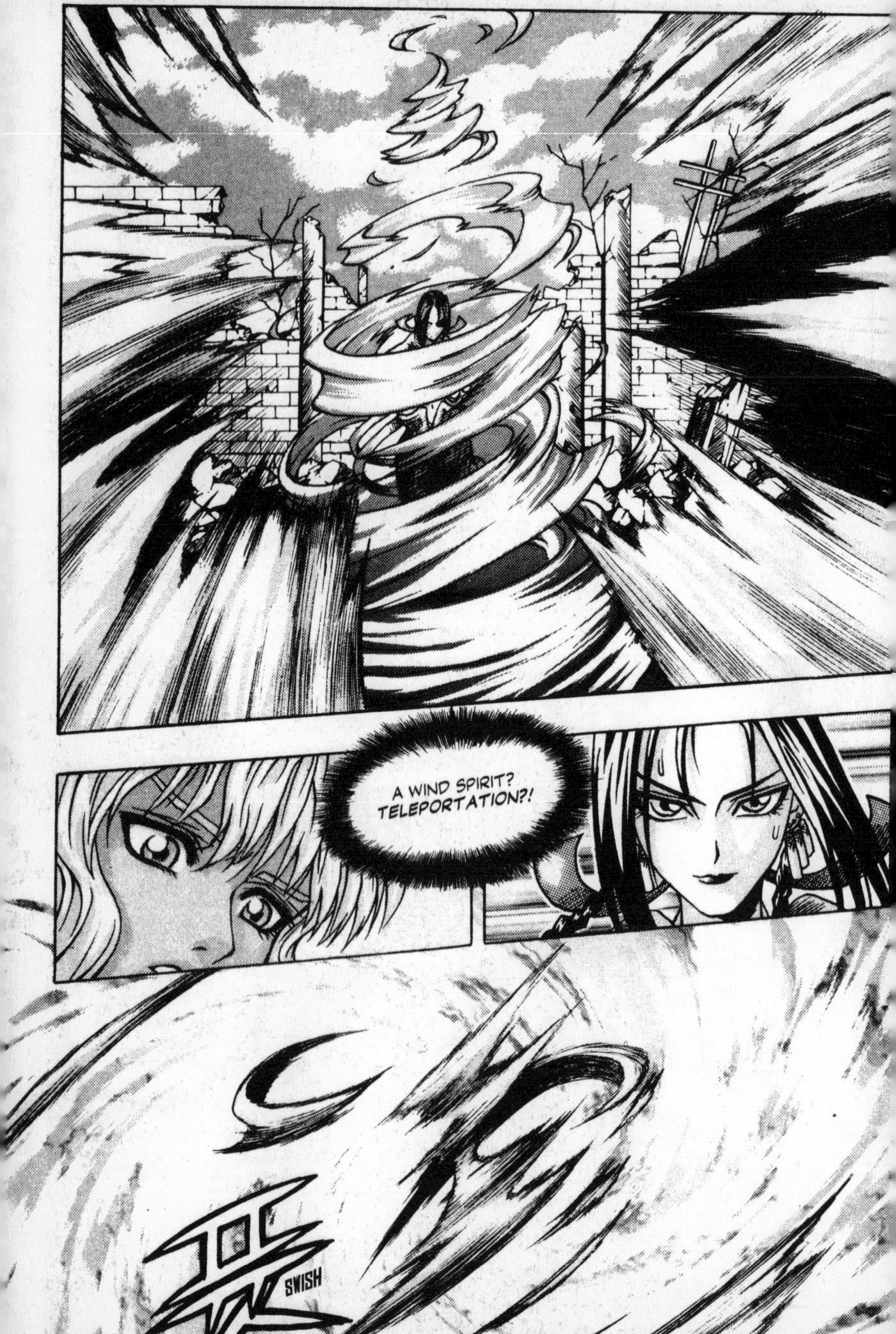
A WIND SPIRIT? TELEPORTATION?!
SWISH

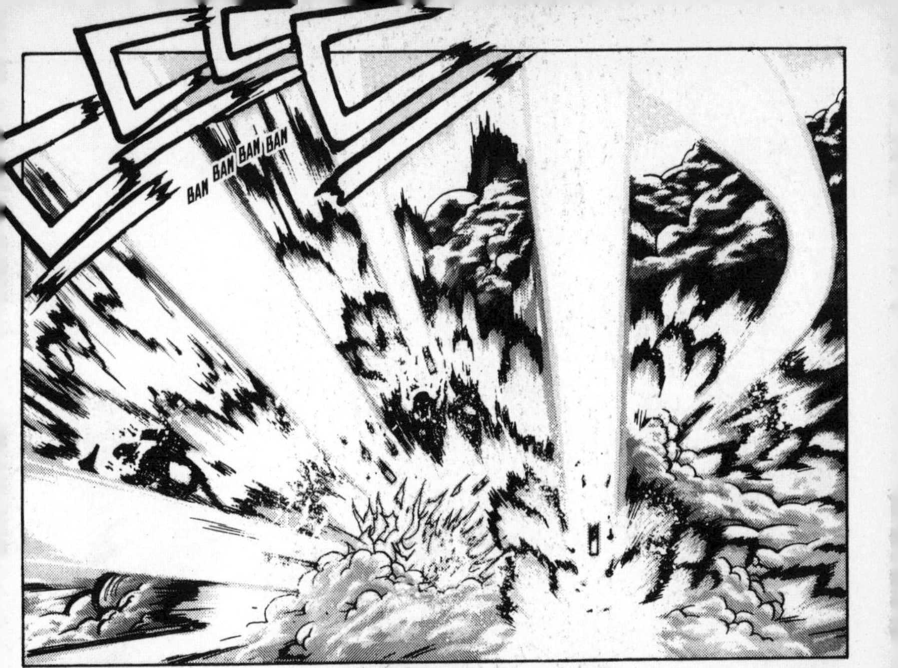
BAM BAM BAM BAM

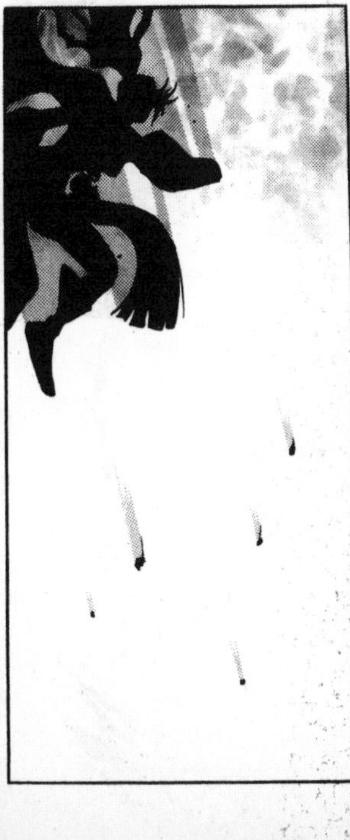

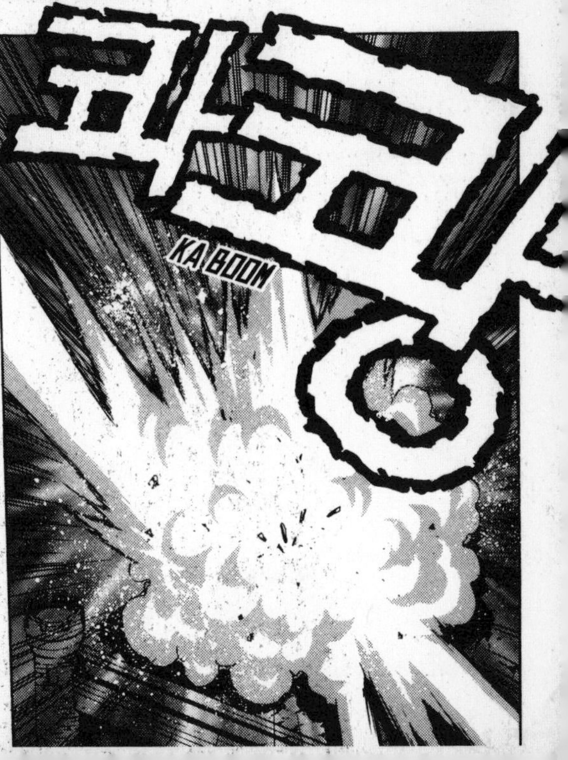
KA BOOM

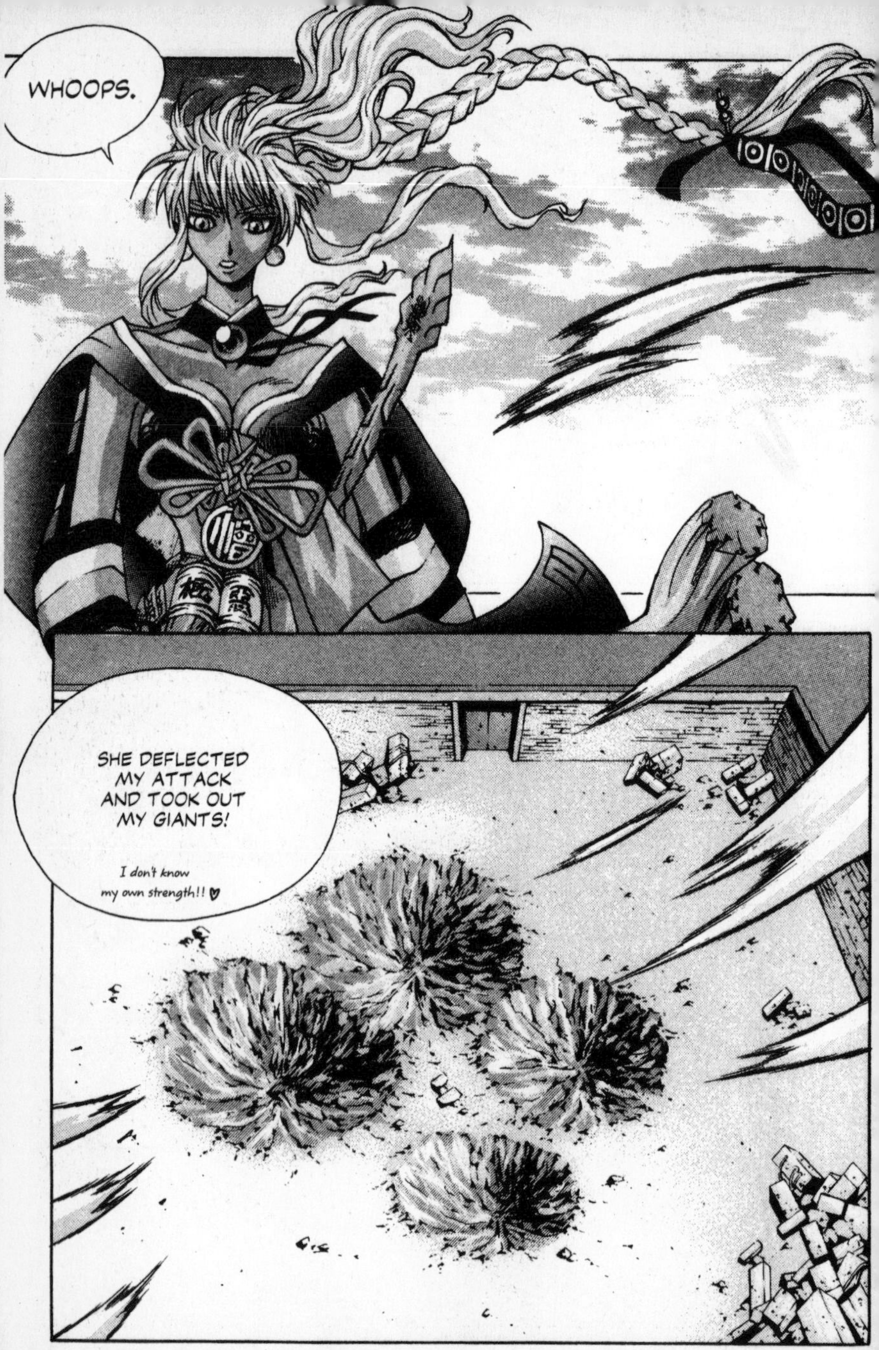
WHOOPS.
SHE DEFLECTED MY ATTACK AND TOOK OUT MY GIANTS!
I don't know my own strength!! ♥

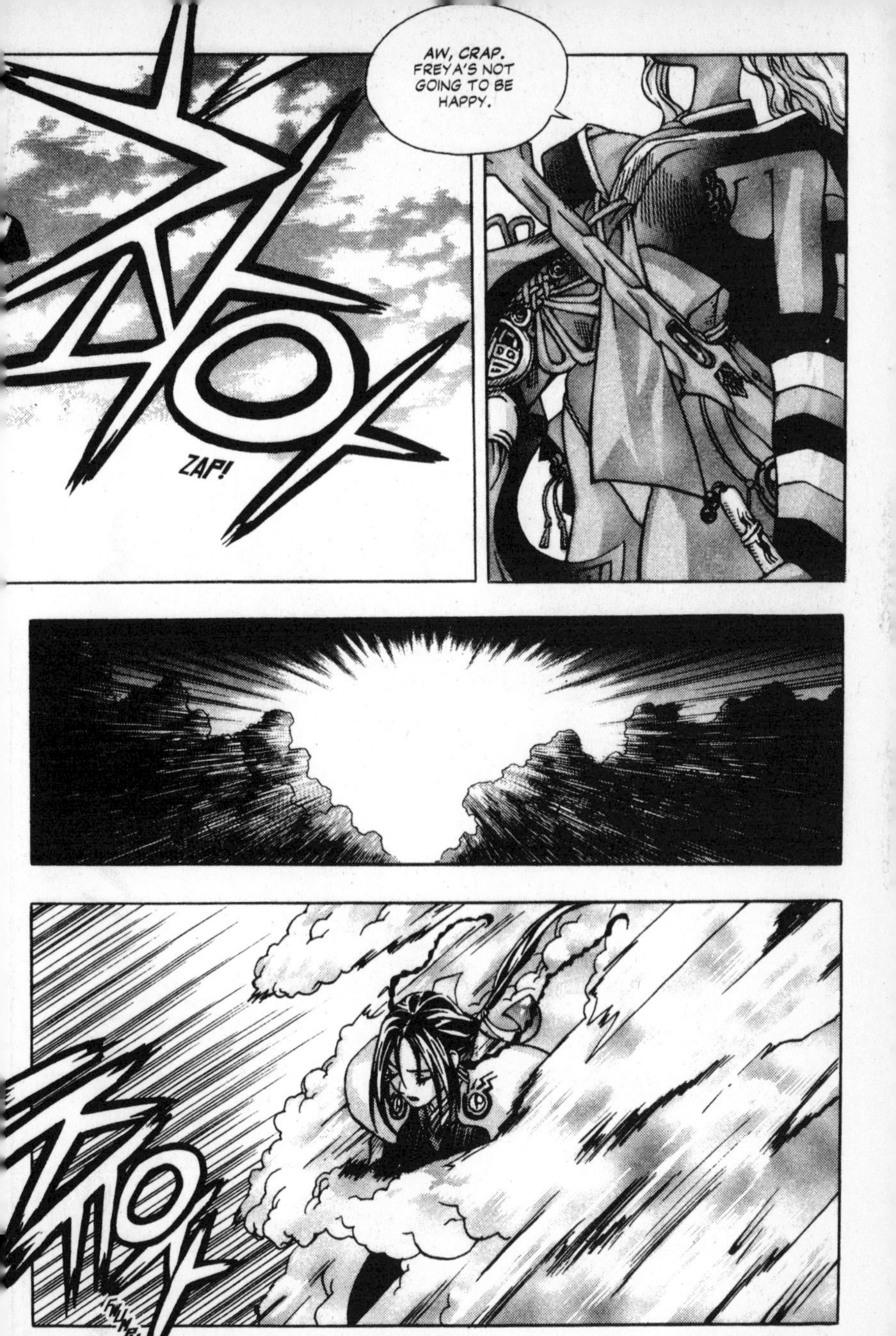
ZAP!
AW, CRAP. FREYA'S NOT GOING TO BE HAPPY.
FWUMPH

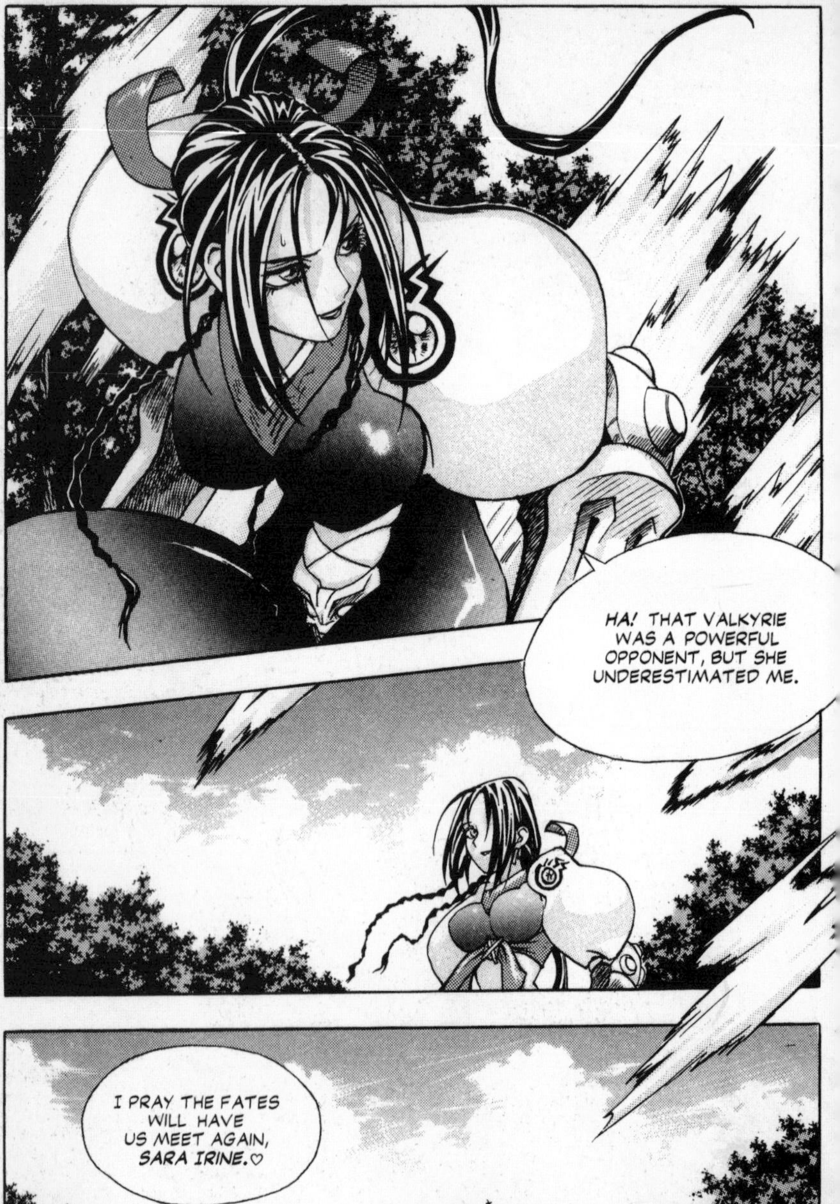
HA! THAT VALKYRIE WAS A POWERFUL OPPONENT, BUT SHE UNDERESTIMATED ME.
I PRAY THE FATES WILL HAVE US MEET AGAIN, SARA IRINE.♡

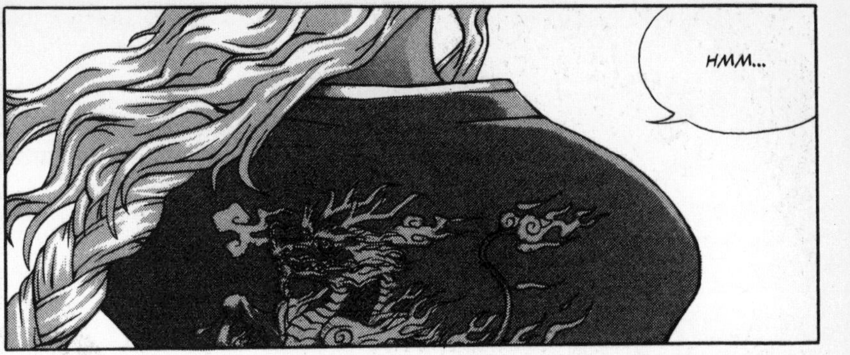
HMM...

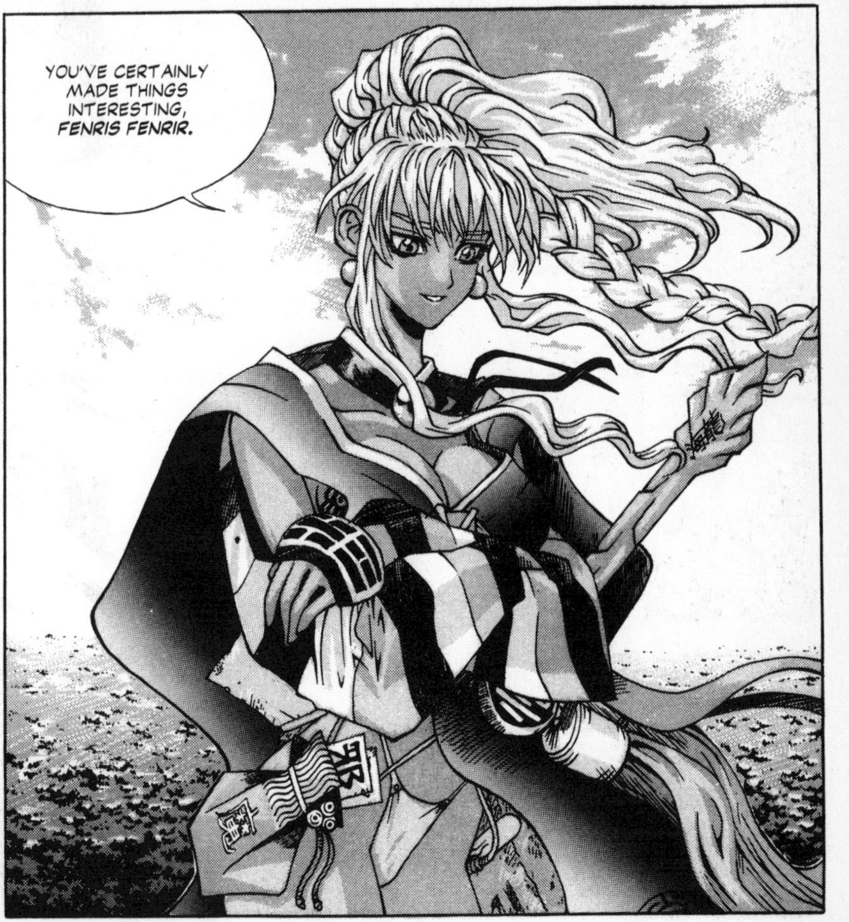
YOU'VE CERTAINLY MADE THINGS INTERESTING, FENRIS FENRIR.

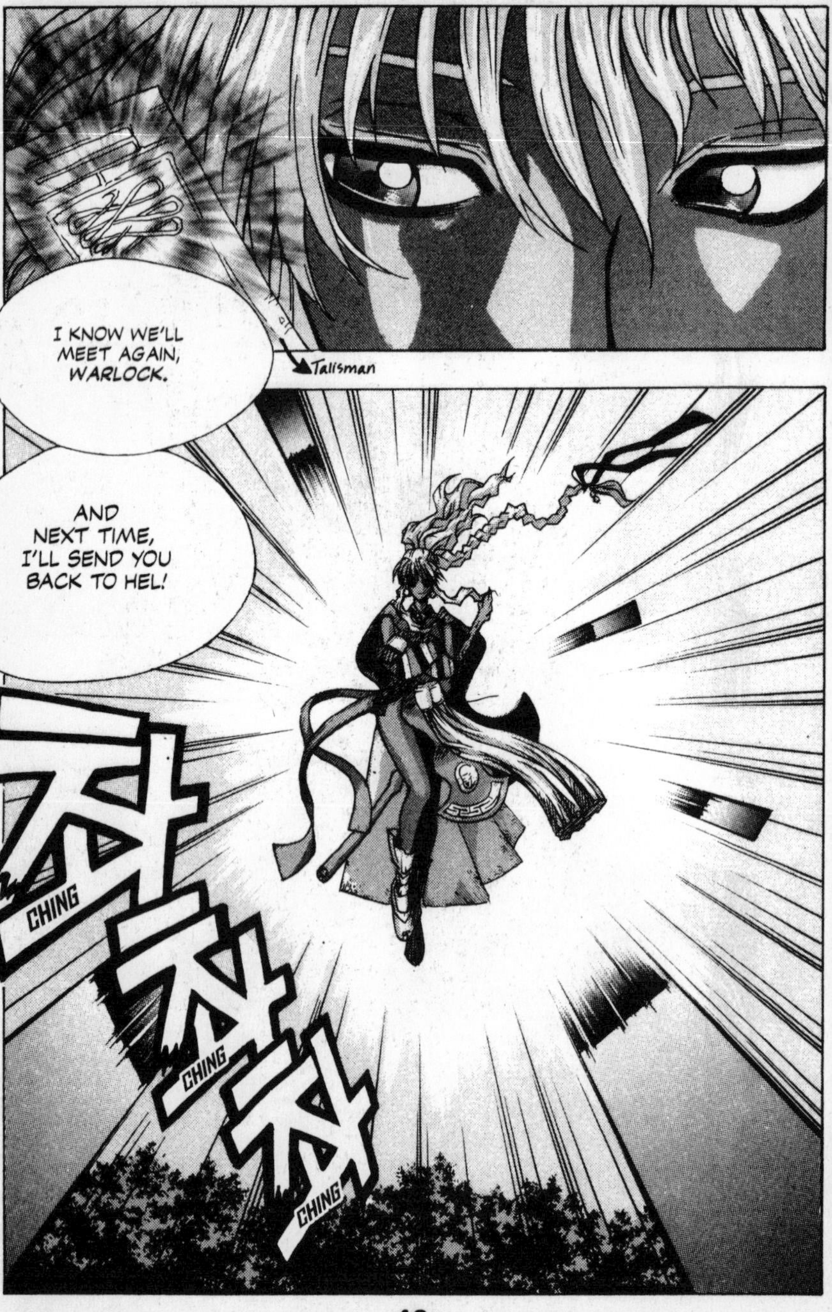

Talisman
I KNOW WE'LL MEET AGAIN, WARLOCK.
AND NEXT TIME, I'LL SEND YOU BACK TO HEL!
CHING
CHING
CHING

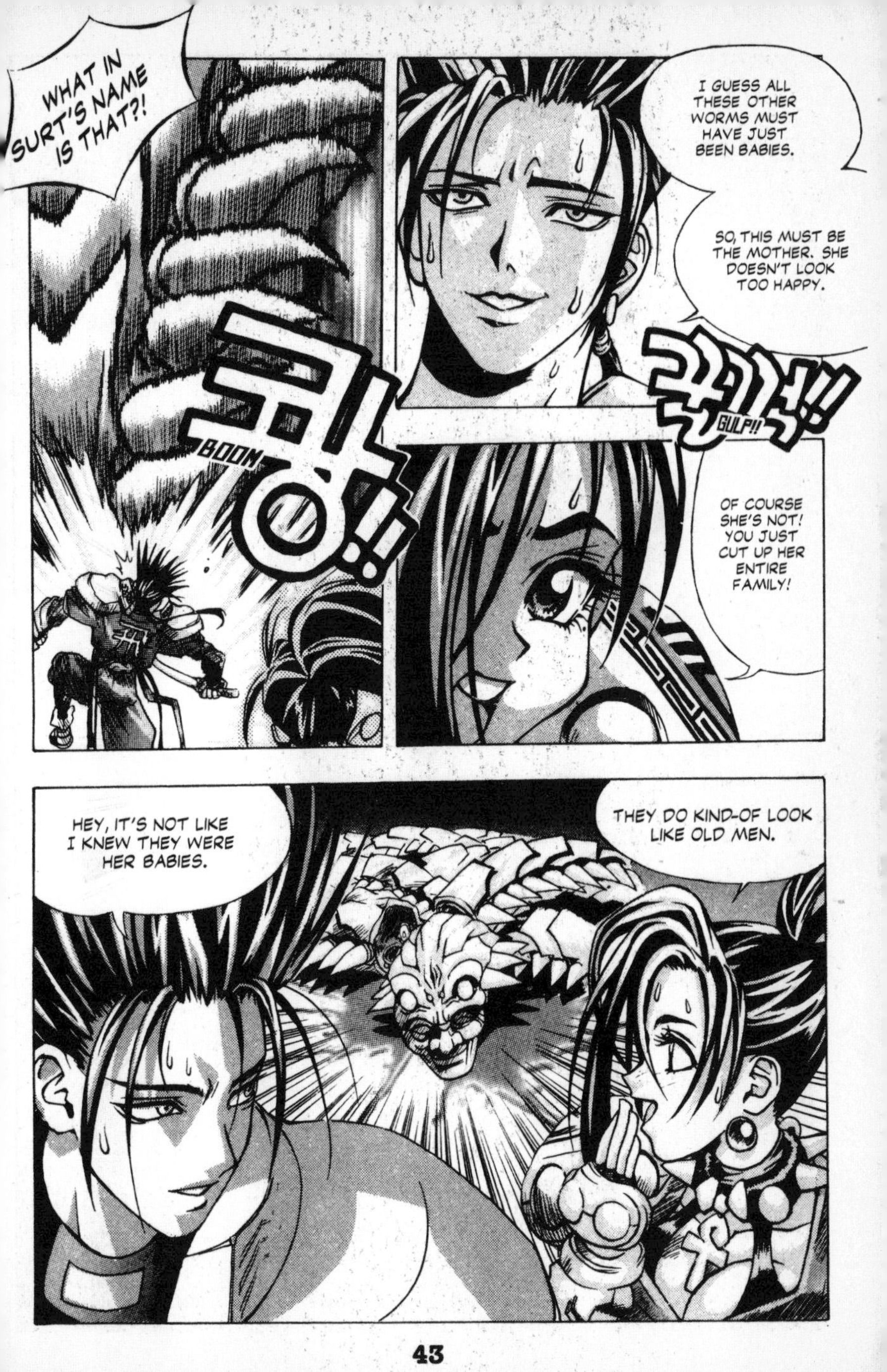
WHAT IN SURT'S NAME IS THAT?!
BOOM
I GUESS ALL THESE OTHER WORMS MUST HAVE JUST BEEN BABIES.
SO, THIS MUST BE THE MOTHER. SHE DOESN'T LOOK TOO HAPPY.
GULP!!
OF COURSE SHE'S NOT! YOU JUST CUT UP HER ENTIRE FAMILY!
HEY, IT'S NOT LIKE I KNEW THEY WERE HER BABIES.
THEY DO KIND-OF LOOK LIKE OLD MEN.

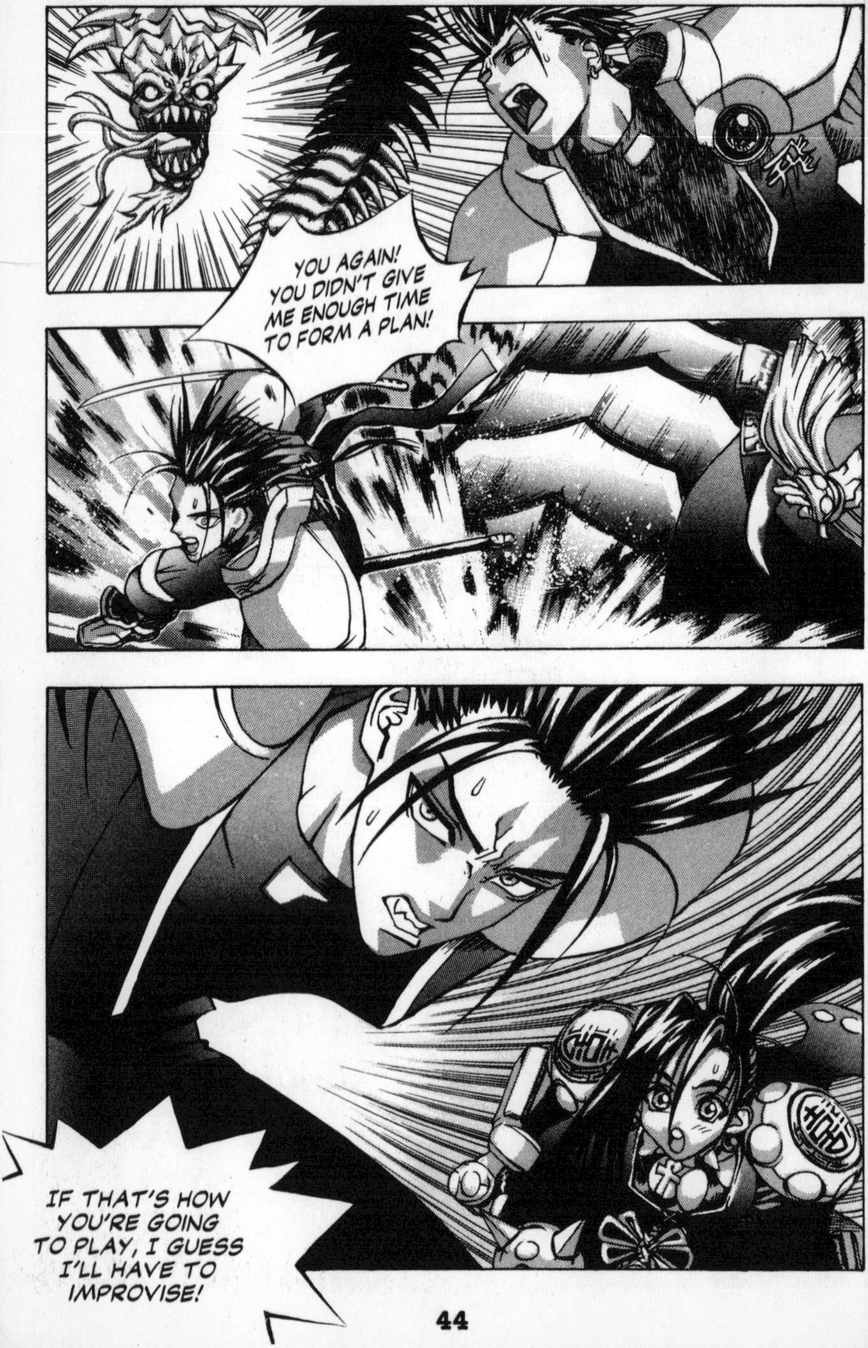
YOU AGAIN! YOU DIDN'T GIVE ME ENOUGH TIME TO FORM A PLAN!
IF THAT'S HOW YOU'RE GOING TO PLAY, I GUESS I'LL HAVE TO IMPROVISE!

RAGNARÖK

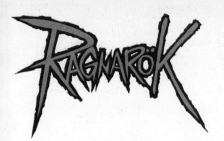

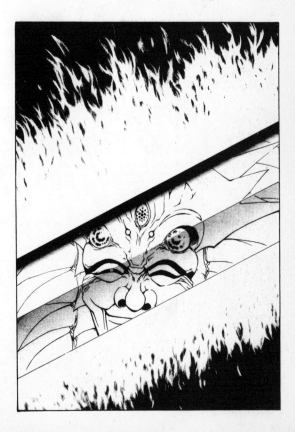

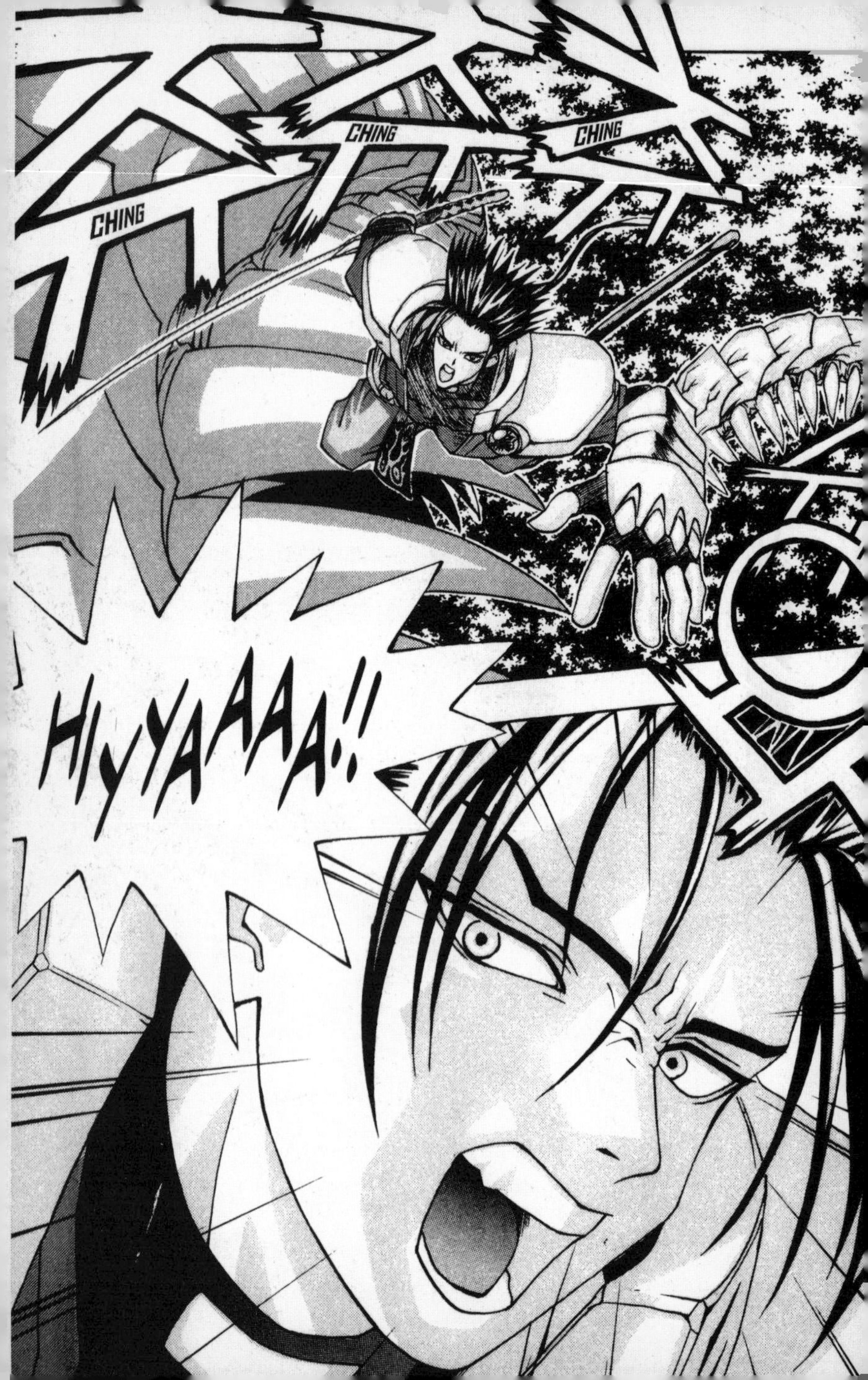
CHING
CHING
CHING
HIYAAAA!!

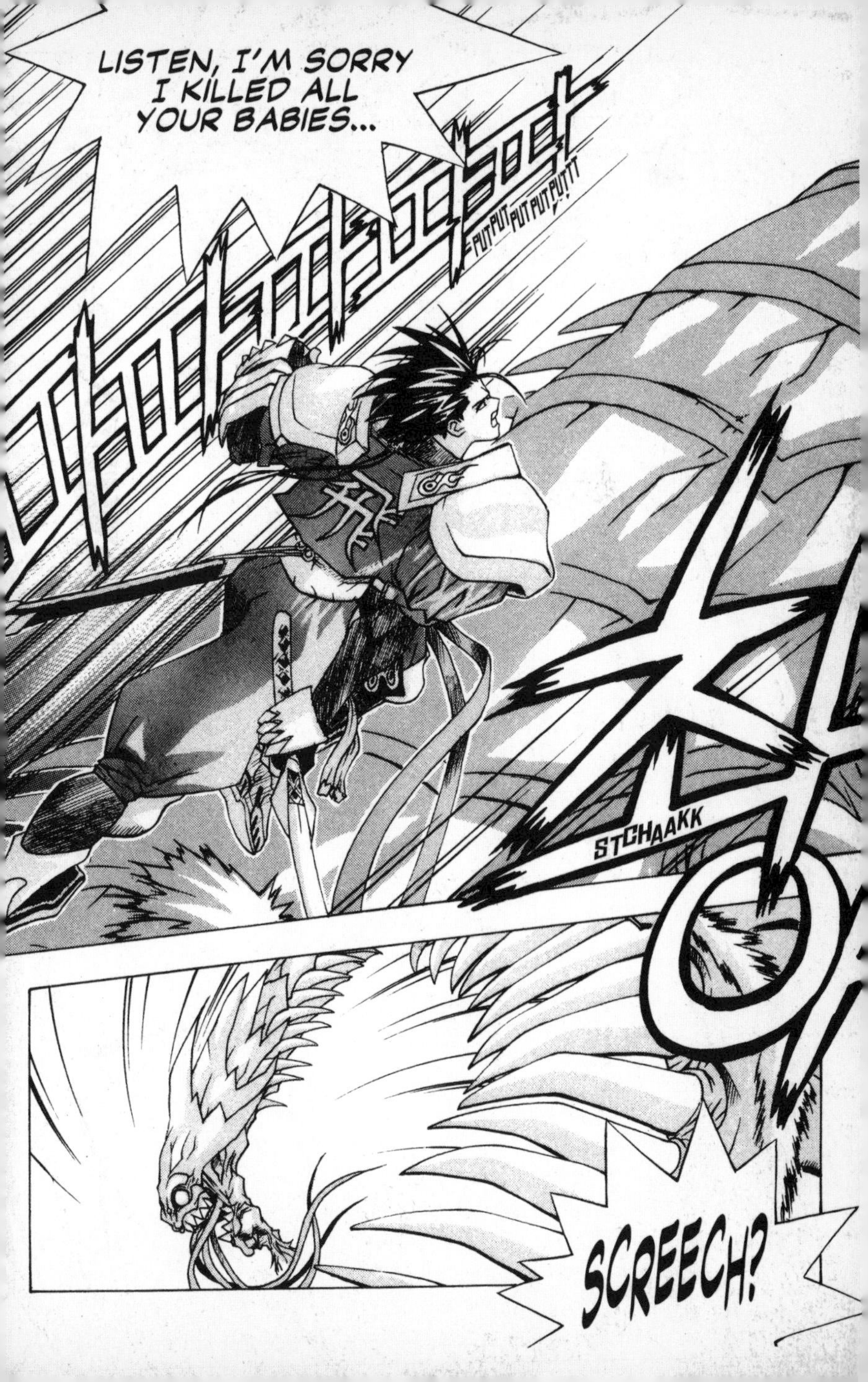
LISTEN, I'M SORRY I KILLED ALL YOUR BABIES...
PUT PUT PUT PUT PUTTT
STCHAAKK
SCREECH?

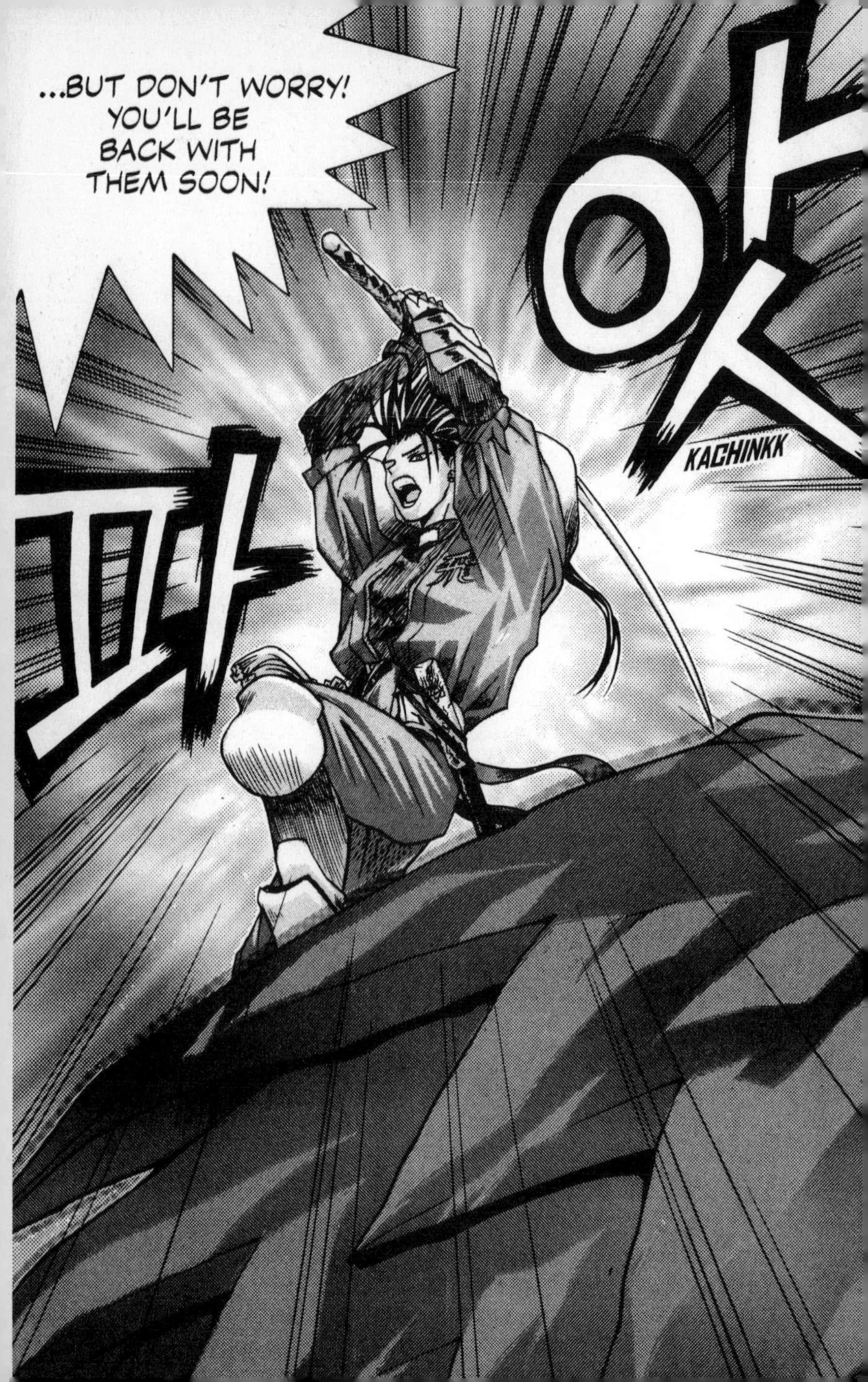
...BUT DON'T WORRY! YOU'LL BE BACK WITH THEM SOON!
KACHINKK

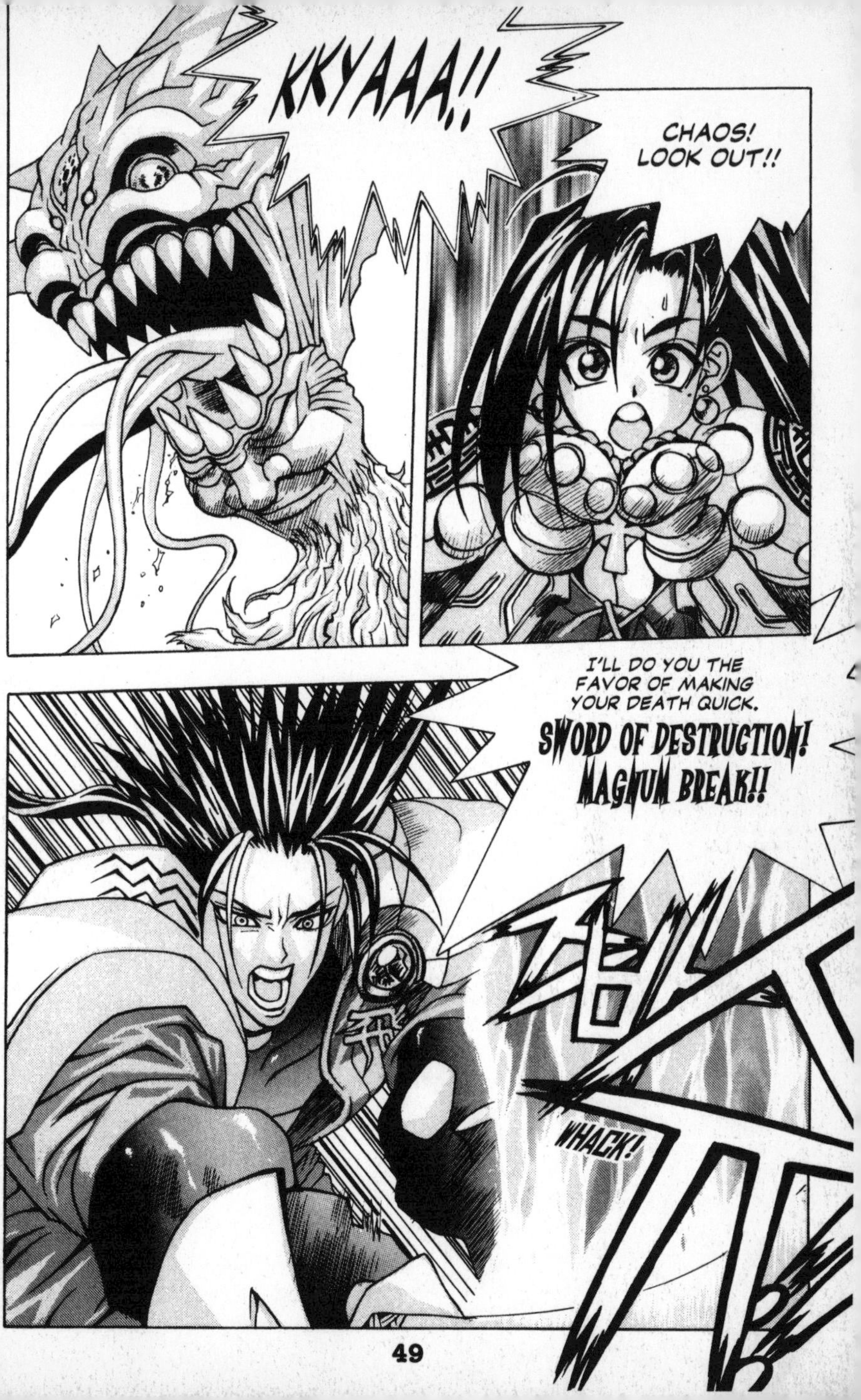
KKYAAA!!
CHAOS! LOOK OUT!!
I'LL DO YOU THE FAVOR OF MAKING YOUR DEATH QUICK.
SWORD OF DESTRUCTION! MAGNUM BREAK!!
WHACK!

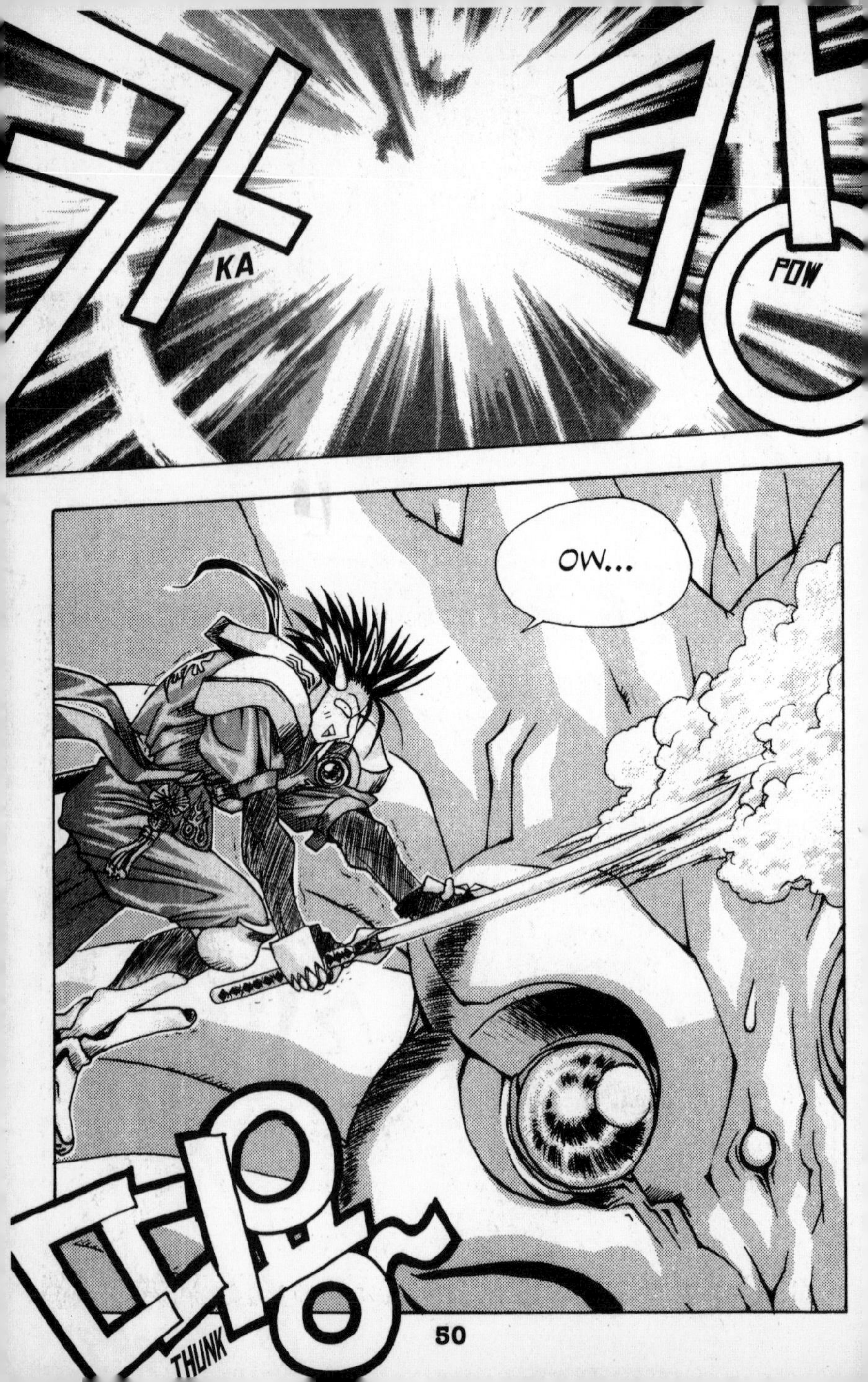
KA
POW
OW...
THUNK

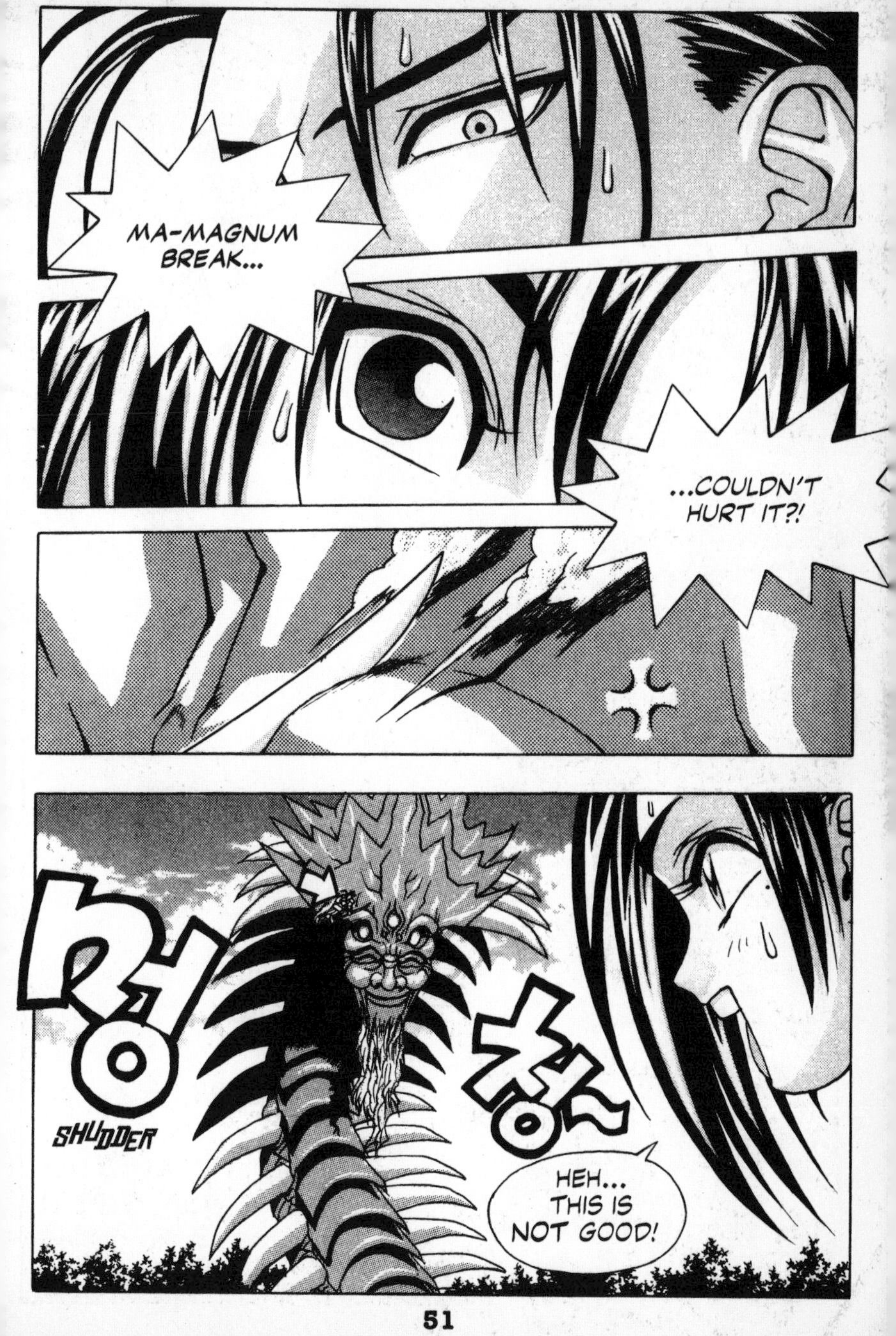
MA-MAGNUM BREAK...
...COULDN'T HURT IT?!
SHUDDER
HEH... THIS IS NOT GOOD!

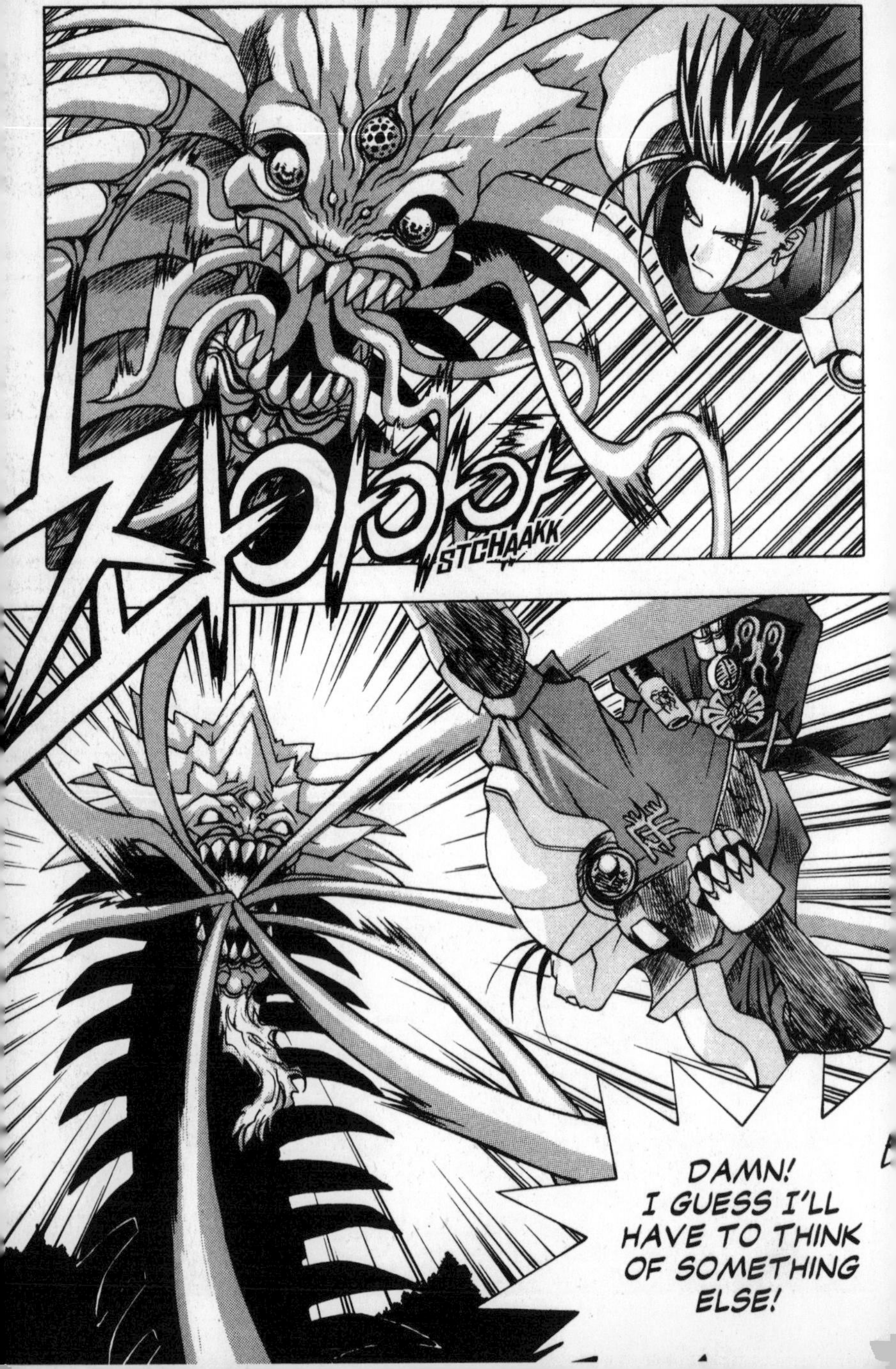
STCHAAKK
DAMN! I GUESS I'LL HAVE TO THINK OF SOMETHING ELSE!

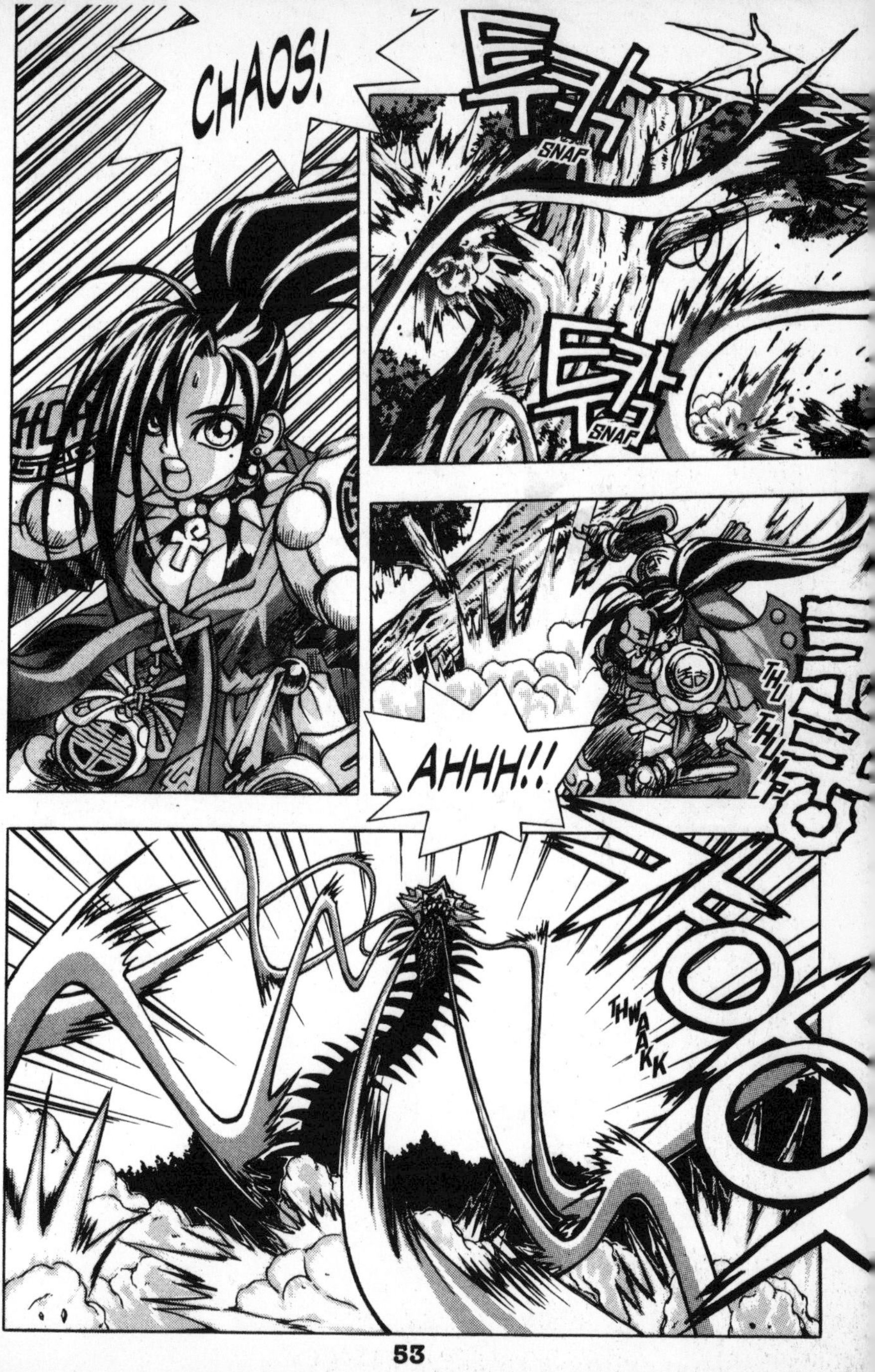
CHAOS!
SNAP
SNAP
AHHH!!
THU THUMP
THWAAKK

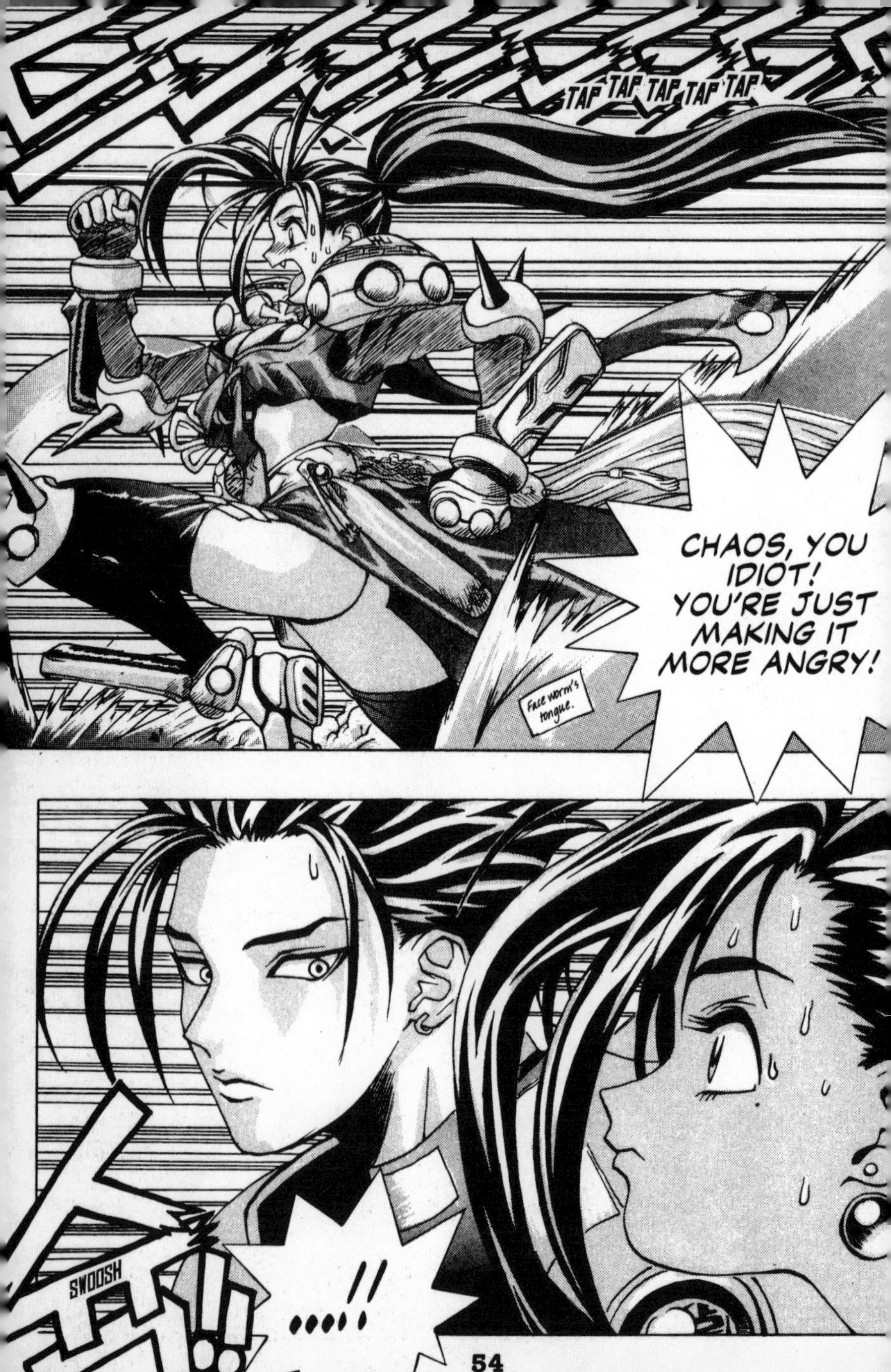
TAP TAP TAP TAP TAP
CHAOS, YOU IDIOT! YOU'RE JUST MAKING IT MORE ANGRY!
Face worm's tongue.
SWOOSH
....!!

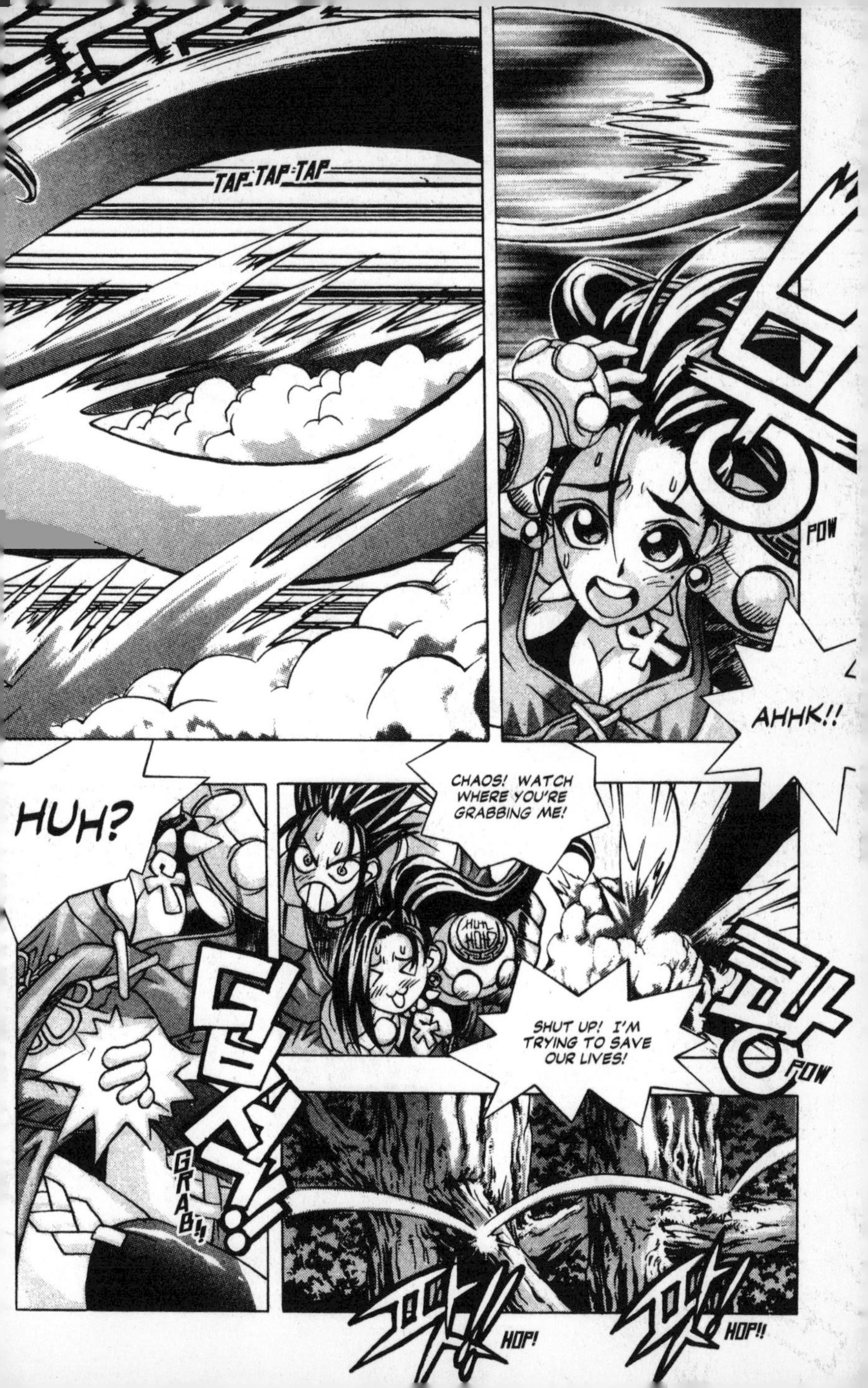
TAP-TAP-TAP
POW
AHHK!!
HUH?
CHAOS! WATCH WHERE YOU'RE GRABBING ME!
GRAB!!
SHUT UP! I'M TRYING TO SAVE OUR LIVES!
POW
HOP!
HOP!!

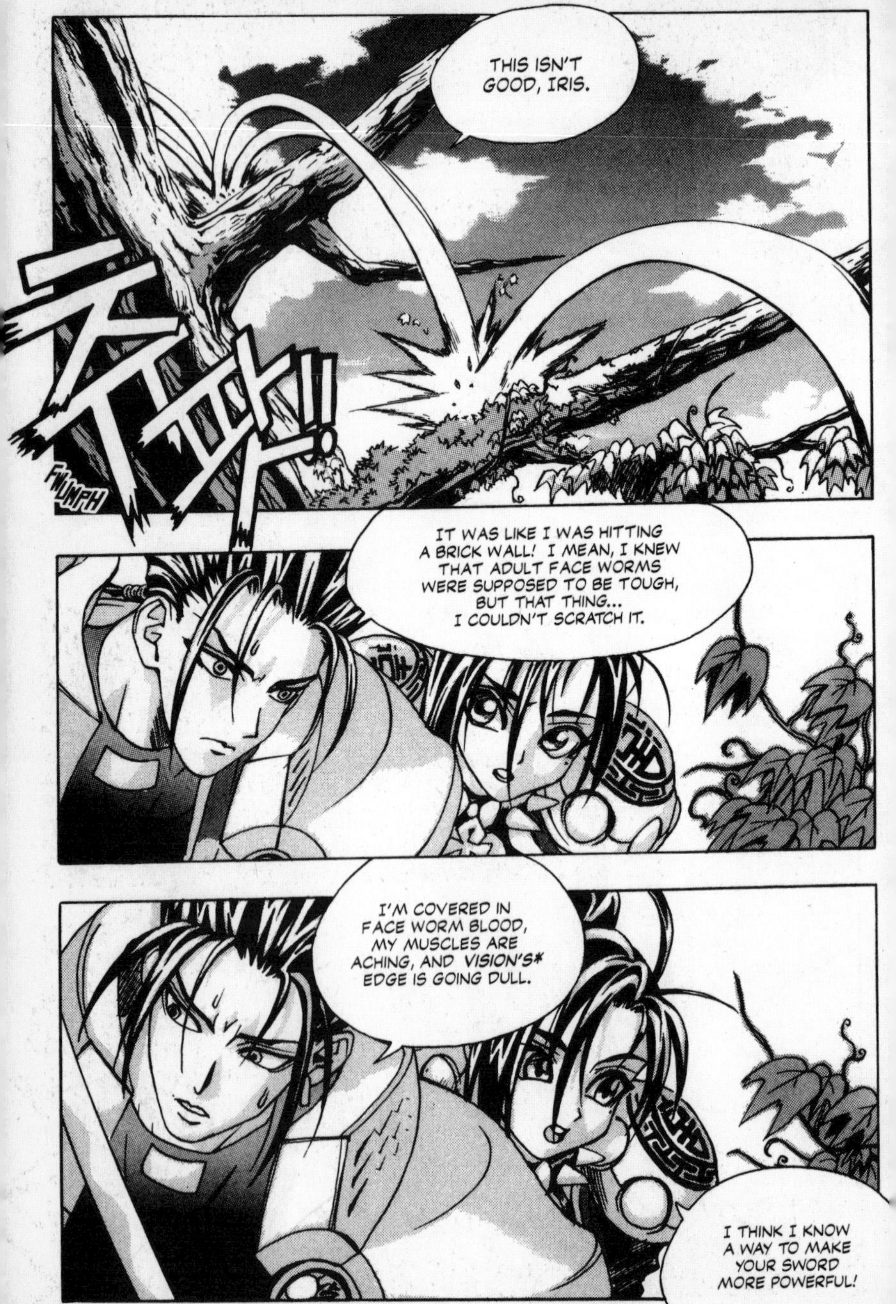
THIS ISN'T GOOD, IRIS.
FWUMPH
IT WAS LIKE I WAS HITTING A BRICK WALL! I MEAN, I KNEW THAT ADULT FACE WORMS WERE SUPPOSED TO BE TOUGH, BUT THAT THING... I COULDN'T SCRATCH IT.
I'M COVERED IN FACE WORM BLOOD, MY MUSCLES ARE ACHING, AND VISION'S* EDGE IS GOING DULL.
I THINK I KNOW A WAY TO MAKE YOUR SWORD MORE POWERFUL!

* VISION: CHAOS'S SWORD, AN ENCHANTED BLADE.

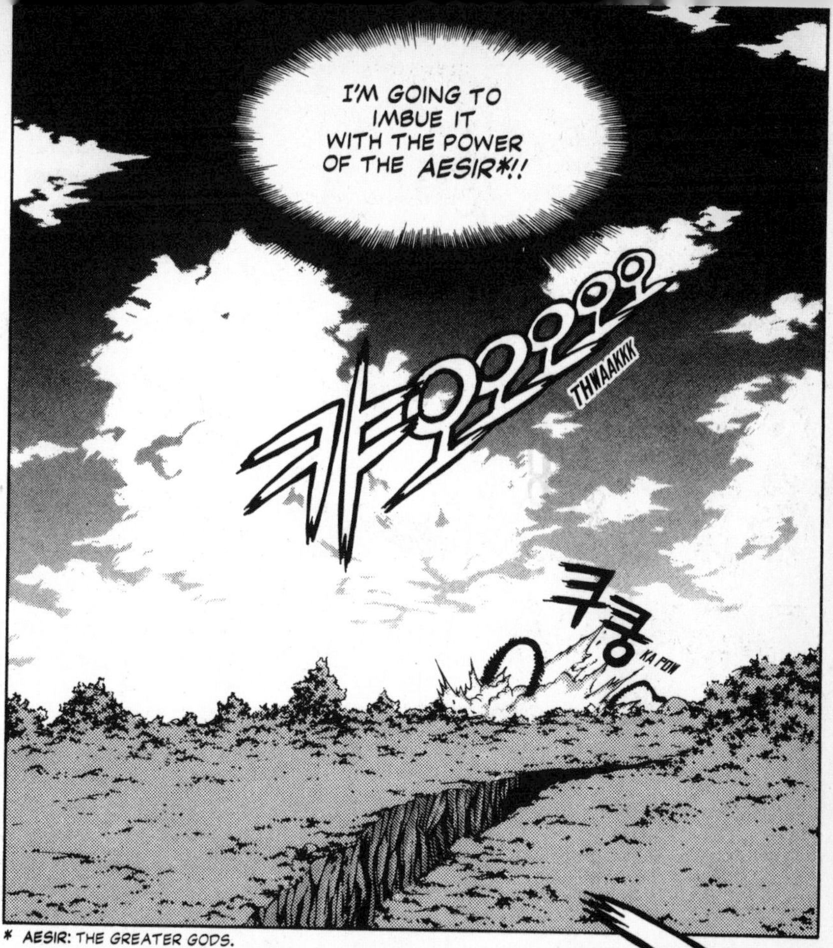
I'M GOING TO IMBUE IT WITH THE POWER OF THE AESIR*!!
THWAAKKK
쿠쿵
KA POW

* AESIR: THE GREATER GODS.

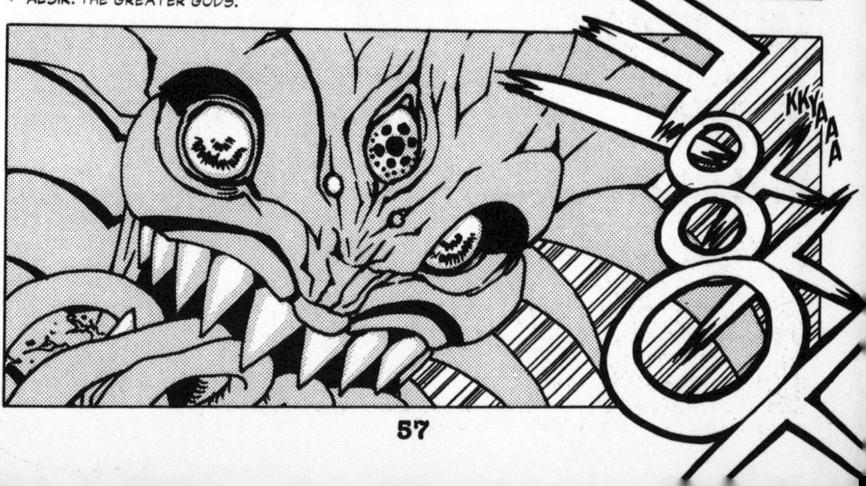
KKYAAA

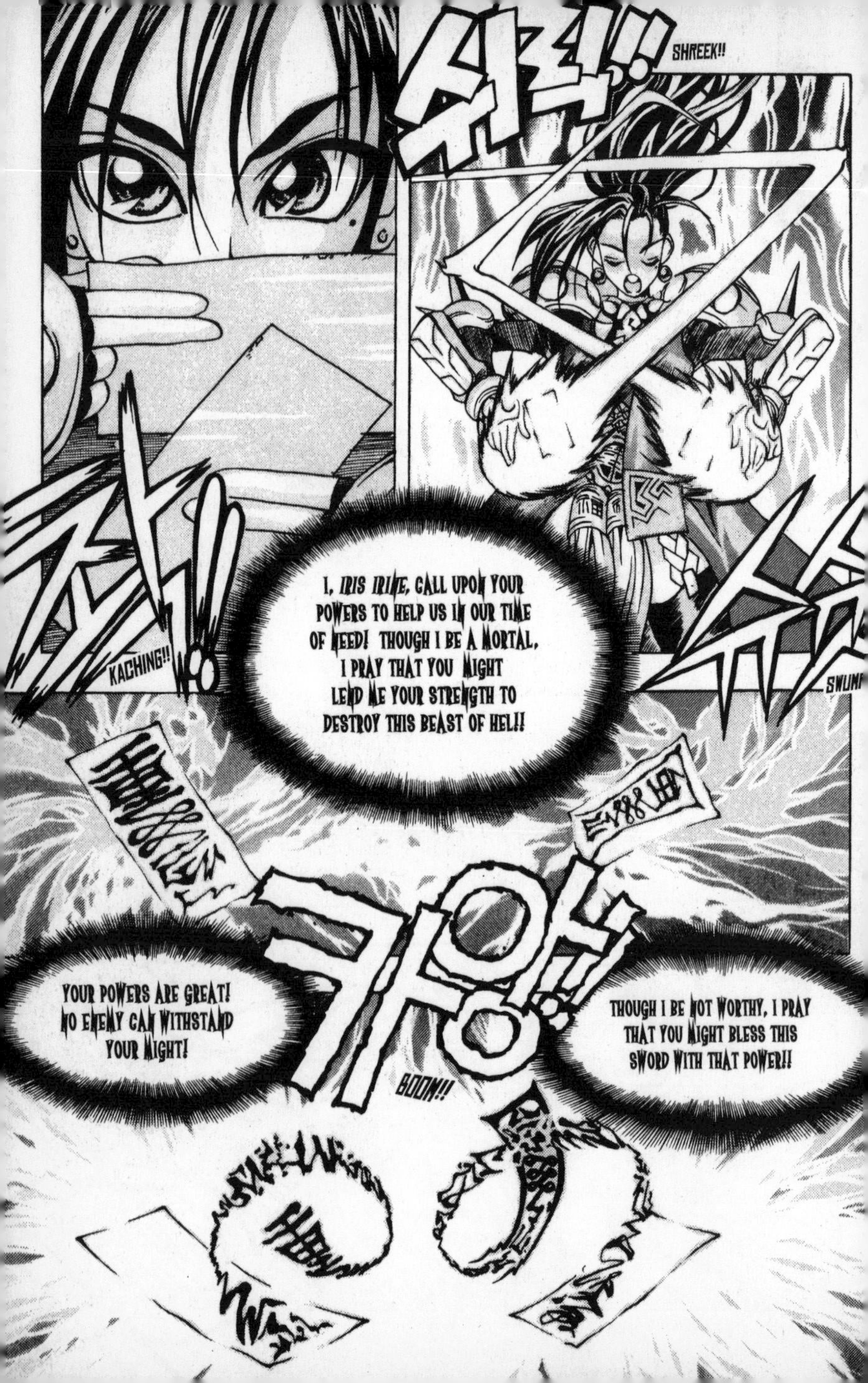
KACHING!!
SHREEK!!
SWUM
I, IRIS IRINE, CALL UPON YOUR POWERS TO HELP US IN OUR TIME OF NEED! THOUGH I BE A MORTAL, I PRAY THAT YOU MIGHT LEND ME YOUR STRENGTH TO DESTROY THIS BEAST OF HEL!!
YOUR POWERS ARE GREAT! NO ENEMY CAN WITHSTAND YOUR MIGHT!
BOOM!!
THOUGH I BE NOT WORTHY, I PRAY THAT YOU MIGHT BLESS THIS SWORD WITH THAT POWER!!

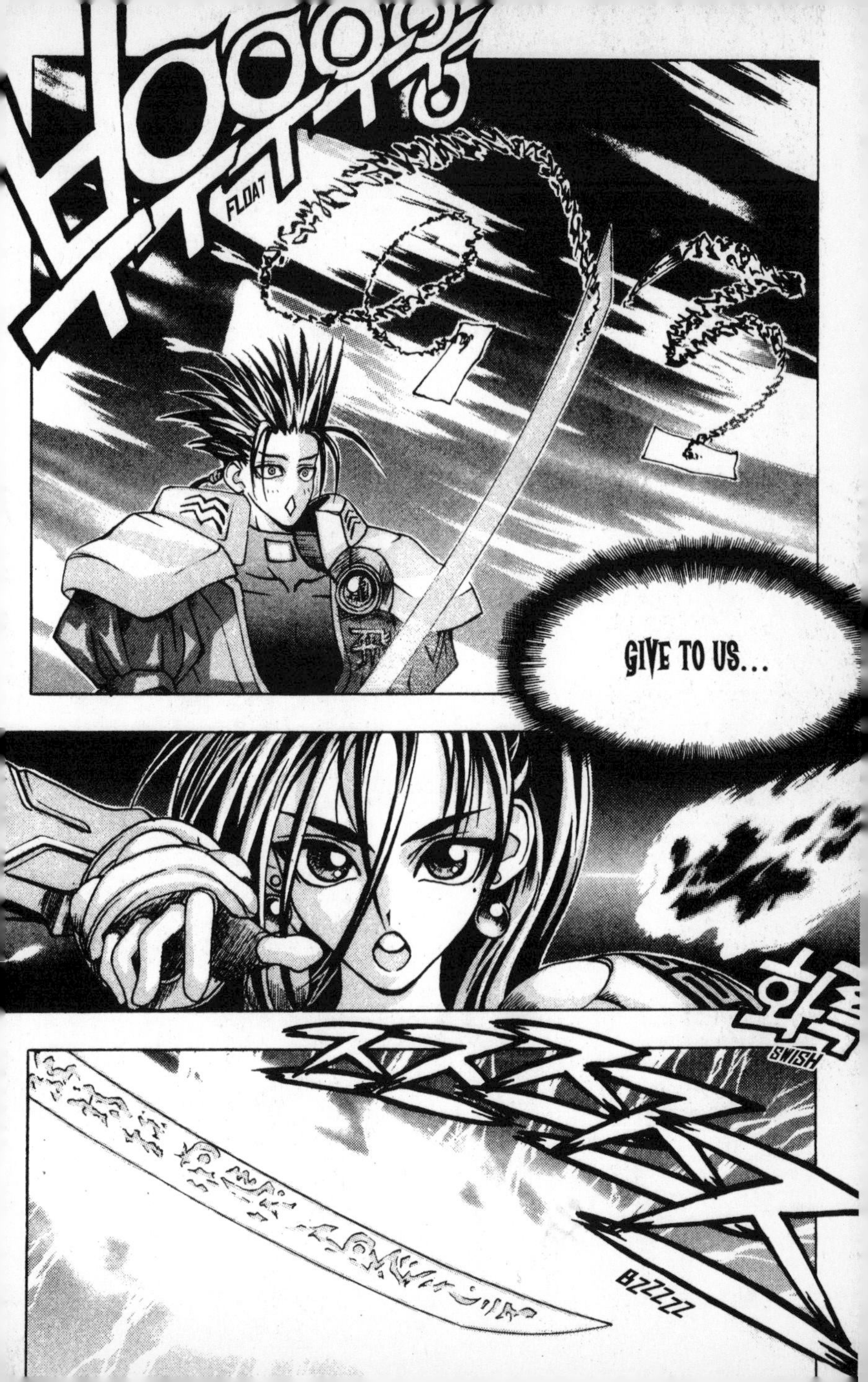
FLOAT
GIVE TO US...
SWISH
BZZZZZ

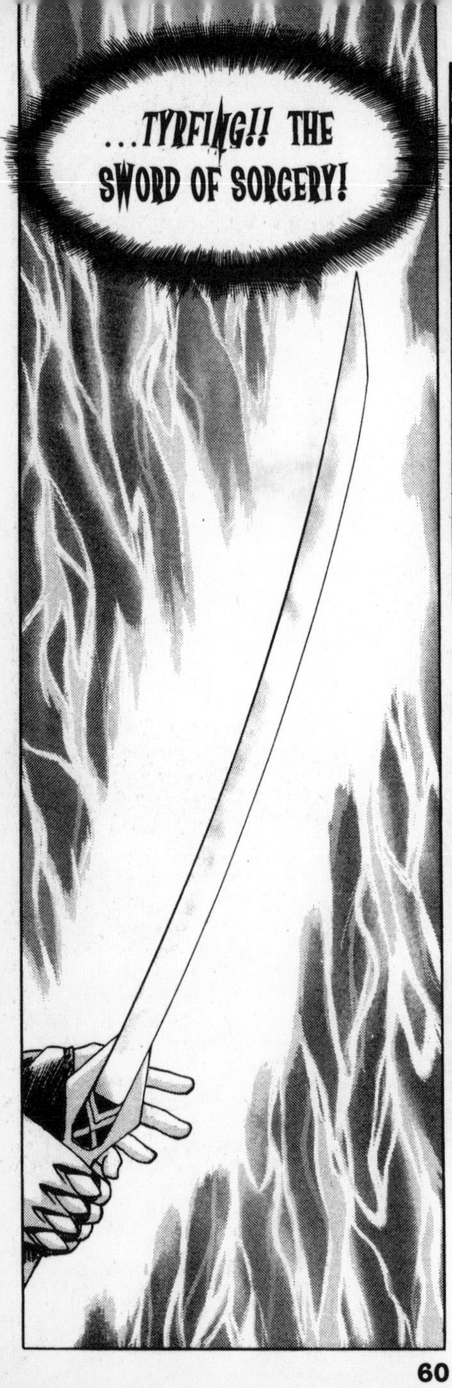
...TYRFING!! THE SWORD OF SORCERY!

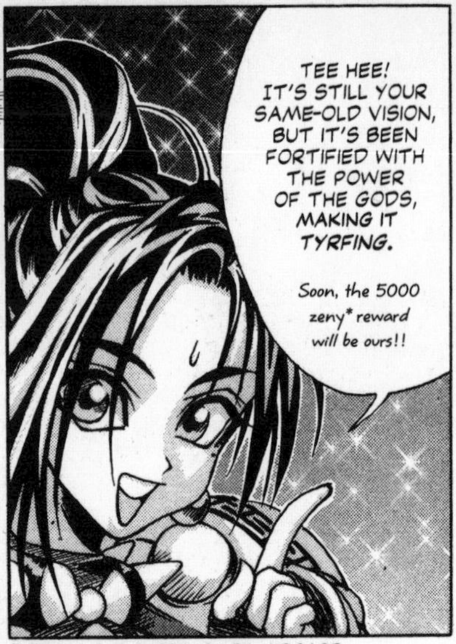
TEE HEE! IT'S STILL YOUR SAME-OLD VISION, BUT IT'S BEEN FORTIFIED WITH THE POWER OF THE GODS, MAKING IT TYRFING.
Soon, the 5000 zeny* reward will be ours!!

* ZENY: THE CURRENCY OF MIDGARD.

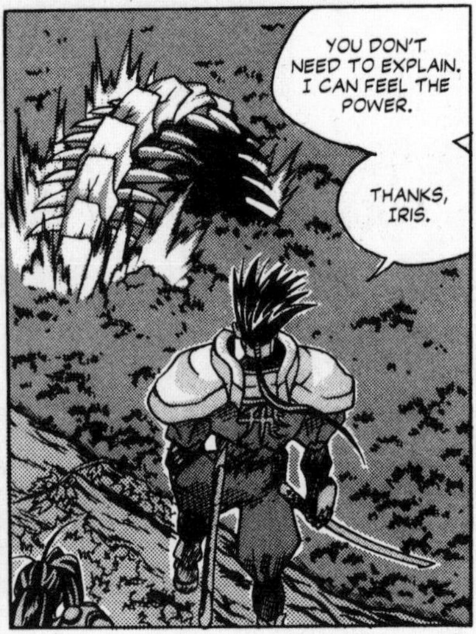
YOU DON'T NEED TO EXPLAIN. I CAN FEEL THE POWER.
THANKS, IRIS.

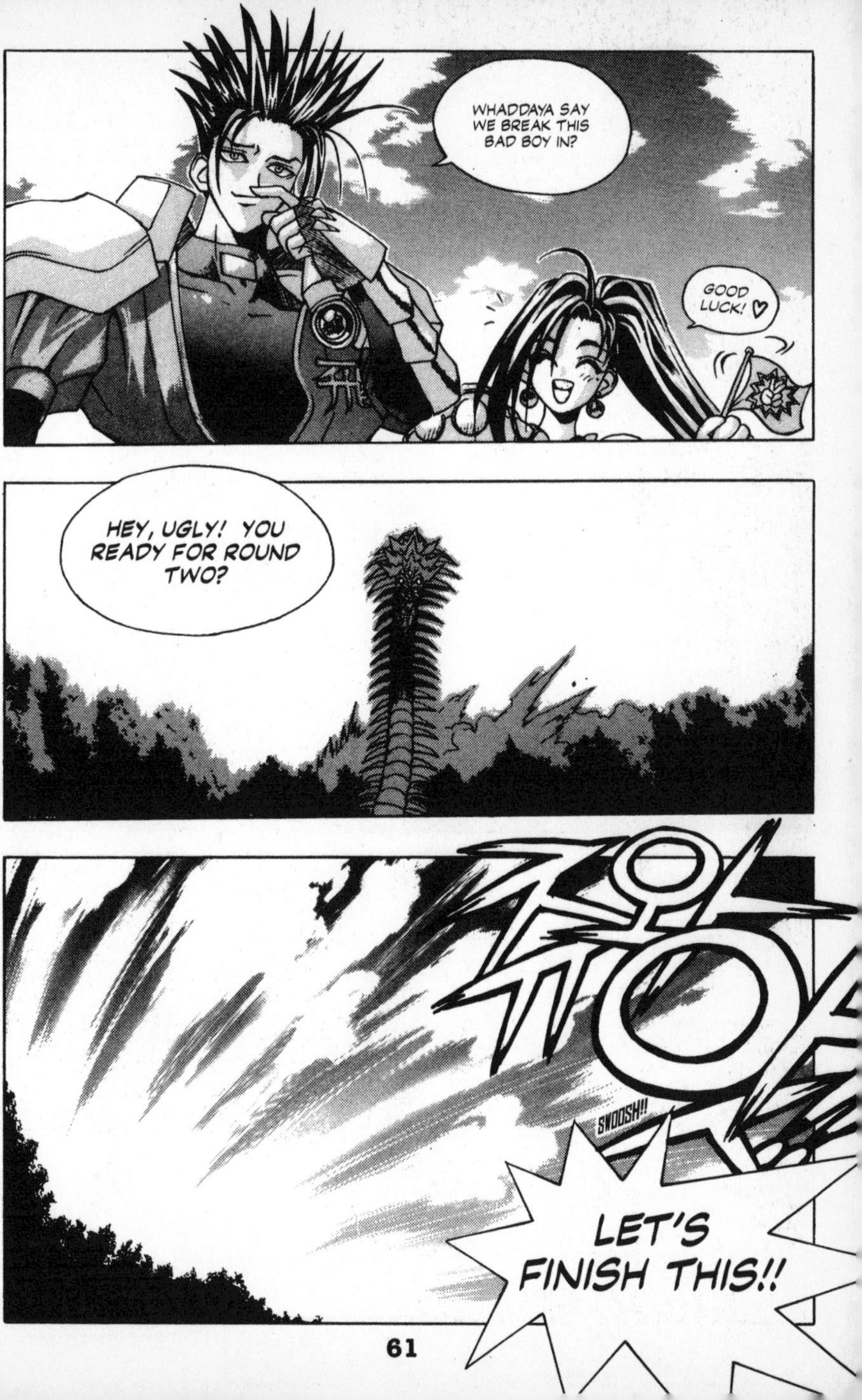
WHADDAYA SAY WE BREAK THIS BAD BOY IN?
GOOD LUCK! ♡
HEY, UGLY! YOU READY FOR ROUND TWO?
SWOOSH!!
LET'S FINISH THIS!!

THE VILLAGE OF ALBERTA: A PORT TOWN ON THE SOUTHEAST COAST OF THE MIDGARD KINGDOM.

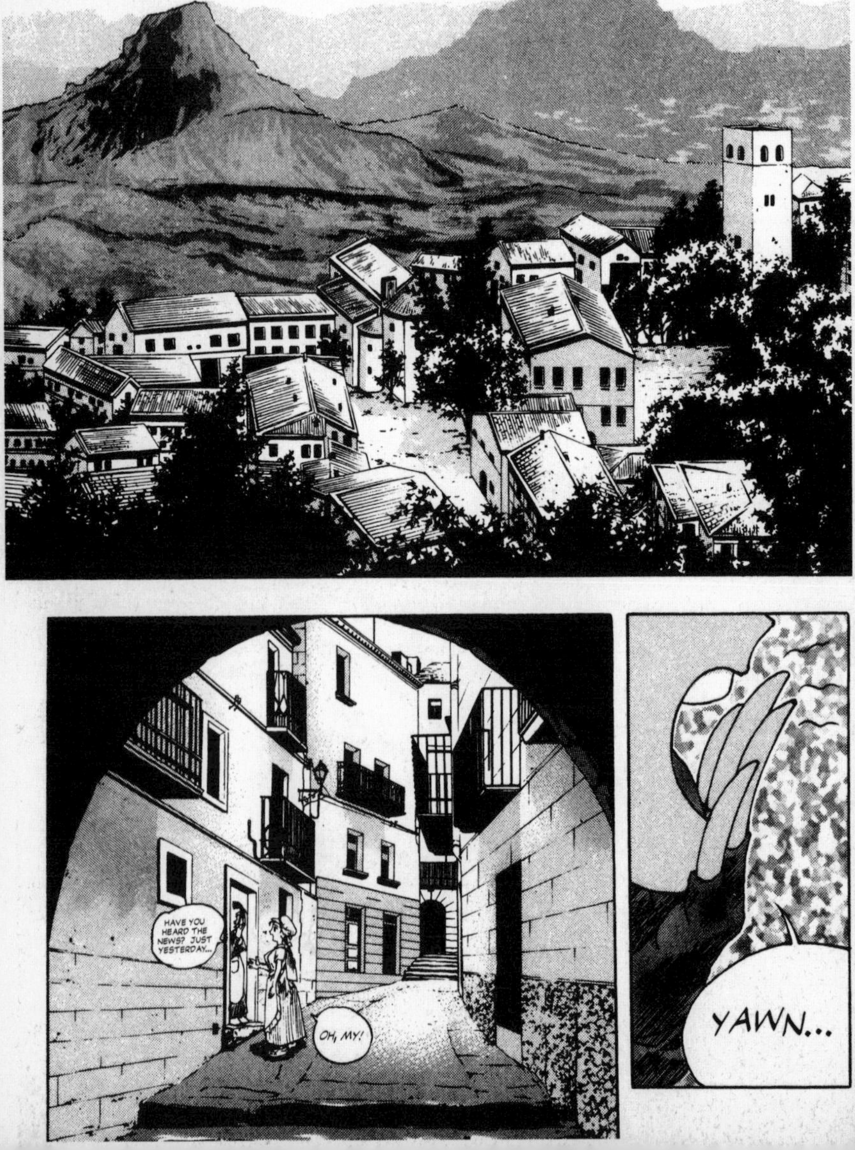
HAVE YOU HEARD THE NEWS? JUST YESTERDAY...
OH, MY!
YAWN...

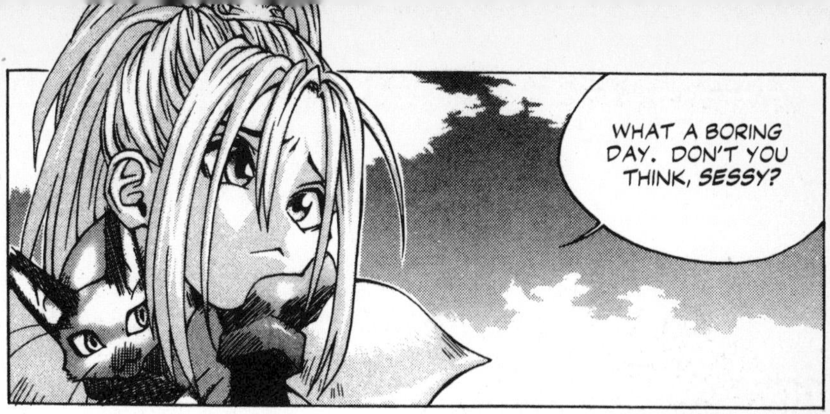
WHAT A BORING DAY. DON'T YOU THINK, SESSY?

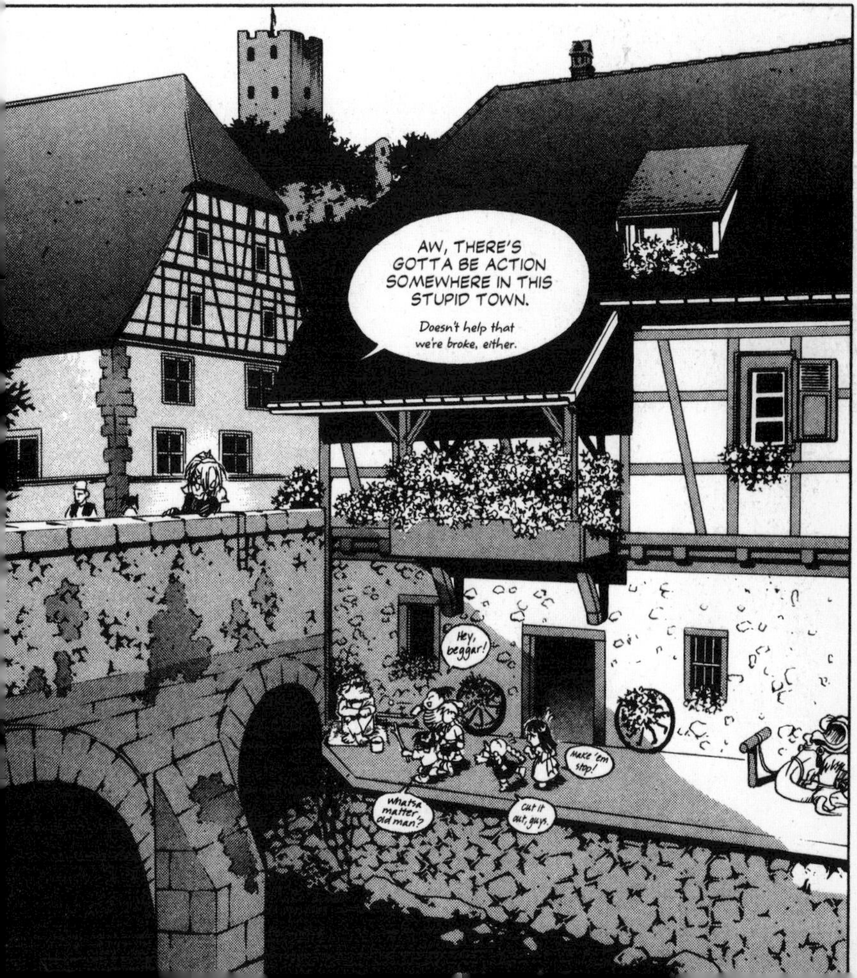
AW, THERE'S GOTTA BE ACTION SOMEWHERE IN THIS STUPID TOWN.
Doesn't help that we're broke, either.
Hey, beggar!
whatsa matter, old man?
Cut it out, guys.
Make 'em stop!

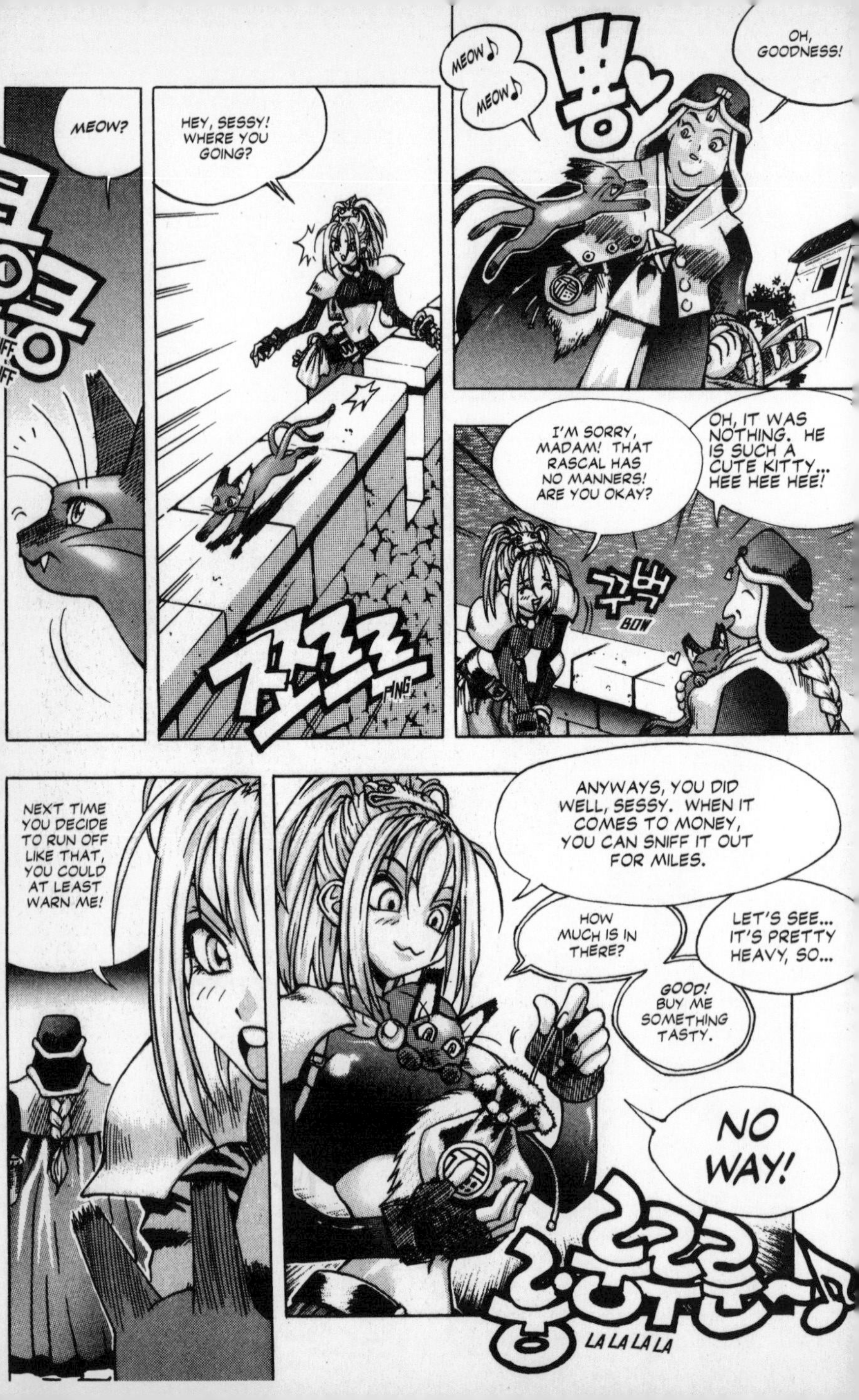

MEOW?
SNIFF SNIFF
HEY, SESSY! WHERE YOU GOING?
PING
MEOW♪ MEOW♪
뿅
OH, GOODNESS!
I'M SORRY, MADAM! THAT RASCAL HAS NO MANNERS! ARE YOU OKAY?
OH, IT WAS NOTHING. HE IS SUCH A CUTE KITTY... HEE HEE HEE!
꾸벅
BOW
NEXT TIME YOU DECIDE TO RUN OFF LIKE THAT, YOU COULD AT LEAST WARN ME!
ANYWAYS, YOU DID WELL, SESSY. WHEN IT COMES TO MONEY, YOU CAN SNIFF IT OUT FOR MILES.
HOW MUCH IS IN THERE?
LET'S SEE... IT'S PRETTY HEAVY, SO...
GOOD! BUY ME SOMETHING TASTY.
NO WAY!
LA LA LA LA

RAGNARÖK

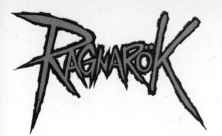

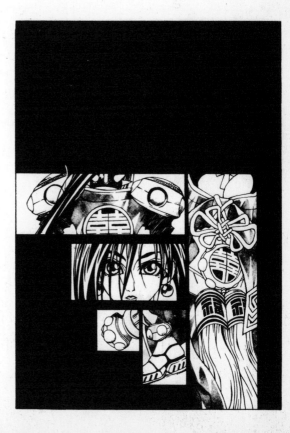

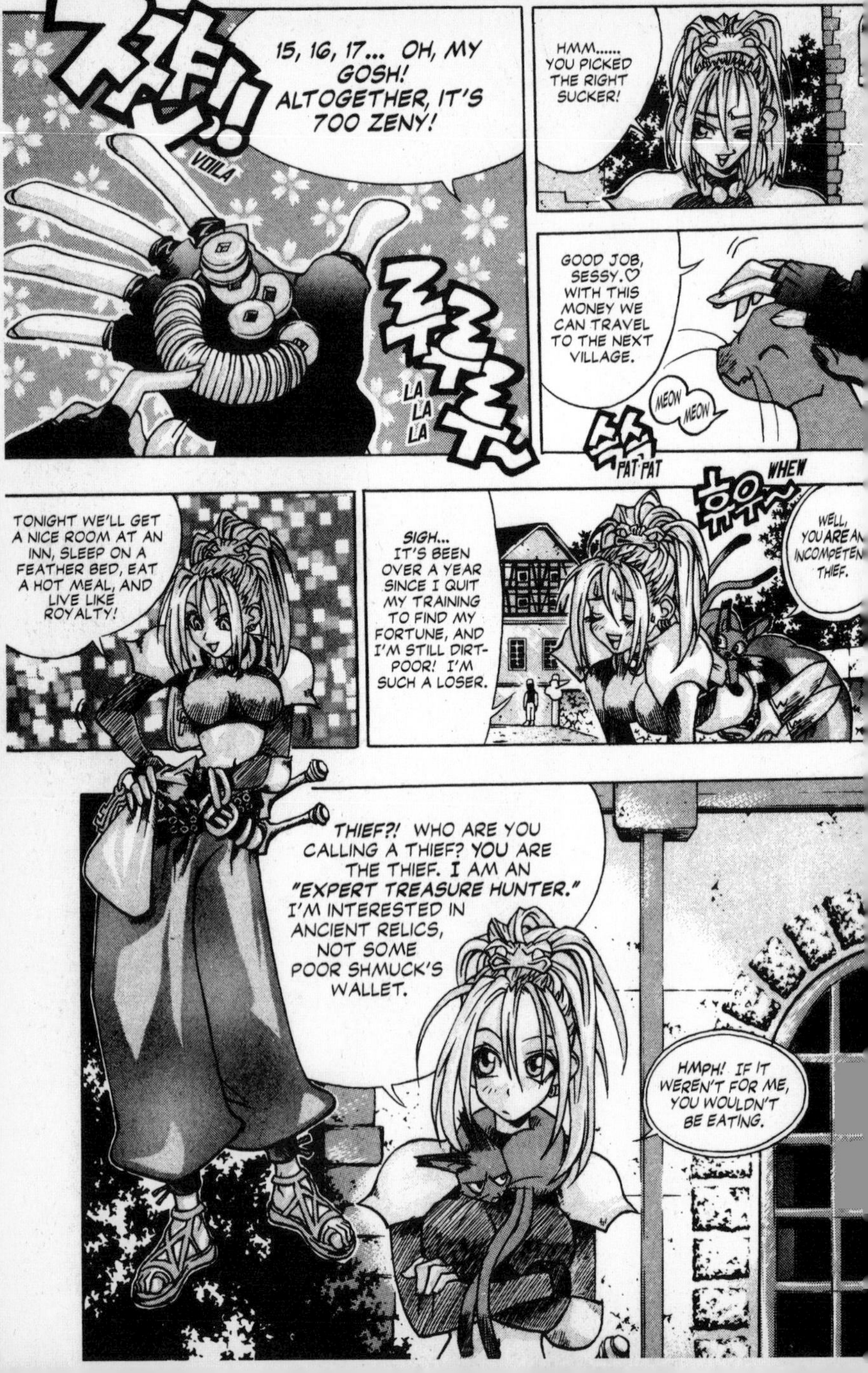
15, 16, 17... OH, MY GOSH! ALTOGETHER, IT'S 700 ZENY!
VOILA
LA LA LA
HMM...... YOU PICKED THE RIGHT SUCKER!
GOOD JOB, SESSY.♡ WITH THIS MONEY WE CAN TRAVEL TO THE NEXT VILLAGE.
MEOW MEOW
PAT PAT
TONIGHT WE'LL GET A NICE ROOM AT AN INN, SLEEP ON A FEATHER BED, EAT A HOT MEAL, AND LIVE LIKE ROYALTY!
SIGH... IT'S BEEN OVER A YEAR SINCE I QUIT MY TRAINING TO FIND MY FORTUNE, AND I'M STILL DIRT-POOR! I'M SUCH A LOSER.
휴우~
WHEW
WELL, YOU ARE AN INCOMPETEN THIEF.
THIEF?! WHO ARE YOU CALLING A THIEF? YOU ARE THE THIEF. I AM AN "EXPERT TREASURE HUNTER." I'M INTERESTED IN ANCIENT RELICS, NOT SOME POOR SHMUCK'S WALLET.
HMPH! IF IT WEREN'T FOR ME, YOU WOULDN'T BE EATING.

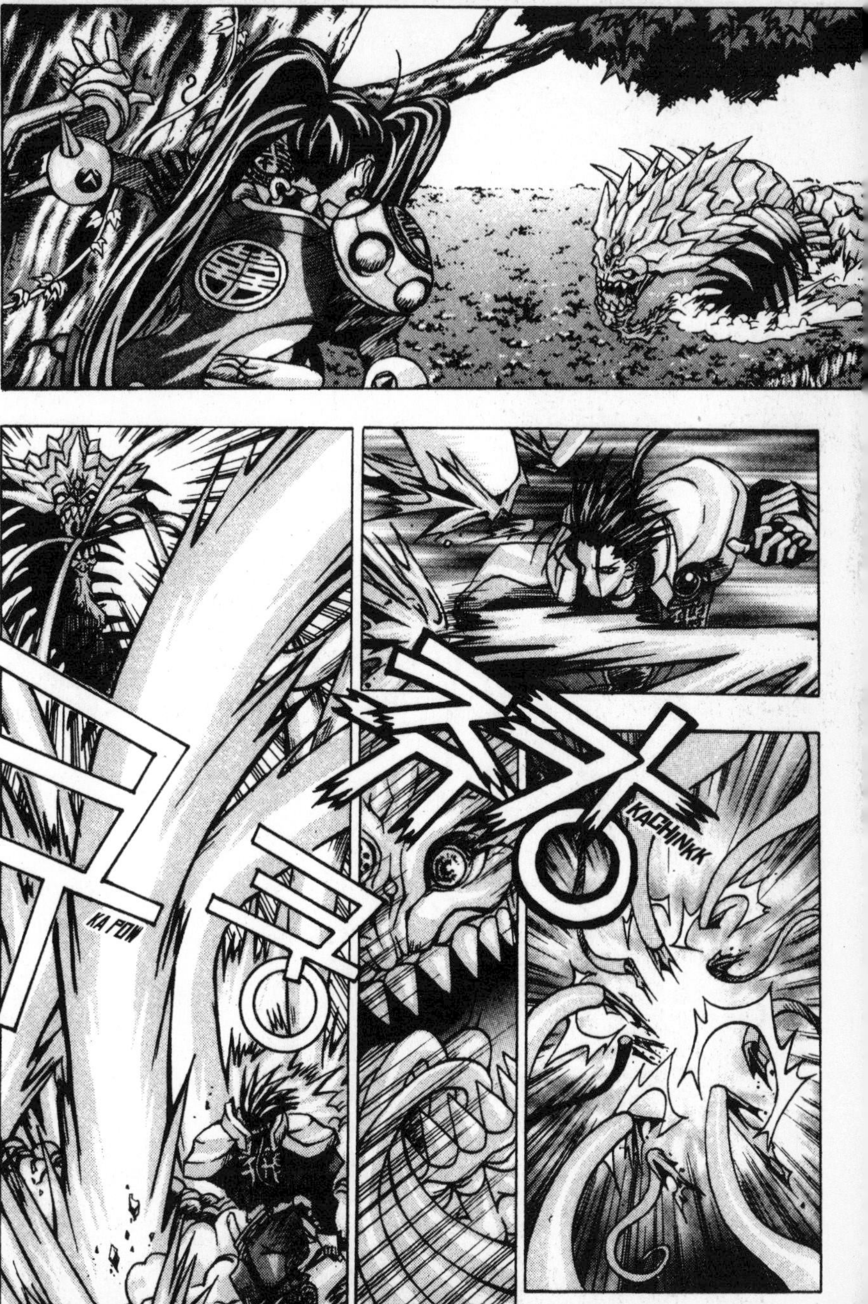
KA POW
KACHINKK

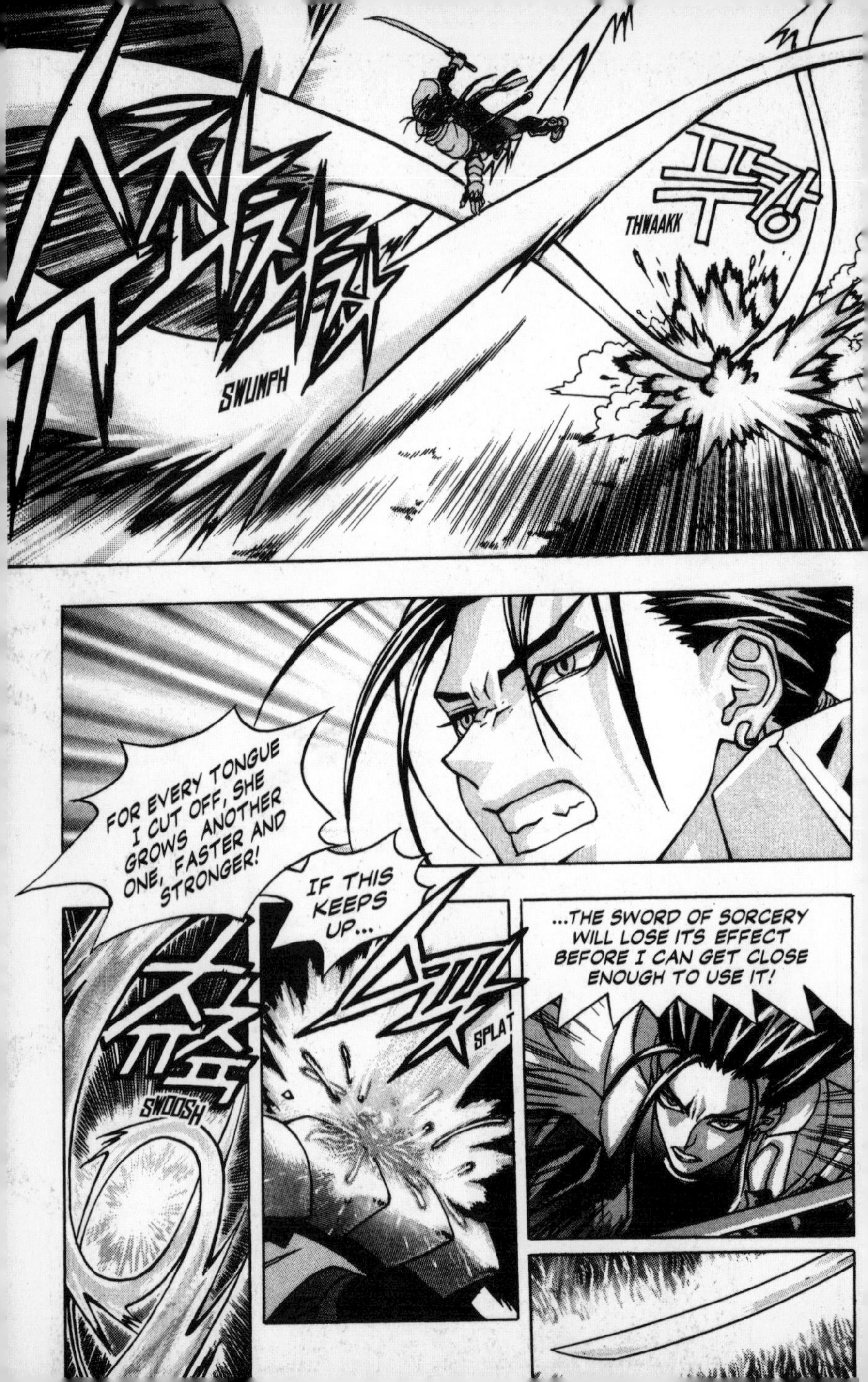
SWUMPH
THWAAKK
FOR EVERY TONGUE I CUT OFF, SHE GROWS ANOTHER ONE, FASTER AND STRONGER!
SWOOSH
IF THIS KEEPS UP...
SPLAT
...THE SWORD OF SORCERY WILL LOSE ITS EFFECT BEFORE I CAN GET CLOSE ENOUGH TO USE IT!

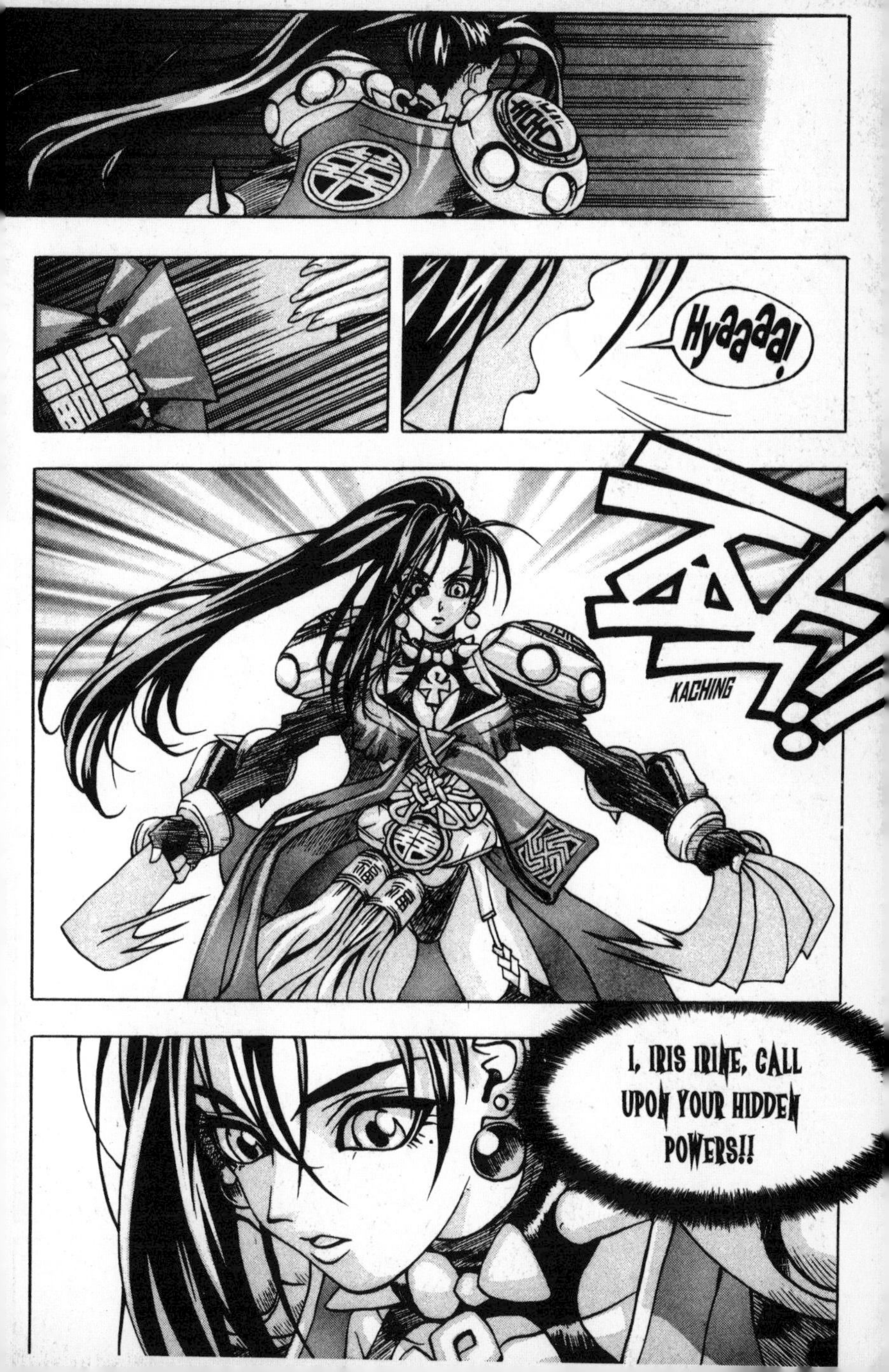
Hyaaaa!
KACHING
I, IRIS IRINE, CALL UPON YOUR HIDDEN POWERS!!

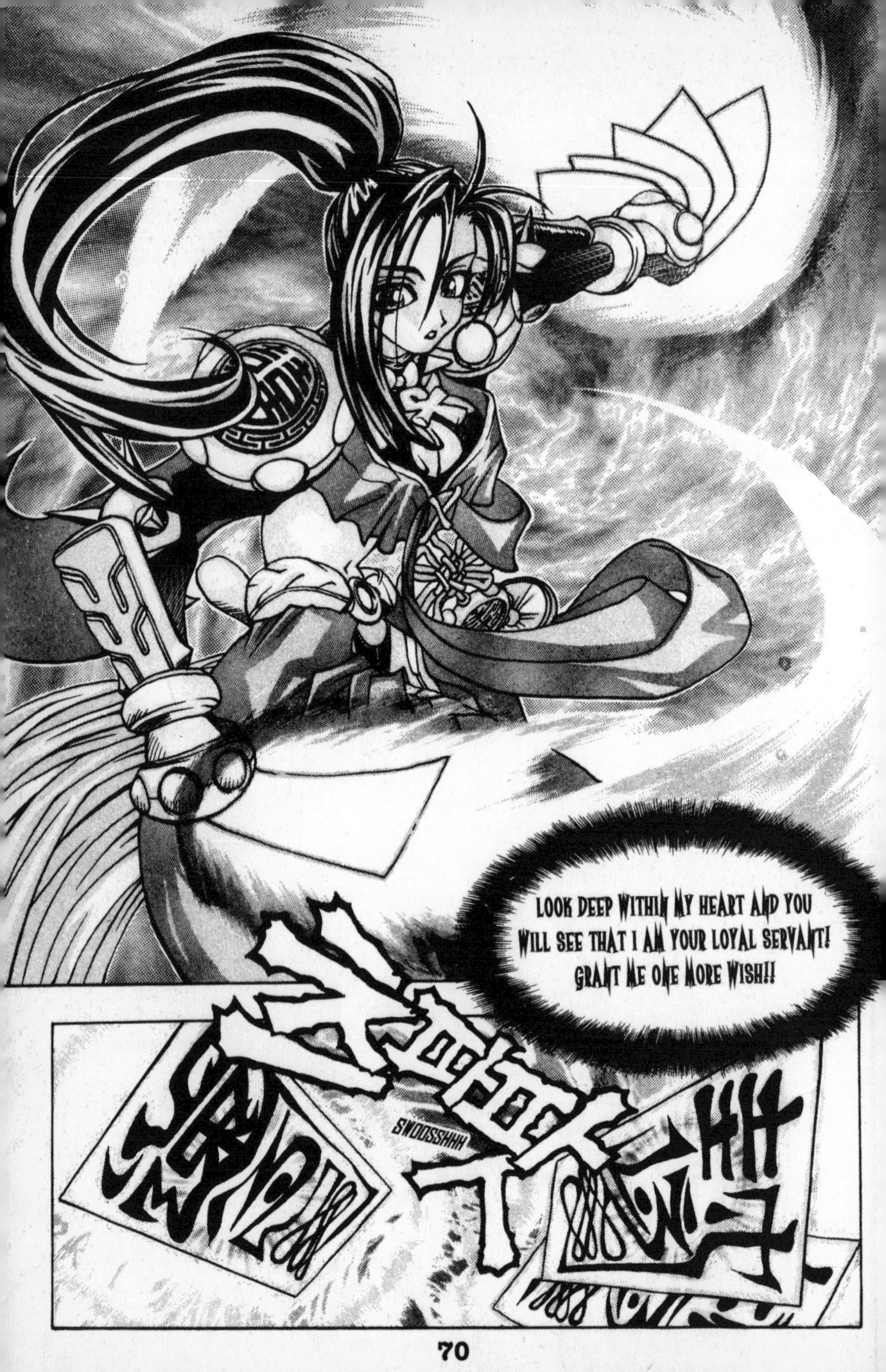
LOOK DEEP WITHIN MY HEART AND YOU WILL SEE THAT I AM YOUR LOYAL SERVANT! GRANT ME ONE MORE WISH!!
SWOOSSHHH

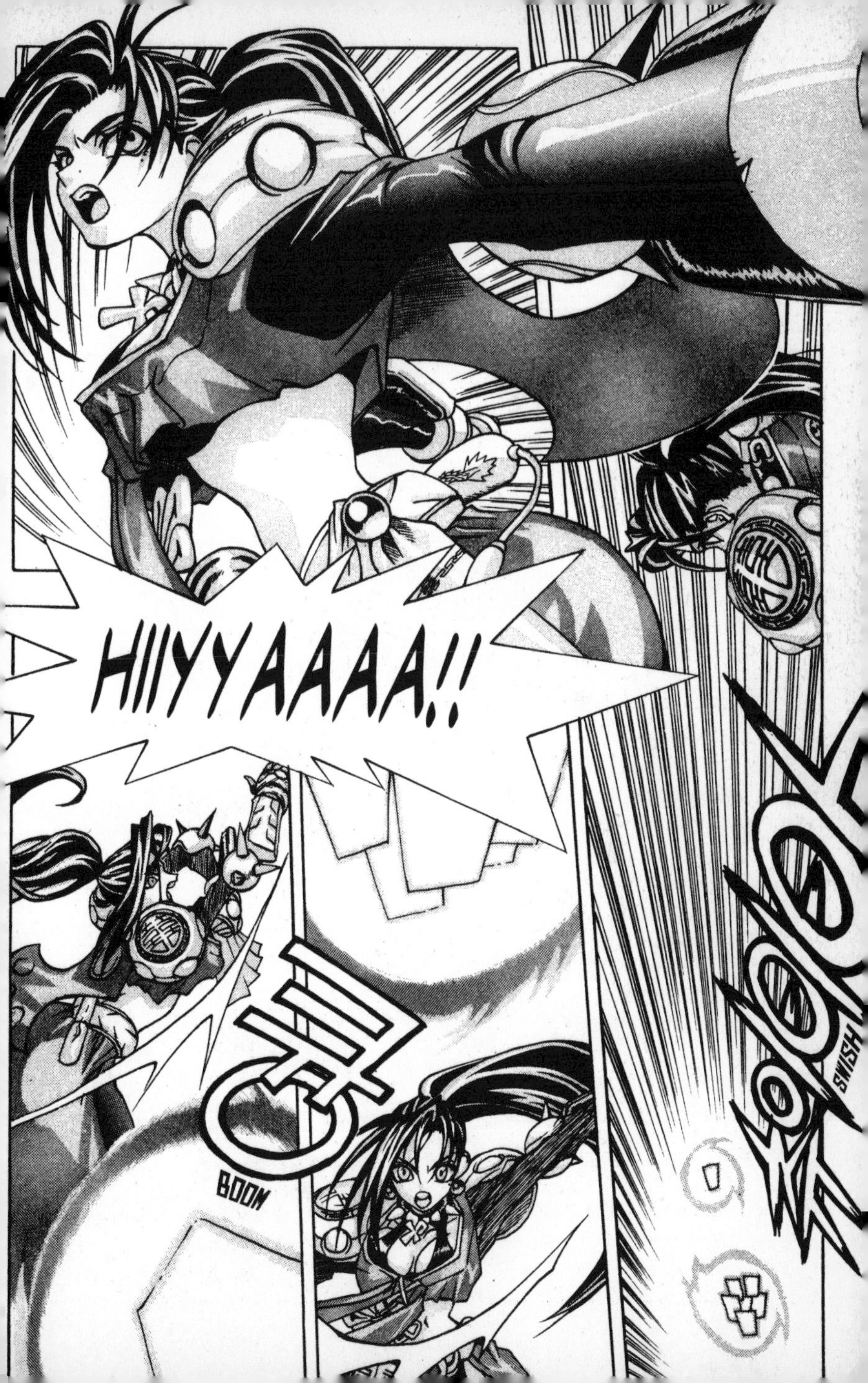
HIIYYAAAA!!
BOOM
SWISH

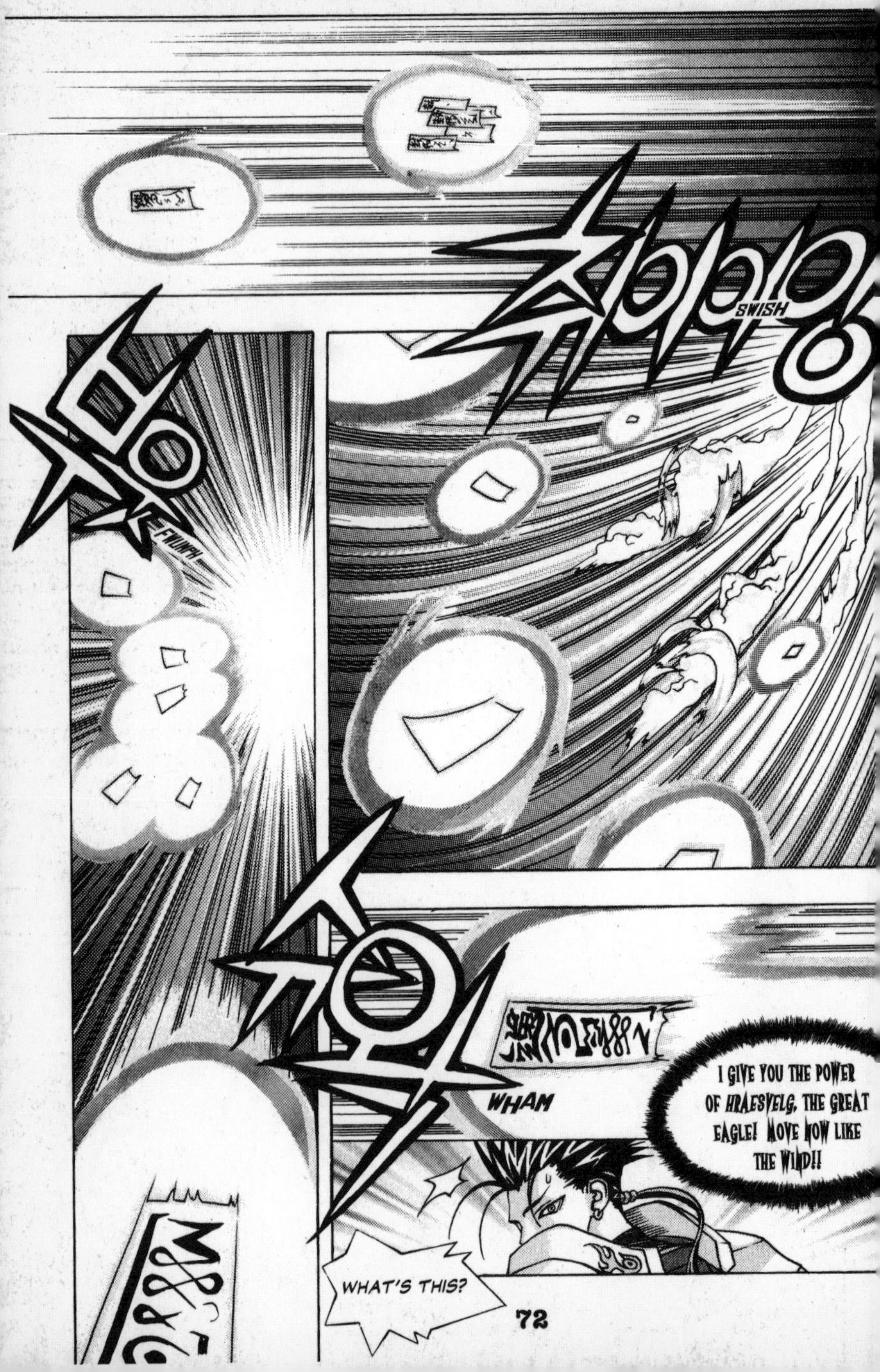
SWISH
FWUMPH
WHAM
I GIVE YOU THE POWER OF HRAESVELG, THE GREAT EAGLE! MOVE NOW LIKE THE WIND!!
WHAT'S THIS?

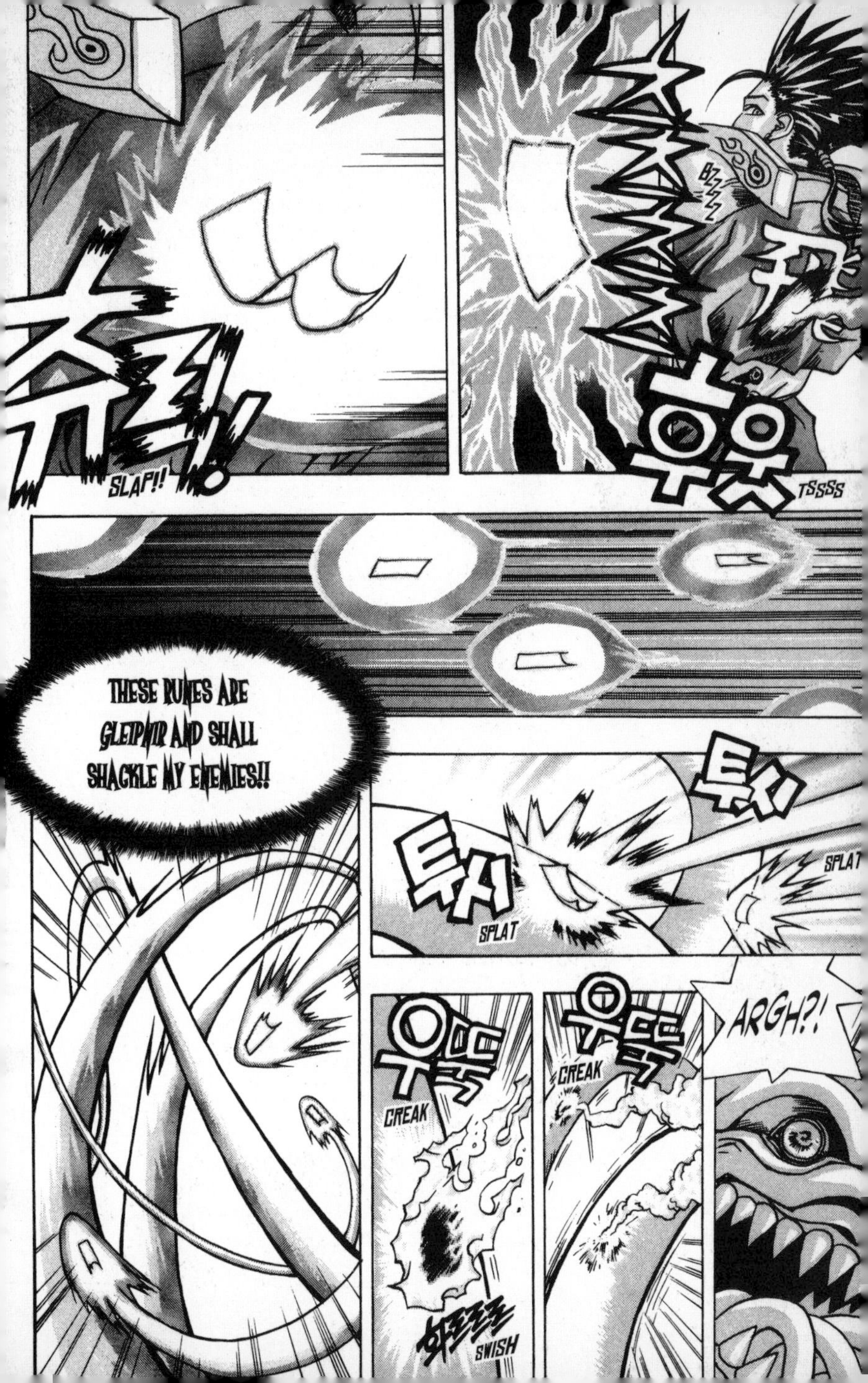
SLAP!!
BZZZZ
TSSSS
THESE RUNES ARE GLEIPNIR AND SHALL SHACKLE MY ENEMIES!!
SPLAT
SPLAT
CREAK
CREAK
ARGH?!
SWISH

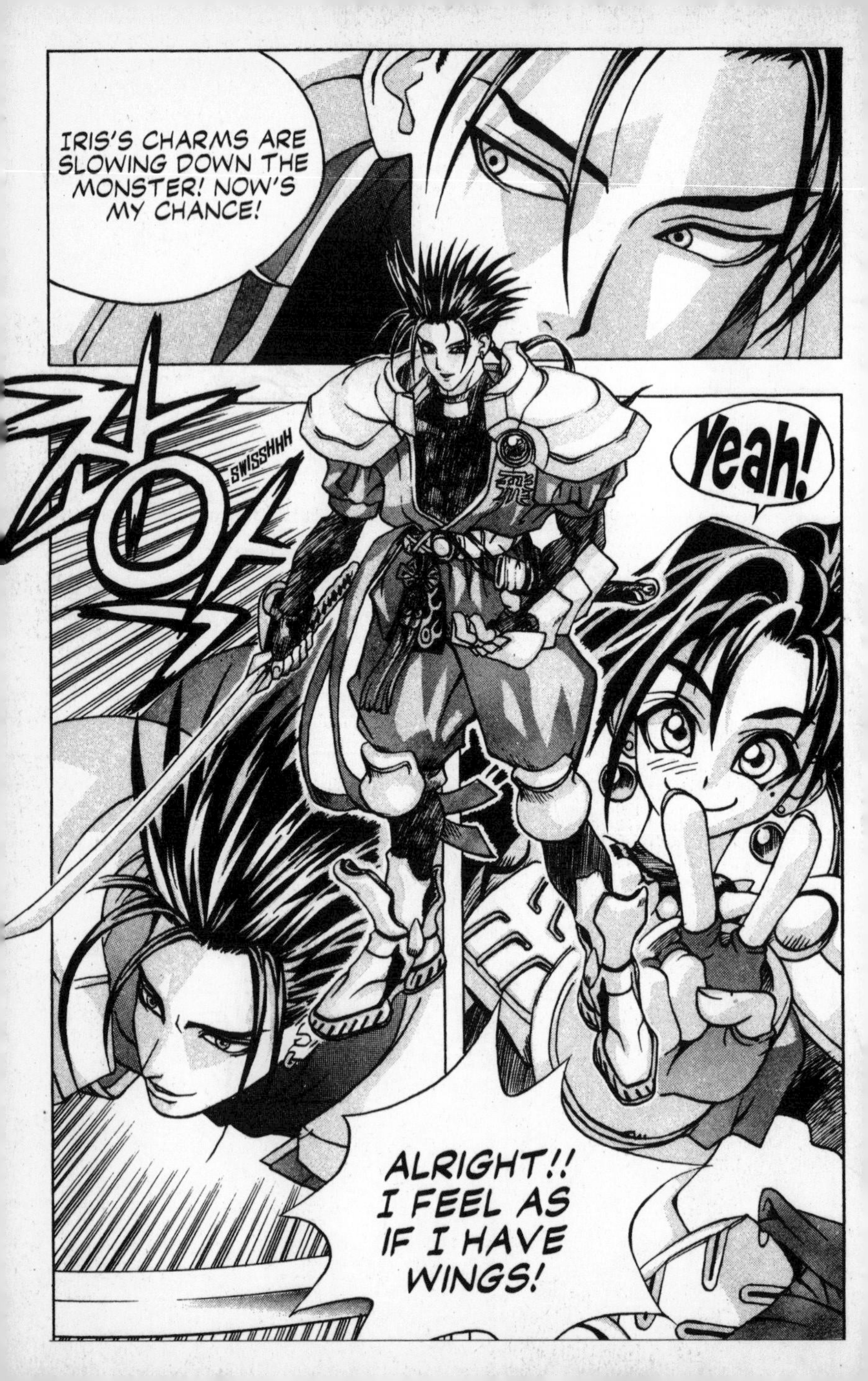
IRIS'S CHARMS ARE SLOWING DOWN THE MONSTER! NOW'S MY CHANCE!
SWISSHHH
Yeah!
ALRIGHT!! I FEEL AS IF I HAVE WINGS!

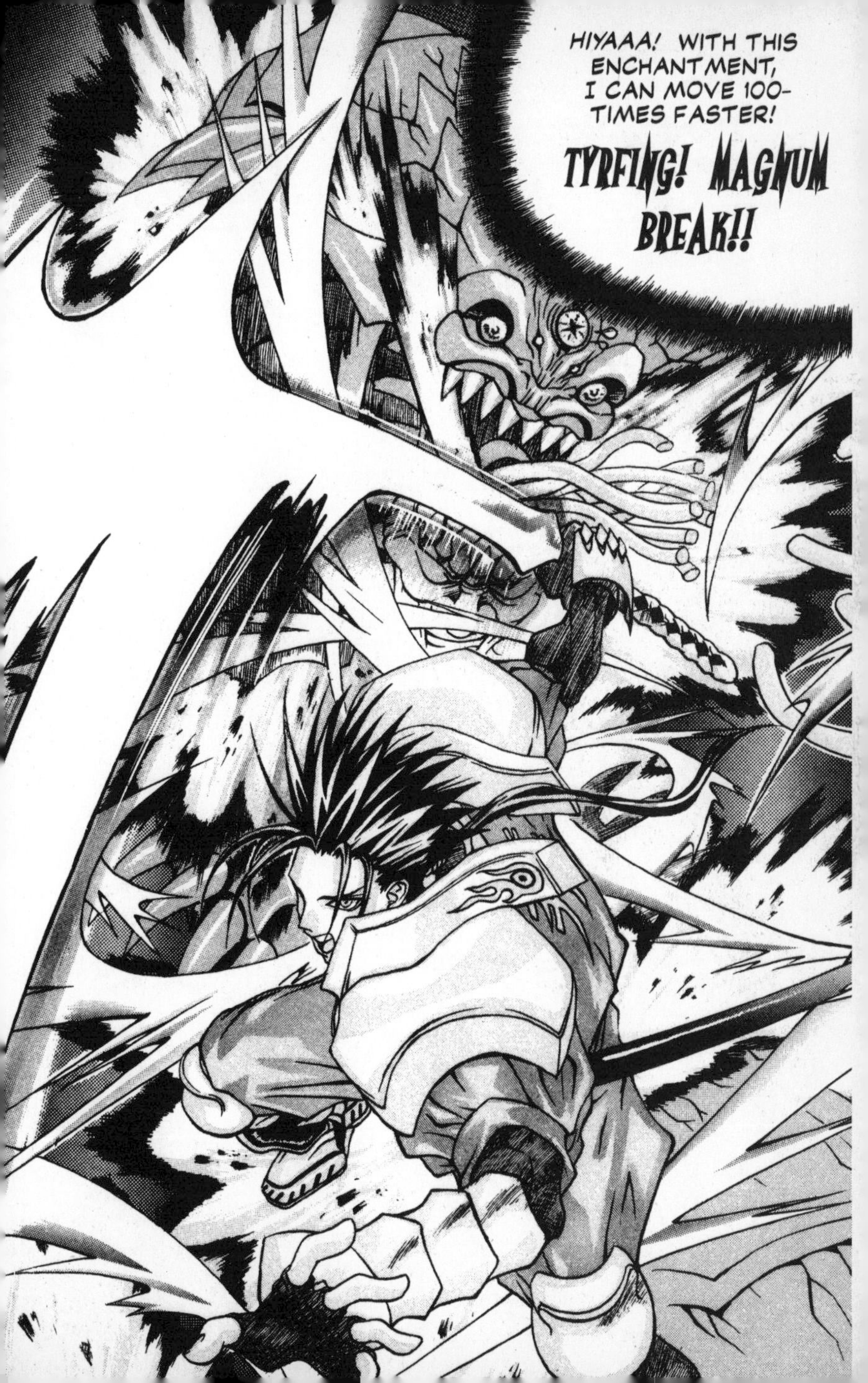
HIYAAA! WITH THIS ENCHANTMENT, I CAN MOVE 100-TIMES FASTER!
TYRFING! MAGNUM BREAK!!

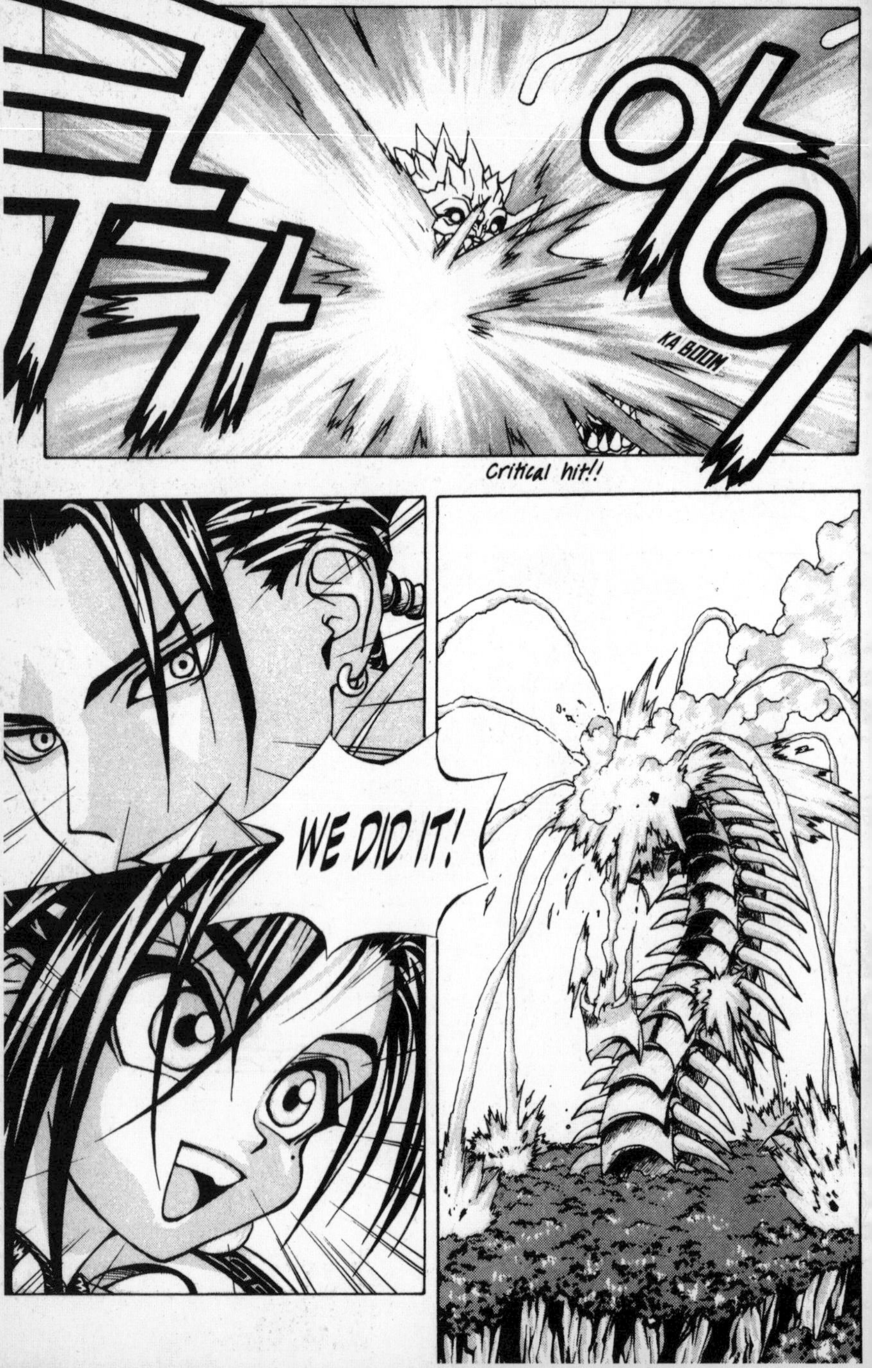
KA BOOM
Critical hit!!
WE DID IT!

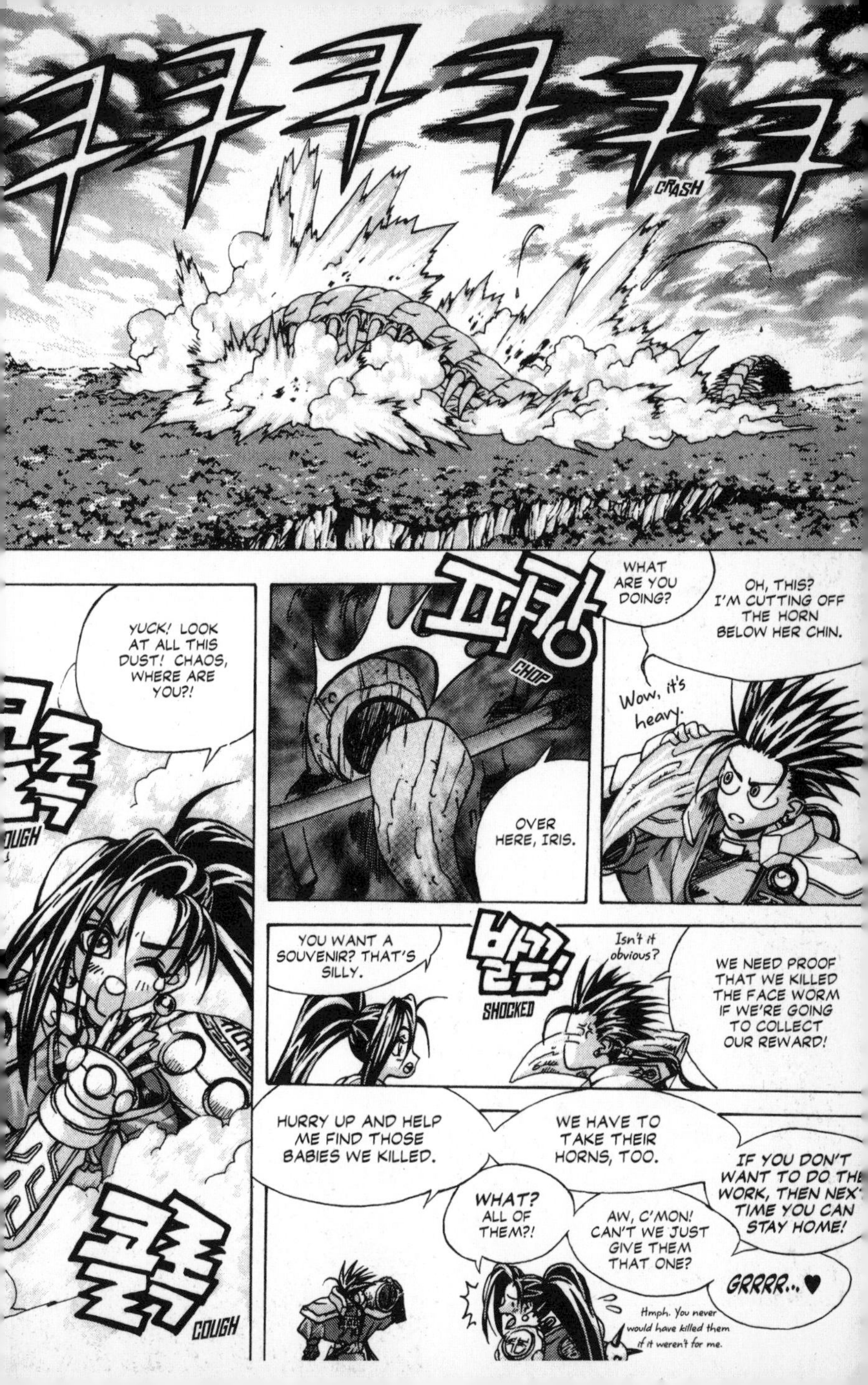
CRASH
YUCK! LOOK AT ALL THIS DUST! CHAOS, WHERE ARE YOU?!
COUGH
COUGH
CHOP
OVER HERE, IRIS.
WHAT ARE YOU DOING?
OH, THIS? I'M CUTTING OFF THE HORN BELOW HER CHIN.
Wow, it's heavy.
YOU WANT A SOUVENIR? THAT'S SILLY.
SHOCKED
Isn't it obvious?
WE NEED PROOF THAT WE KILLED THE FACE WORM IF WE'RE GOING TO COLLECT OUR REWARD!
HURRY UP AND HELP ME FIND THOSE BABIES WE KILLED.
WE HAVE TO TAKE THEIR HORNS, TOO.
WHAT? ALL OF THEM?!
AW, C'MON! CAN'T WE JUST GIVE THEM THAT ONE?
IF YOU DON'T WANT TO DO THE WORK, THEN NEX' TIME YOU CAN STAY HOME!
GRRRR...♥
Hmph. You never would have killed them if it weren't for me.

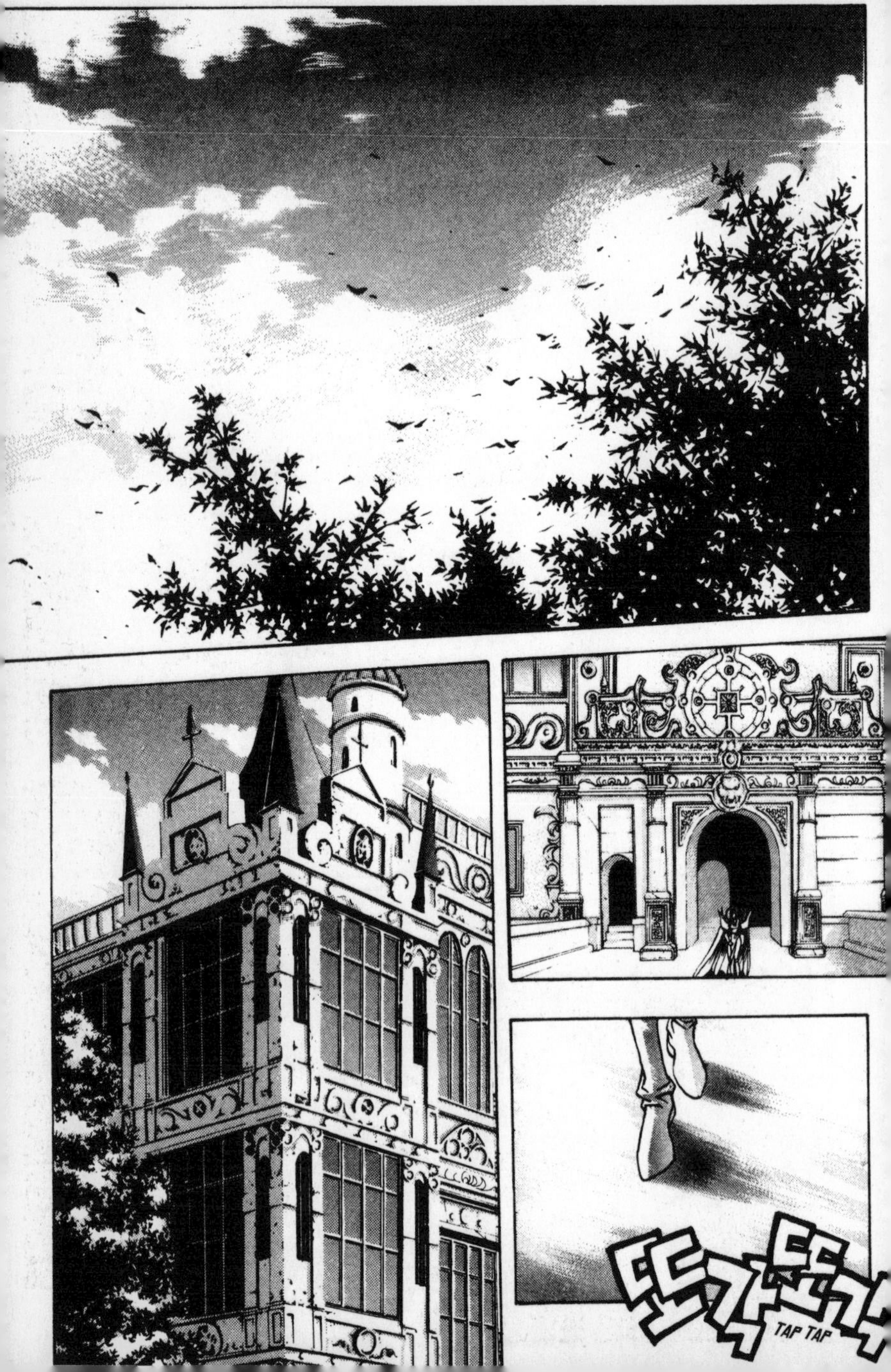
또각 또각
TAP TAP

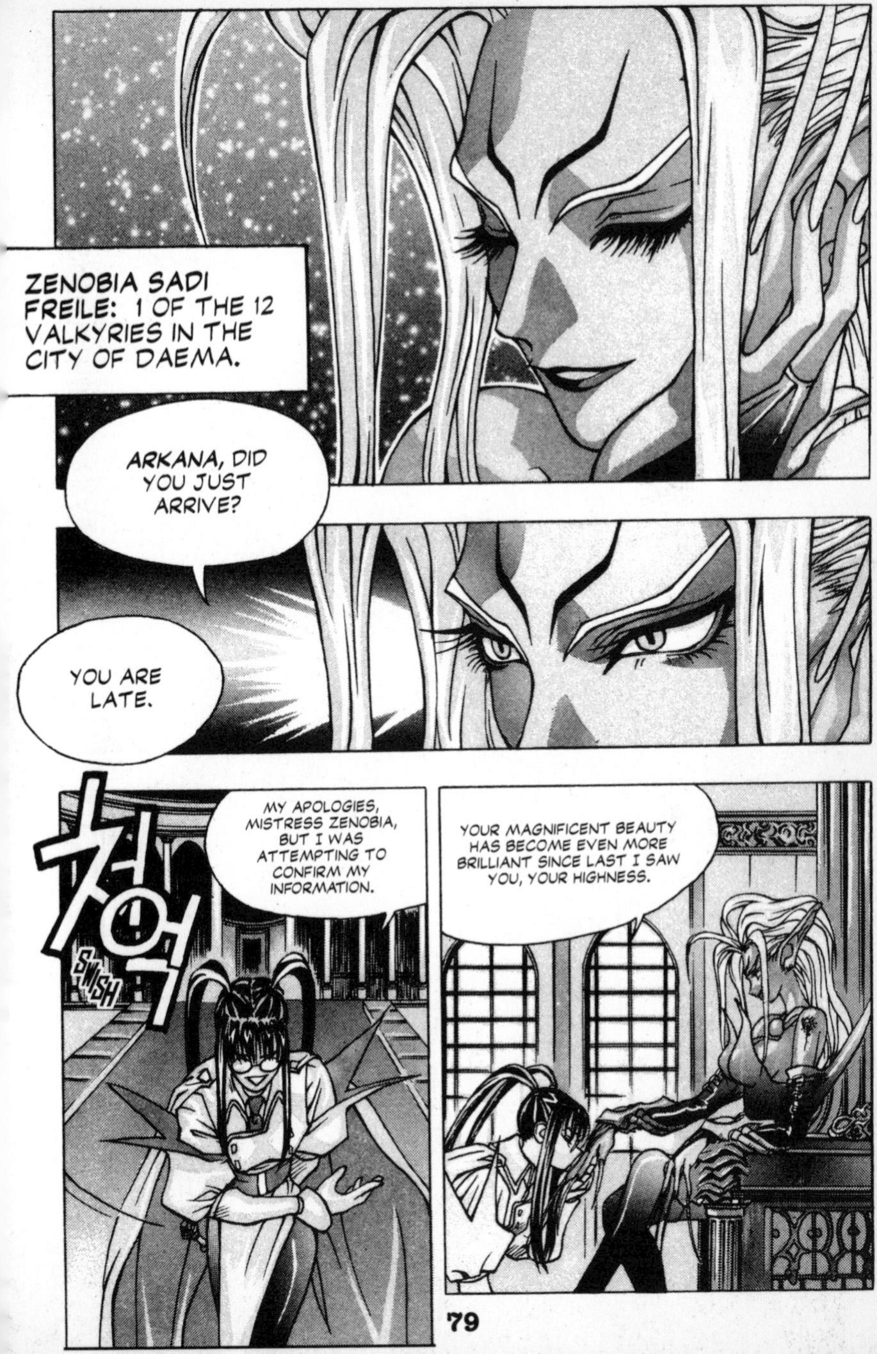
ZENOBIA SADI FREILE: 1 OF THE 12 VALKYRIES IN THE CITY OF DAEMA.
ARKANA, DID YOU JUST ARRIVE?
YOU ARE LATE.
SWISH
MY APOLOGIES, MISTRESS ZENOBIA, BUT I WAS ATTEMPTING TO CONFIRM MY INFORMATION.
YOUR MAGNIFICENT BEAUTY HAS BECOME EVEN MORE BRILLIANT SINCE LAST I SAW YOU, YOUR HIGHNESS.

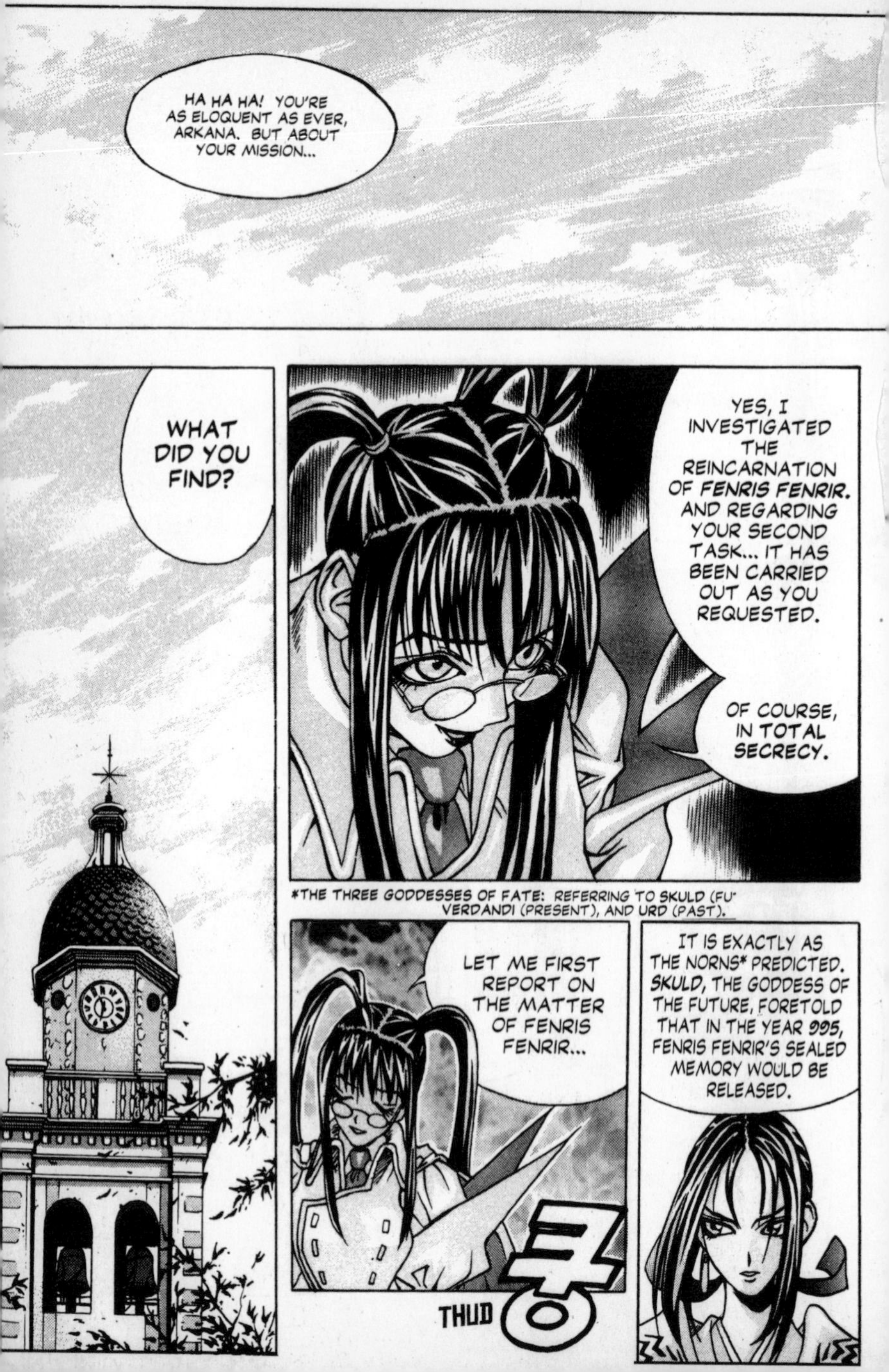

HA HA HA! YOU'RE AS ELOQUENT AS EVER, ARKANA. BUT ABOUT YOUR MISSION...
WHAT DID YOU FIND?
YES, I INVESTIGATED THE REINCARNATION OF FENRIS FENRIR. AND REGARDING YOUR SECOND TASK... IT HAS BEEN CARRIED OUT AS YOU REQUESTED.
OF COURSE, IN TOTAL SECRECY.
LET ME FIRST REPORT ON THE MATTER OF FENRIS FENRIR...
쿵
THUD
IT IS EXACTLY AS THE NORNS* PREDICTED. SKULD, THE GODDESS OF THE FUTURE, FORETOLD THAT IN THE YEAR 995, FENRIS FENRIR'S SEALED MEMORY WOULD BE RELEASED.

*THE THREE GODDESSES OF FATE: REFERRING TO SKULD (FU VERDANDI (PRESENT), AND URD (PAST).

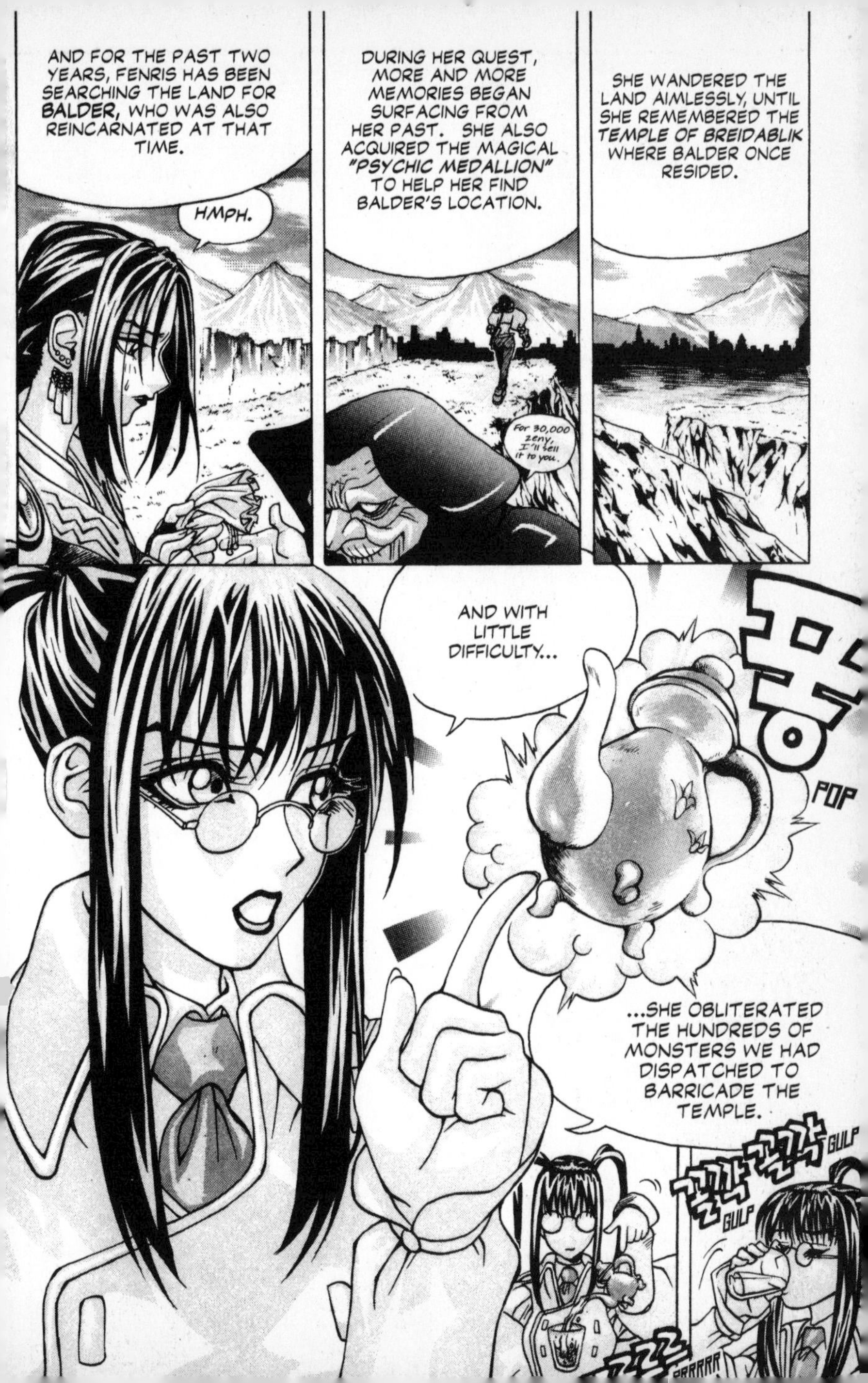

AND FOR THE PAST TWO YEARS, FENRIS HAS BEEN SEARCHING THE LAND FOR BALDER, WHO WAS ALSO REINCARNATED AT THAT TIME.
HMPH.
DURING HER QUEST, MORE AND MORE MEMORIES BEGAN SURFACING FROM HER PAST. SHE ALSO ACQUIRED THE MAGICAL "PSYCHIC MEDALLION" TO HELP HER FIND BALDER'S LOCATION.
For 30,000 zeny, I'll sell it to you.
SHE WANDERED THE LAND AIMLESSLY, UNTIL SHE REMEMBERED THE TEMPLE OF BREIDABLIK WHERE BALDER ONCE RESIDED.
AND WITH LITTLE DIFFICULTY...
POP
...SHE OBLITERATED THE HUNDREDS OF MONSTERS WE HAD DISPATCHED TO BARRICADE THE TEMPLE.
GULP
GULP

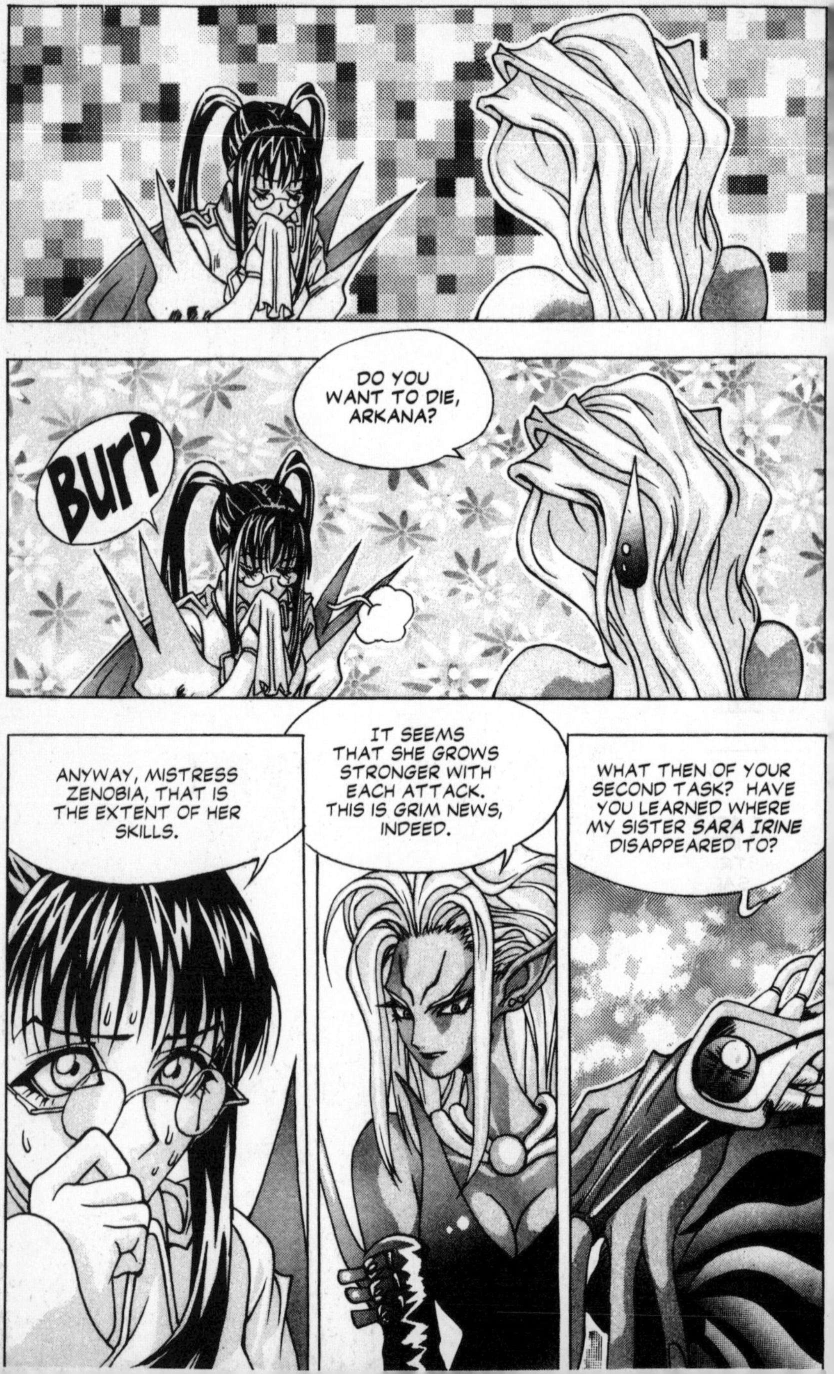
DO YOU WANT TO DIE, ARKANA?
BURP
ANYWAY, MISTRESS ZENOBIA, THAT IS THE EXTENT OF HER SKILLS.
IT SEEMS THAT SHE GROWS STRONGER WITH EACH ATTACK. THIS IS GRIM NEWS, INDEED.
WHAT THEN OF YOUR SECOND TASK? HAVE YOU LEARNED WHERE MY SISTER *SARA IRINE* DISAPPEARED TO?

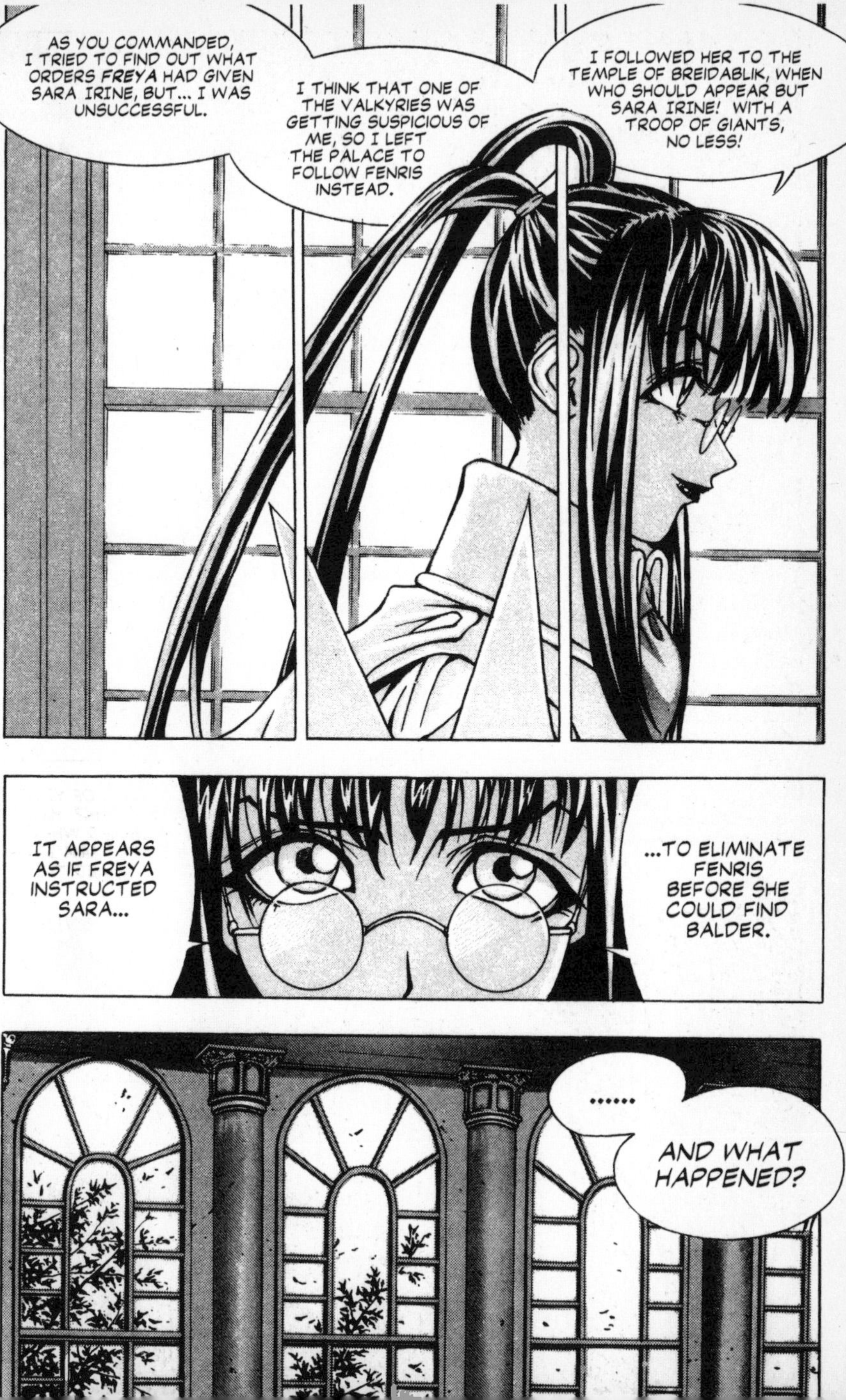
AS YOU COMMANDED, I TRIED TO FIND OUT WHAT ORDERS FREYA HAD GIVEN SARA IRINE, BUT... I WAS UNSUCCESSFUL.
I THINK THAT ONE OF THE VALKYRIES WAS GETTING SUSPICIOUS OF ME, SO I LEFT THE PALACE TO FOLLOW FENRIS INSTEAD.
I FOLLOWED HER TO THE TEMPLE OF BREIDABLIK, WHEN WHO SHOULD APPEAR BUT SARA IRINE! WITH A TROOP OF GIANTS, NO LESS!
IT APPEARS AS IF FREYA INSTRUCTED SARA...
...TO ELIMINATE FENRIS BEFORE SHE COULD FIND BALDER.
......
AND WHAT HAPPENED?

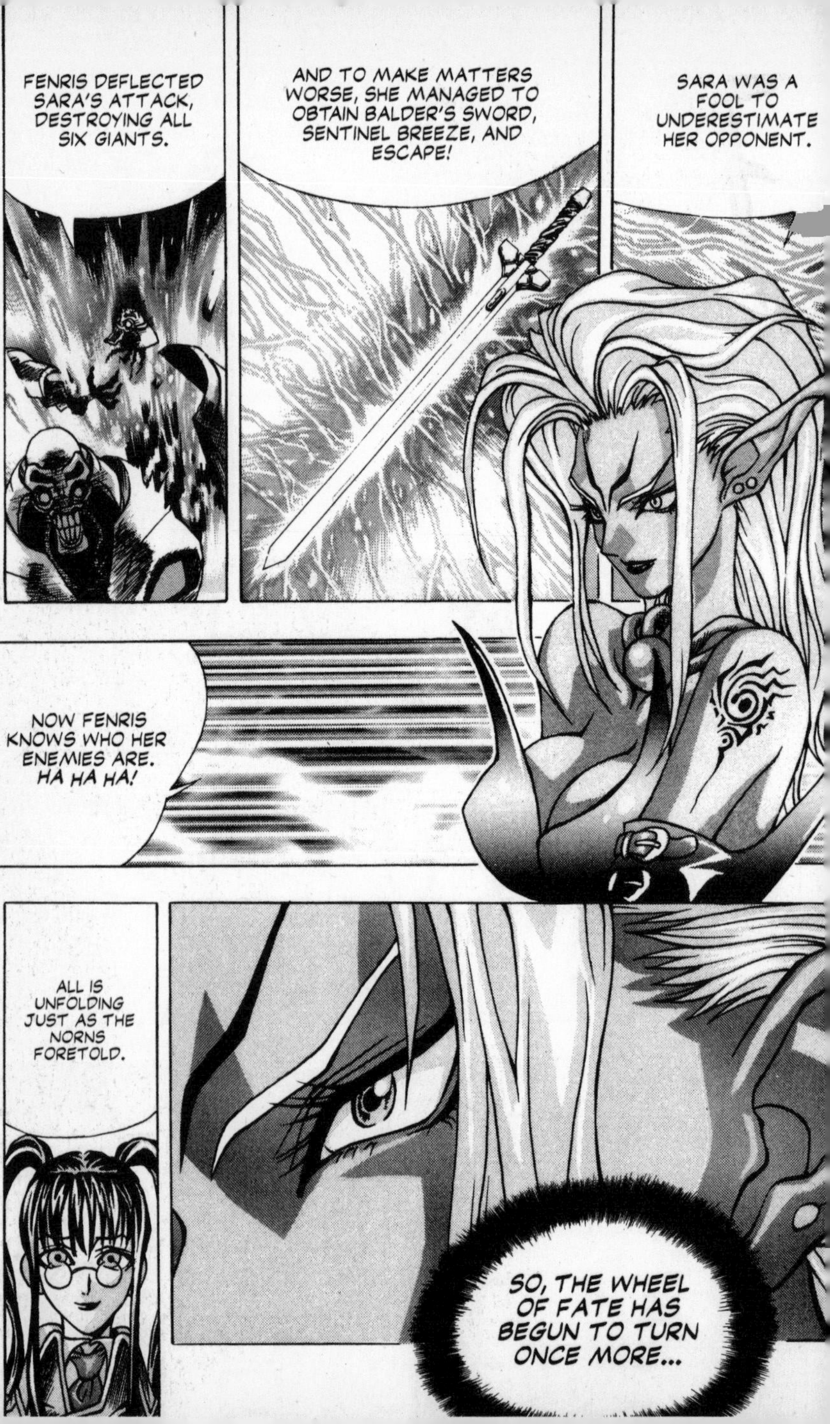
FENRIS DEFLECTED SARA'S ATTACK, DESTROYING ALL SIX GIANTS.
AND TO MAKE MATTERS WORSE, SHE MANAGED TO OBTAIN BALDER'S SWORD, SENTINEL BREEZE, AND ESCAPE!
SARA WAS A FOOL TO UNDERESTIMATE HER OPPONENT.
NOW FENRIS KNOWS WHO HER ENEMIES ARE. HA HA HA!
ALL IS UNFOLDING JUST AS THE NORNS FORETOLD.
SO, THE WHEEL OF FATE HAS BEGUN TO TURN ONCE MORE...

RAGNARÖK

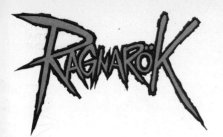

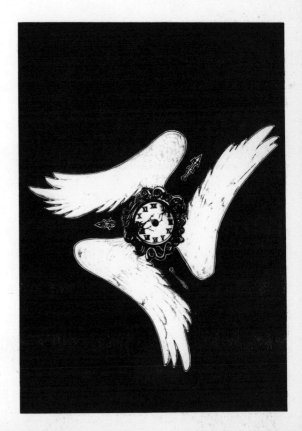

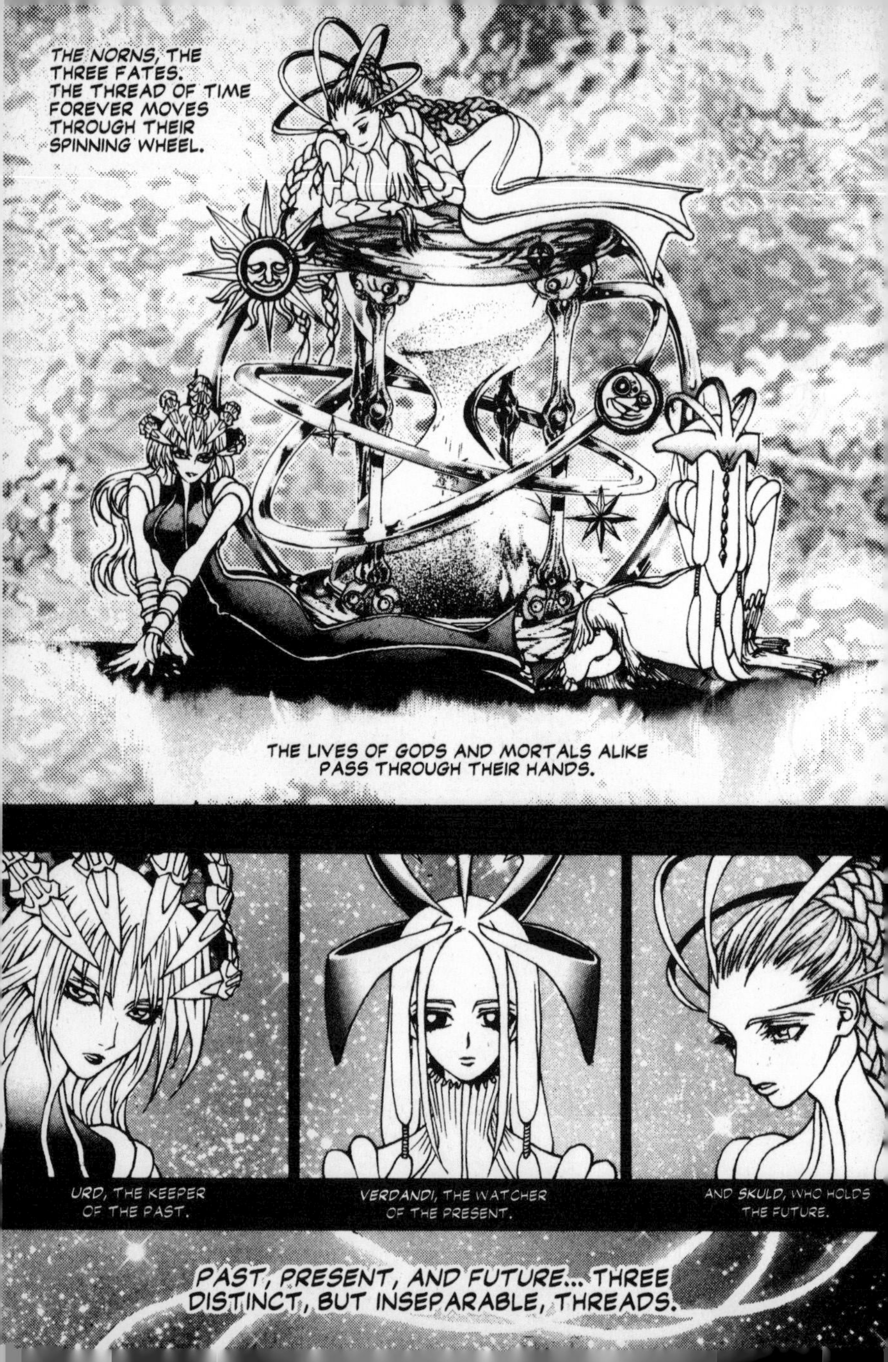
THE NORNS, THE THREE FATES. THE THREAD OF TIME FOREVER MOVES THROUGH THEIR SPINNING WHEEL.
THE LIVES OF GODS AND MORTALS ALIKE PASS THROUGH THEIR HANDS.
URD, THE KEEPER OF THE PAST.
VERDANDI, THE WATCHER OF THE PRESENT.
AND SKULD, WHO HOLDS THE FUTURE.
PAST, PRESENT, AND FUTURE... THREE DISTINCT, BUT INSEPARABLE, THREADS.

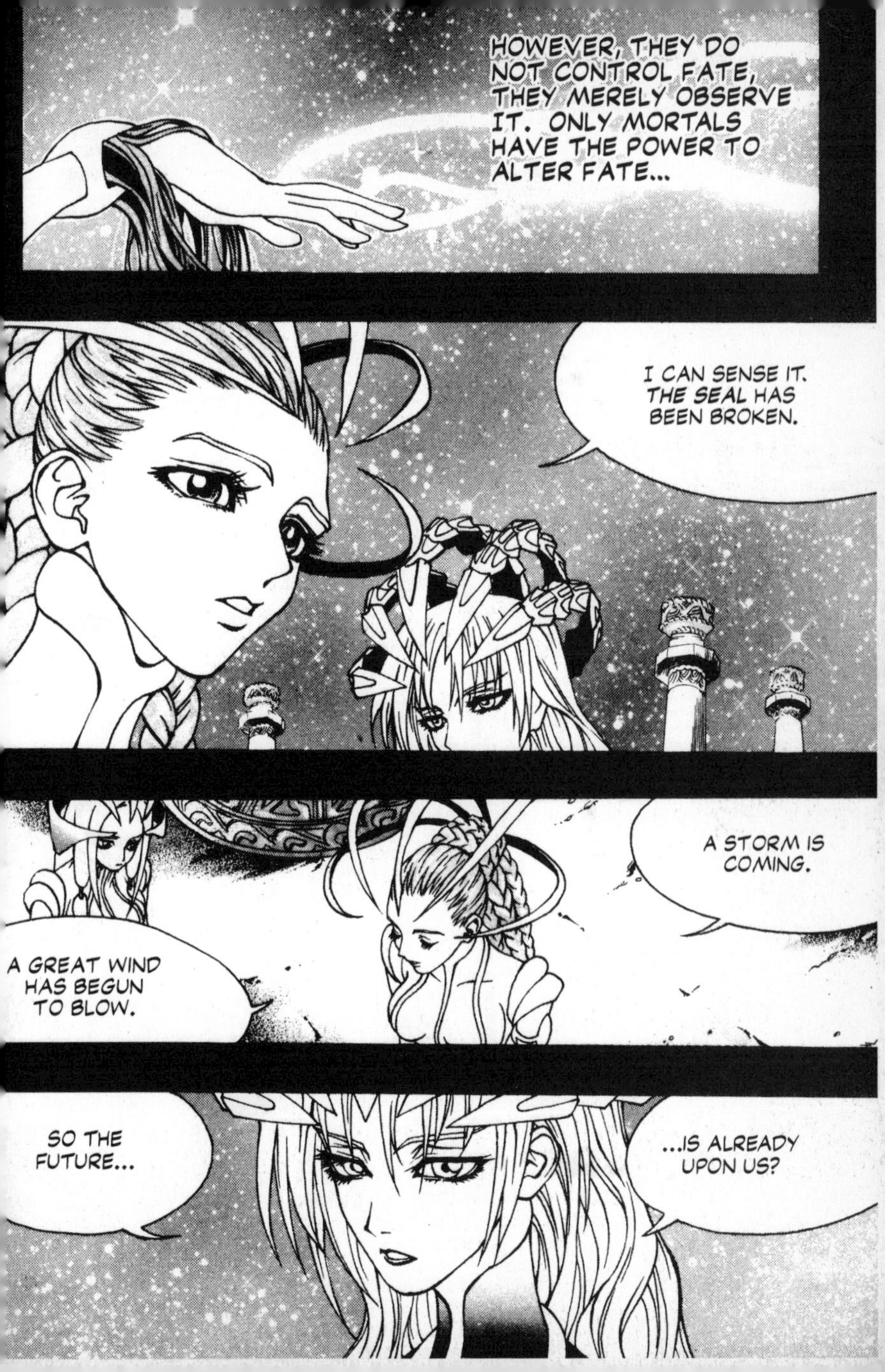
HOWEVER, THEY DO NOT CONTROL FATE, THEY MERELY OBSERVE IT. ONLY MORTALS HAVE THE POWER TO ALTER FATE...
I CAN SENSE IT. THE SEAL HAS BEEN BROKEN.
A STORM IS COMING.
A GREAT WIND HAS BEGUN TO BLOW.
SO THE FUTURE...
...IS ALREADY UPON US?

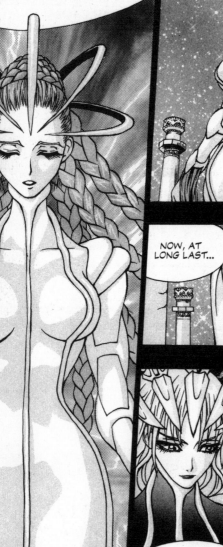

IT IS A TIME OF GREAT CONFUSION THAT WILL CHANGE THE NATURE OF THE UNIVERSE.

1000 YEARS AGO, FREE WILL WAS SHACKLED AND CHANGE WAS KEPT AT BAY.

NOW, AT LONG LAST...

...THE PROMISED DAY HAS ARRIVED.

YES. THE WORLD IS EMERGING FROM A THOUSAND-YEAR SLUMBER.

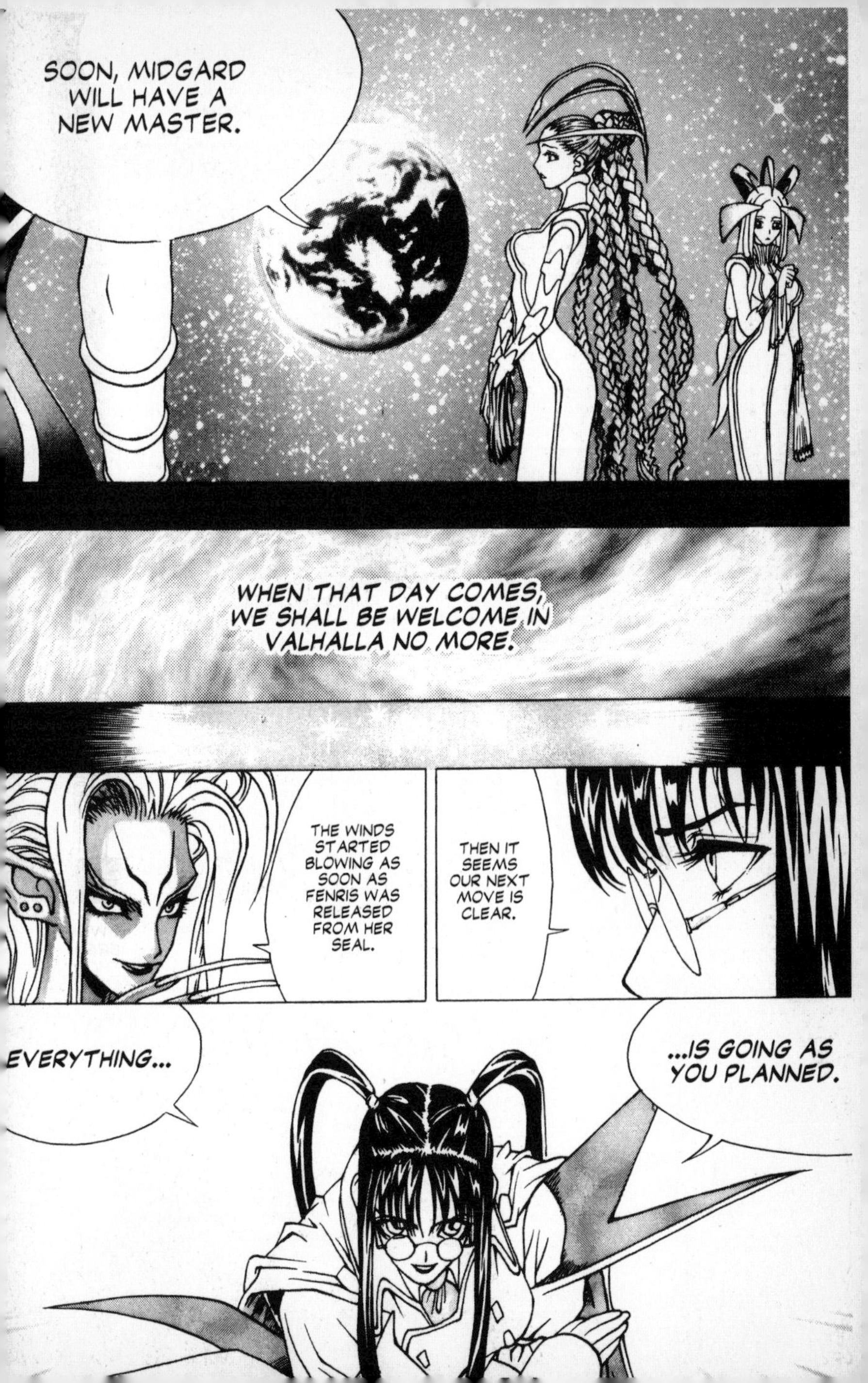
SOON, MIDGARD WILL HAVE A NEW MASTER.
WHEN THAT DAY COMES, WE SHALL BE WELCOME IN VALHALLA NO MORE.
THE WINDS STARTED BLOWING AS SOON AS FENRIS WAS RELEASED FROM HER SEAL.
THEN IT SEEMS OUR NEXT MOVE IS CLEAR.
EVERYTHING...
...IS GOING AS YOU PLANNED.

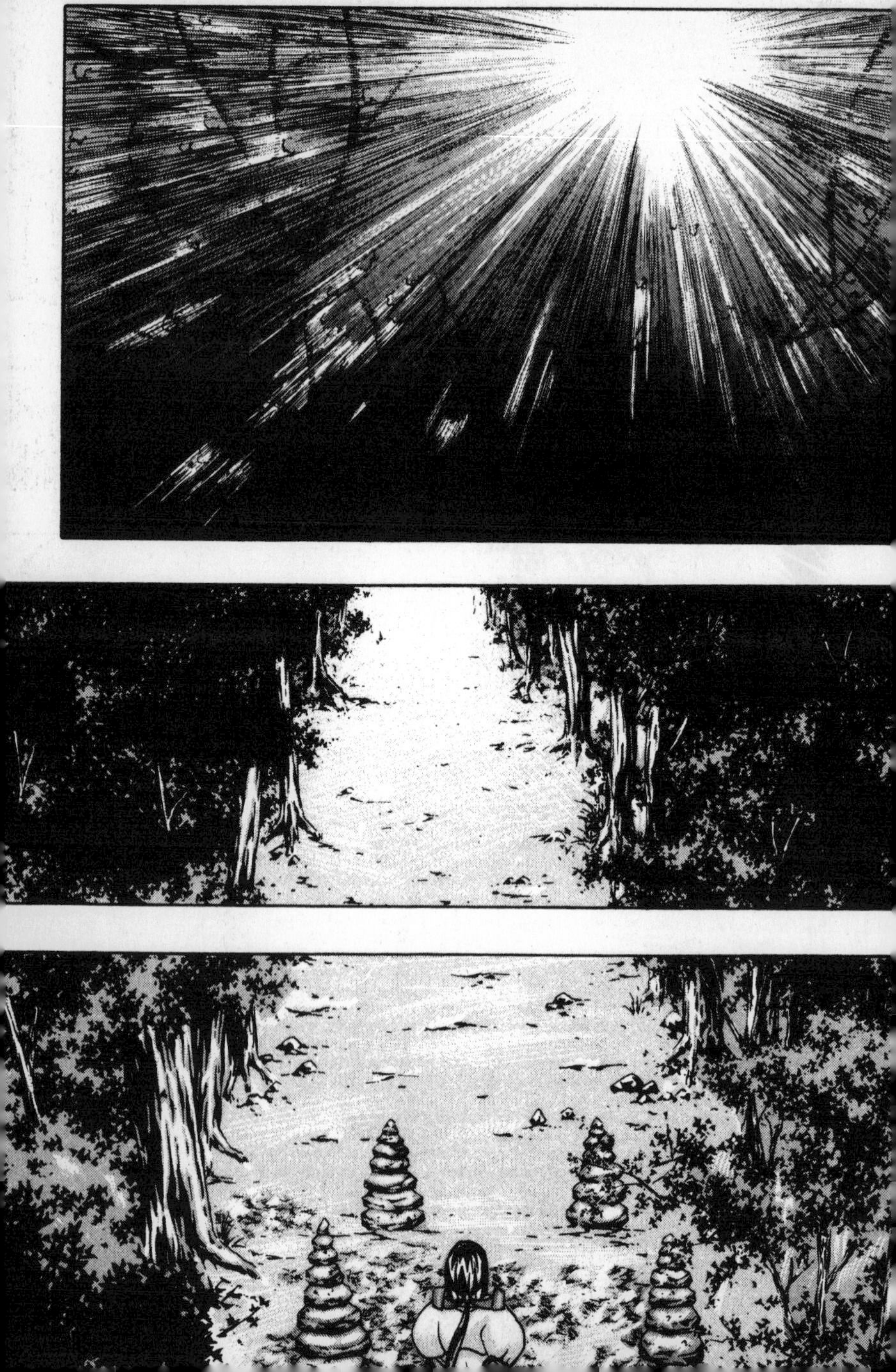

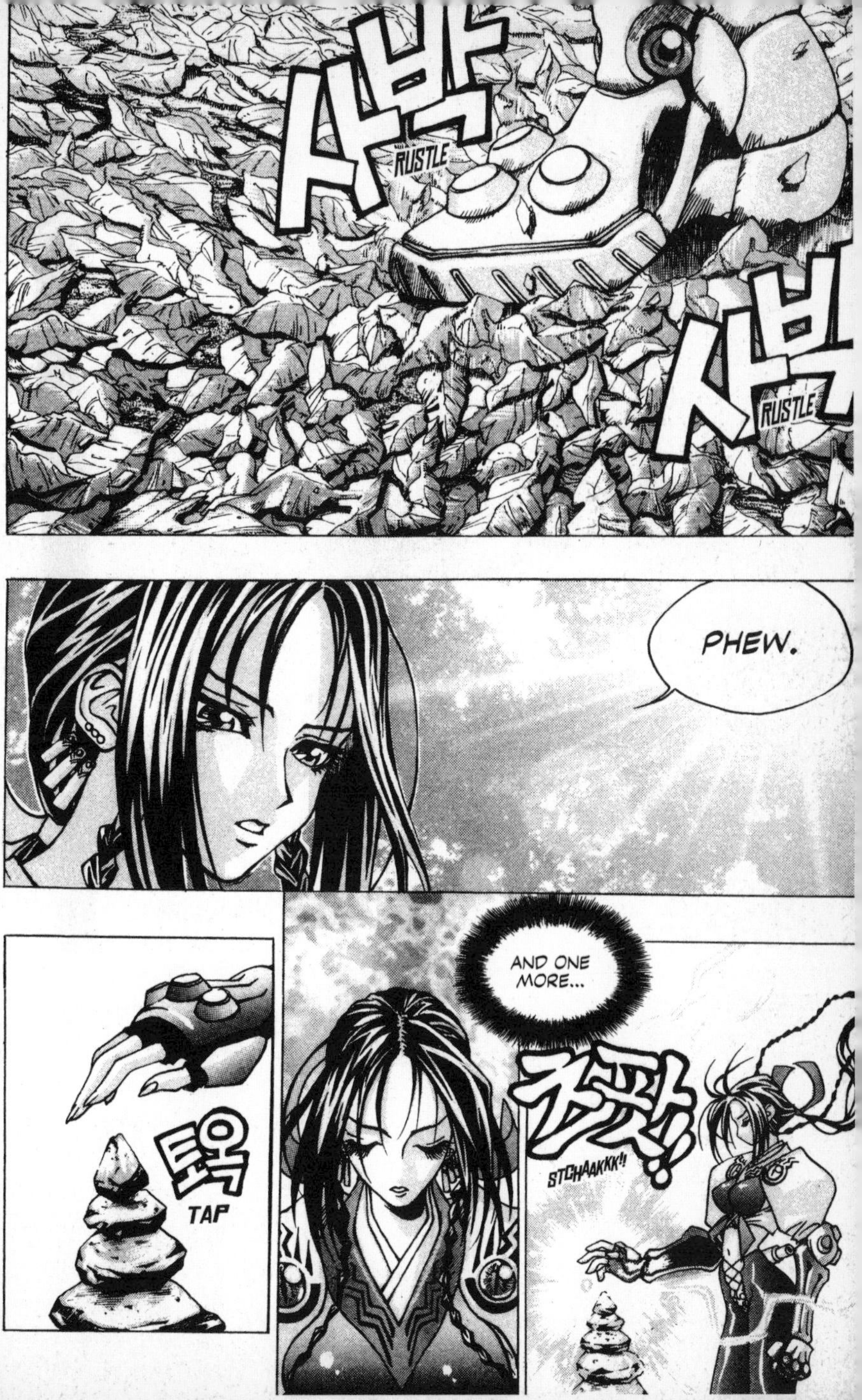
RUSTLE
RUSTLE
PHEW.
TAP
AND ONE MORE...
STCHAAKKK!!

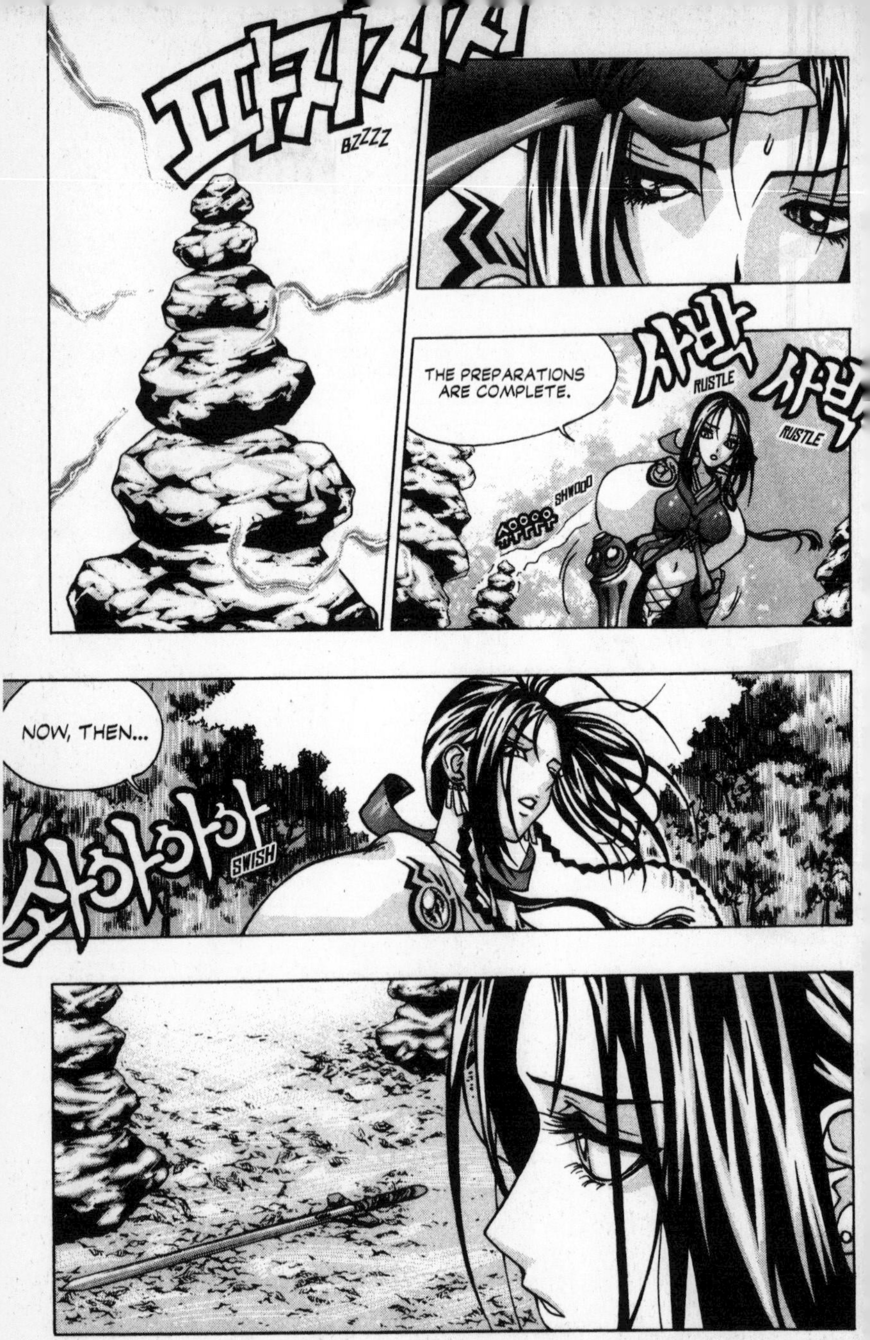
BZZZZ
THE PREPARATIONS ARE COMPLETE.
사락
RUSTLE
사락
RUSTLE
슈우우우
SHWOOO
NOW, THEN...
사아아아
SWISH

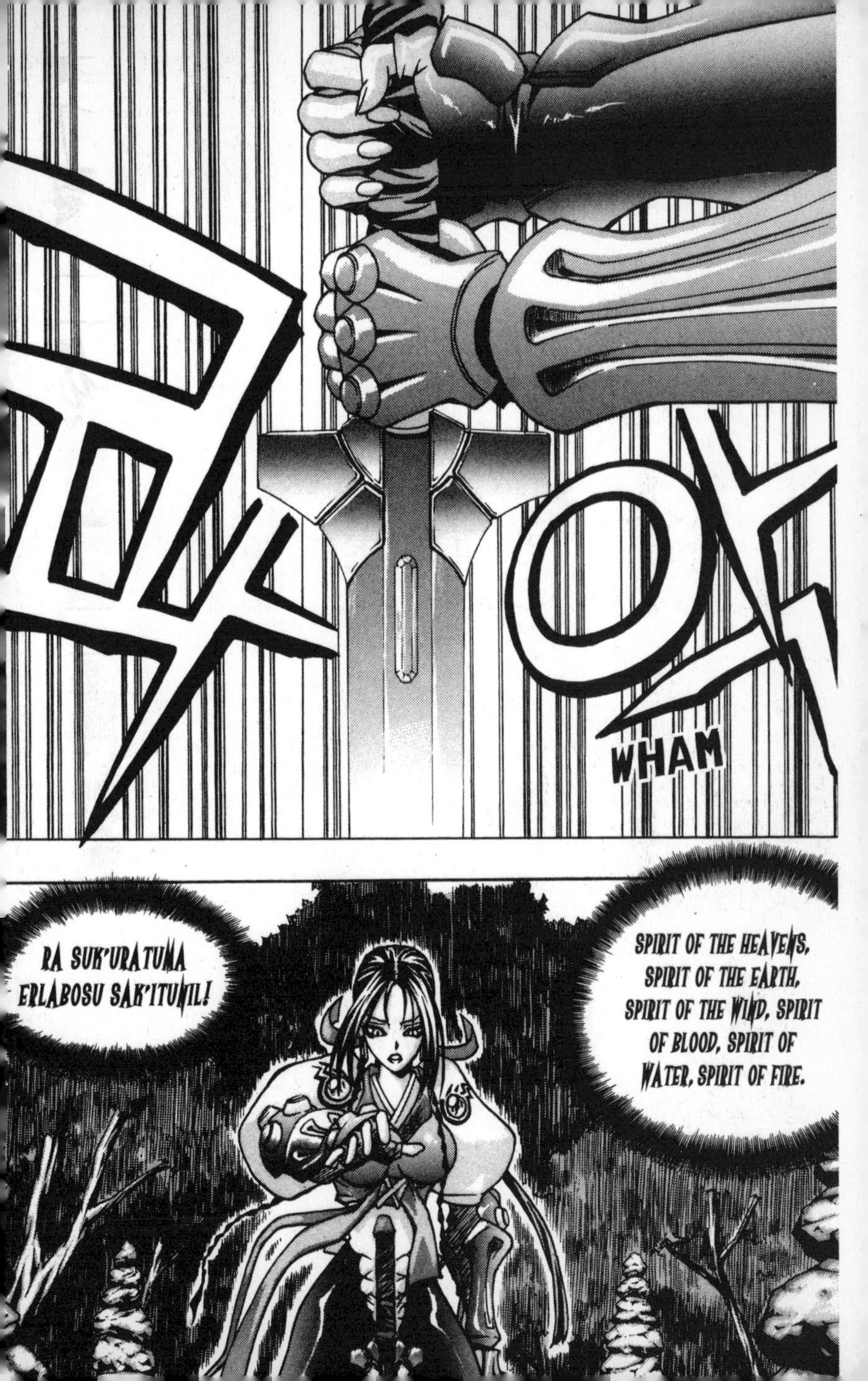
WHAM
RA SUK'URATUMA ERLABOSU SAK'ITUNIL!
SPIRIT OF THE HEAVENS, SPIRIT OF THE EARTH, SPIRIT OF THE WIND, SPIRIT OF BLOOD, SPIRIT OF WATER, SPIRIT OF FIRE.

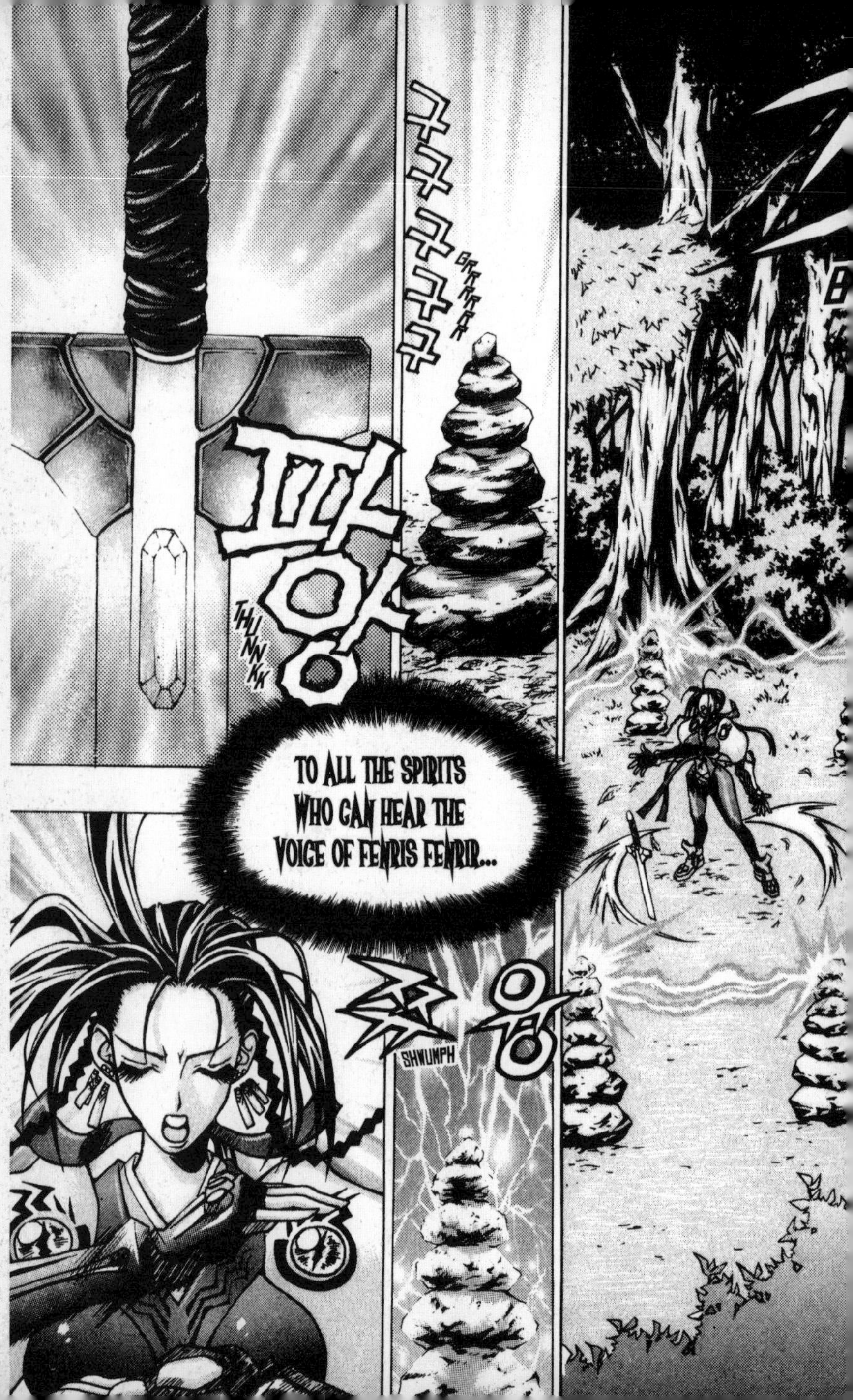
GRRRRR
THUNNKK
TO ALL THE SPIRITS WHO CAN HEAR THE VOICE OF FENRIS FENRIR...
SHWUMPH

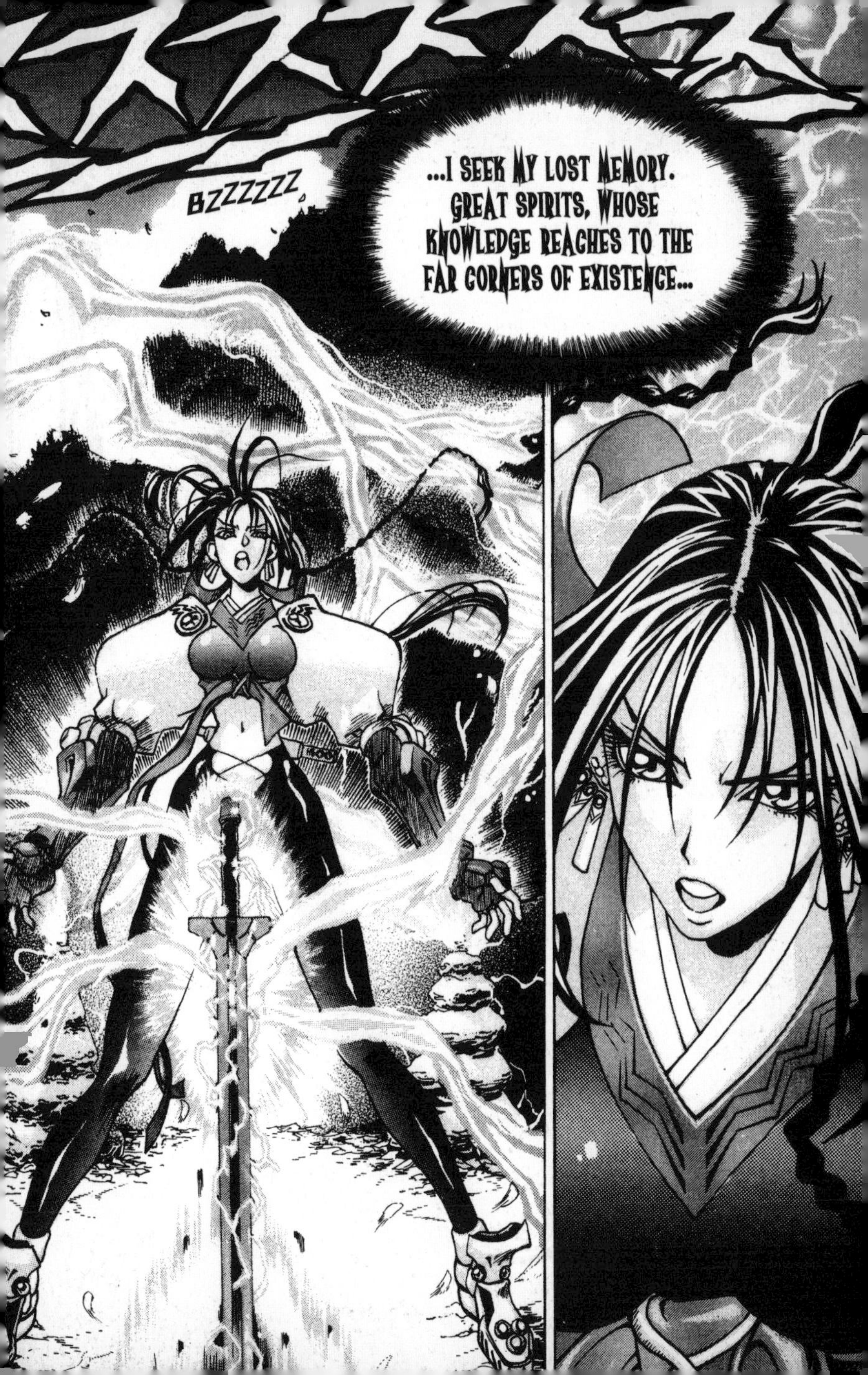
BZZZZZZ
...I SEEK MY LOST MEMORY. GREAT SPIRITS, WHOSE KNOWLEDGE REACHES TO THE FAR CORNERS OF EXISTENCE...

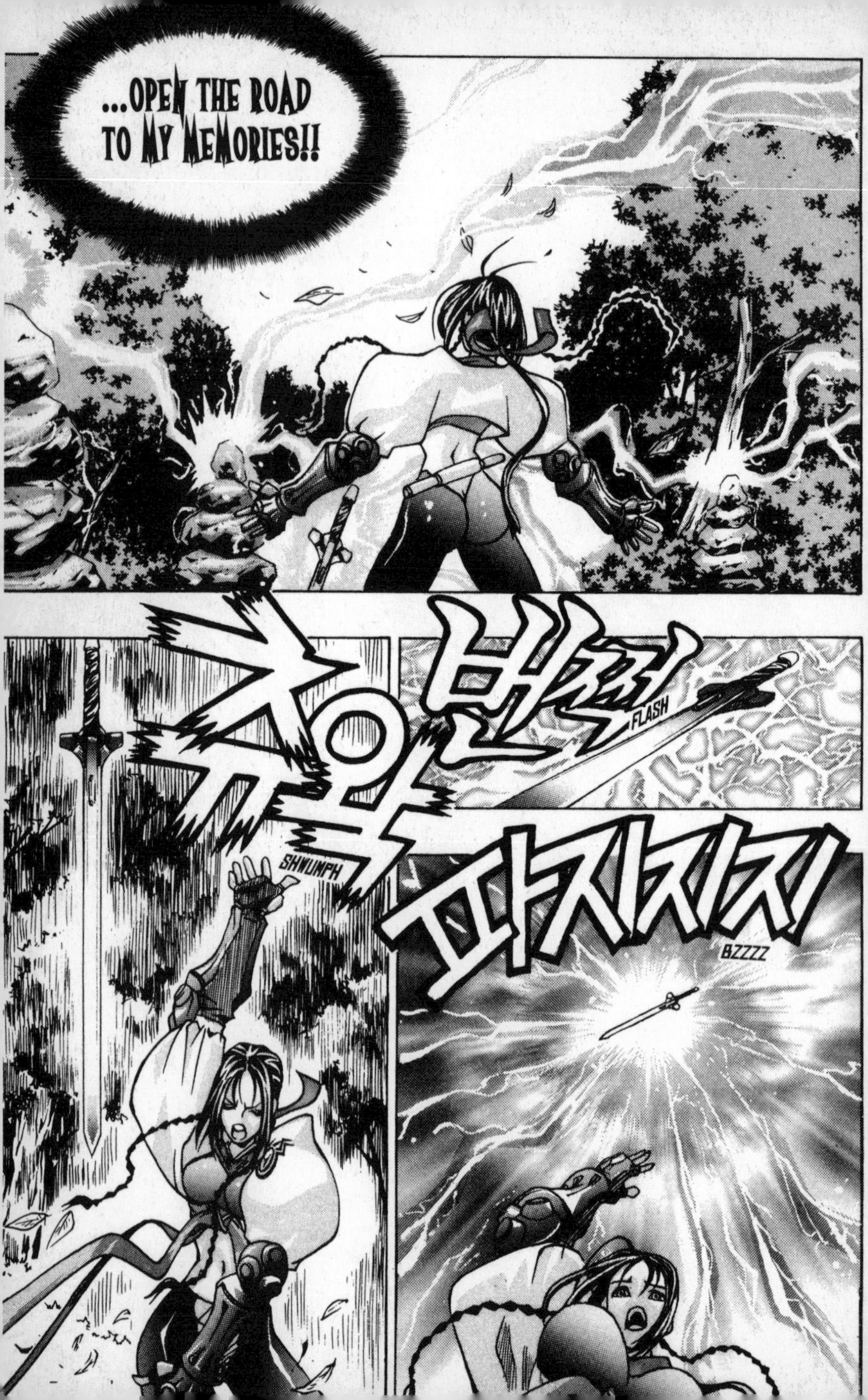
...OPEN THE ROAD TO MY MEMORIES!!
SHWUMPH
FLASH
BZZZZ

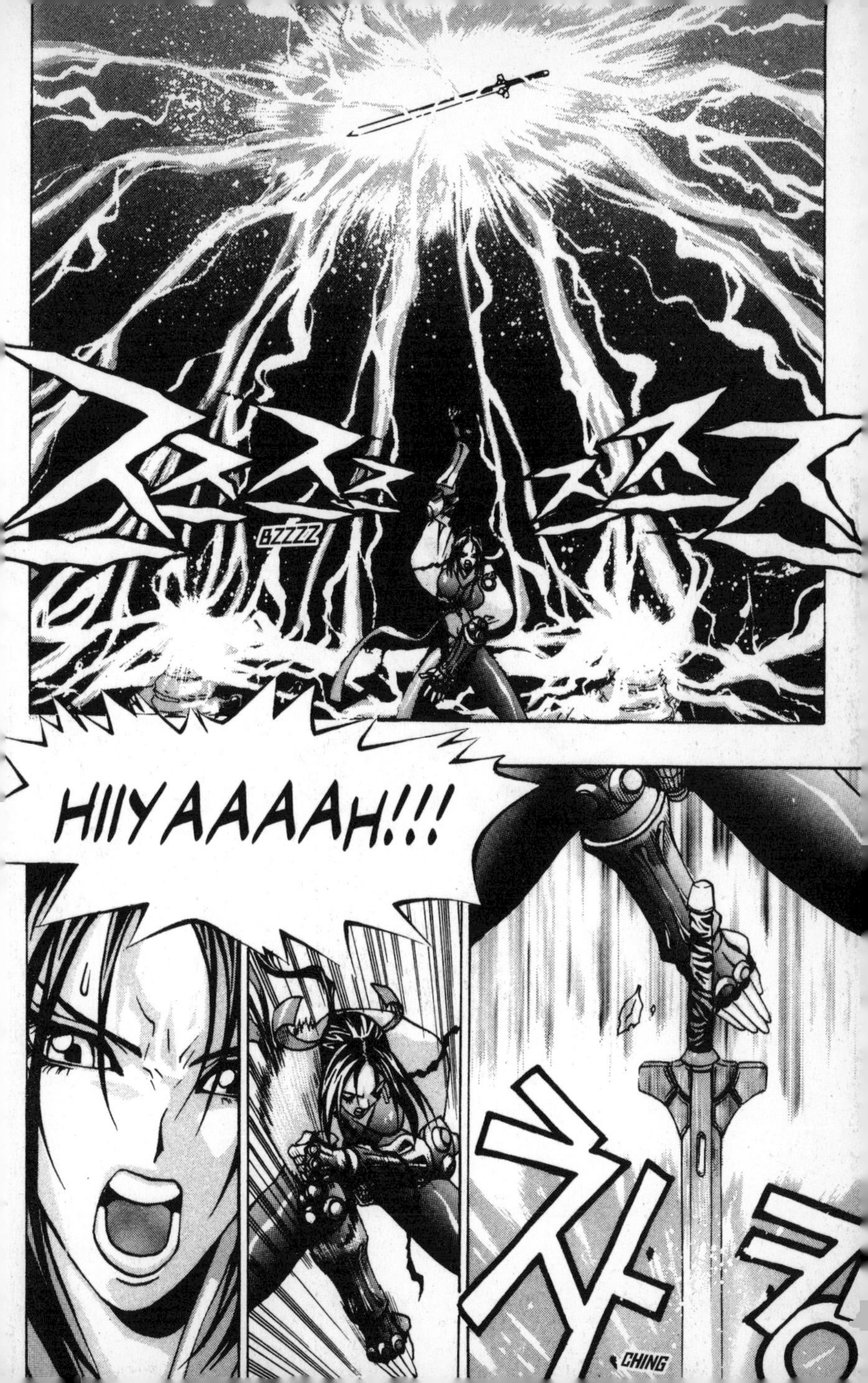
BZZZZ
HIIYAAAAAH!!!
CHING

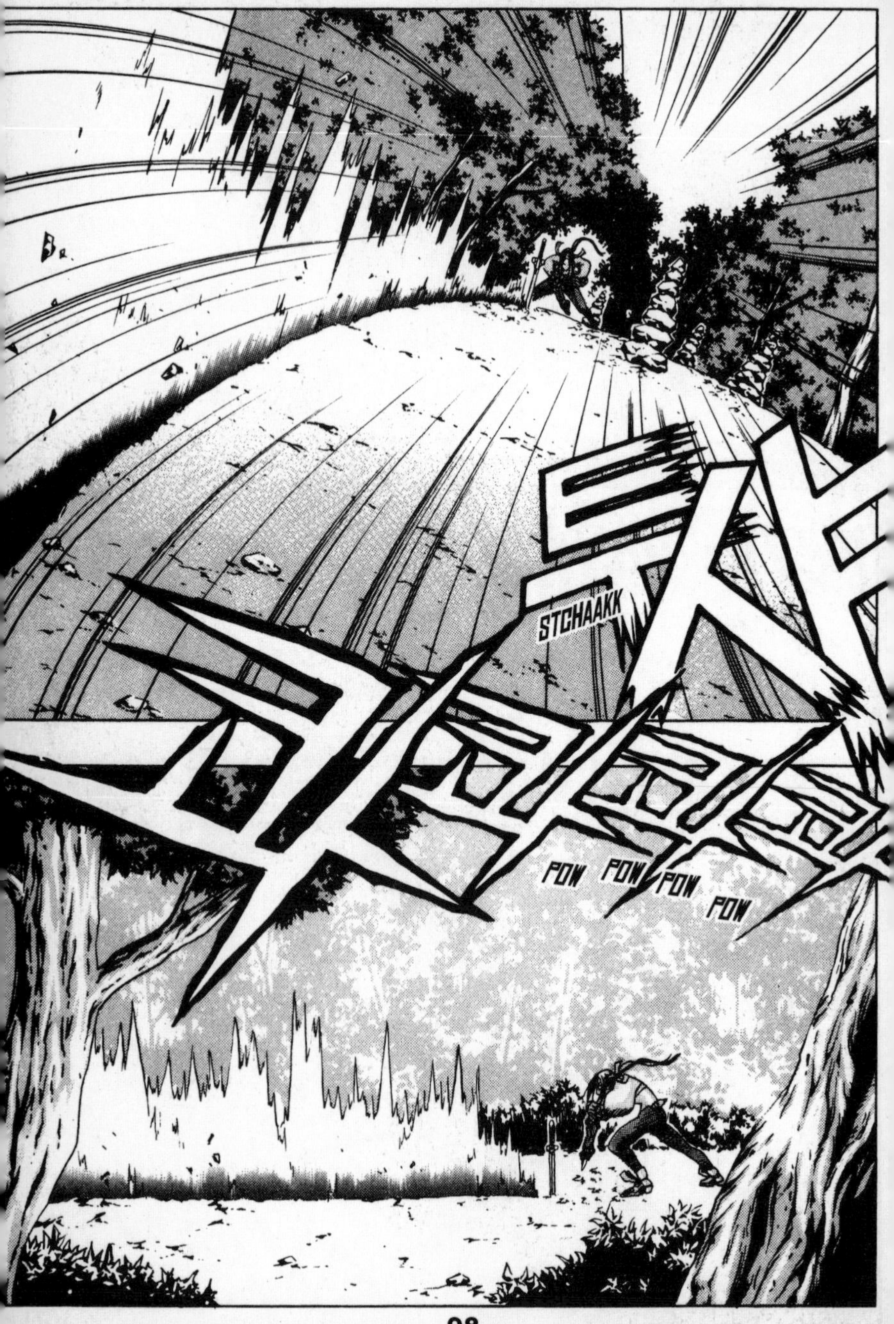
STCHAAKK
POW POW POW POW

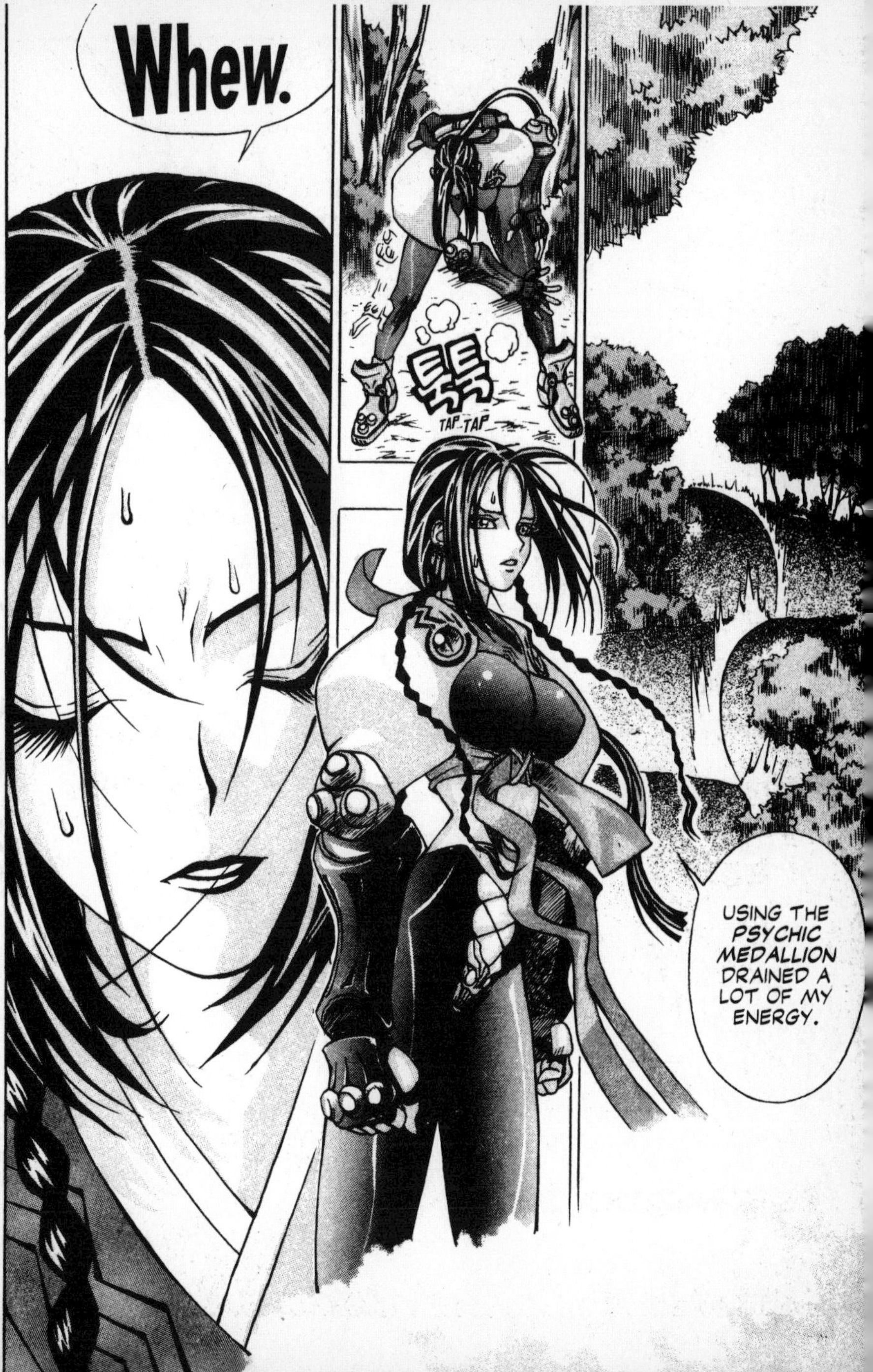
Whew.
TAP TAP
USING THE PSYCHIC MEDALLION DRAINED A LOT OF MY ENERGY.

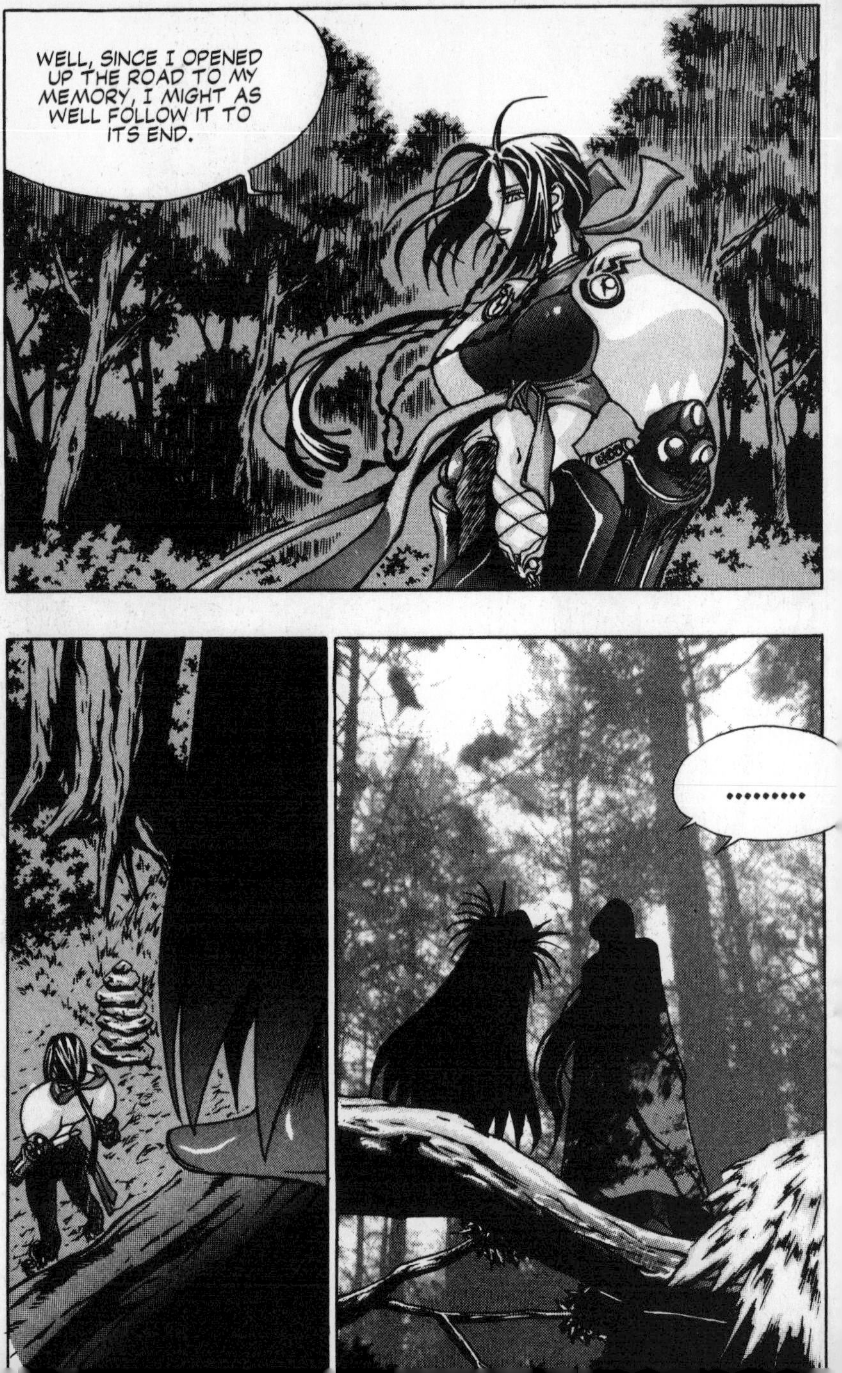
WELL, SINCE I OPENED UP THE ROAD TO MY MEMORY, I MIGHT AS WELL FOLLOW IT TO ITS END.
....

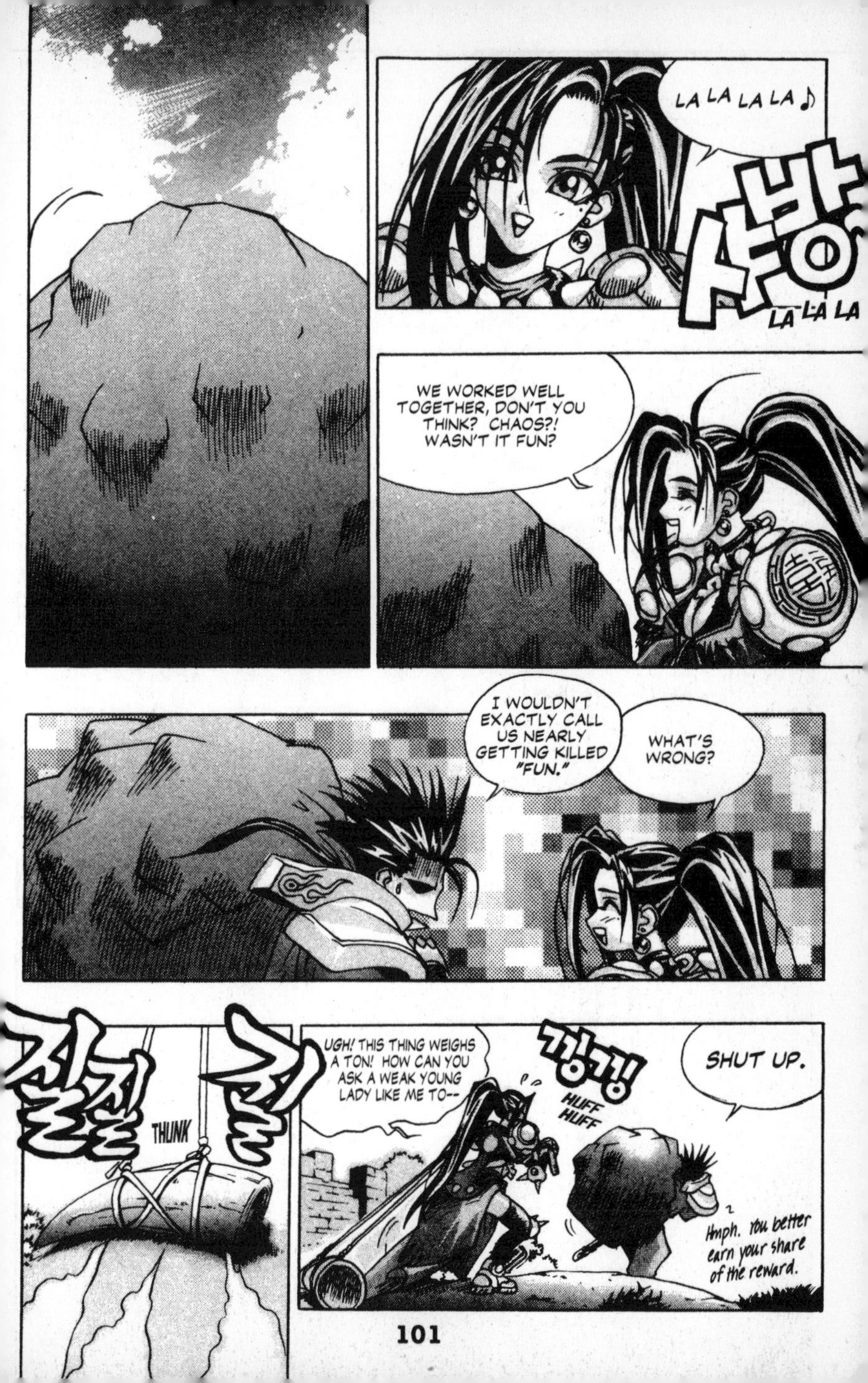
LA LA LA LA ♪
LA LA LA
WE WORKED WELL TOGETHER, DON'T YOU THINK? CHAOS?! WASN'T IT FUN?
I WOULDN'T EXACTLY CALL US NEARLY GETTING KILLED "FUN."
WHAT'S WRONG?
THUNK
UGH! THIS THING WEIGHS A TON! HOW CAN YOU ASK A WEAK YOUNG LADY LIKE ME TO--
HUFF HUFF
SHUT UP.
Hmph. You better earn your share of the reward.

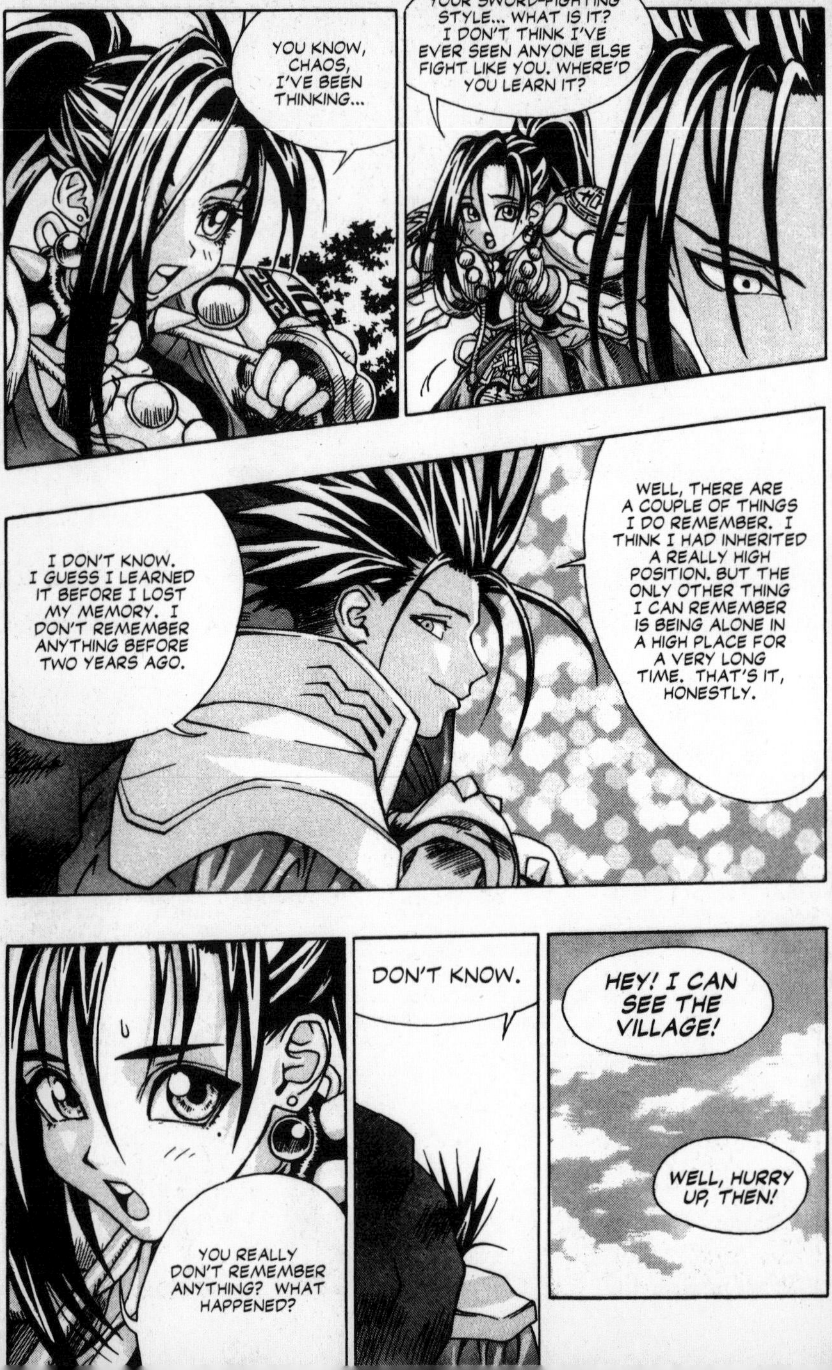
YOU KNOW, CHAOS, I'VE BEEN THINKING...
YOUR SWORD-FIGHTING STYLE... WHAT IS IT? I DON'T THINK I'VE EVER SEEN ANYONE ELSE FIGHT LIKE YOU. WHERE'D YOU LEARN IT?
I DON'T KNOW. I GUESS I LEARNED IT BEFORE I LOST MY MEMORY. I DON'T REMEMBER ANYTHING BEFORE TWO YEARS AGO.
WELL, THERE ARE A COUPLE OF THINGS I DO REMEMBER. I THINK I HAD INHERITED A REALLY HIGH POSITION. BUT THE ONLY OTHER THING I CAN REMEMBER IS BEING ALONE IN A HIGH PLACE FOR A VERY LONG TIME. THAT'S IT, HONESTLY.
YOU REALLY DON'T REMEMBER ANYTHING? WHAT HAPPENED?
DON'T KNOW.
HEY! I CAN SEE THE VILLAGE!
WELL, HURRY UP, THEN!

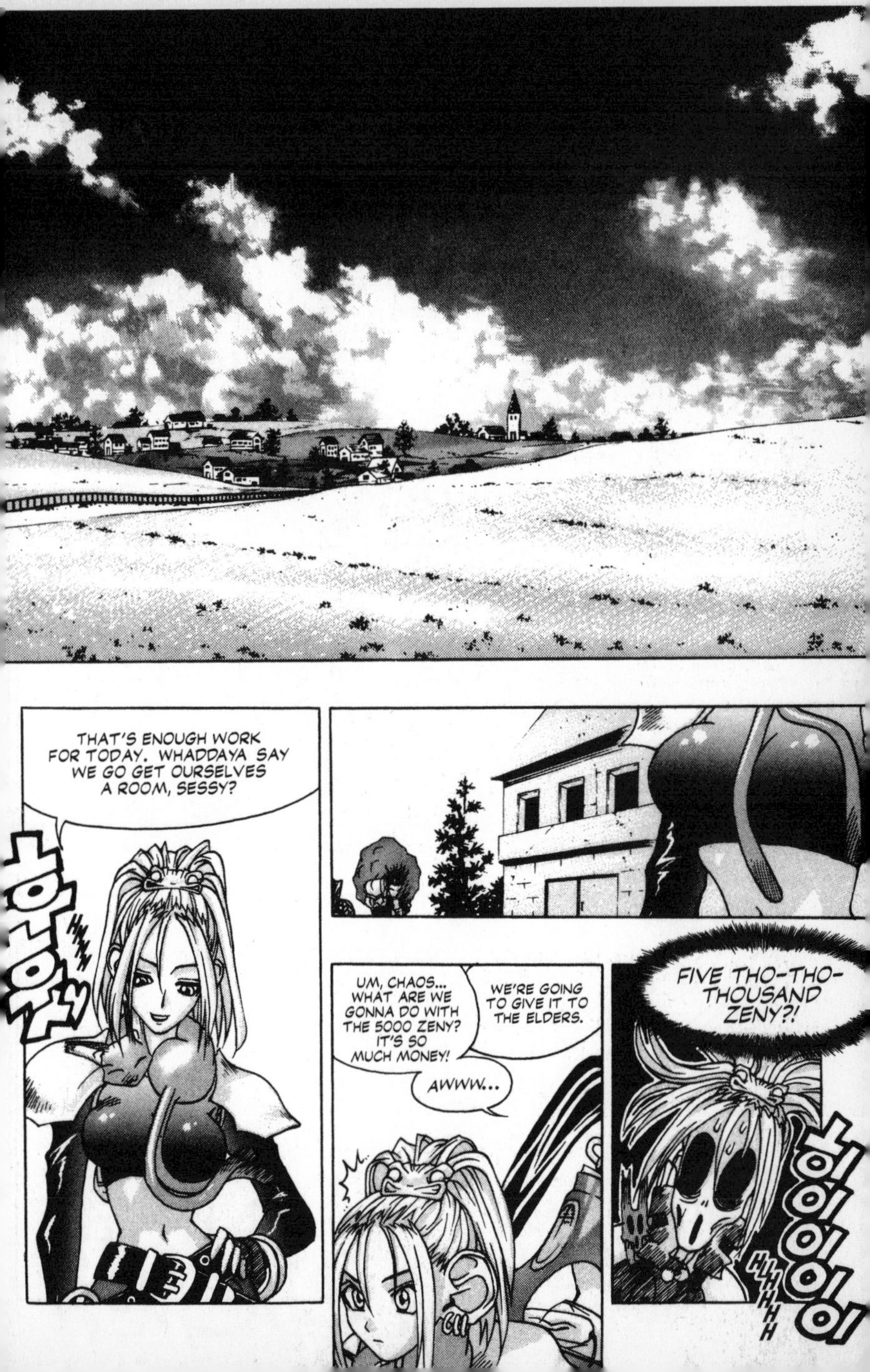
THAT'S ENOUGH WORK FOR TODAY. WHADDAYA SAY WE GO GET OURSELVES A ROOM, SESSY?
UM, CHAOS... WHAT ARE WE GONNA DO WITH THE 5000 ZENY? IT'S SO MUCH MONEY!
WE'RE GOING TO GIVE IT TO THE ELDERS.
AWWW...
FIVE THO-THO-THOUSAND ZENY?!

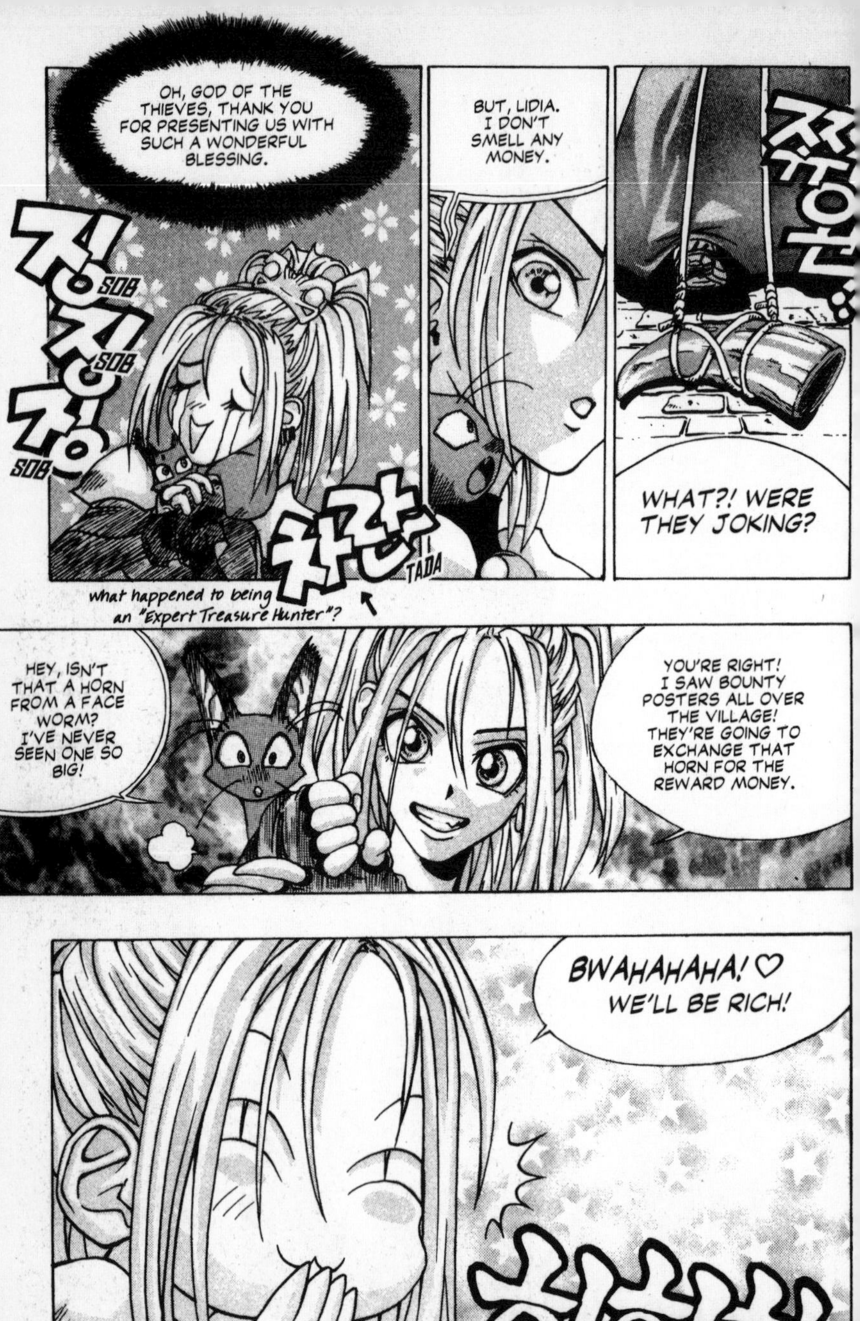
OH, GOD OF THE THIEVES, THANK YOU FOR PRESENTING US WITH SUCH A WONDERFUL BLESSING.
징징징
SOB SOB SOB
짜잔
TADA
what happened to being an "Expert Treasure Hunter"?
BUT, LIDIA. I DON'T SMELL ANY MONEY.
WHAT?! WERE THEY JOKING?
HEY, ISN'T THAT A HORN FROM A FACE WORM? I'VE NEVER SEEN ONE SO BIG!
YOU'RE RIGHT! I SAW BOUNTY POSTERS ALL OVER THE VILLAGE! THEY'RE GOING TO EXCHANGE THAT HORN FOR THE REWARD MONEY.
BWAHAHAHA! ♡ WE'LL BE RICH!
히히히
HE HE HE!

RAGNARÖK

GET THE

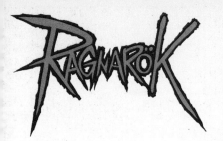

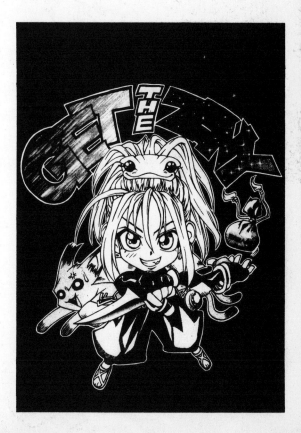

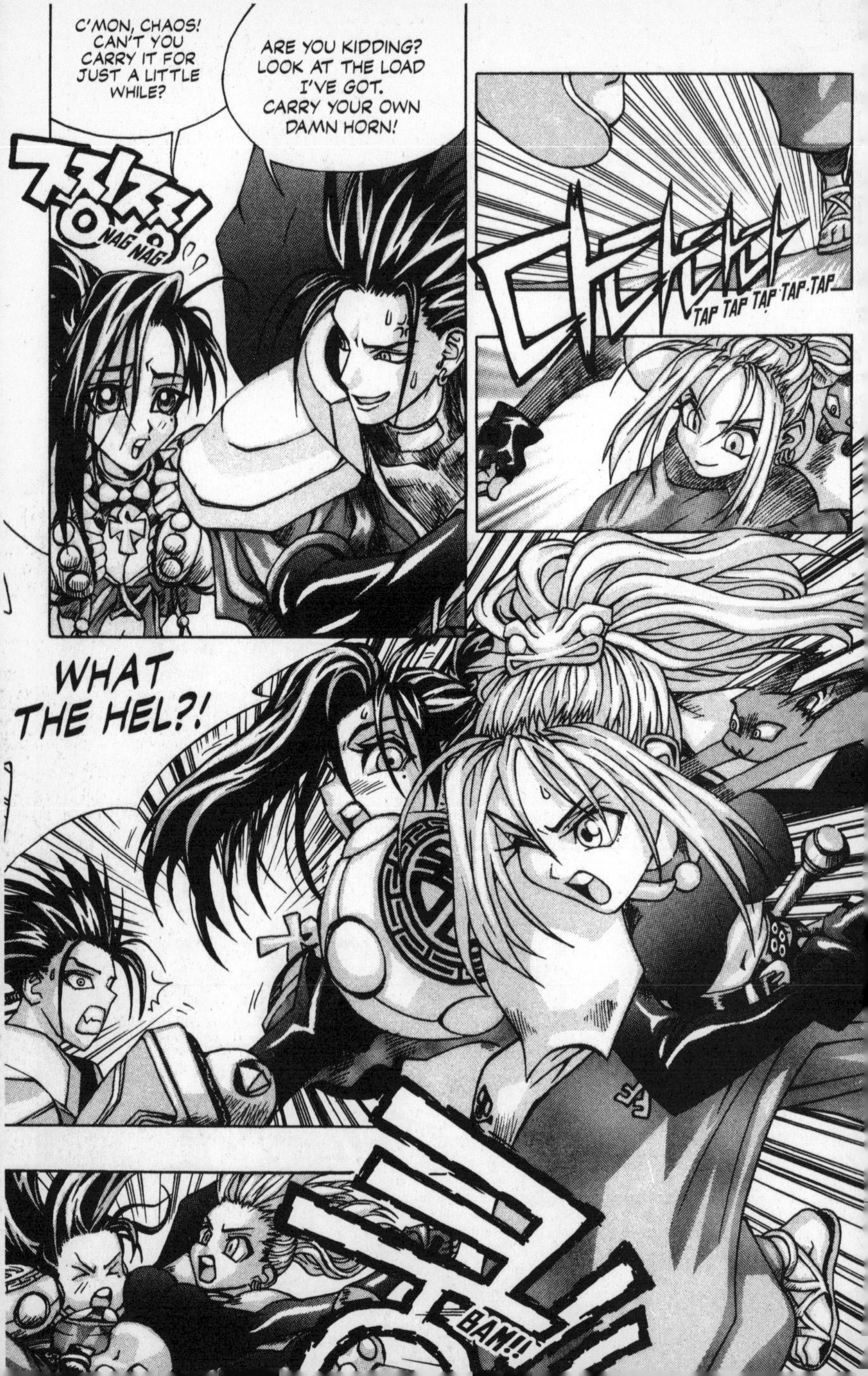
C'MON, CHAOS! CAN'T YOU CARRY IT FOR JUST A LITTLE WHILE?
ARE YOU KIDDING? LOOK AT THE LOAD I'VE GOT. CARRY YOUR OWN DAMN HORN!
NAG NAG
TAP TAP TAP TAP TAP
WHAT THE HEL?!
BAM!!

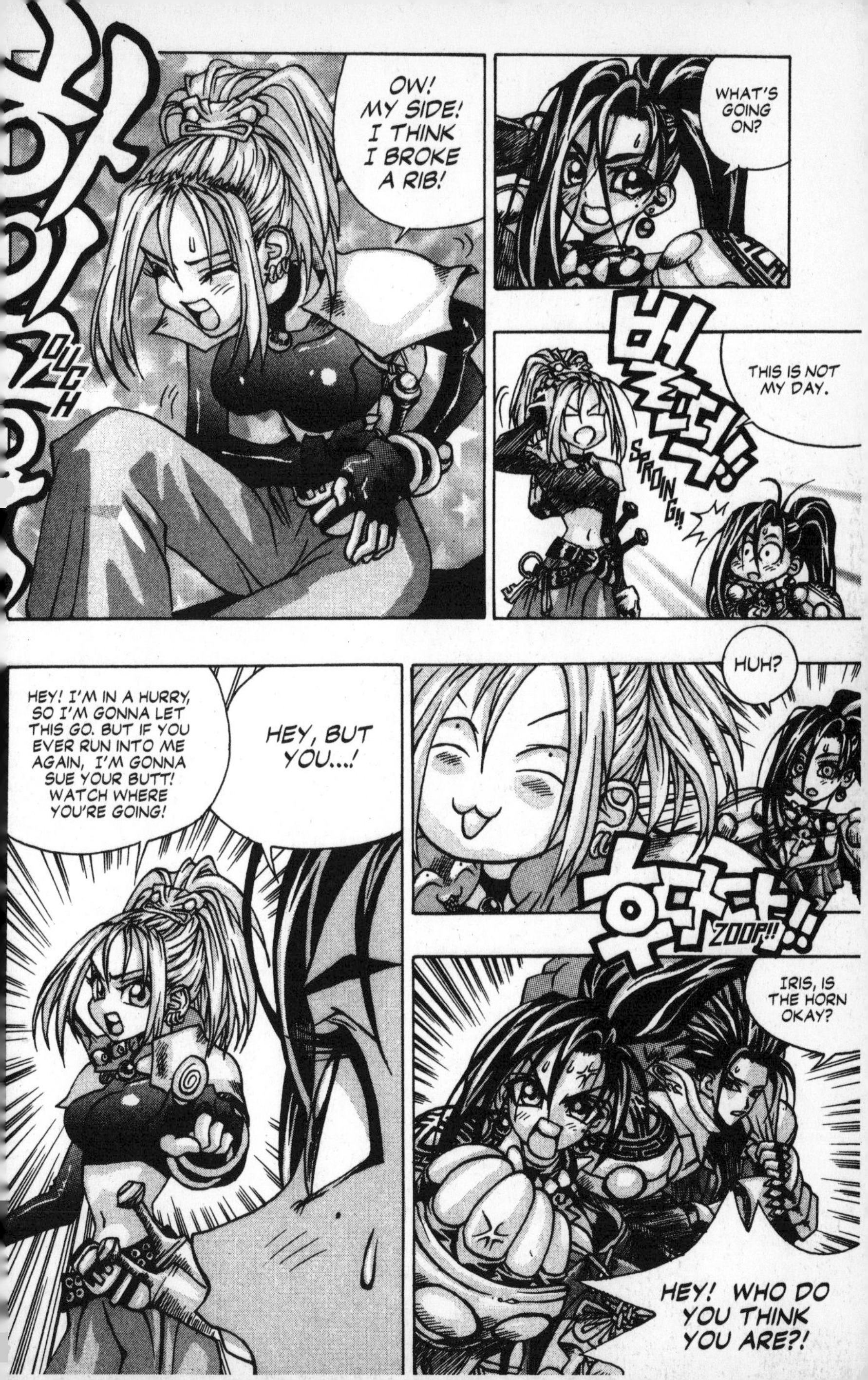
OW! MY SIDE! I THINK I BROKE A RIB!
OUCH
WHAT'S GOING ON?
SPROING!!
THIS IS NOT MY DAY.
HEY! I'M IN A HURRY, SO I'M GONNA LET THIS GO. BUT IF YOU EVER RUN INTO ME AGAIN, I'M GONNA SUE YOUR BUTT! WATCH WHERE YOU'RE GOING!
HEY, BUT YOU...!
HUH?
ZOOP!!
IRIS, IS THE HORN OKAY?
HEY! WHO DO YOU THINK YOU ARE?!

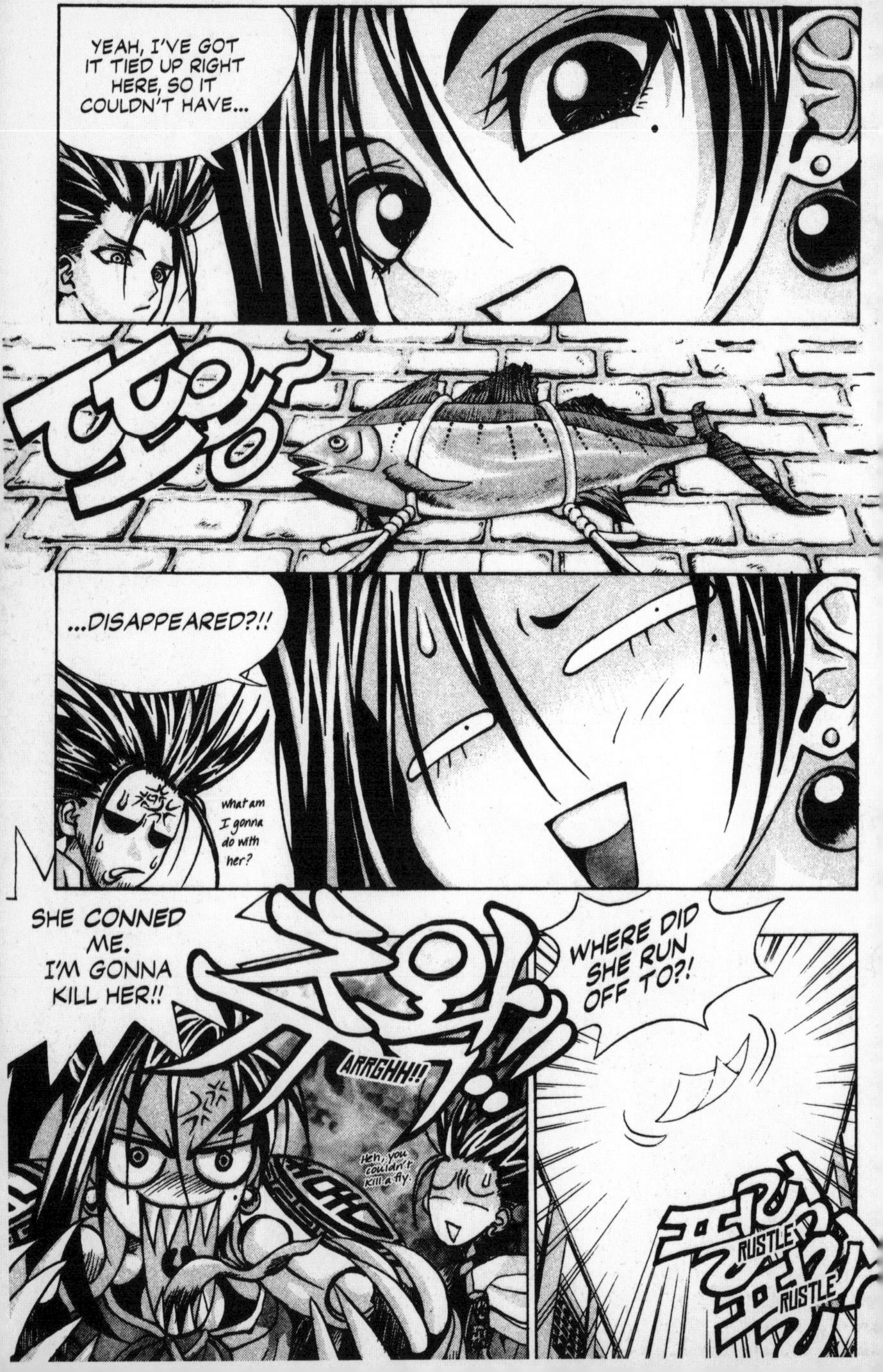
YEAH, I'VE GOT IT TIED UP RIGHT HERE, SO IT COULDN'T HAVE...
...DISAPPEARED?!!
what am I gonna do with her?
SHE CONNED ME. I'M GONNA KILL HER!!
ARRGHH!!
Heh, you couldn't kill a fly.
WHERE DID SHE RUN OFF TO?!
RUSTLE
RUSTLE

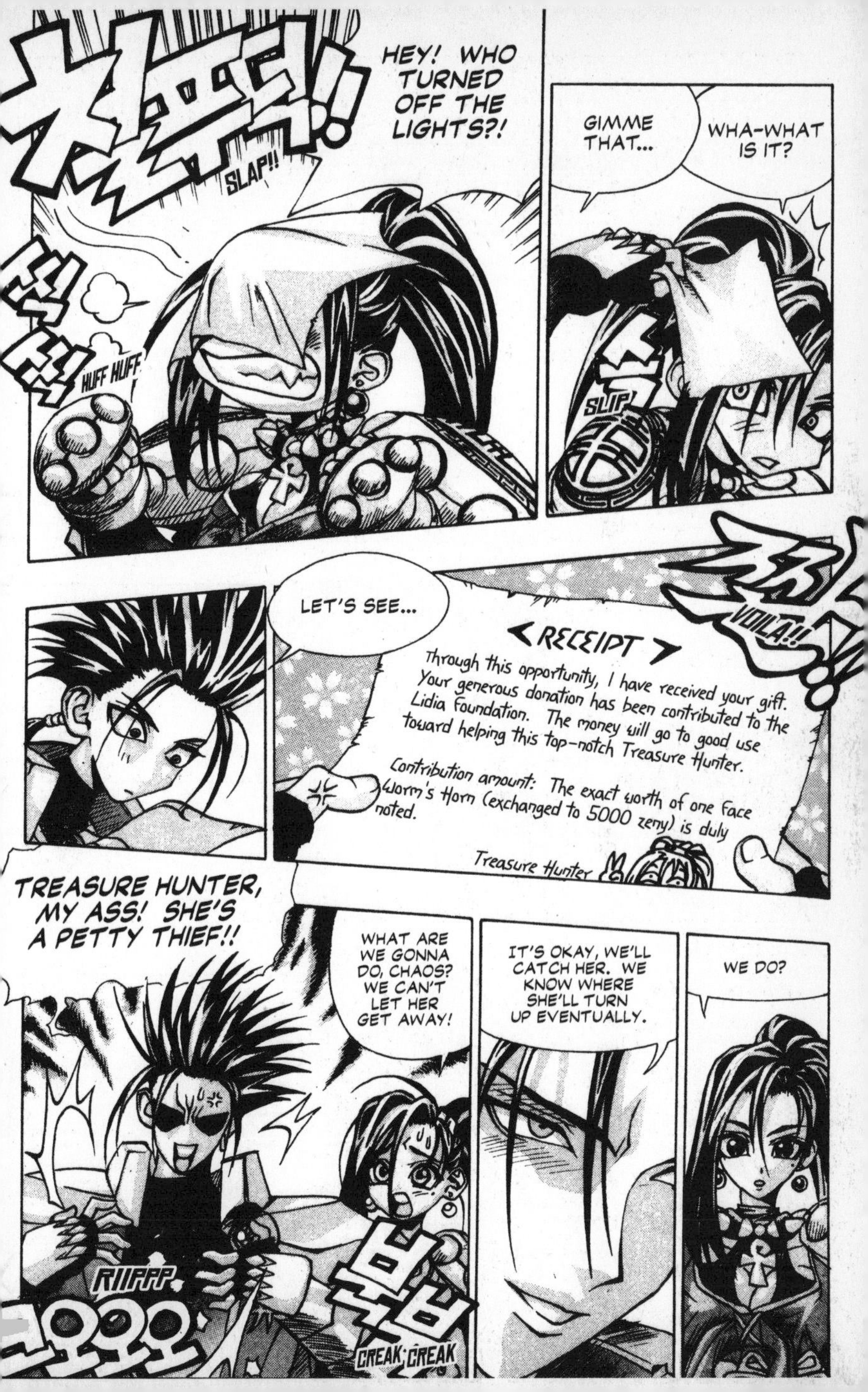
HEY! WHO TURNED OFF THE LIGHTS?!
SLAP!!
HUFF HUFF
GIMME THAT...
WHA-WHAT IS IT?
SLIP
VOILA!!
LET'S SEE...
< RECEIPT >
Through this opportunity, I have received your gift. Your generous donation has been contributed to the Lidia Foundation. The money will go to good use toward helping this top-notch Treasure Hunter.
Contribution amount: The exact worth of one Face Worm's Horn (exchanged to 5000 zeny) is duly noted.
Treasure Hunter
TREASURE HUNTER, MY ASS! SHE'S A PETTY THIEF!!
WHAT ARE WE GONNA DO, CHAOS? WE CAN'T LET HER GET AWAY!
RIIPPP
CREAK CREAK
IT'S OKAY, WE'LL CATCH HER. WE KNOW WHERE SHE'LL TURN UP EVENTUALLY.
WE DO?

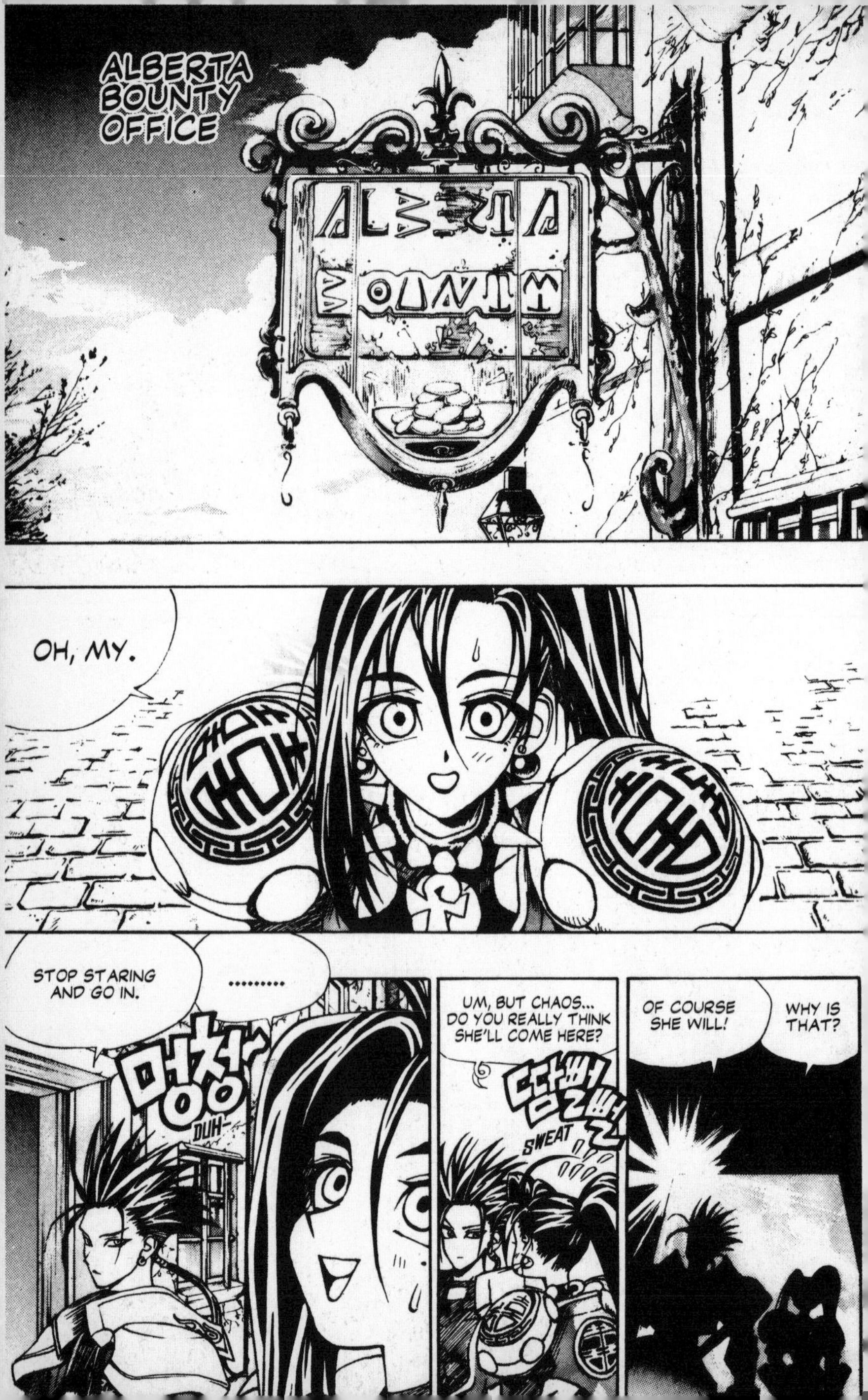

ALBERTA BOUNTY OFFICE
OH, MY.
STOP STARING AND GO IN.
....
DUH-
UM, BUT CHAOS... DO YOU REALLY THINK SHE'LL COME HERE?
SWEAT
OF COURSE SHE WILL!
WHY IS THAT?

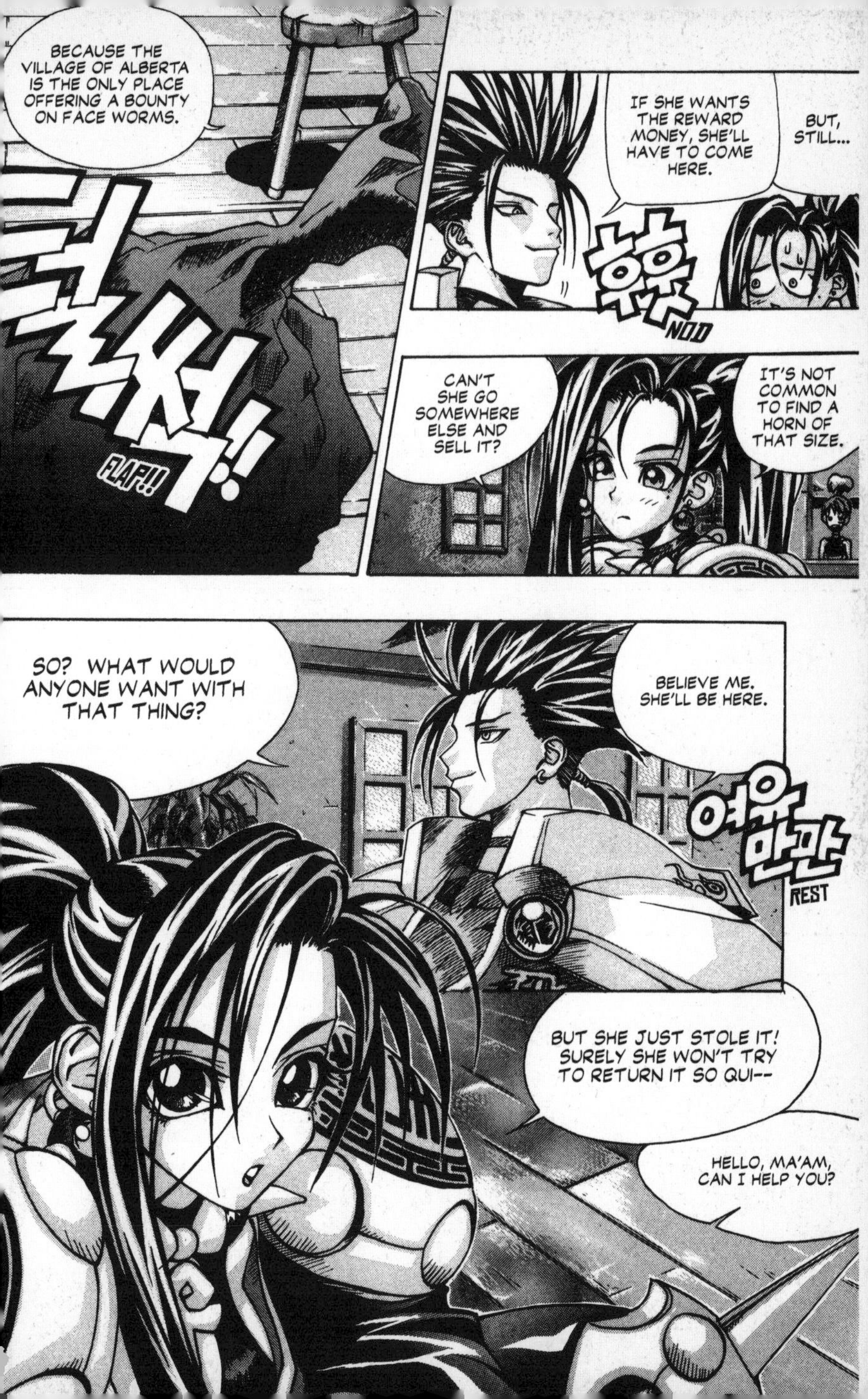
BECAUSE THE VILLAGE OF ALBERTA IS THE ONLY PLACE OFFERING A BOUNTY ON FACE WORMS.
FLAP!!
IF SHE WANTS THE REWARD MONEY, SHE'LL HAVE TO COME HERE.
BUT, STILL...
NOD
CAN'T SHE GO SOMEWHERE ELSE AND SELL IT?
IT'S NOT COMMON TO FIND A HORN OF THAT SIZE.
SO? WHAT WOULD ANYONE WANT WITH THAT THING?
BELIEVE ME. SHE'LL BE HERE.
여유만만
REST
BUT SHE JUST STOLE IT! SURELY SHE WON'T TRY TO RETURN IT SO QUI--
HELLO, MA'AM, CAN I HELP YOU?

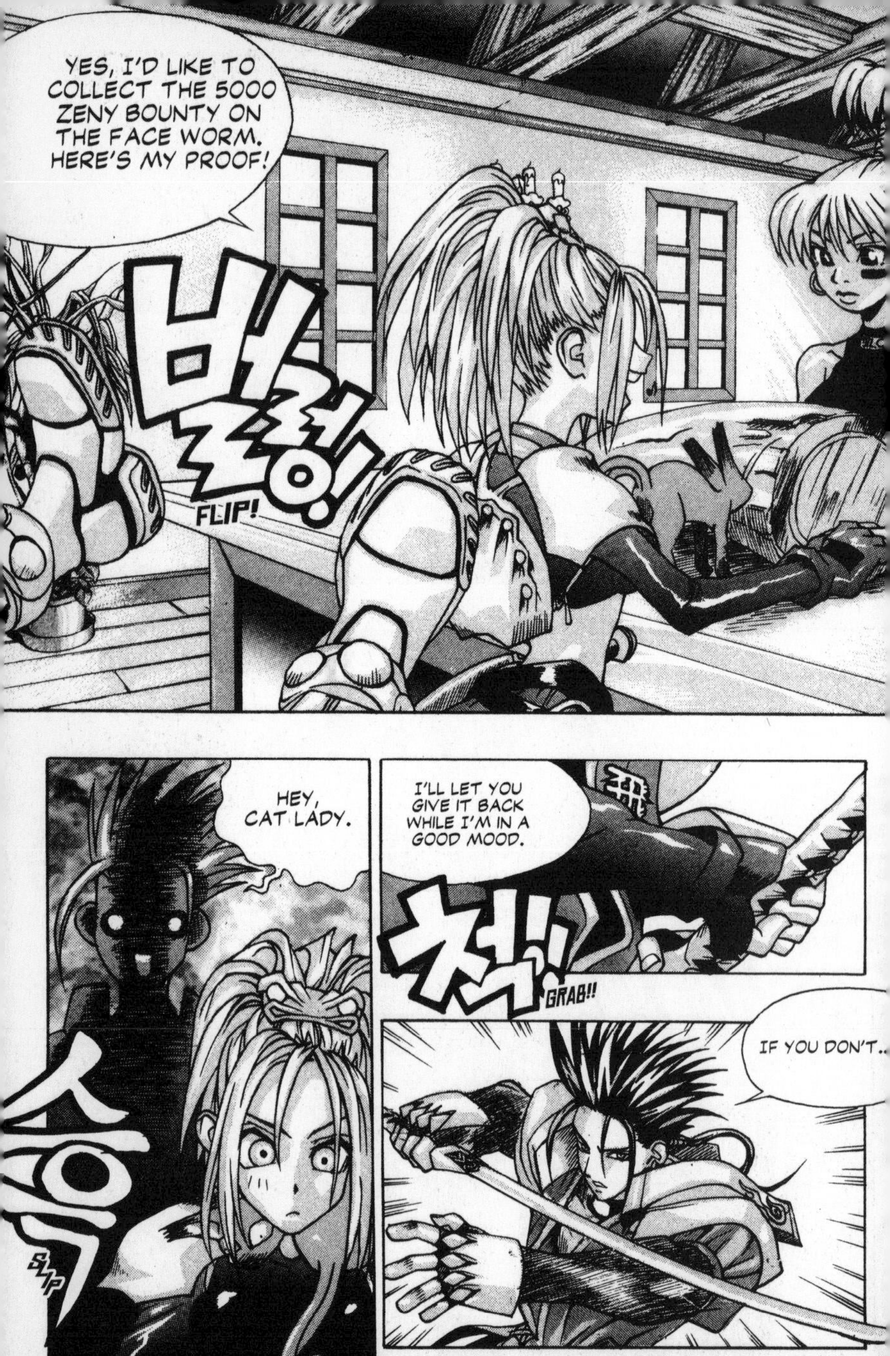
YES, I'D LIKE TO COLLECT THE 5000 ZENY BOUNTY ON THE FACE WORM. HERE'S MY PROOF!
FLIP!
HEY, CAT LADY.
SLIP
I'LL LET YOU GIVE IT BACK WHILE I'M IN A GOOD MOOD.
척!
GRAB!!
IF YOU DON'T...

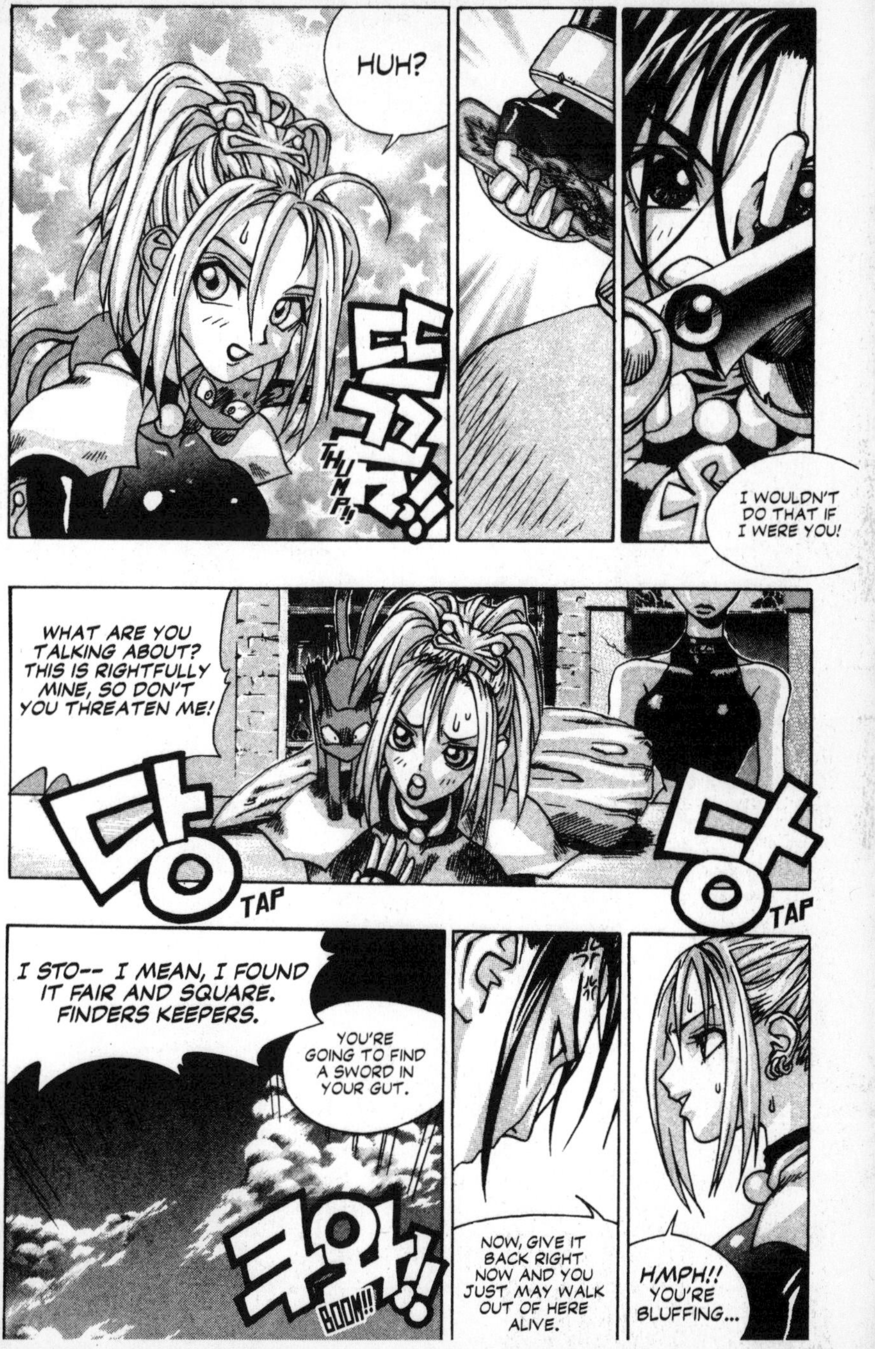
HUH?
THUMP!!
I WOULDN'T DO THAT IF I WERE YOU!
WHAT ARE YOU TALKING ABOUT? THIS IS RIGHTFULLY MINE, SO DON'T YOU THREATEN ME!
TAP
TAP
I STO-- I MEAN, I FOUND IT FAIR AND SQUARE. FINDERS KEEPERS.
YOU'RE GOING TO FIND A SWORD IN YOUR GUT.
BOOM!!
NOW, GIVE IT BACK RIGHT NOW AND YOU JUST MAY WALK OUT OF HERE ALIVE.
HMPH!! YOU'RE BLUFFING...

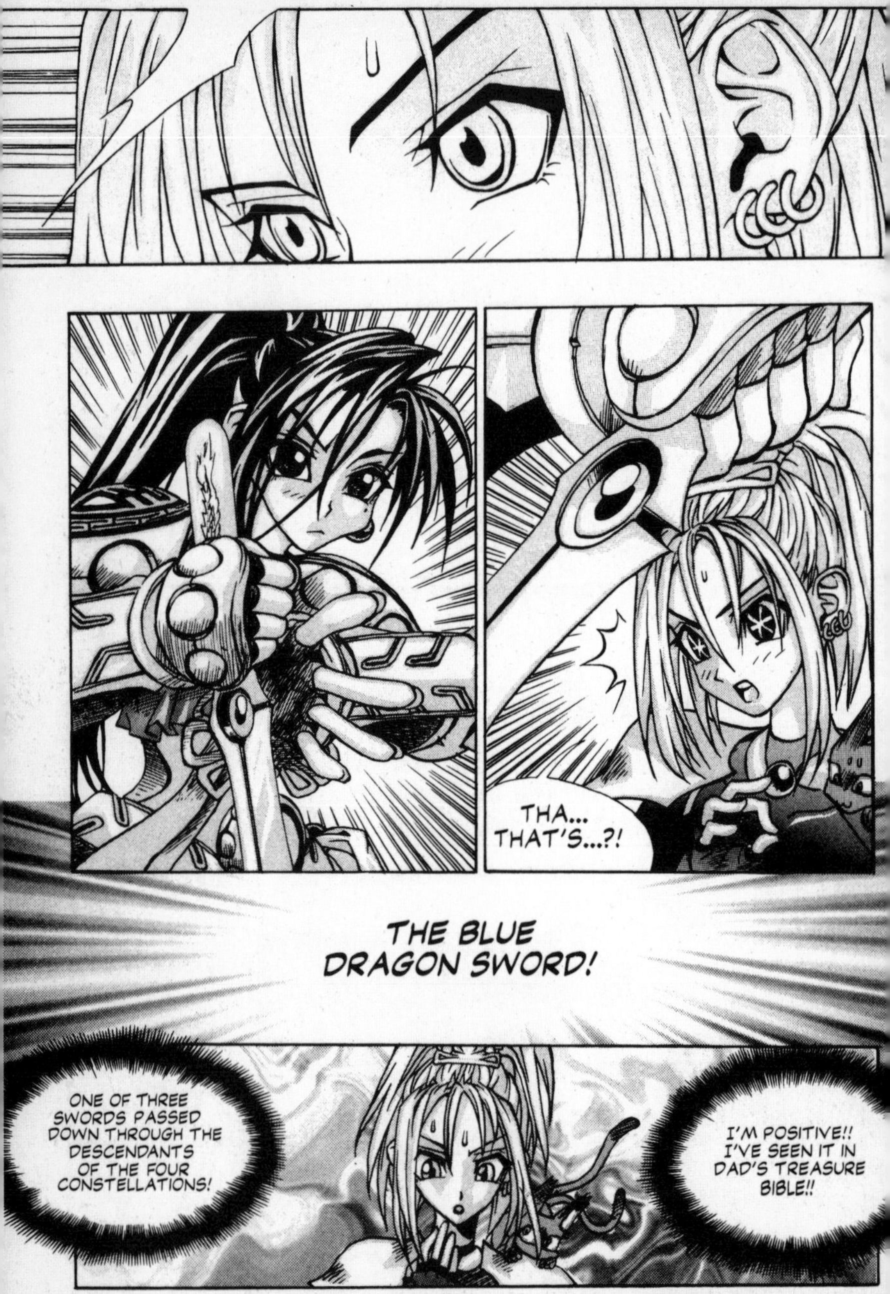
THA... THAT'S...?!
THE BLUE DRAGON SWORD!
ONE OF THREE SWORDS PASSED DOWN THROUGH THE DESCENDANTS OF THE FOUR CONSTELLATIONS!
I'M POSITIVE!! I'VE SEEN IT IN DAD'S TREASURE BIBLE!!

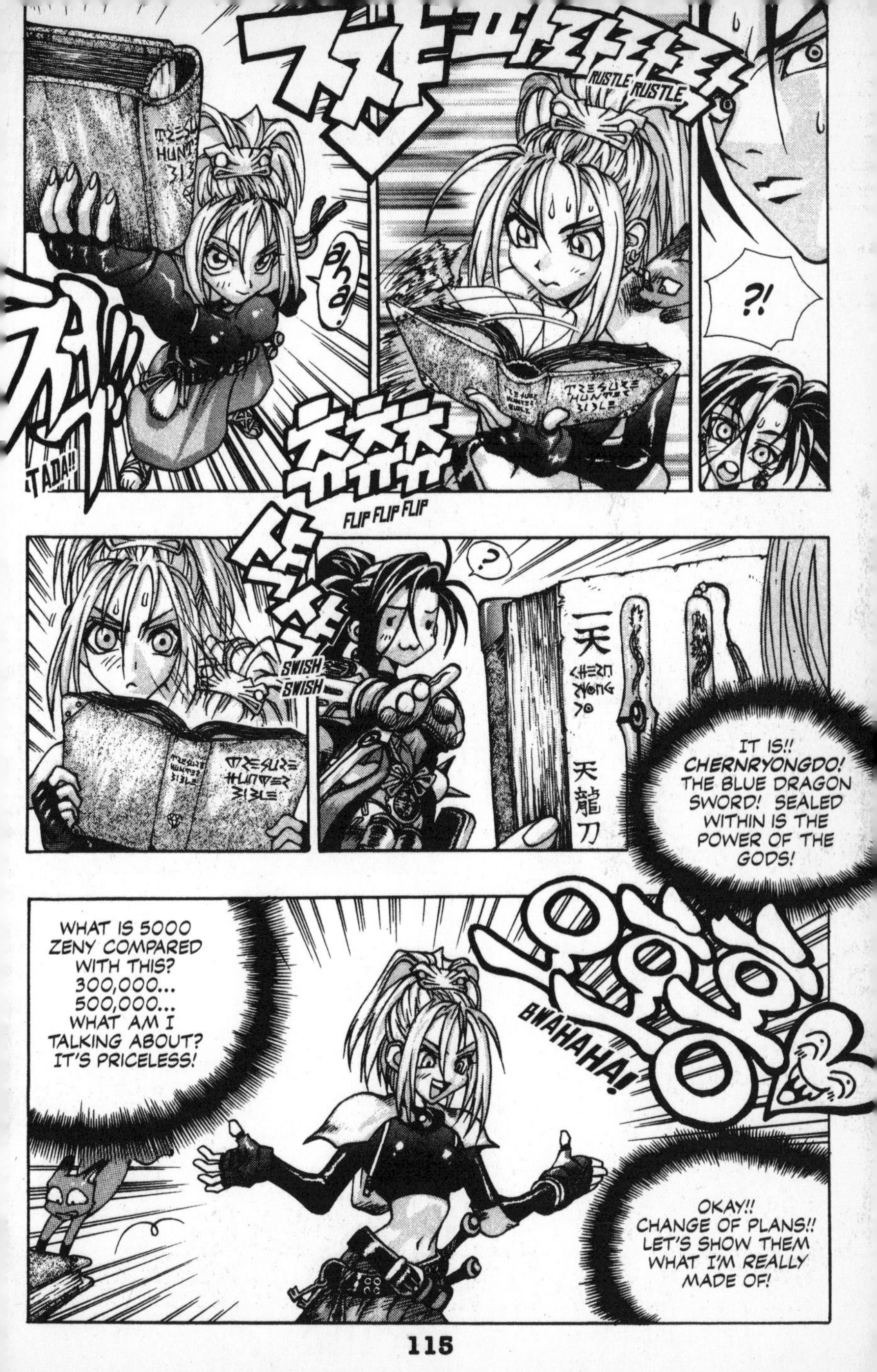
RUSTLE RUSTLE
¡TADA!!
?!
FLIP FLIP FLIP
?
SWISH SWISH
一天
CHERN RYONG DO
天龍刀
IT IS!! CHERNRYONGDO! THE BLUE DRAGON SWORD! SEALED WITHIN IS THE POWER OF THE GODS!
WHAT IS 5000 ZENY COMPARED WITH THIS? 300,000... 500,000... WHAT AM I TALKING ABOUT? IT'S PRICELESS!
BWAHAHA!
OKAY!! CHANGE OF PLANS!! LET'S SHOW THEM WHAT I'M REALLY MADE OF!

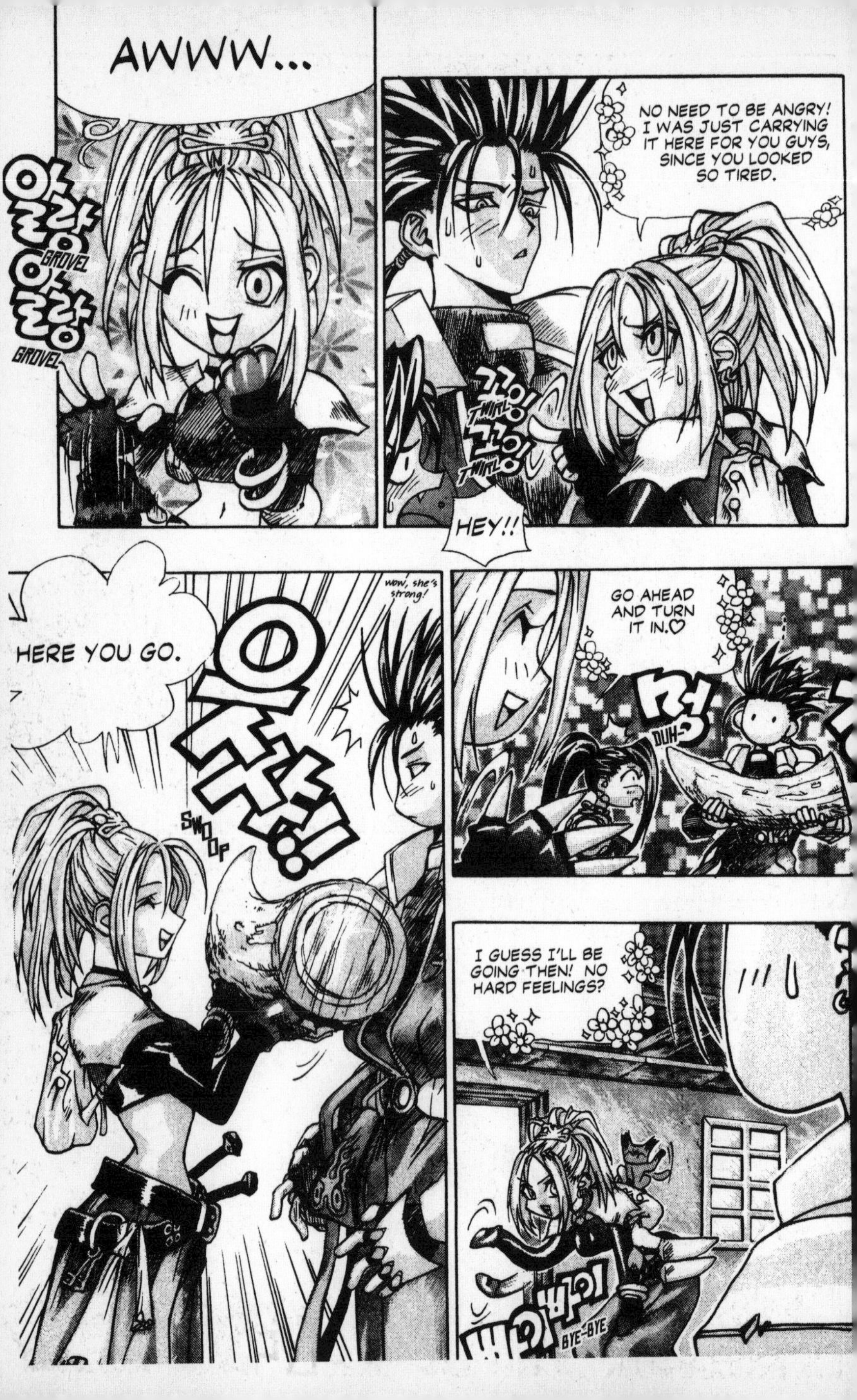
AWWW...
알랑알랑
GROVEL
GROVEL
NO NEED TO BE ANGRY! I WAS JUST CARRYING IT HERE FOR YOU GUYS, SINCE YOU LOOKED SO TIRED.
TWIRL
TWIRL
HEY!!
HERE YOU GO.
wow, she's strong!
SWOOP
GO AHEAD AND TURN IT IN.♡
DUH-
I GUESS I'LL BE GOING THEN! NO HARD FEELINGS?
바이바이
BYE-BYE

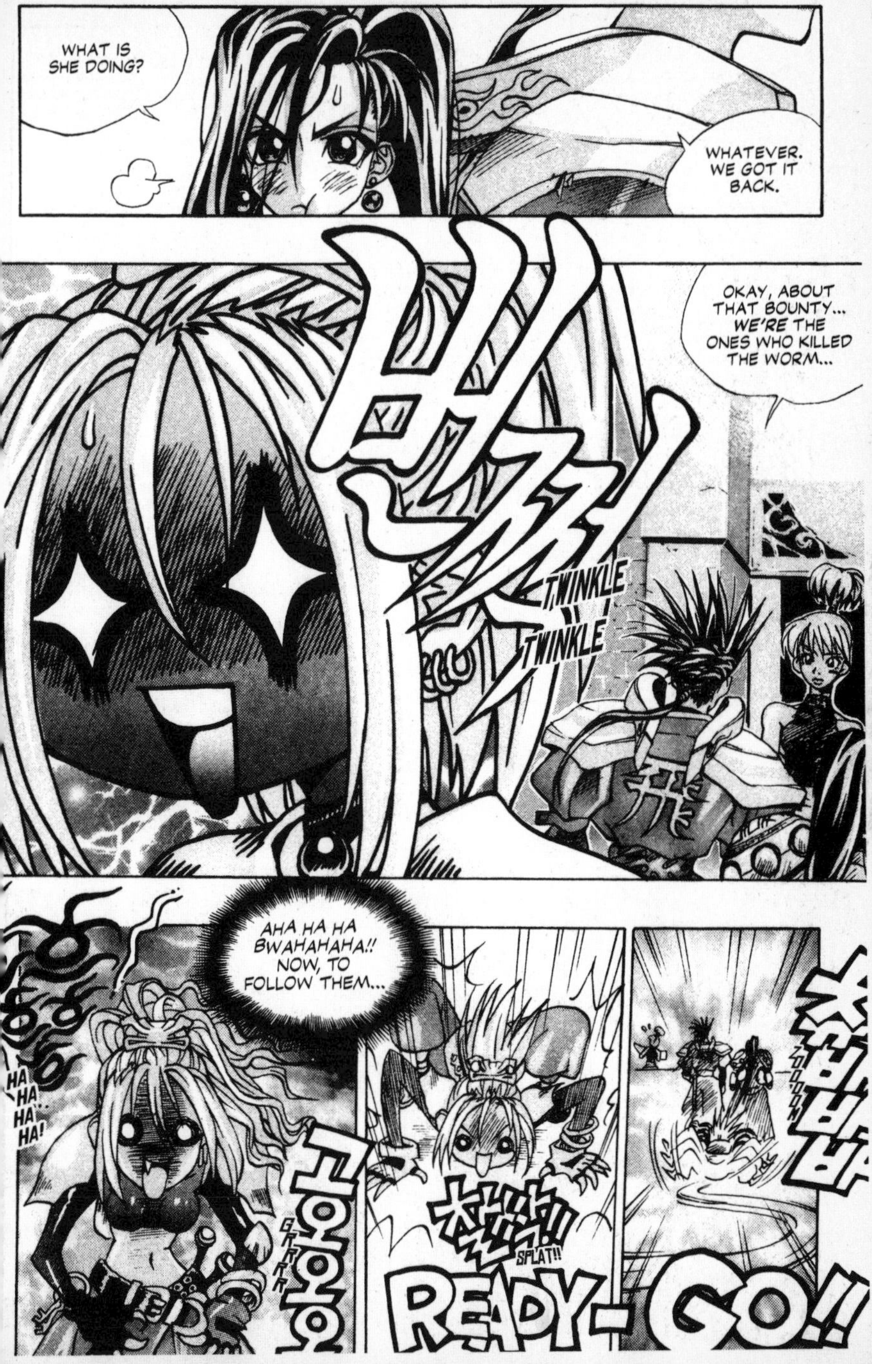
WHAT IS SHE DOING?
WHATEVER. WE GOT IT BACK.
OKAY, ABOUT THAT BOUNTY... WE'RE THE ONES WHO KILLED THE WORM...
TWINKLE TWINKLE
AHA HA HA BWAHAHAHA!! NOW, TO FOLLOW THEM...
HA HA... HA HA HA!
GRRRR
SPLAT!!
ZOOOOM
READY-GO!!

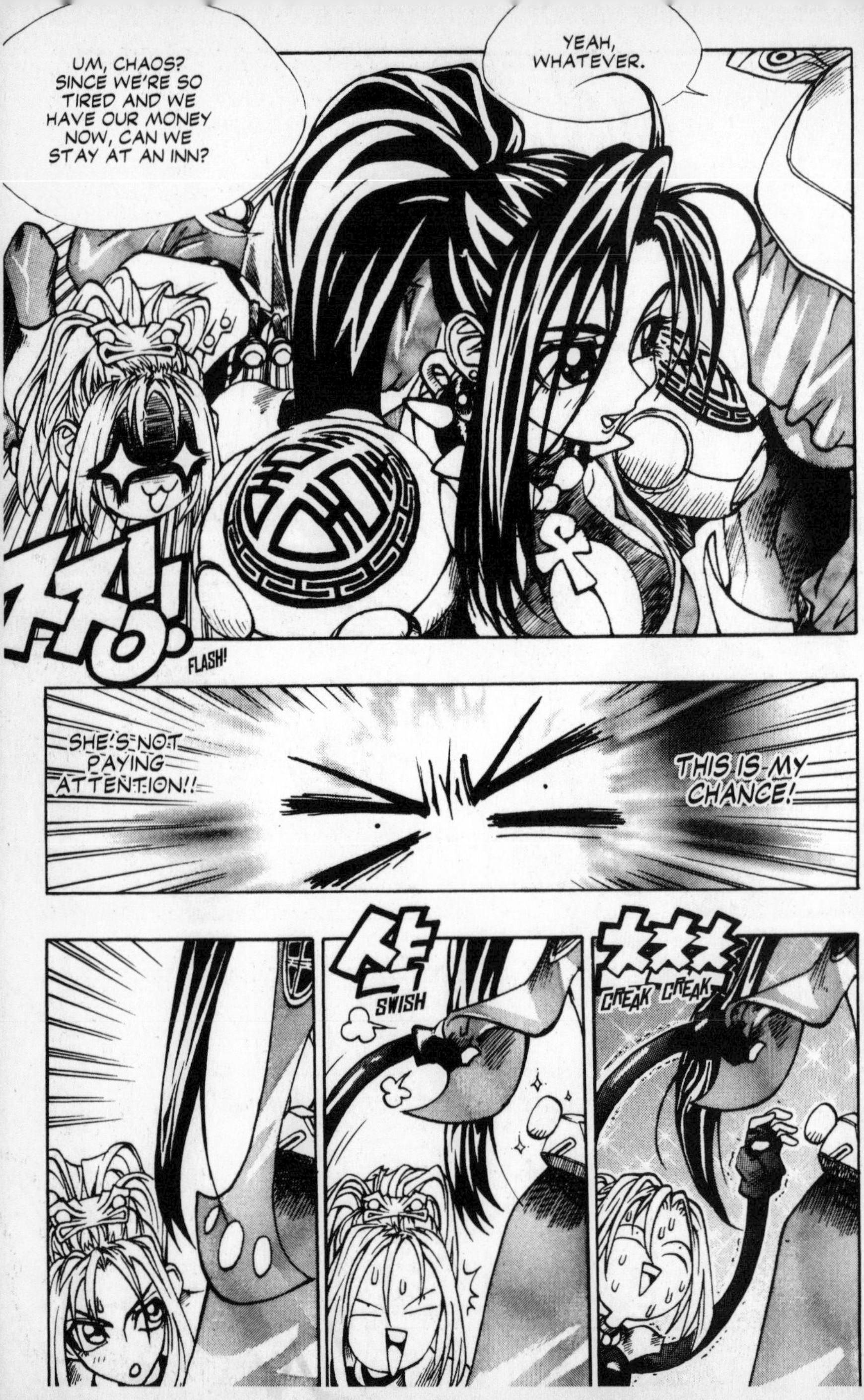
UM, CHAOS? SINCE WE'RE SO TIRED AND WE HAVE OUR MONEY NOW, CAN WE STAY AT AN INN?
YEAH, WHATEVER.
FLASH!
SHE'S NOT PAYING ATTENTION!!
THIS IS MY CHANCE!
SWISH
CREAK CREAK

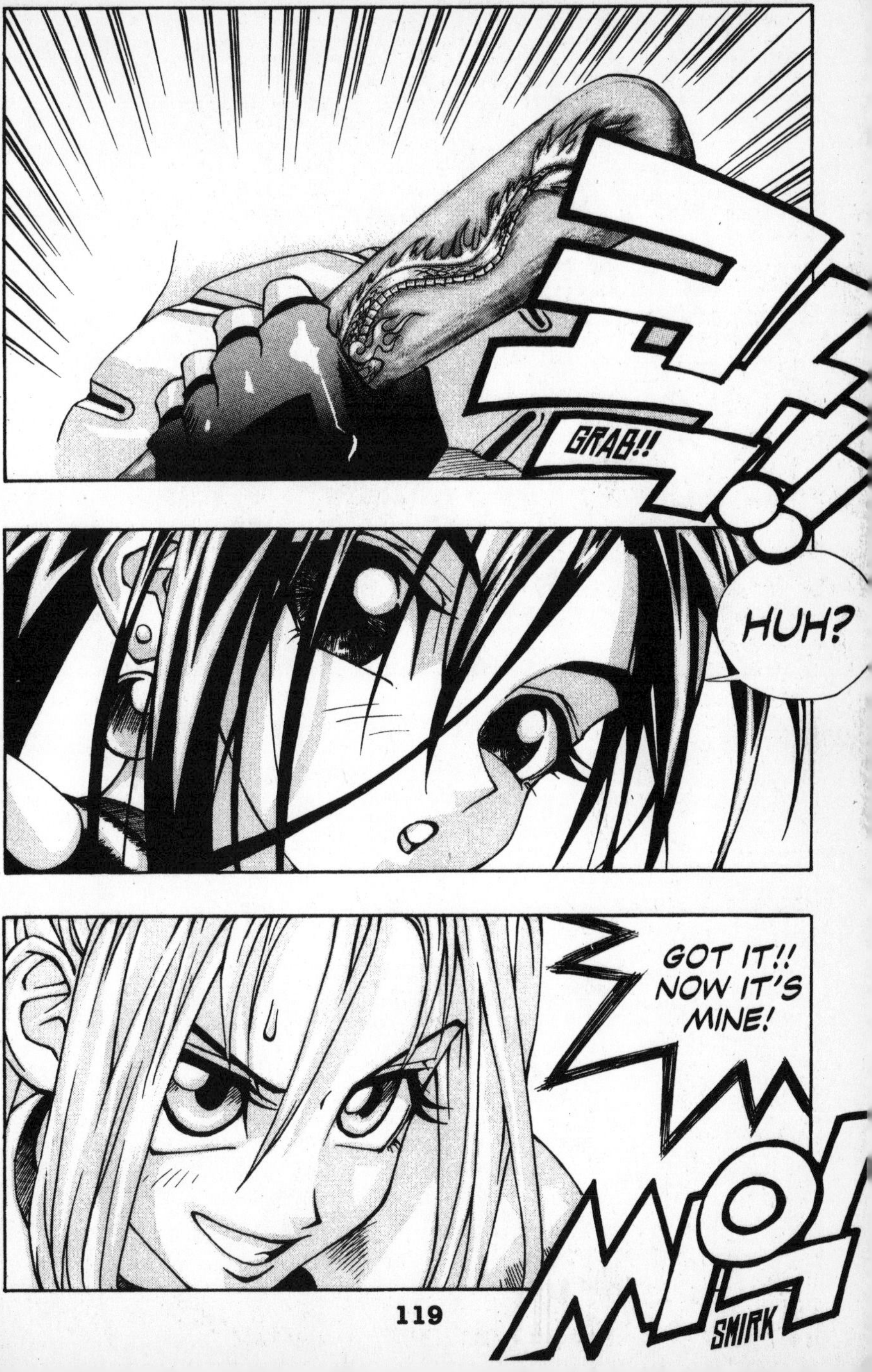
GRAB!!
HUH?
GOT IT!! NOW IT'S MINE!
SMIRK

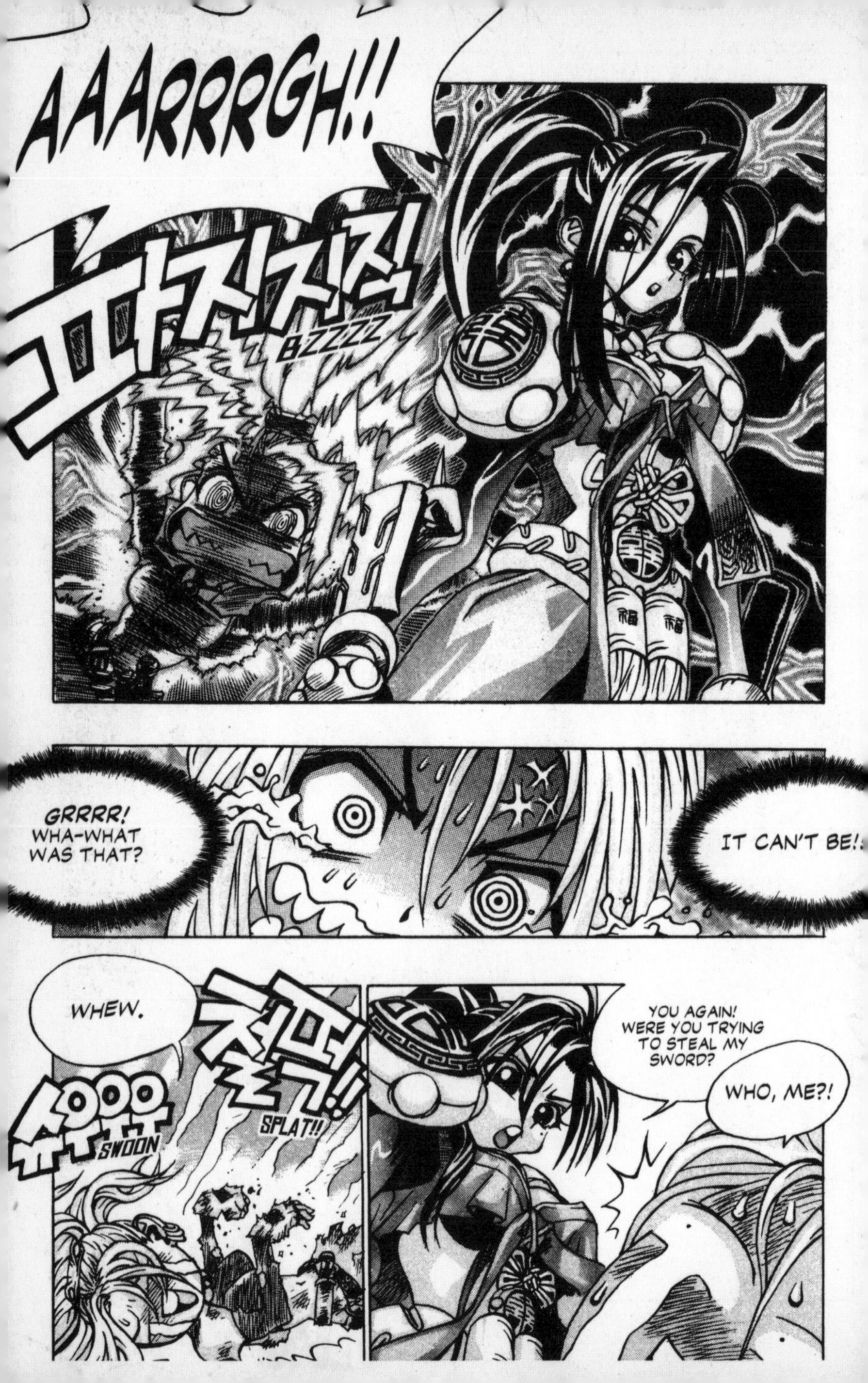
AAARRRGH!!
BZZZZ
GRRRR! WHA-WHAT WAS THAT?
IT CAN'T BE!..
WHEW.
SWOON
SPLAT!!
YOU AGAIN! WERE YOU TRYING TO STEAL MY SWORD?
WHO, ME?!

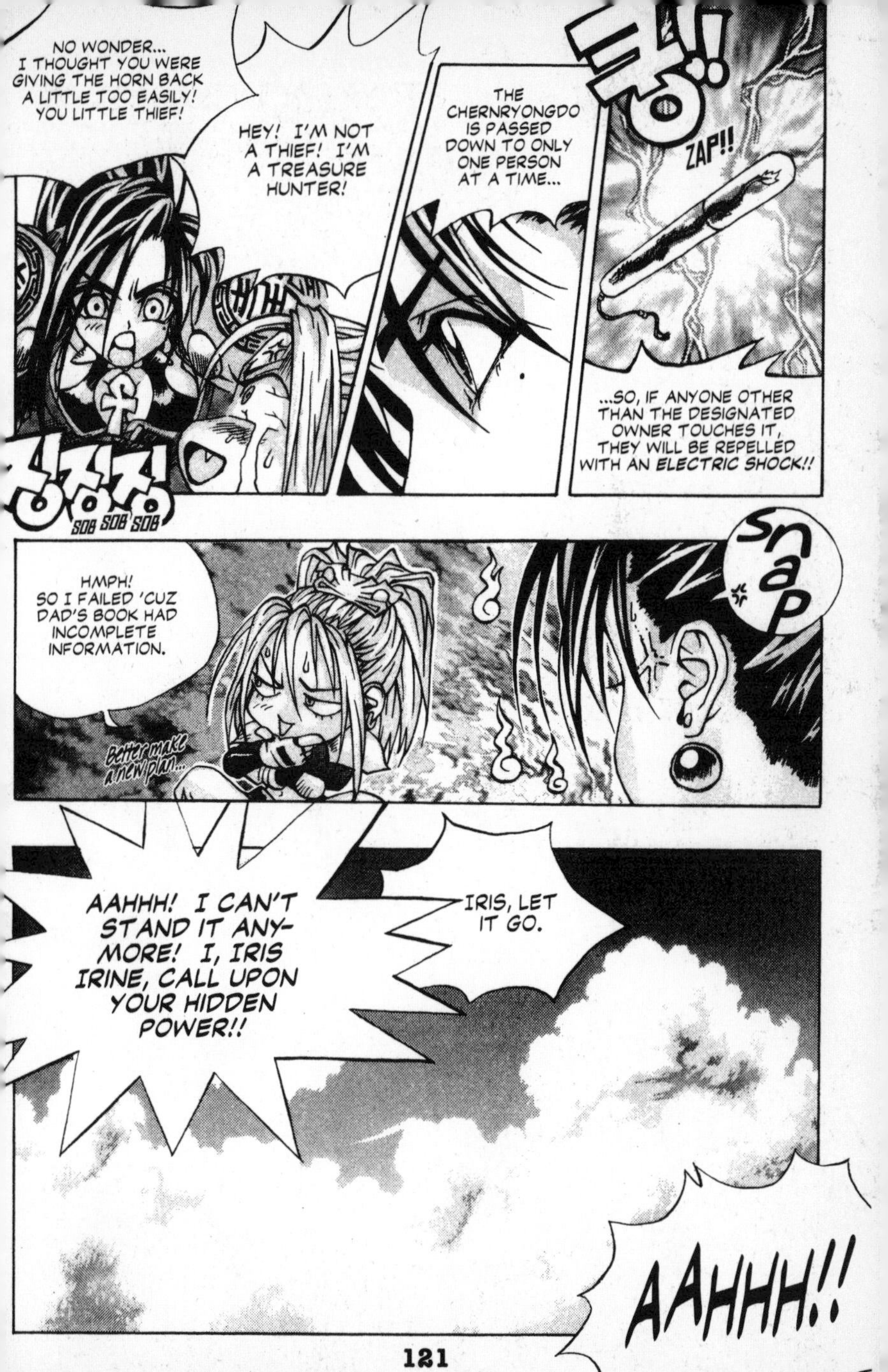

NO WONDER... I THOUGHT YOU WERE GIVING THE HORN BACK A LITTLE TOO EASILY! YOU LITTLE THIEF!
HEY! I'M NOT A THIEF! I'M A TREASURE HUNTER!
SOB SOB SOB
THE CHERNRYONGDO IS PASSED DOWN TO ONLY ONE PERSON AT A TIME...
ZAP!!
...SO, IF ANYONE OTHER THAN THE DESIGNATED OWNER TOUCHES IT, THEY WILL BE REPELLED WITH AN ELECTRIC SHOCK!!
HMPH! SO I FAILED 'CUZ DAD'S BOOK HAD INCOMPLETE INFORMATION.
Better make a new plan...
Snap
AAHHH! I CAN'T STAND IT ANY-MORE! I, IRIS IRINE, CALL UPON YOUR HIDDEN POWER!!
IRIS, LET IT GO.
AAHHH!!

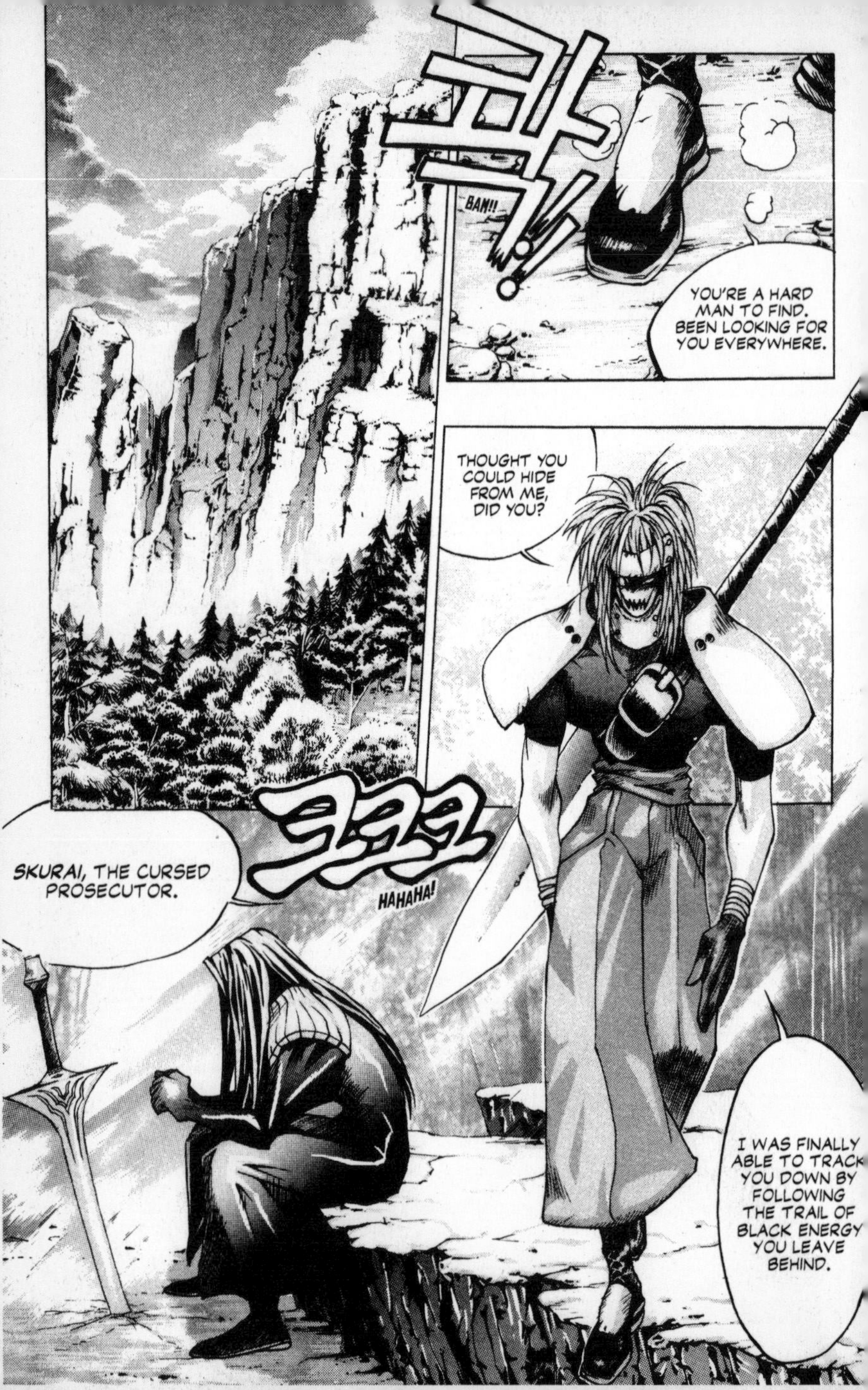
BAM!!
YOU'RE A HARD MAN TO FIND. BEEN LOOKING FOR YOU EVERYWHERE.
THOUGHT YOU COULD HIDE FROM ME, DID YOU?
SKURAI, THE CURSED PROSECUTOR.
HAHAHA!
I WAS FINALLY ABLE TO TRACK YOU DOWN BY FOLLOWING THE TRAIL OF BLACK ENERGY YOU LEAVE BEHIND.

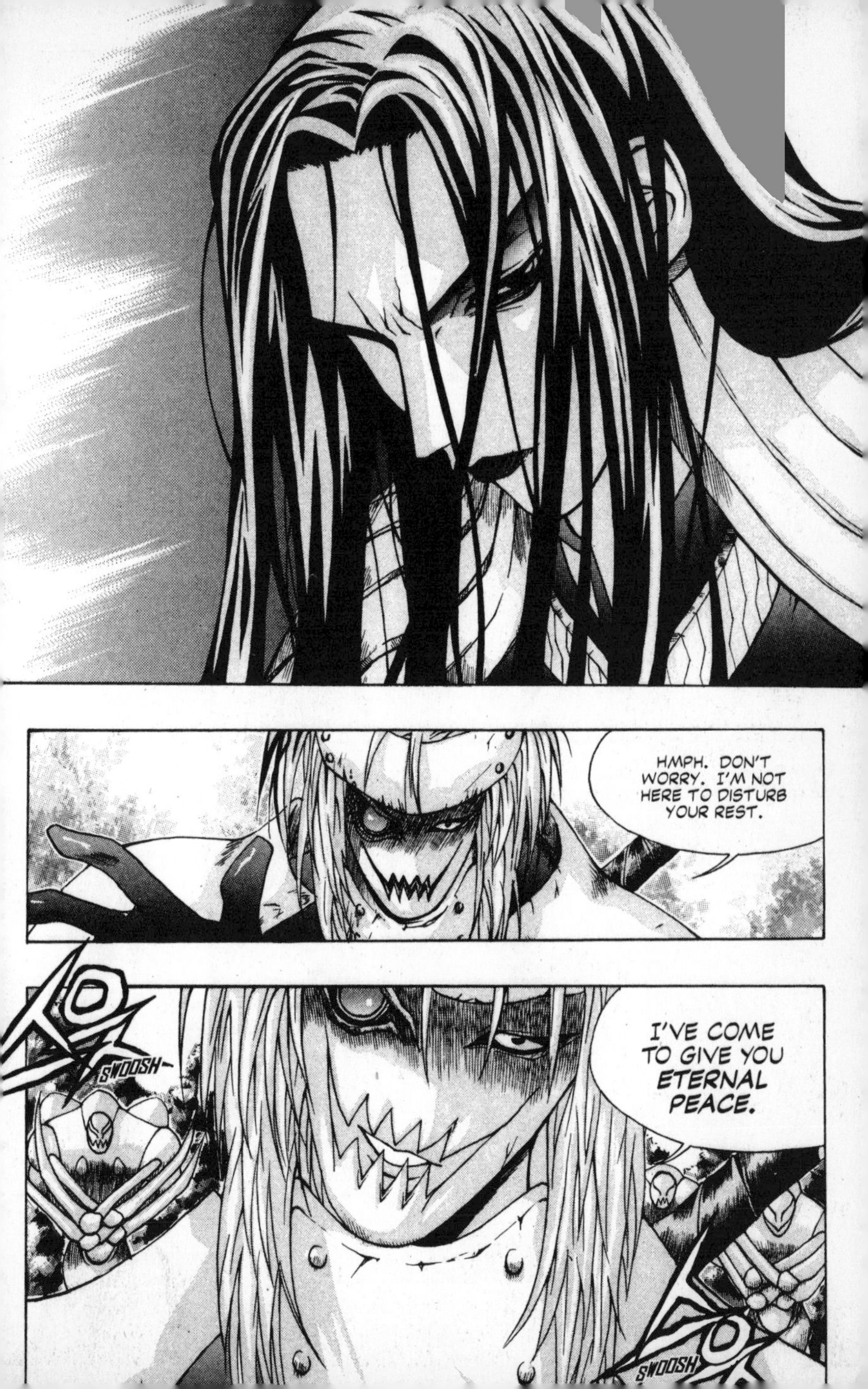
HMPH. DON'T WORRY. I'M NOT HERE TO DISTURB YOUR REST.
SWOOSH
I'VE COME TO GIVE YOU ETERNAL PEACE.
SWOOSH

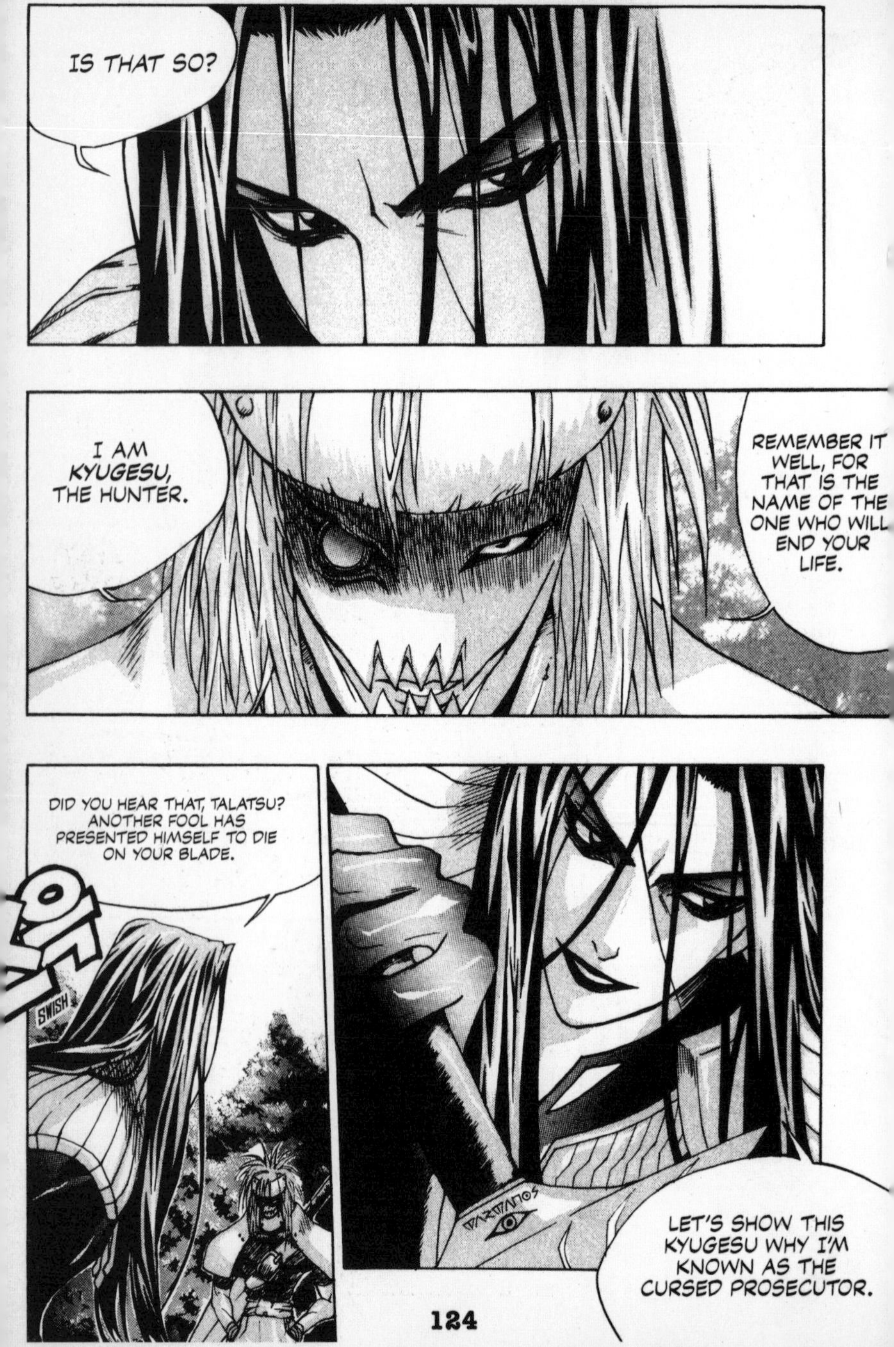
IS THAT SO?
I AM KYUGESU, THE HUNTER.
REMEMBER IT WELL, FOR THAT IS THE NAME OF THE ONE WHO WILL END YOUR LIFE.
DID YOU HEAR THAT, TALATSU? ANOTHER FOOL HAS PRESENTED HIMSELF TO DIE ON YOUR BLADE.
SWISH
LET'S SHOW THIS KYUGESU WHY I'M KNOWN AS THE CURSED PROSECUTOR.

RAGNARÖK

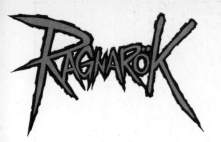

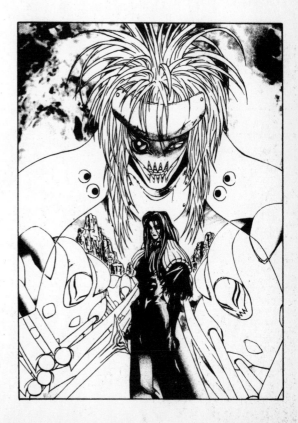

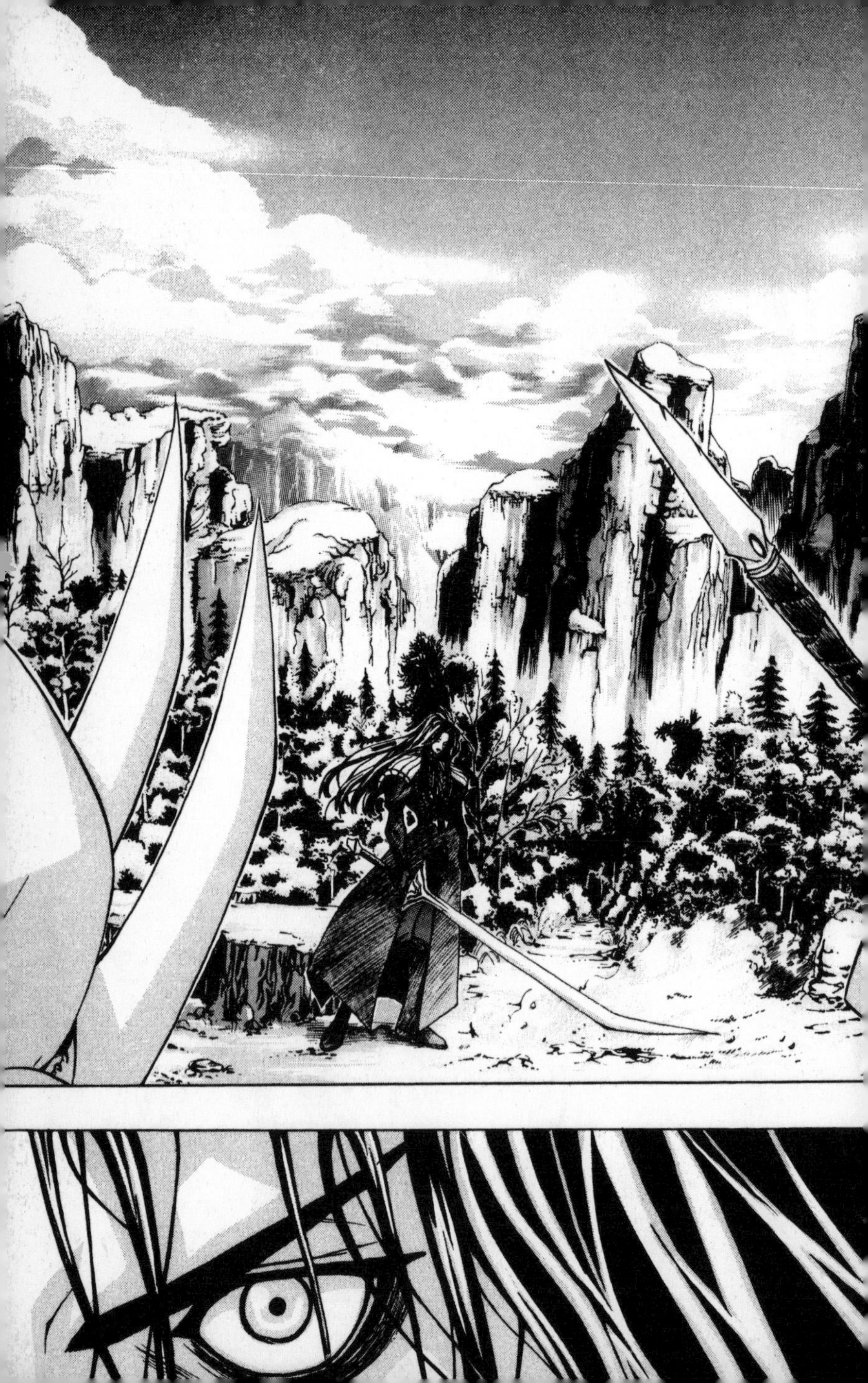

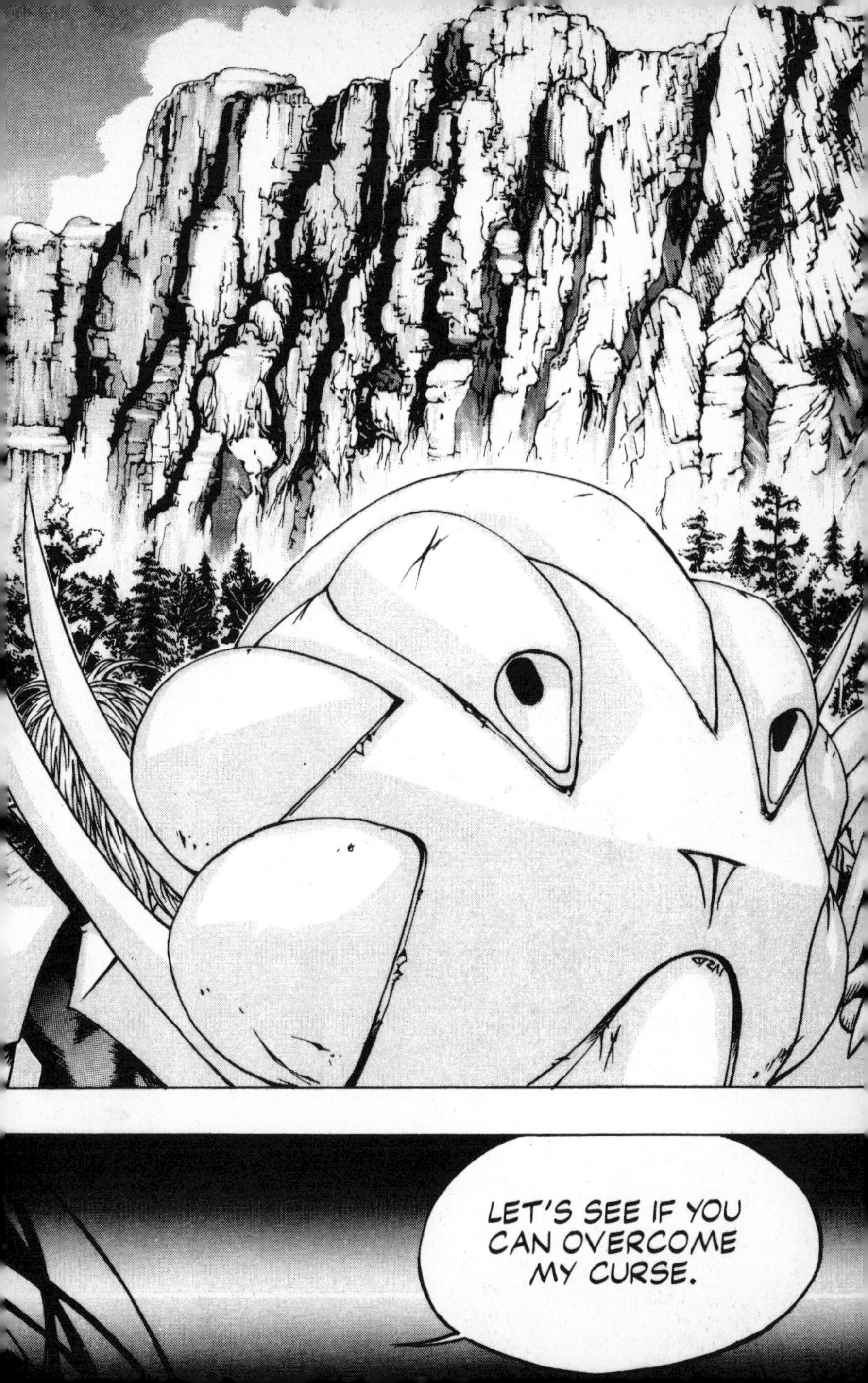
LET'S SEE IF YOU CAN OVERCOME MY CURSE.

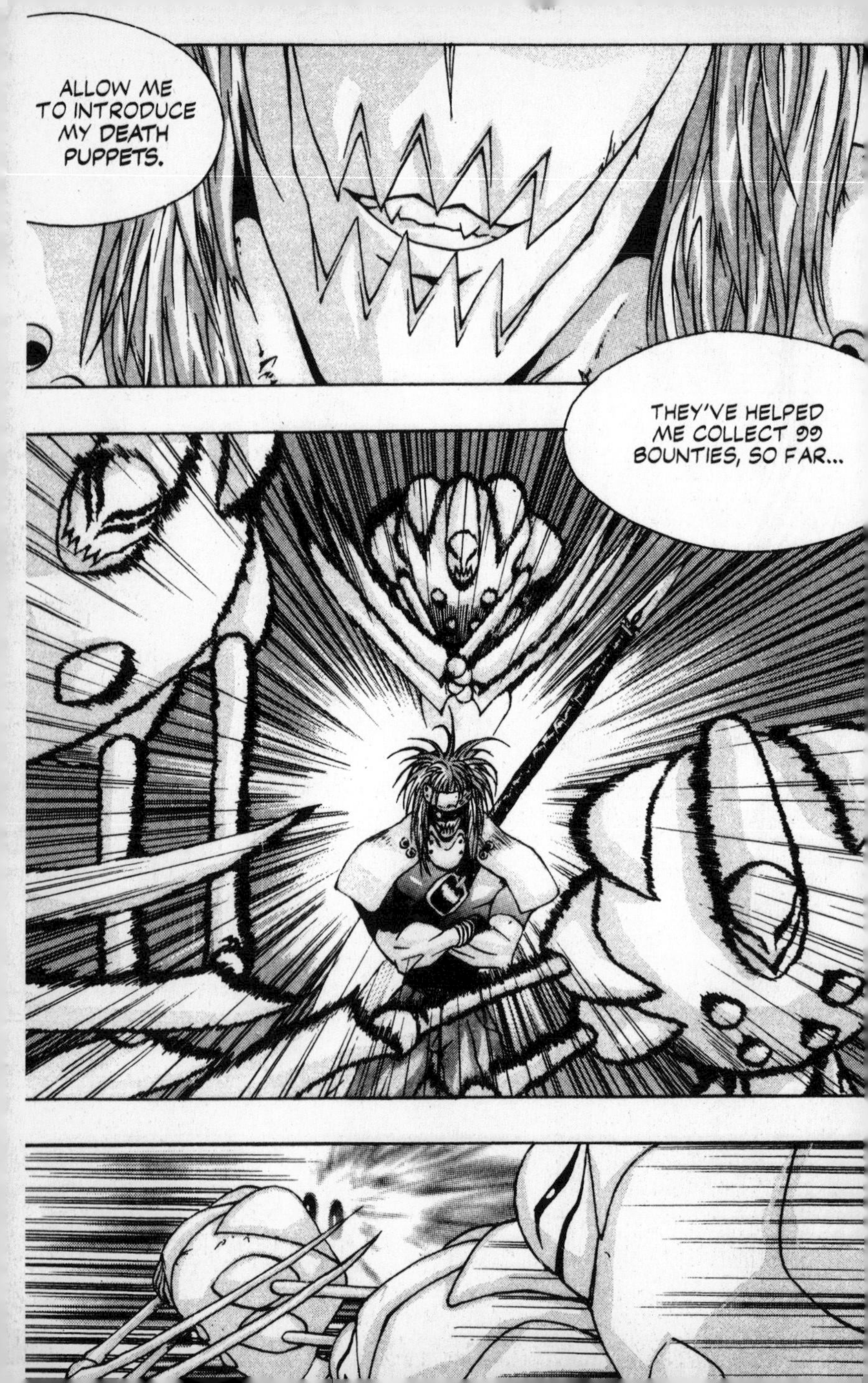
ALLOW ME TO INTRODUCE MY DEATH PUPPETS.
THEY'VE HELPED ME COLLECT 99 BOUNTIES, SO FAR...

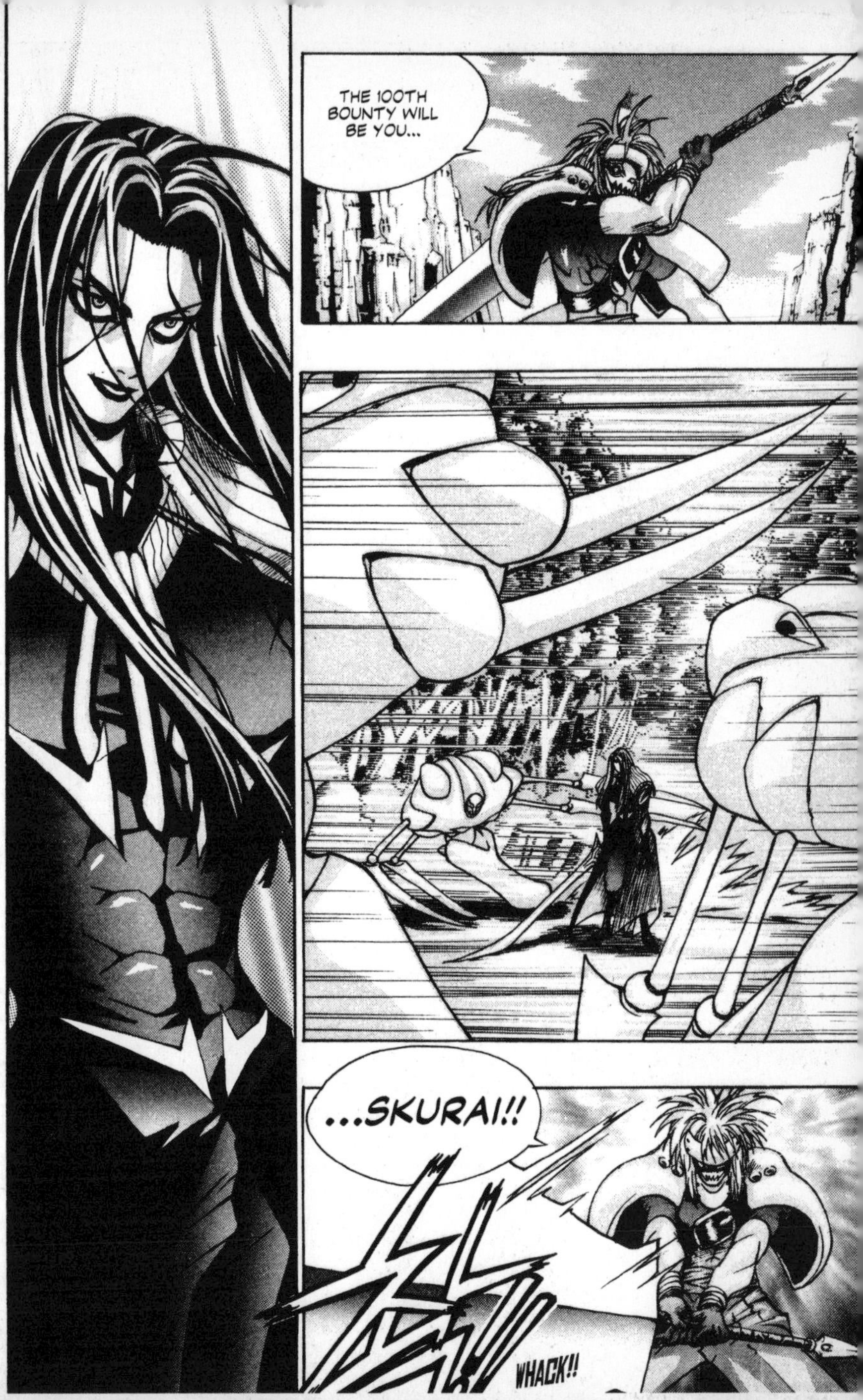
THE 100TH BOUNTY WILL BE YOU...
...SKURAI!!
WHACK!!

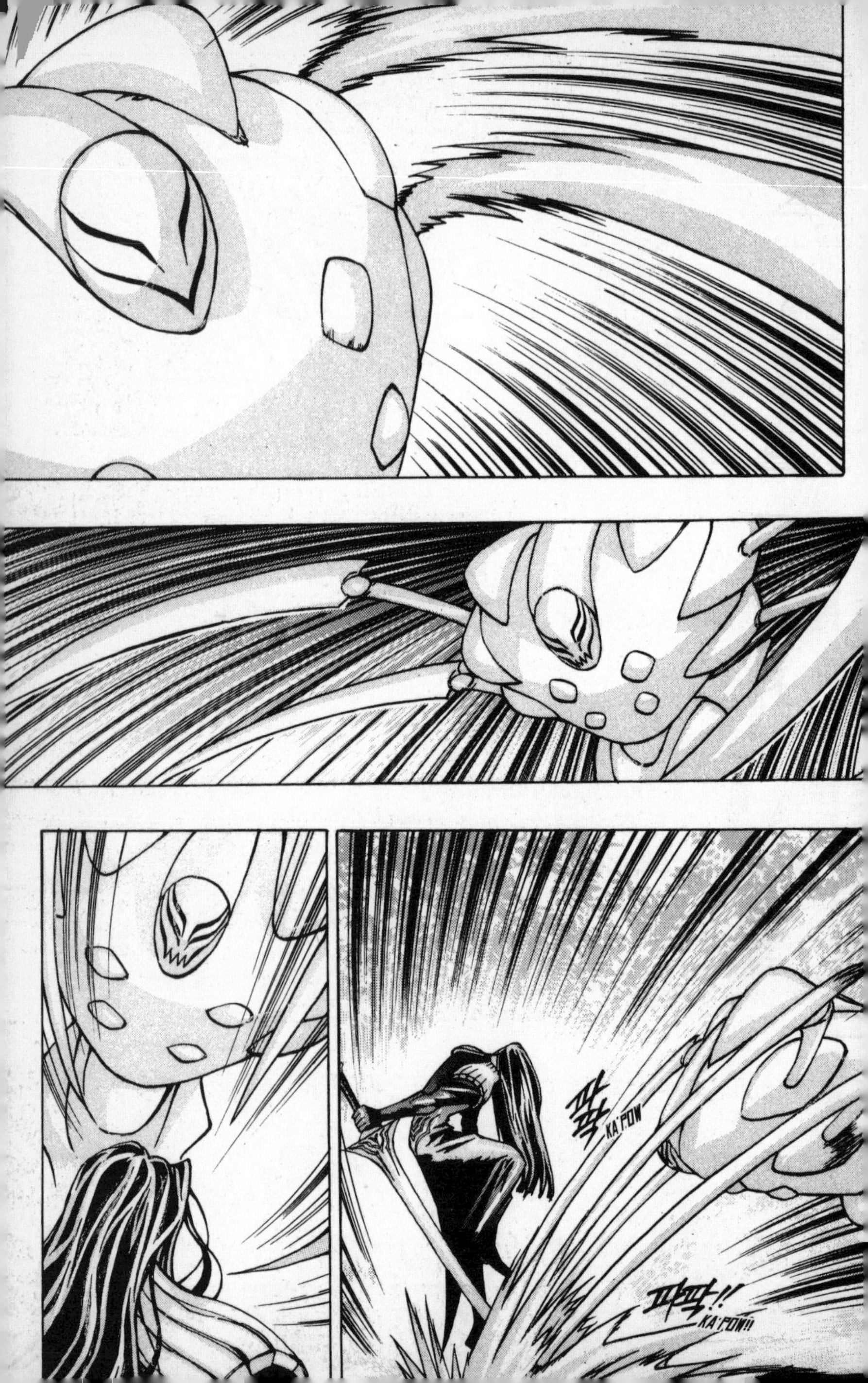

깍
KA'POW
파악!!
KA'POW!!

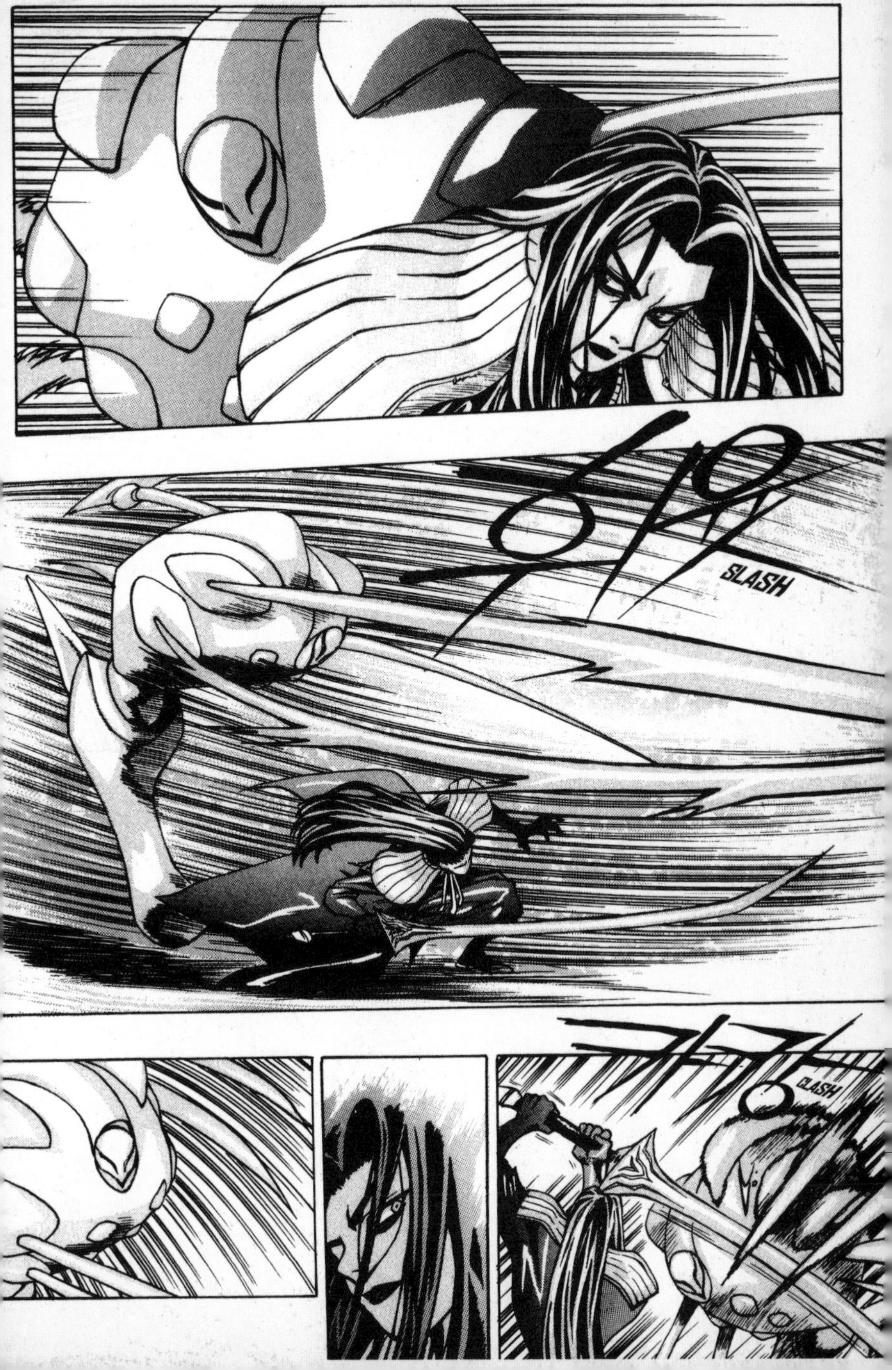
SLASH
CLASH

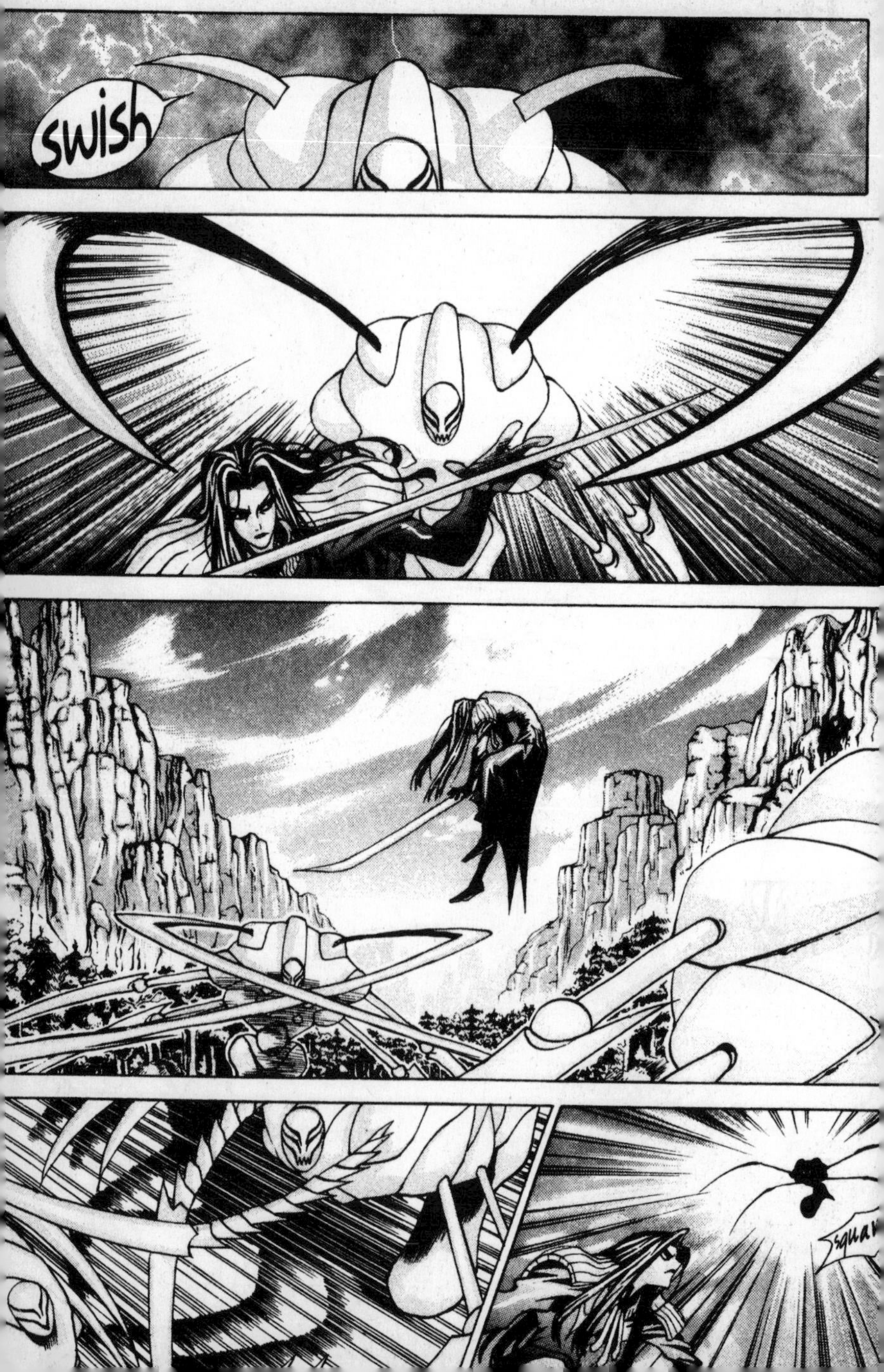
swish
squa

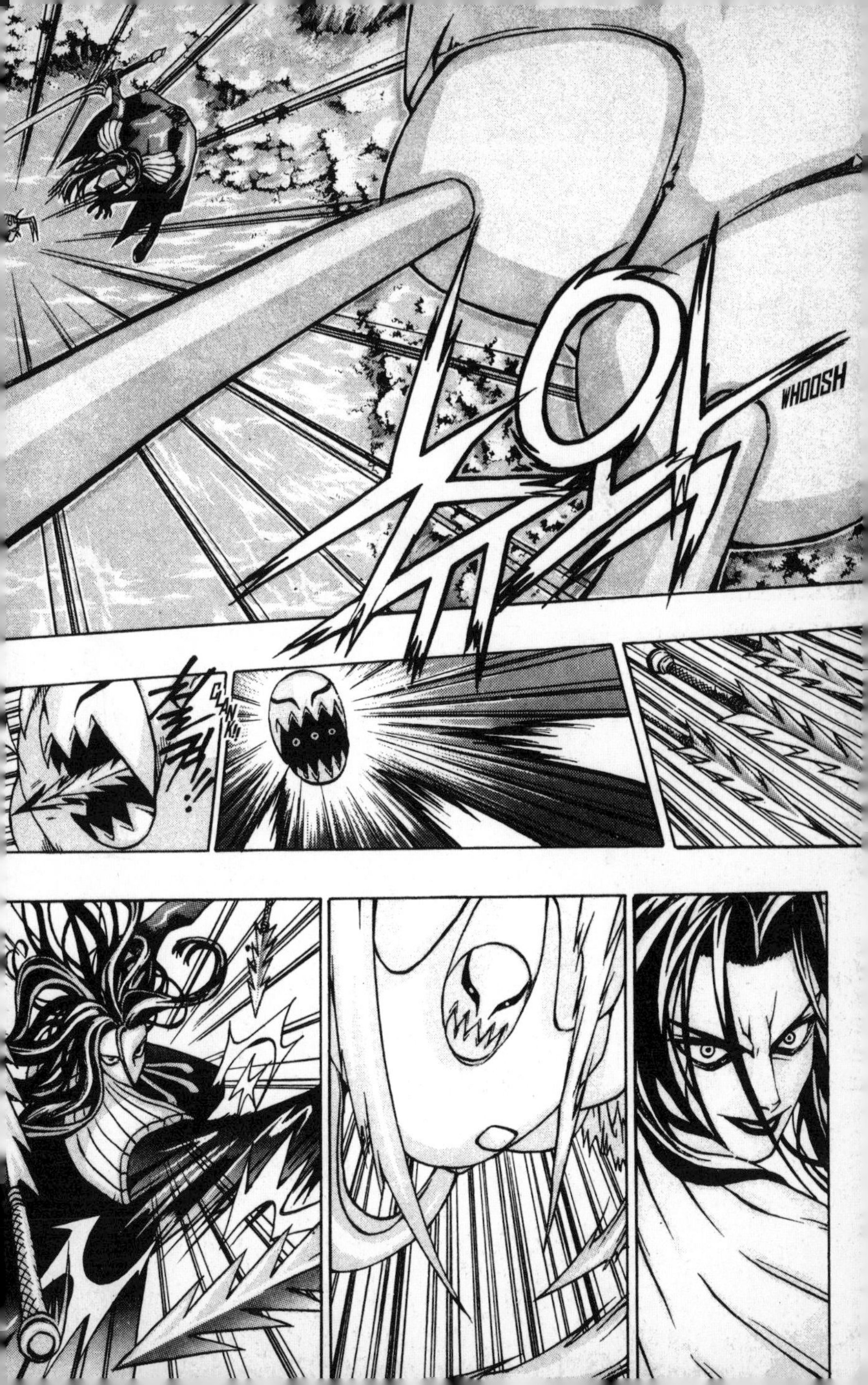
WHOOSH
CLANK!!

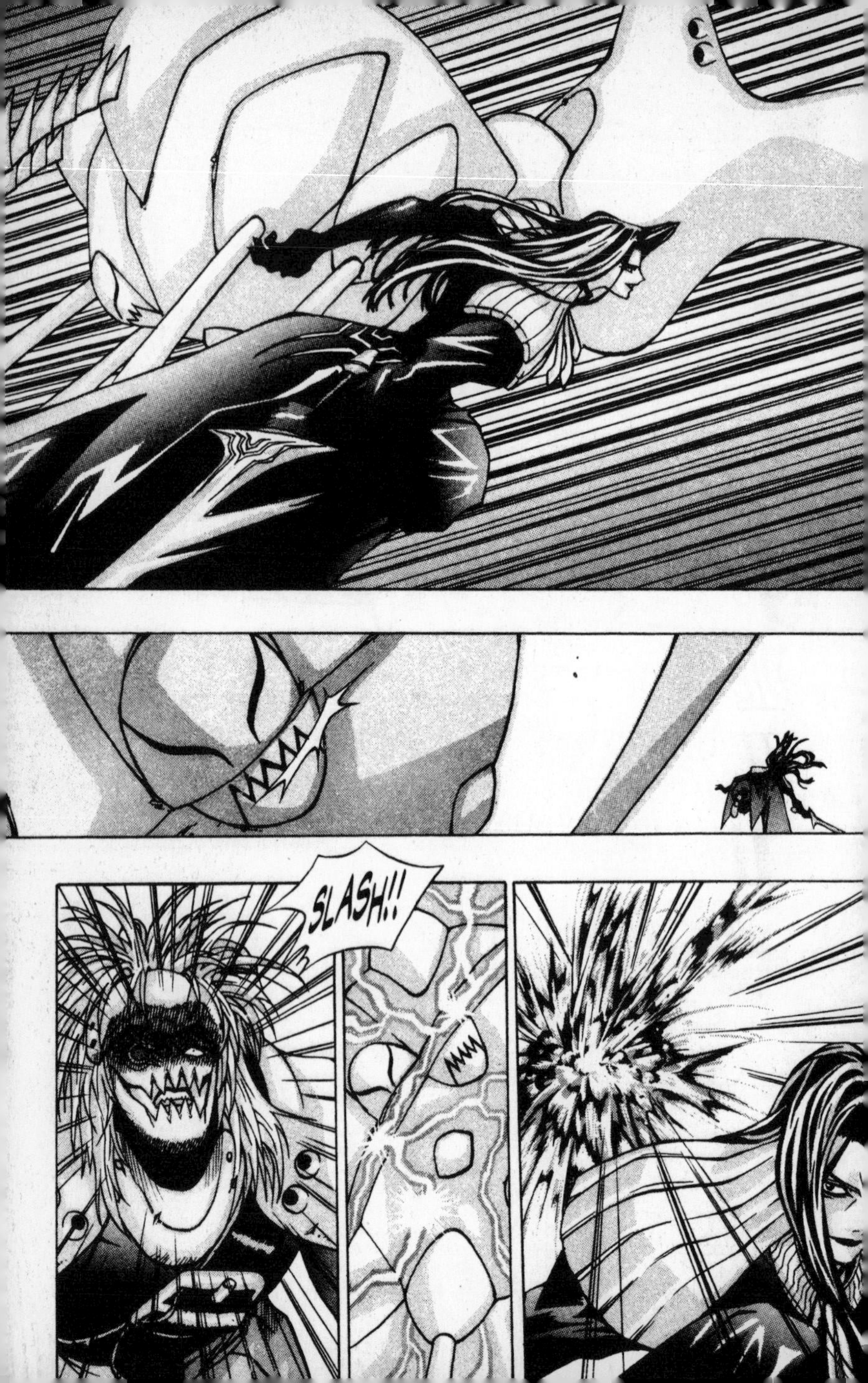
SLASH!!

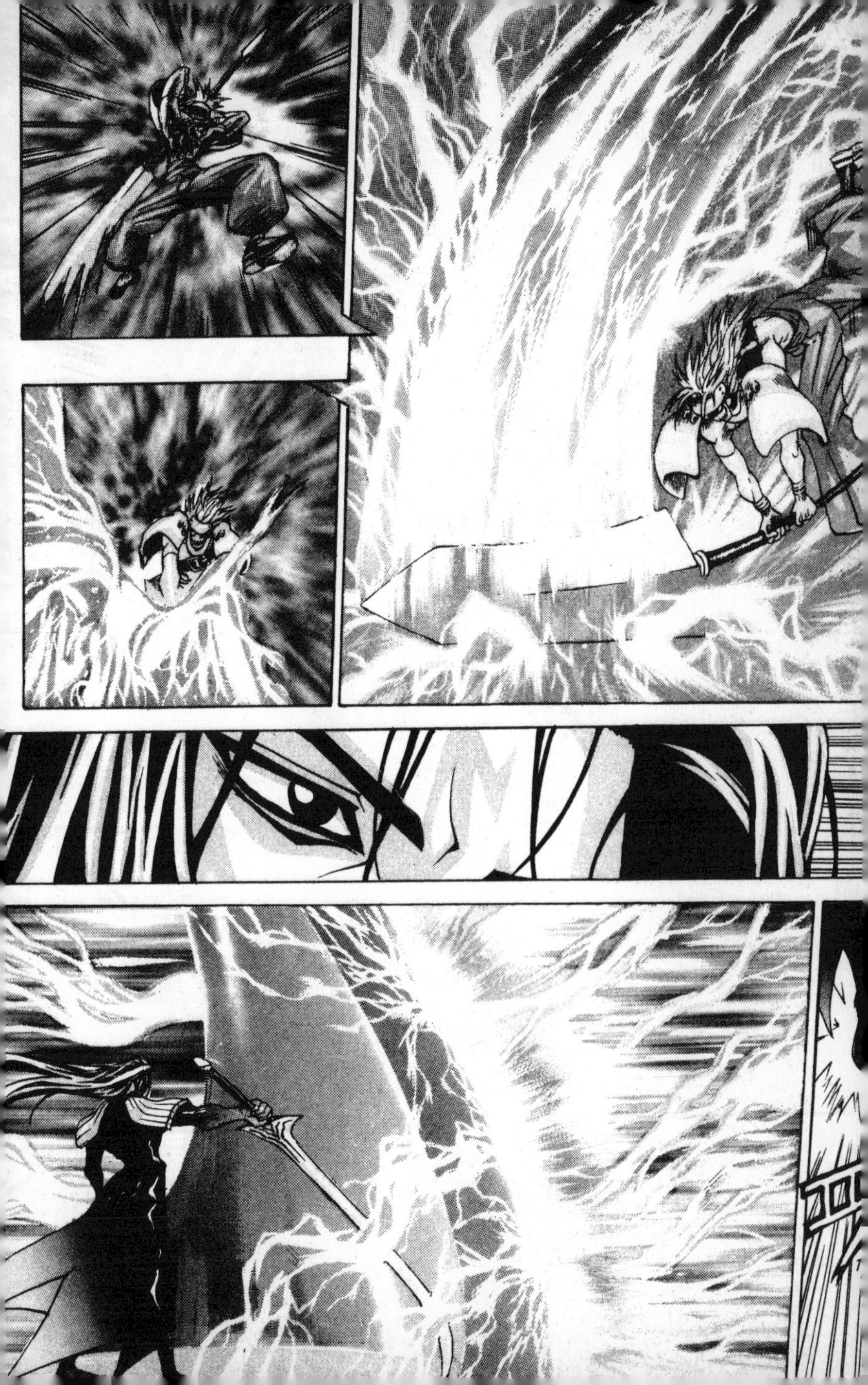

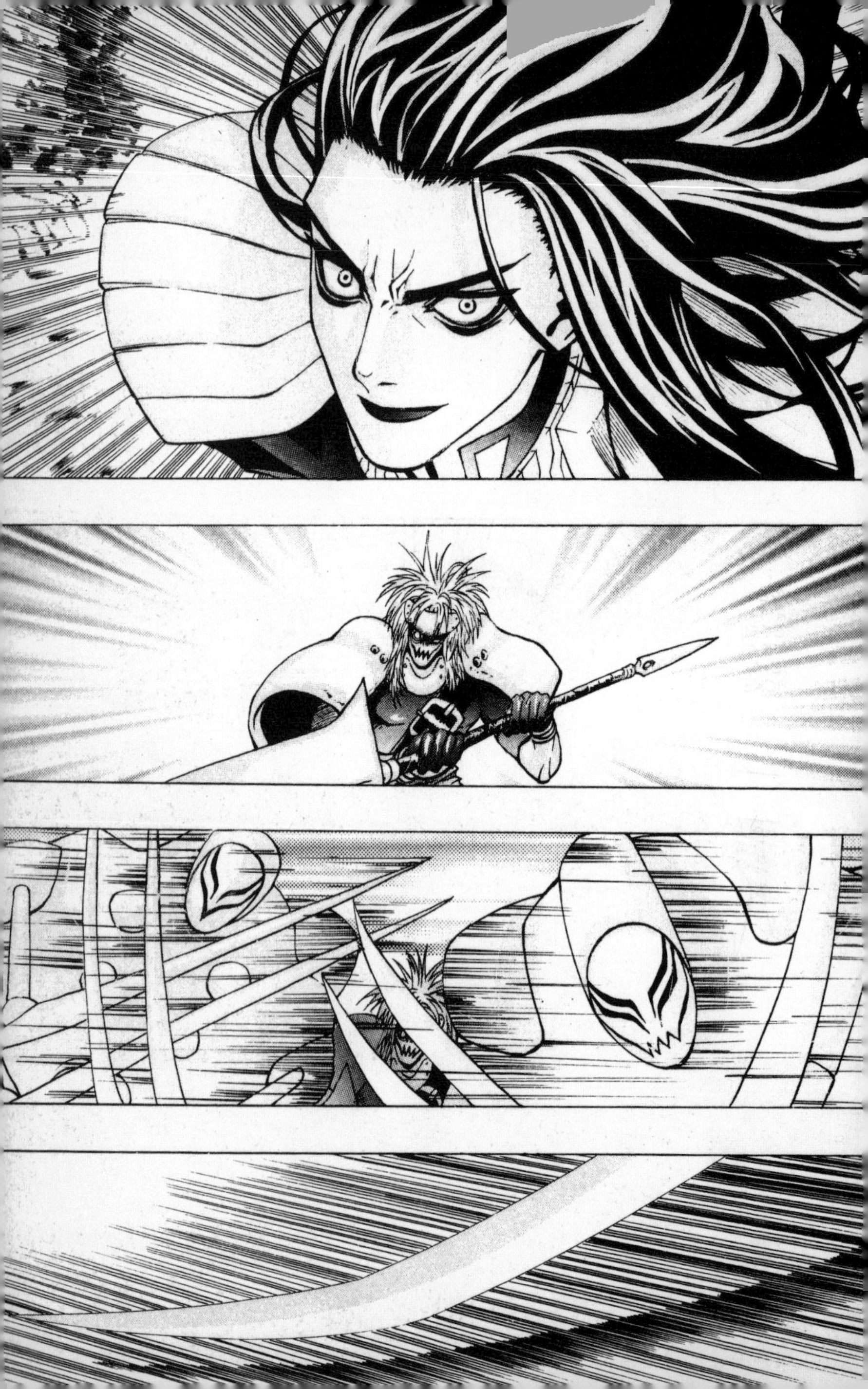

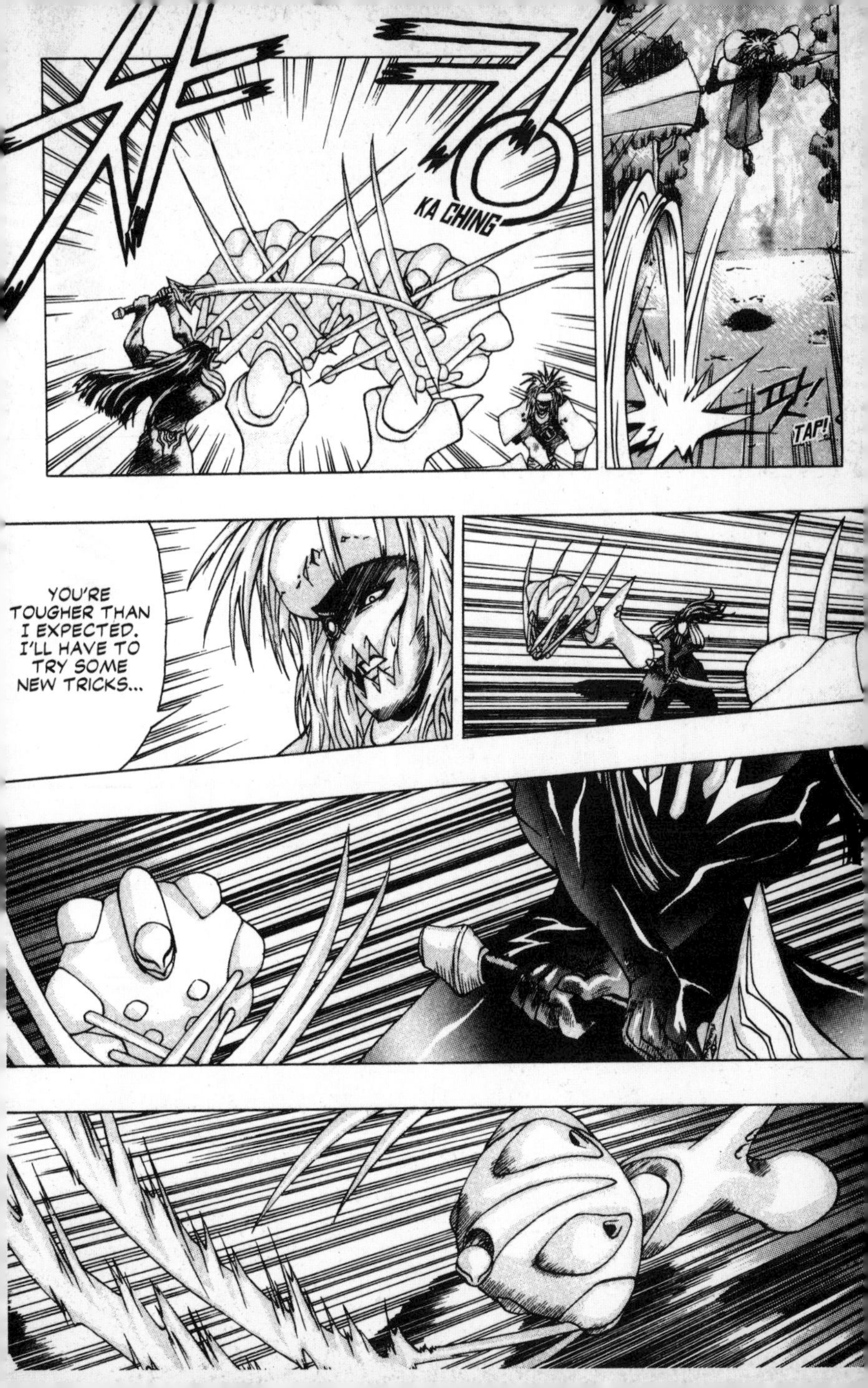
KA CHING
TAP!
YOU'RE TOUGHER THAN I EXPECTED. I'LL HAVE TO TRY SOME NEW TRICKS...

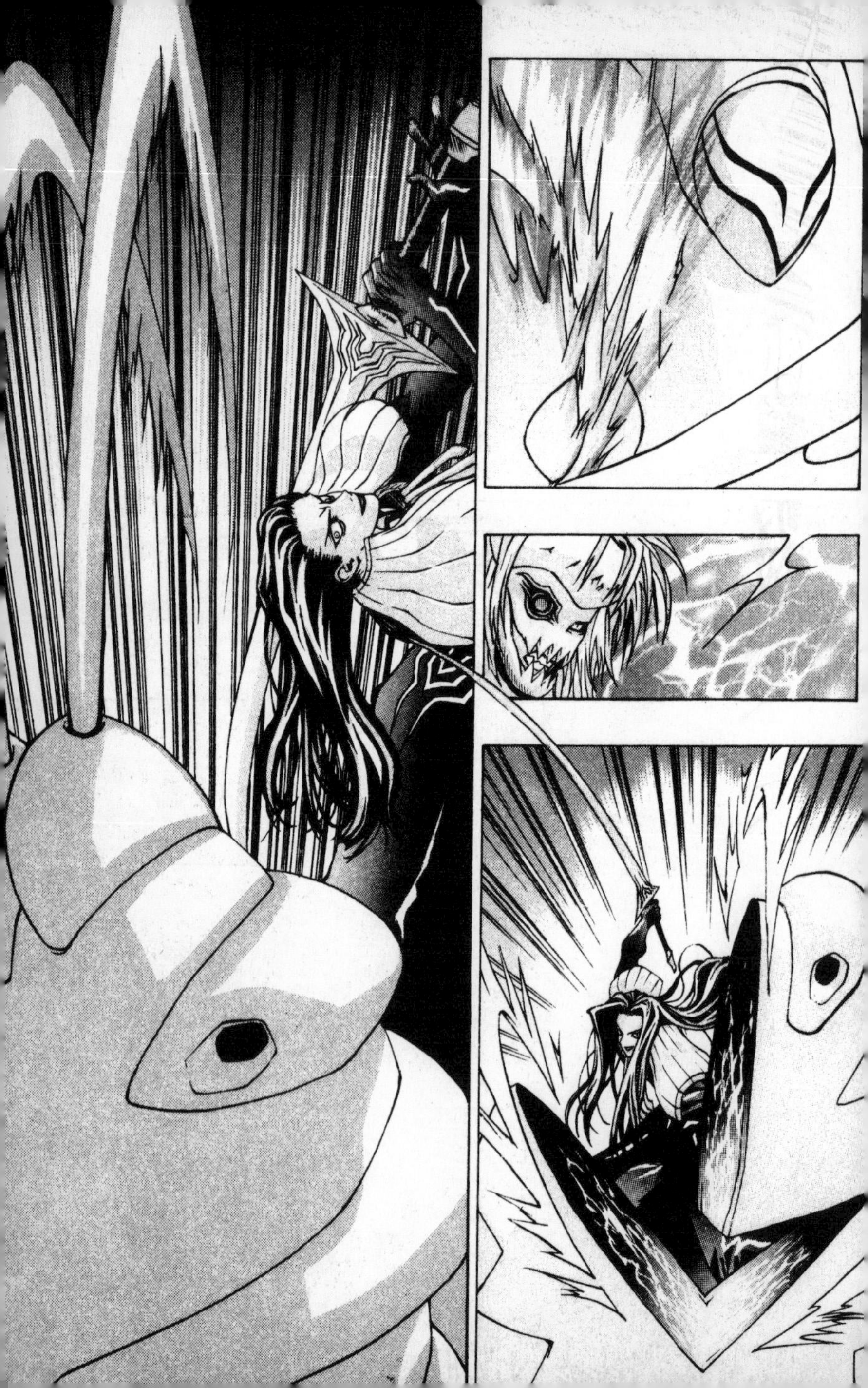

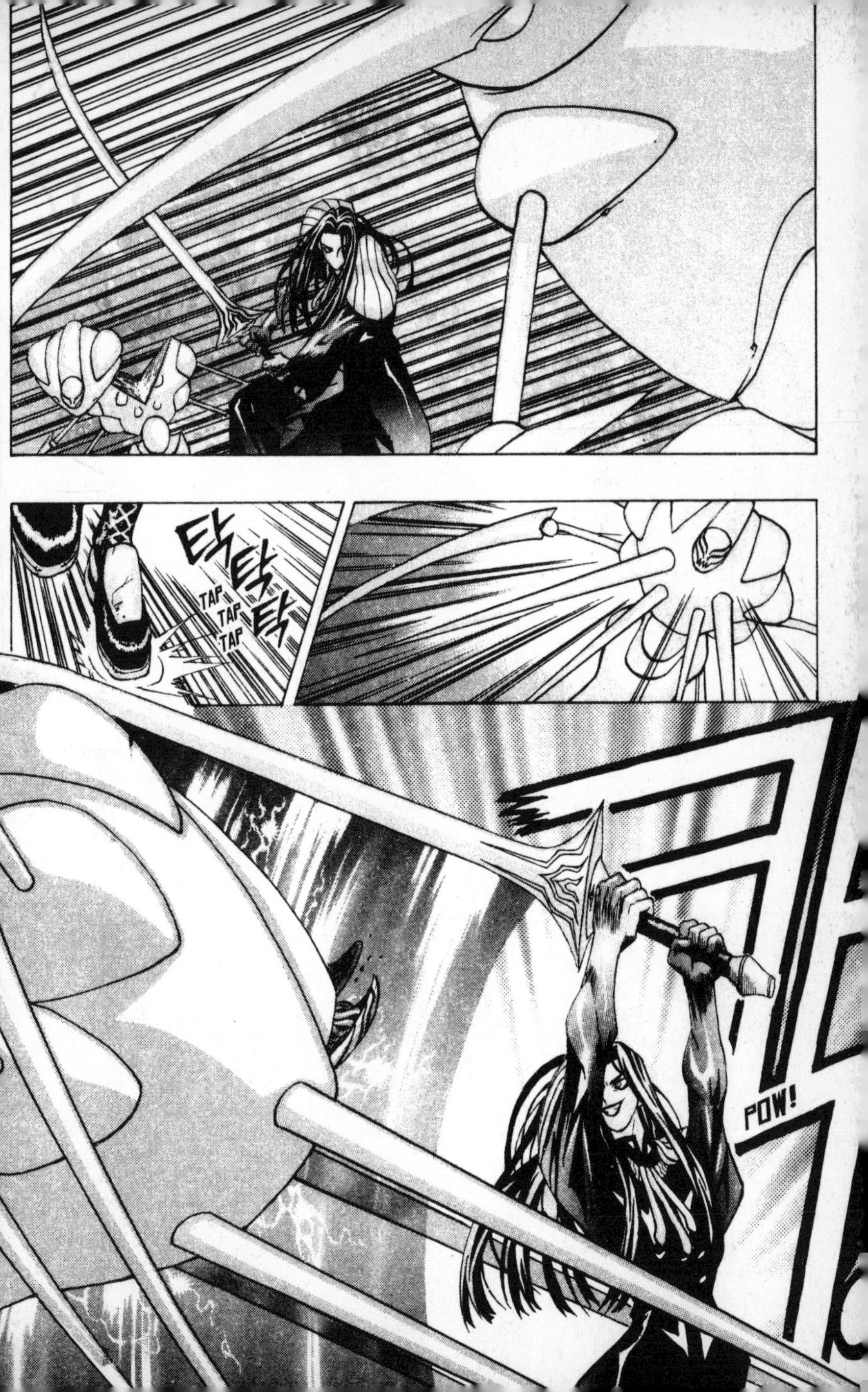
TAP
TAP
TAP
POW!

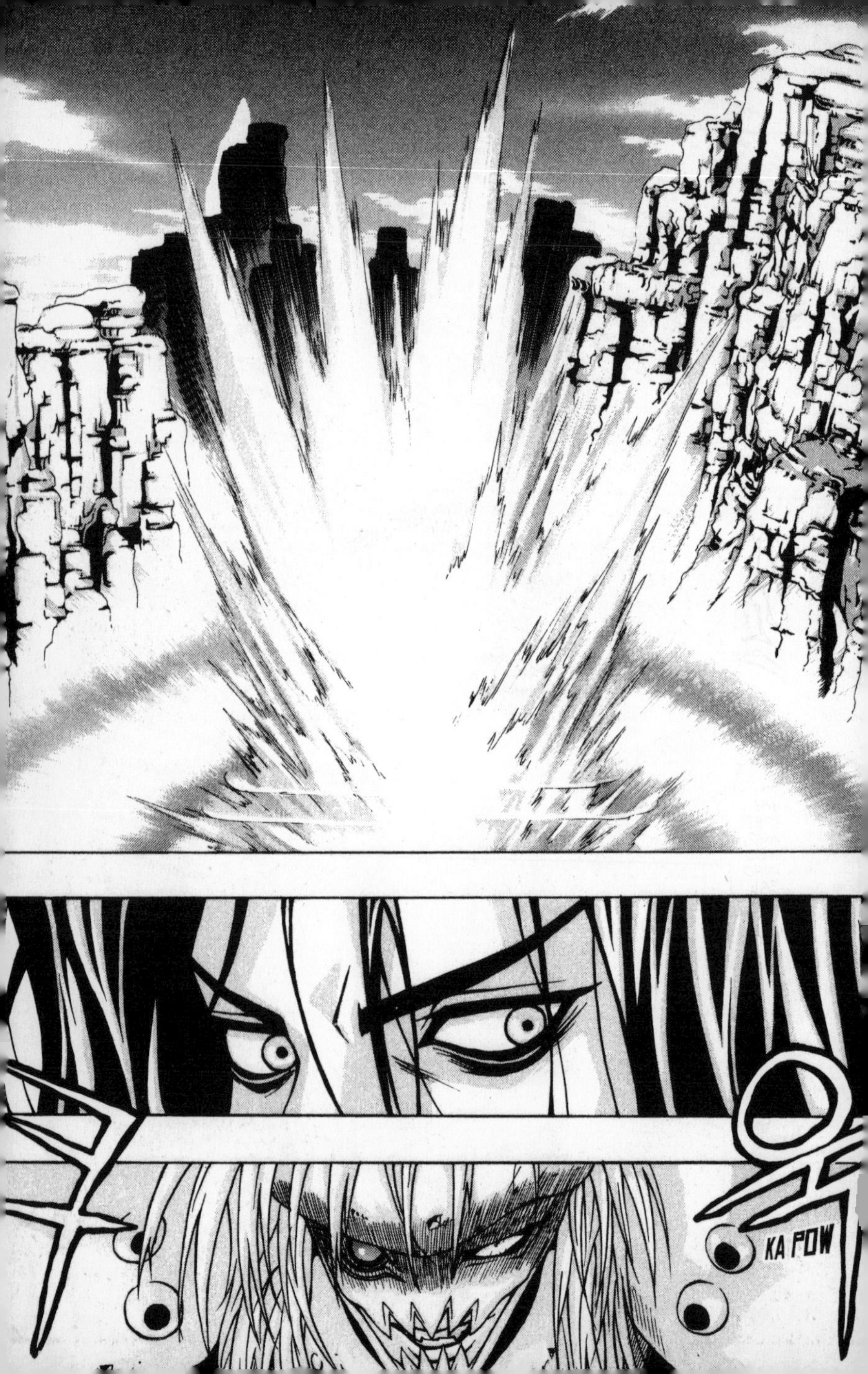
KA POW

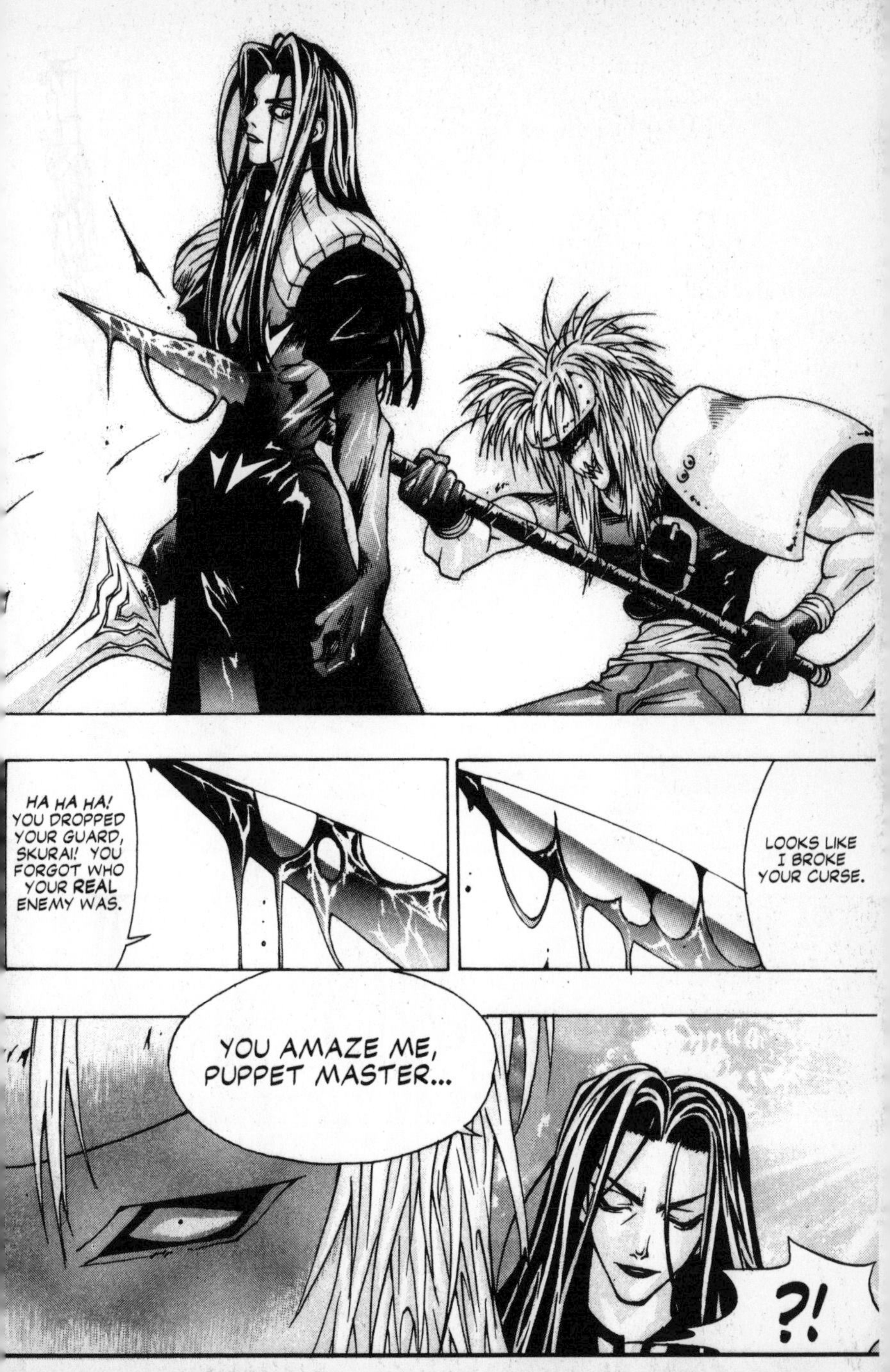

HA HA HA! YOU DROPPED YOUR GUARD, SKURAI! YOU FORGOT WHO YOUR REAL ENEMY WAS.
LOOKS LIKE I BROKE YOUR CURSE.
YOU AMAZE ME, PUPPET MASTER...
?!

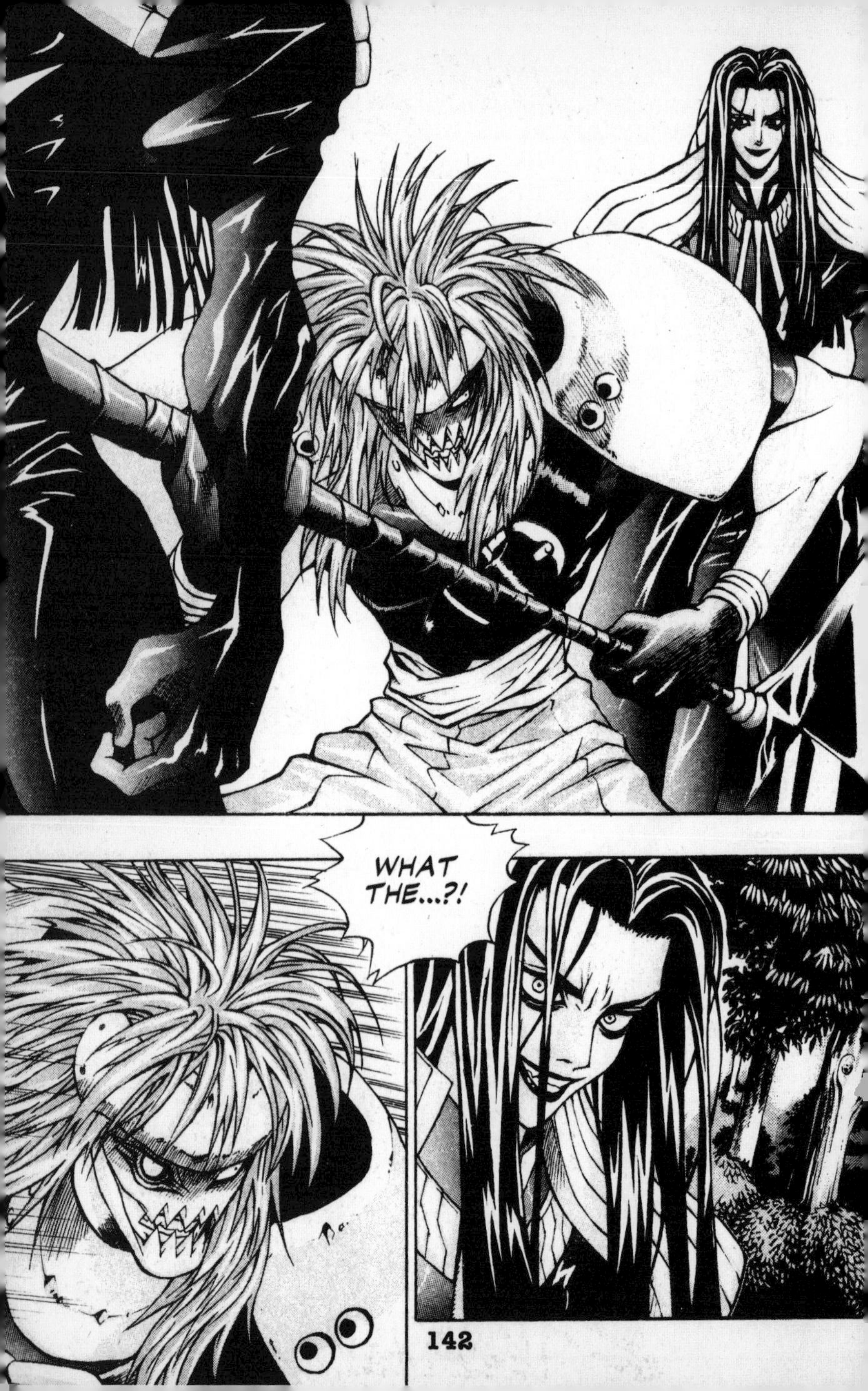
WHAT THE...?!

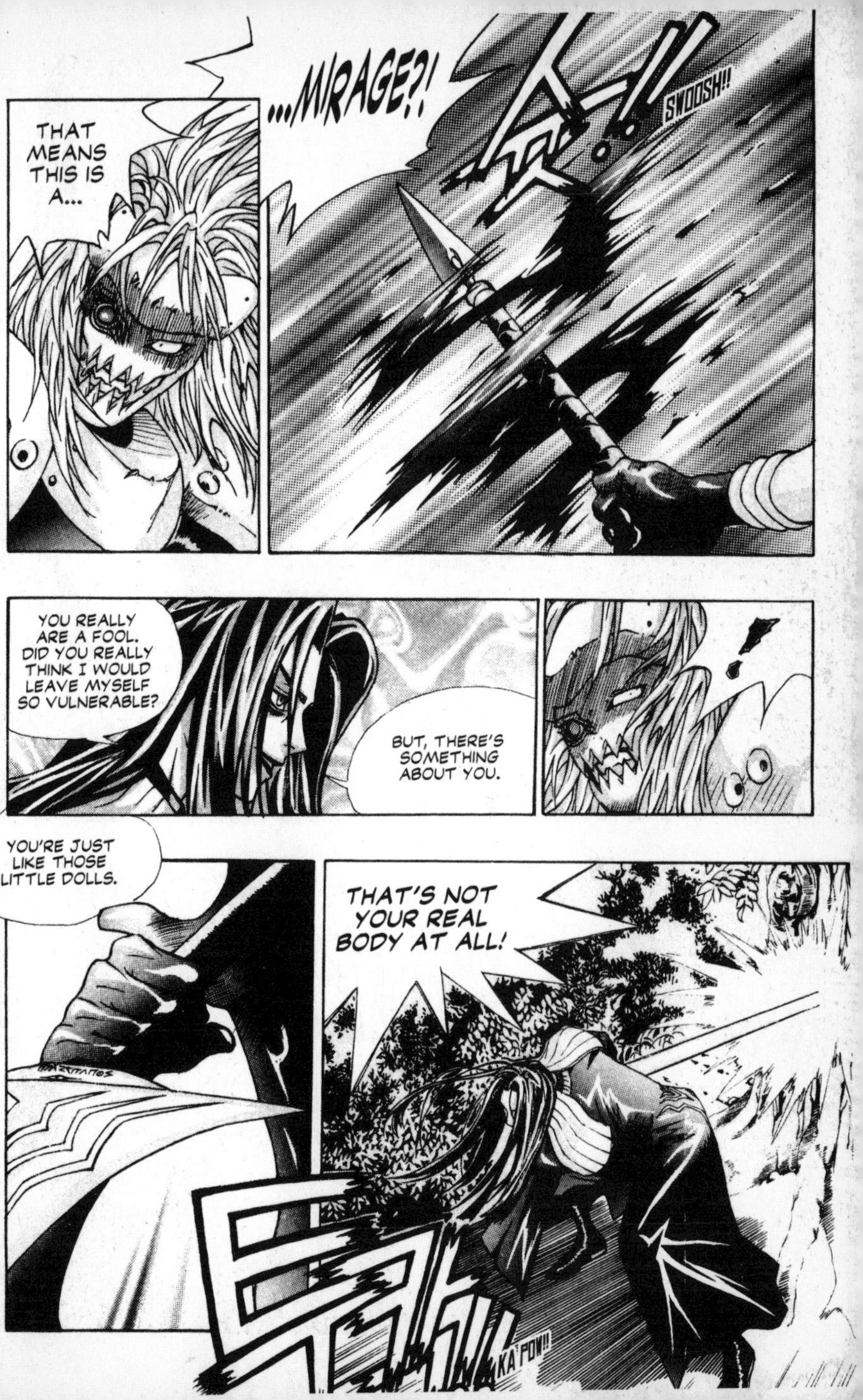
THAT MEANS THIS IS A...
...MIRAGE?!
SWOOSH!!
YOU REALLY ARE A FOOL. DID YOU REALLY THINK I WOULD LEAVE MYSELF SO VULNERABLE?
BUT, THERE'S SOMETHING ABOUT YOU.
YOU'RE JUST LIKE THOSE LITTLE DOLLS.
THAT'S NOT YOUR REAL BODY AT ALL!
KA'POW!!

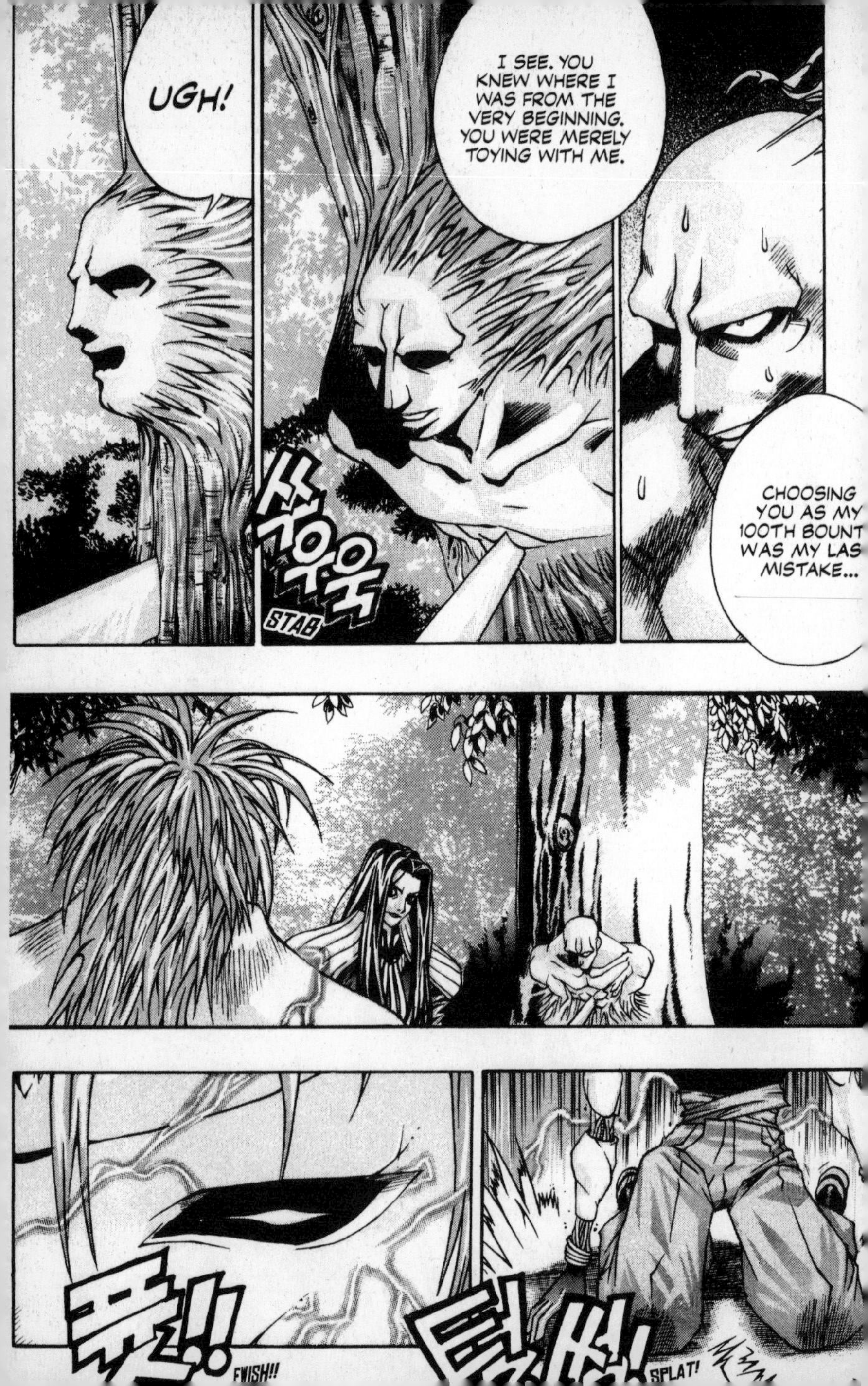
UGH!
I SEE. YOU KNEW WHERE I WAS FROM THE VERY BEGINNING. YOU WERE MERELY TOYING WITH ME.
STAB
CHOOSING YOU AS MY 100TH BOUNT WAS MY LAS MISTAKE...
FWISH!!
SPLAT!

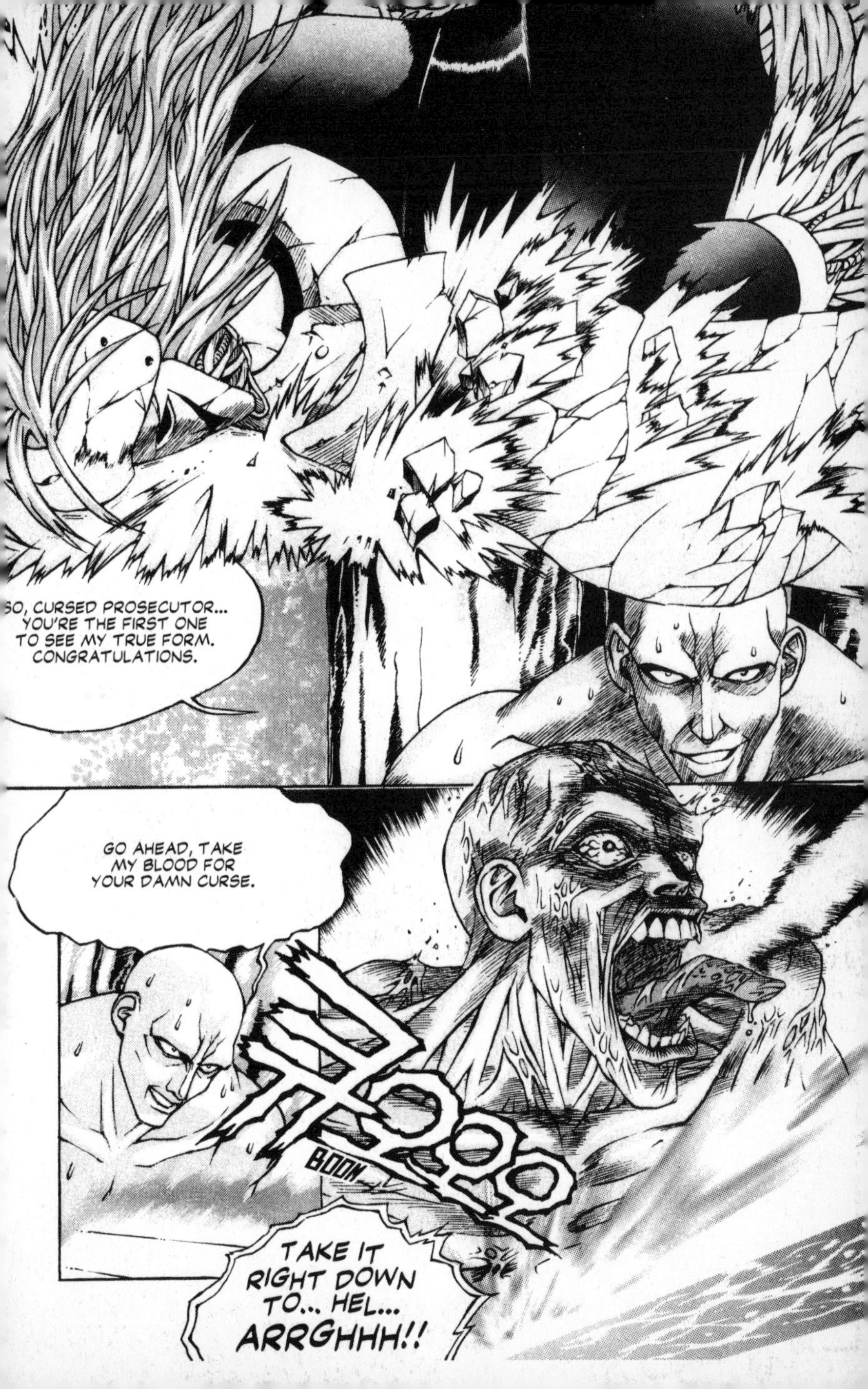
SO, CURSED PROSECUTOR... YOU'RE THE FIRST ONE TO SEE MY TRUE FORM. CONGRATULATIONS.
GO AHEAD, TAKE MY BLOOD FOR YOUR DAMN CURSE.
BOOM
TAKE IT RIGHT DOWN TO... HEL... ARRGHHH!!

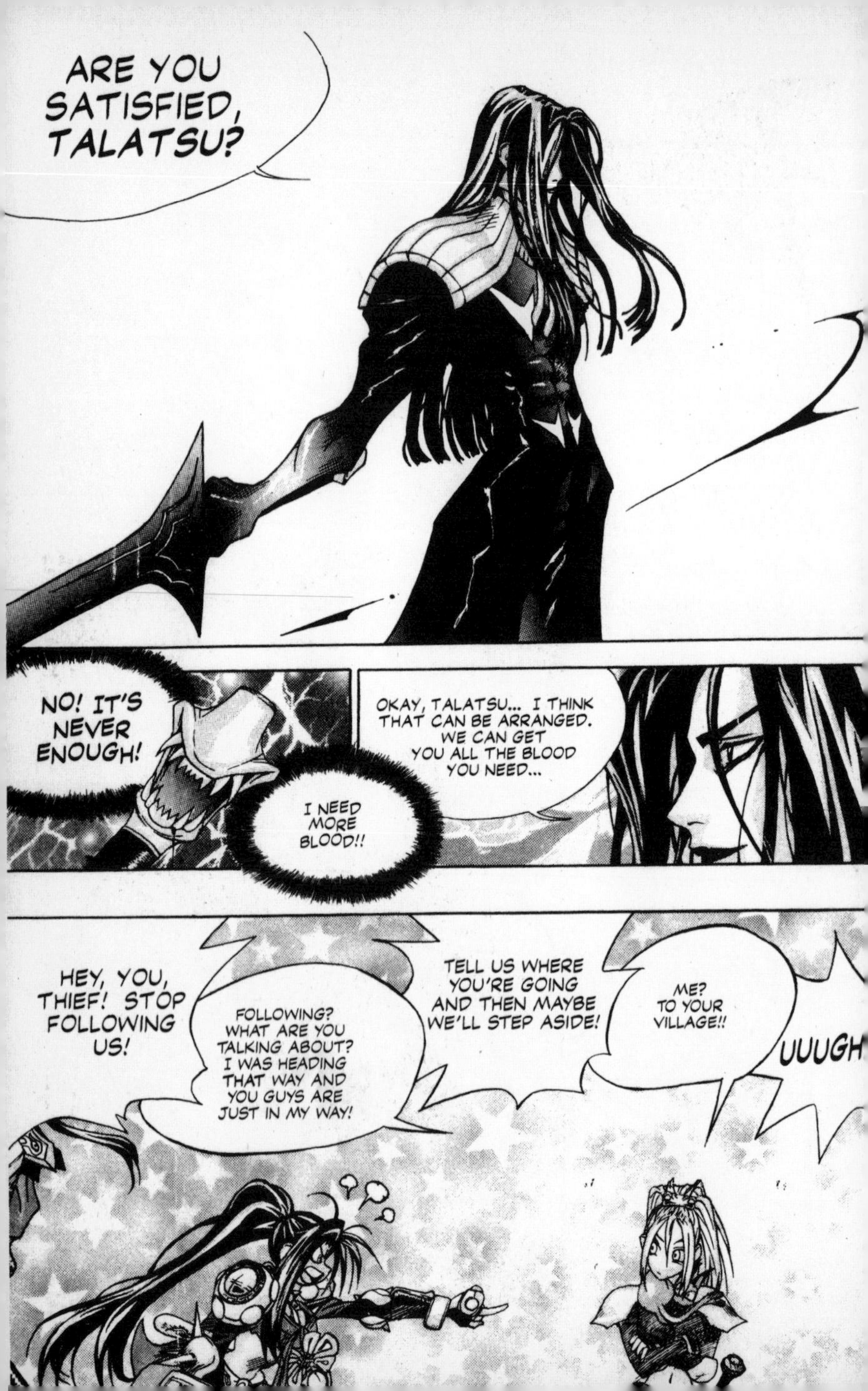
ARE YOU SATISFIED, TALATSU?
NO! IT'S NEVER ENOUGH!
I NEED MORE BLOOD!!
OKAY, TALATSU... I THINK THAT CAN BE ARRANGED. WE CAN GET YOU ALL THE BLOOD YOU NEED...
HEY, YOU, THIEF! STOP FOLLOWING US!
FOLLOWING? WHAT ARE YOU TALKING ABOUT? I WAS HEADING THAT WAY AND YOU GUYS ARE JUST IN MY WAY!
TELL US WHERE YOU'RE GOING AND THEN MAYBE WE'LL STEP ASIDE!
ME? TO YOUR VILLAGE!!
UUUGH

RAGNARÖK

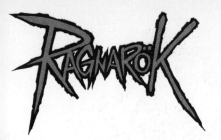

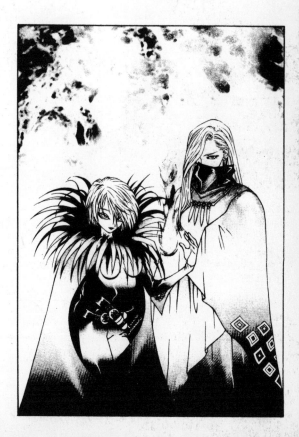

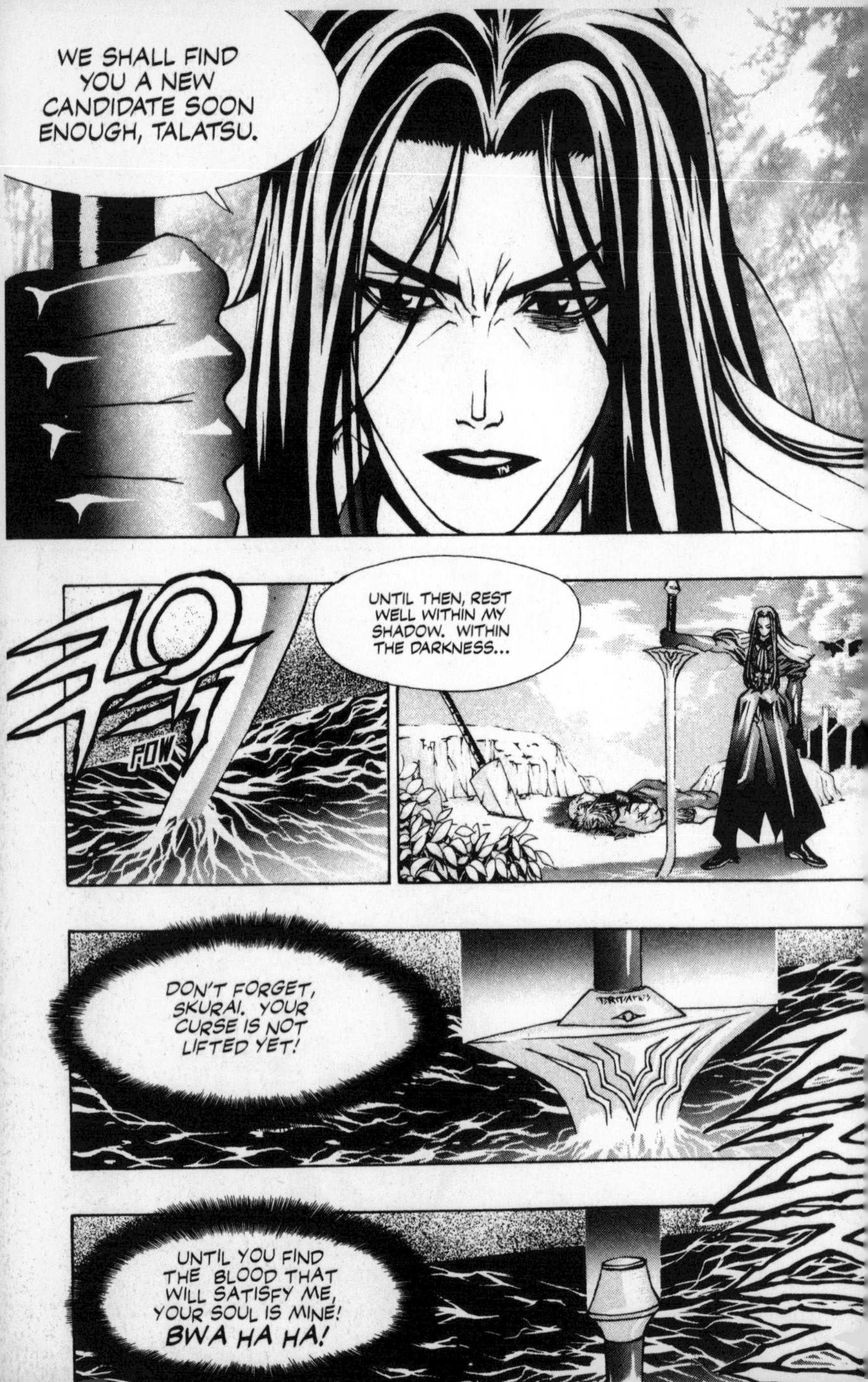
WE SHALL FIND YOU A NEW CANDIDATE SOON ENOUGH, TALATSU.
FOW
UNTIL THEN, REST WELL WITHIN MY SHADOW. WITHIN THE DARKNESS...
DON'T FORGET, SKURAI. YOUR CURSE IS NOT LIFTED YET!
UNTIL YOU FIND THE BLOOD THAT WILL SATISFY ME, YOUR SOUL IS MINE! BWA HA HA!

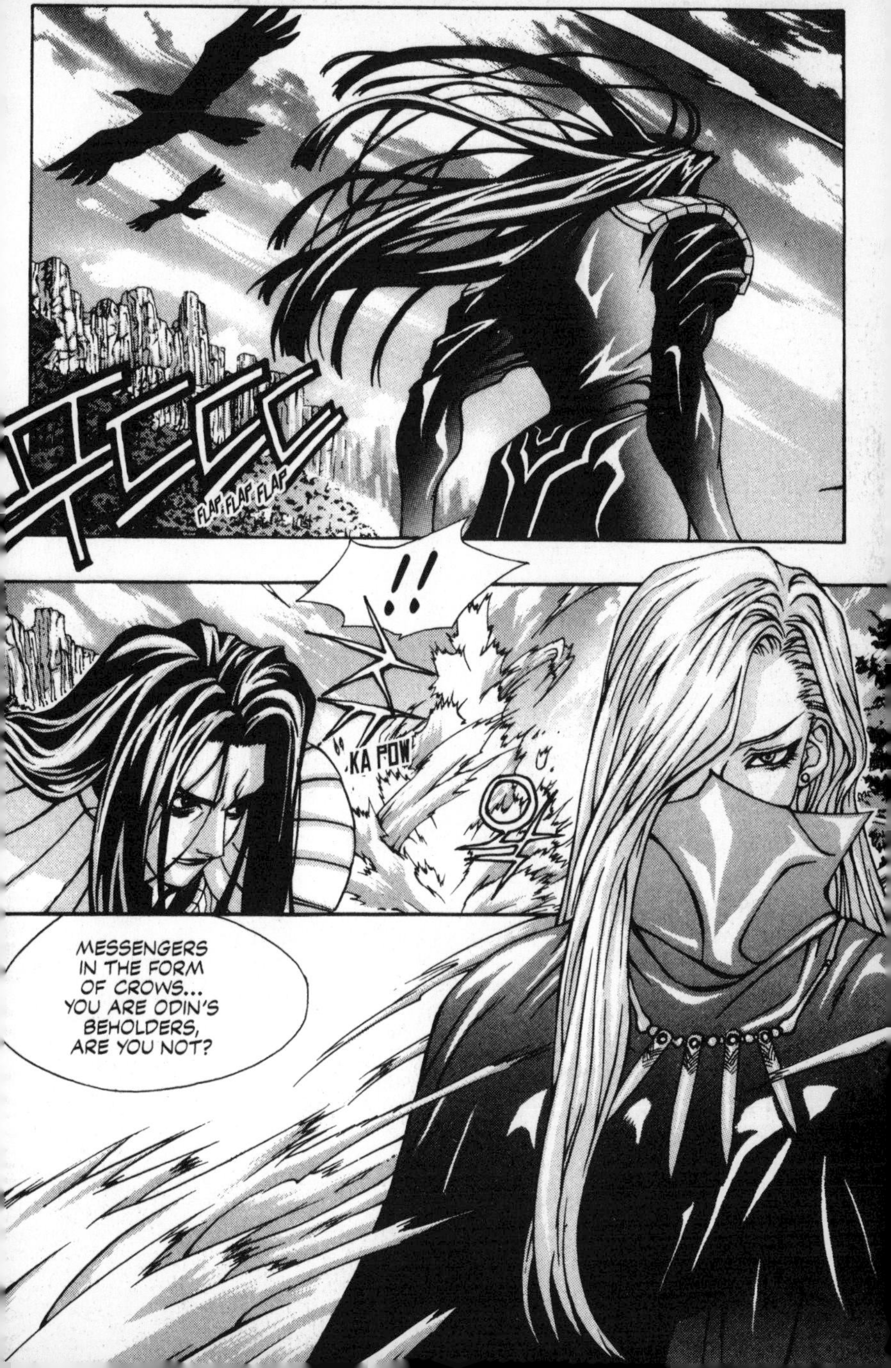
FLAP FLAP FLAP
!!
KA POW
MESSENGERS IN THE FORM OF CROWS... YOU ARE ODIN'S BEHOLDERS, ARE YOU NOT?

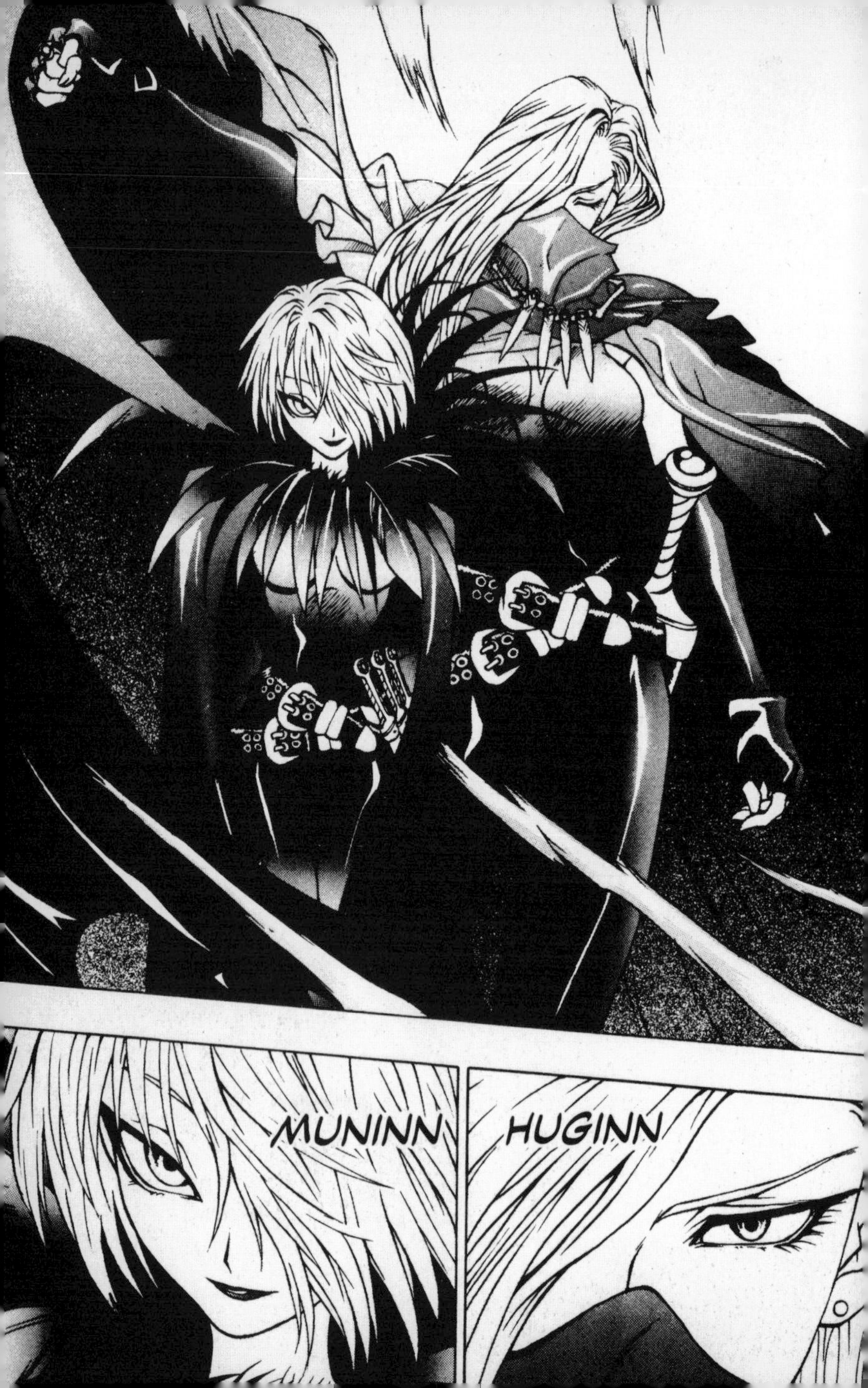
MUNINN
HUGINN

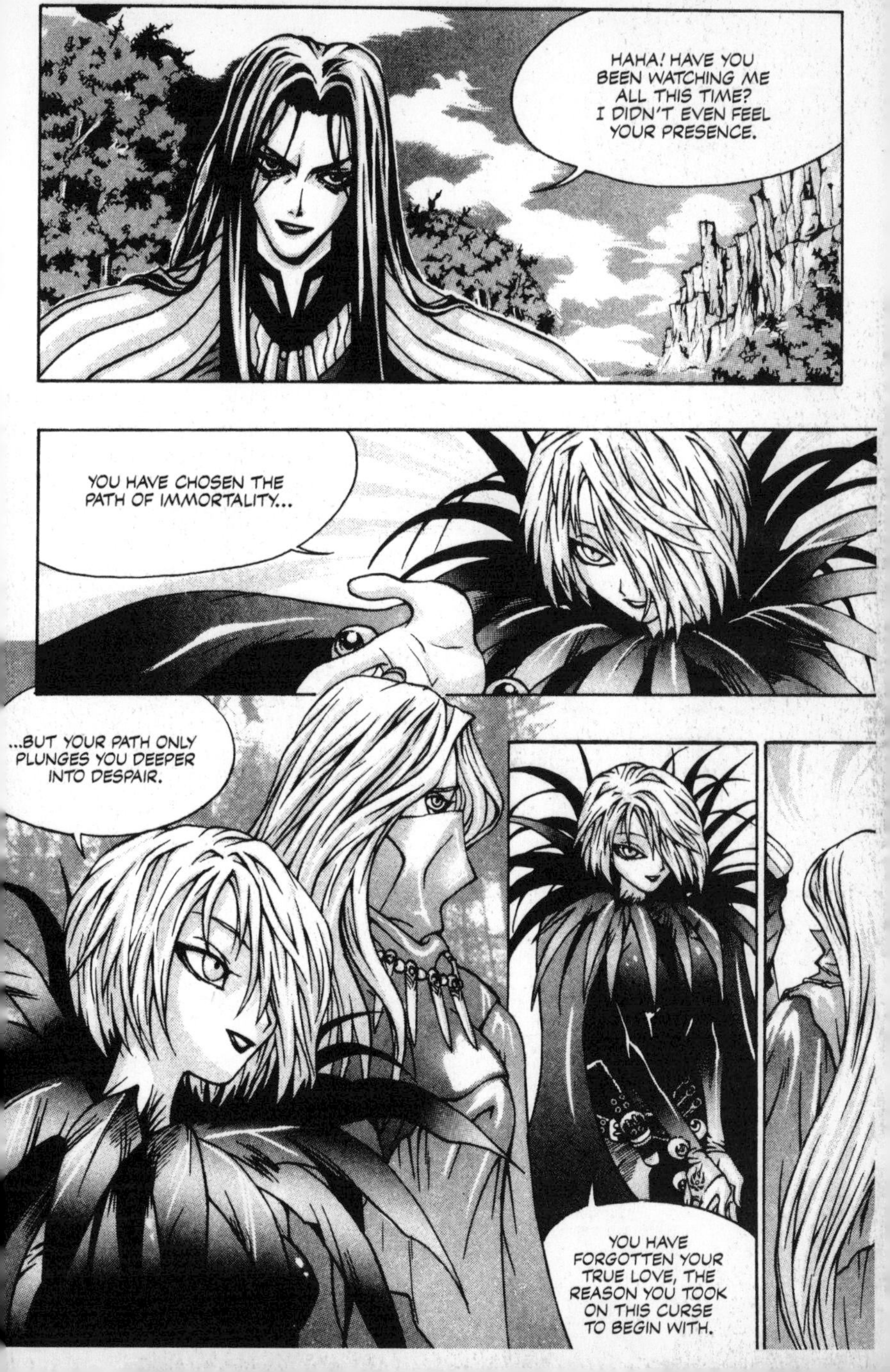
HAHA! HAVE YOU BEEN WATCHING ME ALL THIS TIME? I DIDN'T EVEN FEEL YOUR PRESENCE.
YOU HAVE CHOSEN THE PATH OF IMMORTALITY...
...BUT YOUR PATH ONLY PLUNGES YOU DEEPER INTO DESPAIR.
YOU HAVE FORGOTTEN YOUR TRUE LOVE, THE REASON YOU TOOK ON THIS CURSE TO BEGIN WITH.

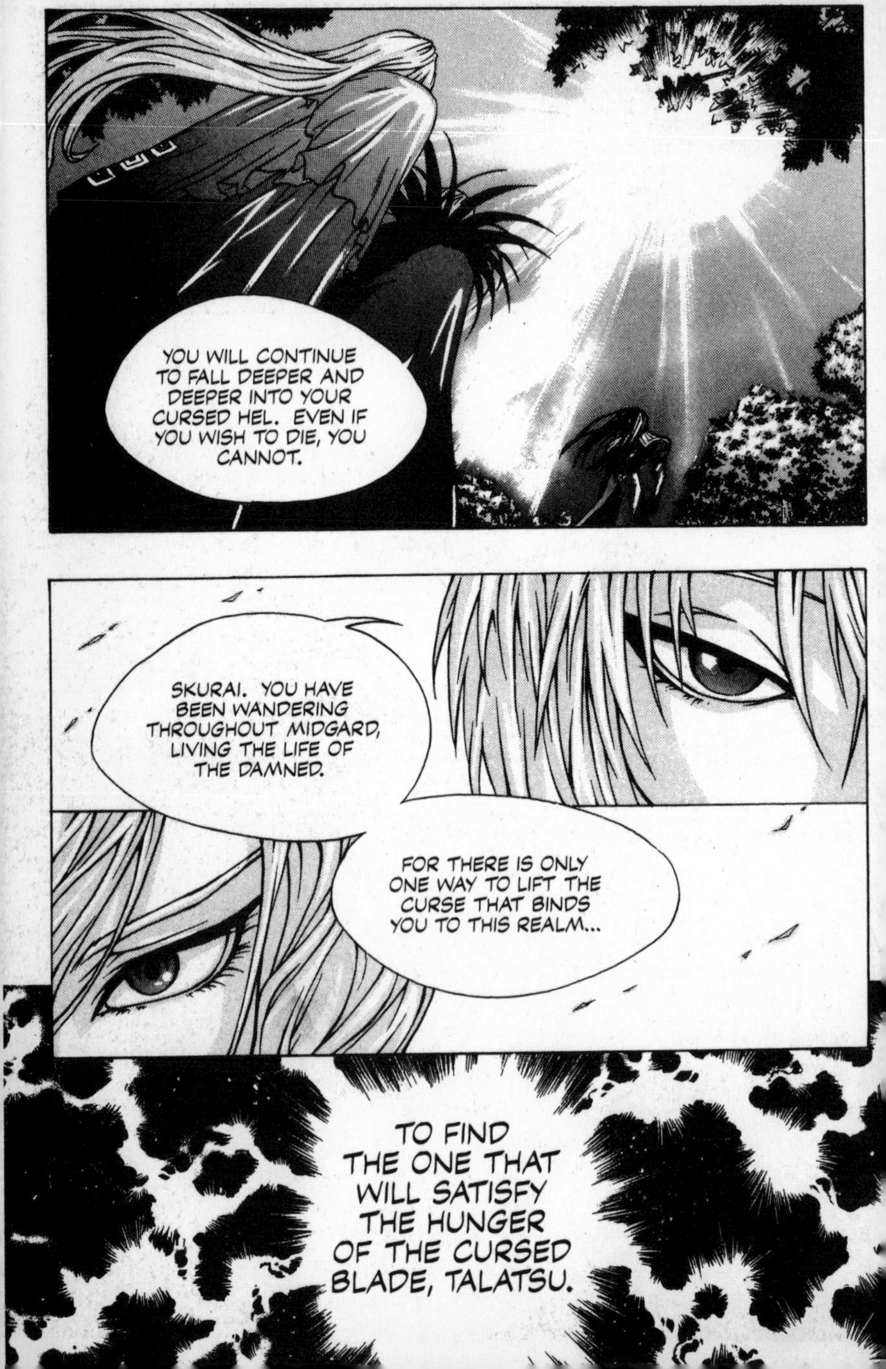
YOU WILL CONTINUE TO FALL DEEPER AND DEEPER INTO YOUR CURSED HEL. EVEN IF YOU WISH TO DIE, YOU CANNOT.
SKURAI. YOU HAVE BEEN WANDERING THROUGHOUT MIDGARD, LIVING THE LIFE OF THE DAMNED.
FOR THERE IS ONLY ONE WAY TO LIFT THE CURSE THAT BINDS YOU TO THIS REALM...
TO FIND THE ONE THAT WILL SATISFY THE HUNGER OF THE CURSED BLADE, TALATSU.

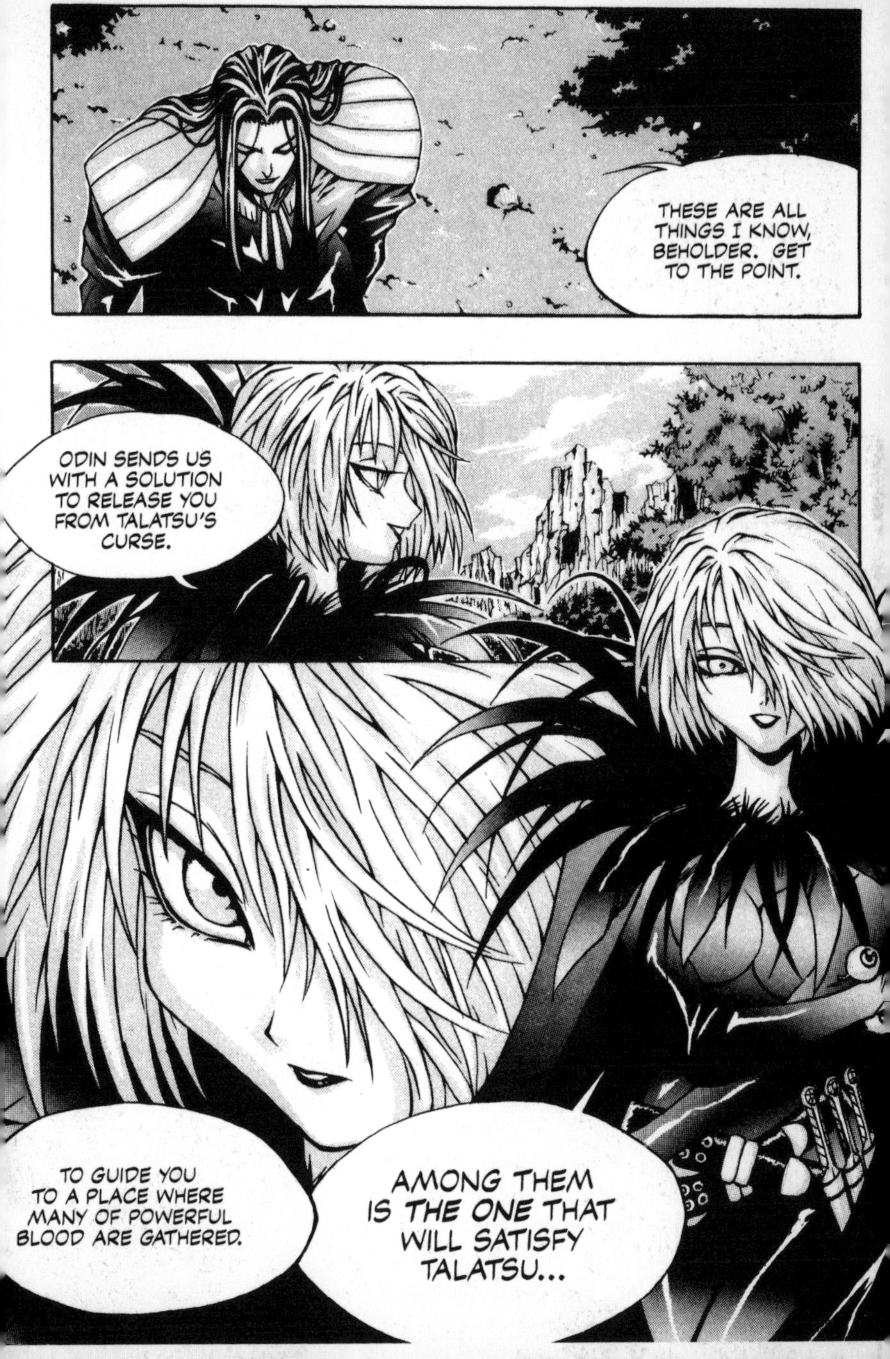
THESE ARE ALL THINGS I KNOW, BEHOLDER. GET TO THE POINT.
ODIN SENDS US WITH A SOLUTION TO RELEASE YOU FROM TALATSU'S CURSE.
TO GUIDE YOU TO A PLACE WHERE MANY OF POWERFUL BLOOD ARE GATHERED.
AMONG THEM IS *THE ONE* THAT WILL SATISFY TALATSU...

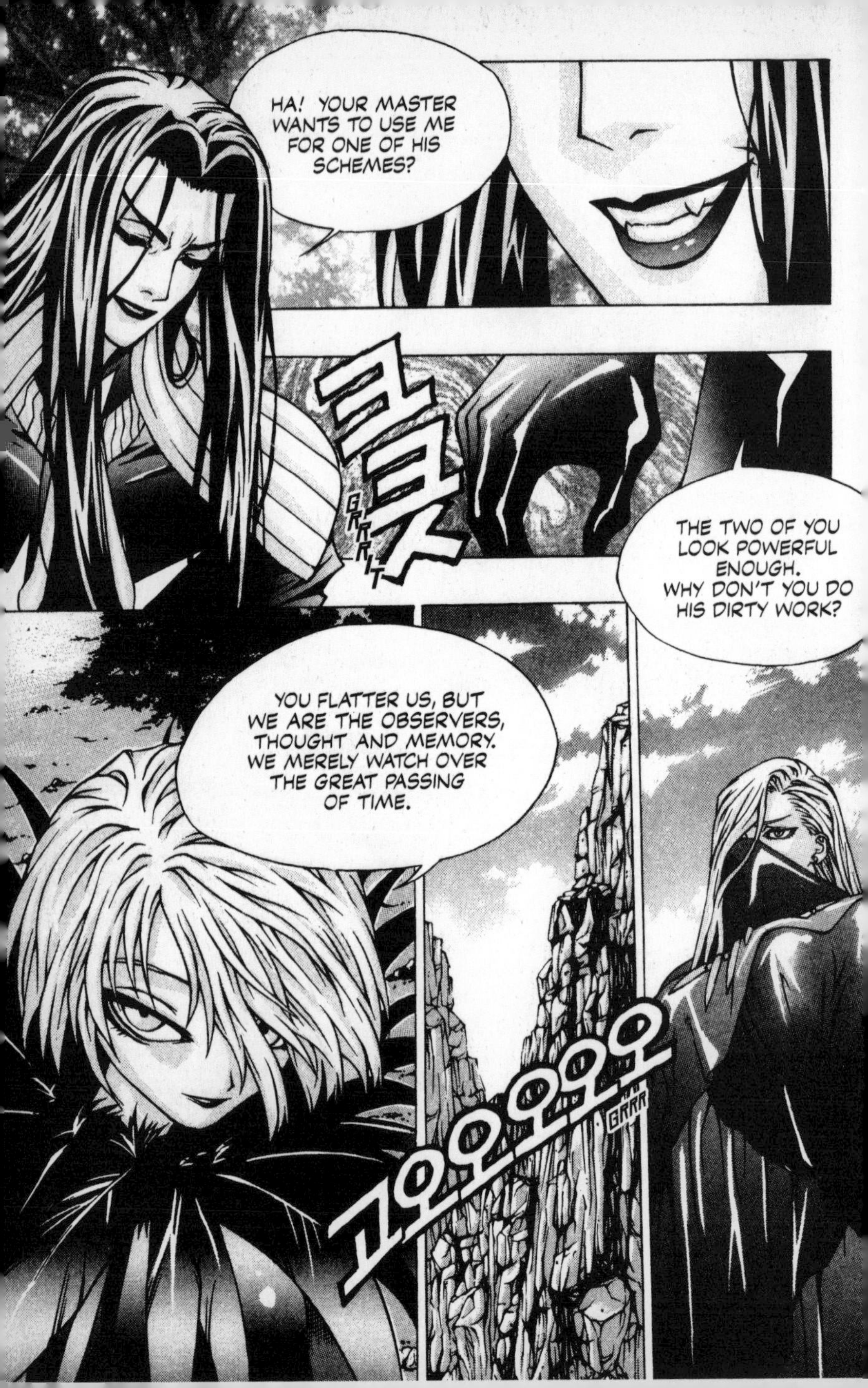
HA! YOUR MASTER WANTS TO USE ME FOR ONE OF HIS SCHEMES?
GRRRIT
THE TWO OF YOU LOOK POWERFUL ENOUGH. WHY DON'T YOU DO HIS DIRTY WORK?
YOU FLATTER US, BUT WE ARE THE OBSERVERS, THOUGHT AND MEMORY. WE MERELY WATCH OVER THE GREAT PASSING OF TIME.
GRRR

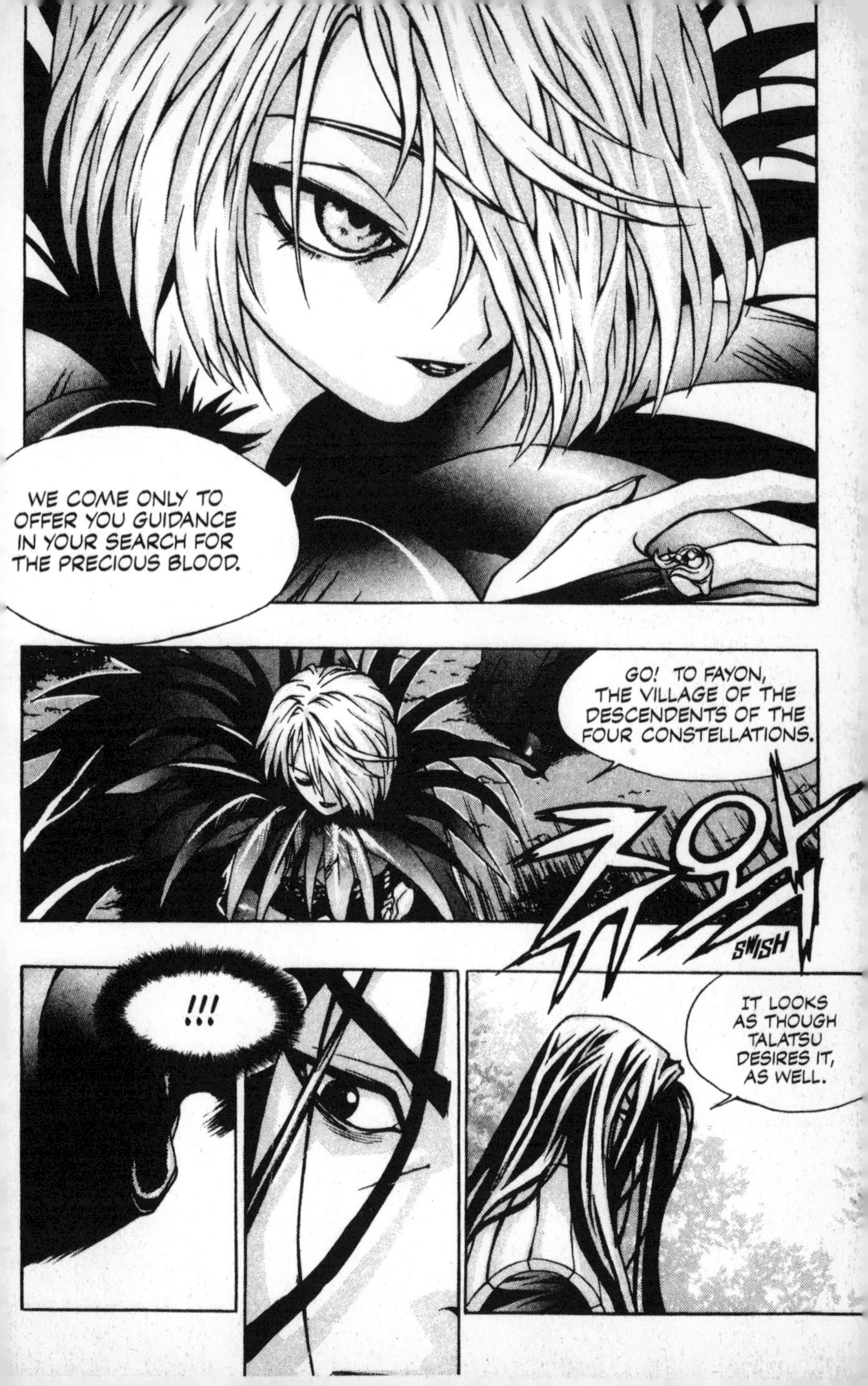
WE COME ONLY TO OFFER YOU GUIDANCE IN YOUR SEARCH FOR THE PRECIOUS BLOOD.
GO! TO FAYON, THE VILLAGE OF THE DESCENDENTS OF THE FOUR CONSTELLATIONS.
SWISH
!!!
IT LOOKS AS THOUGH TALATSU DESIRES IT, AS WELL.

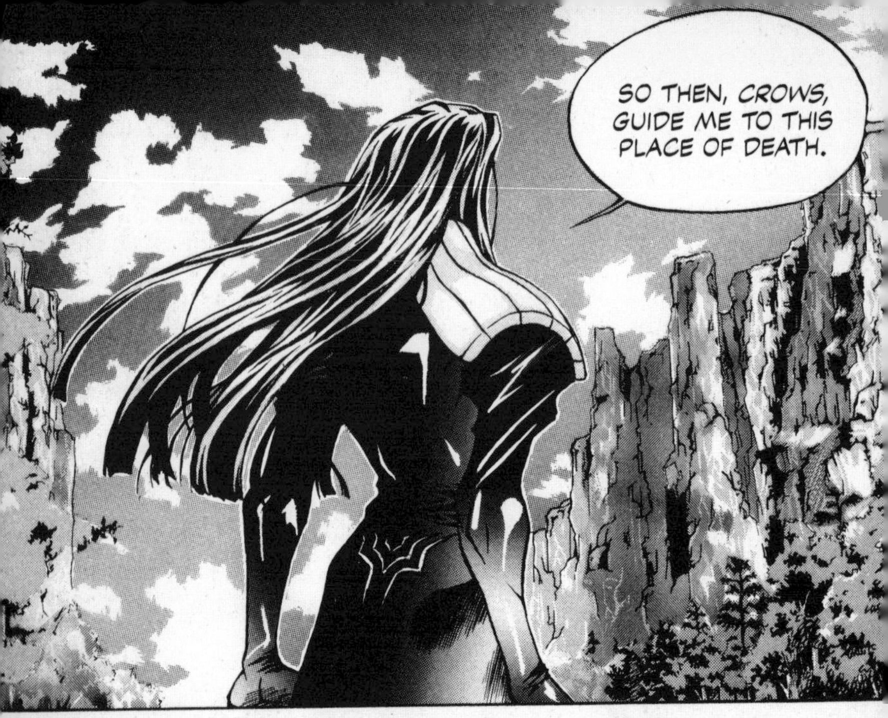
SO THEN, CROWS, GUIDE ME TO THIS PLACE OF DEATH.

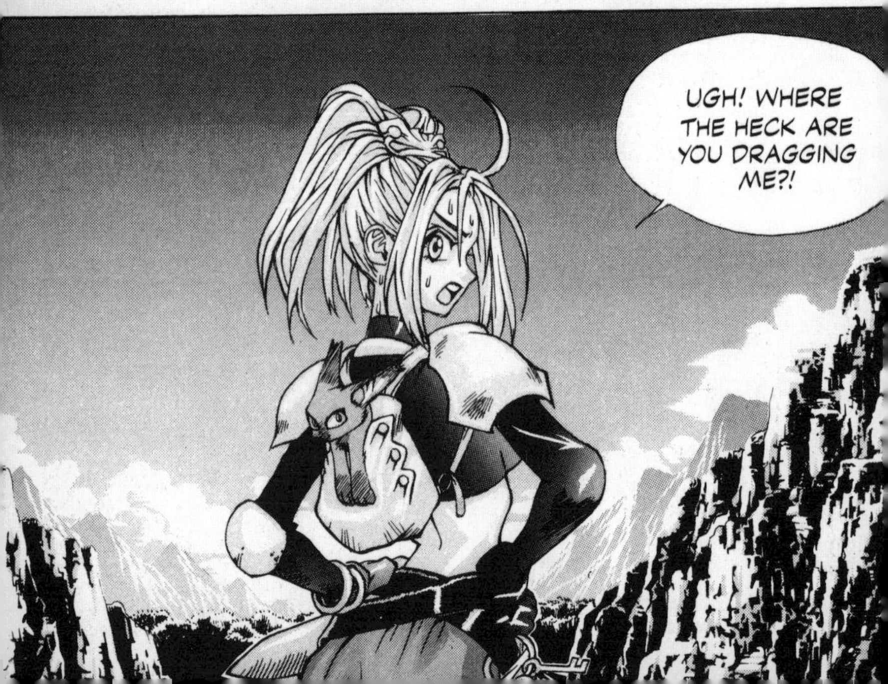
UGH! WHERE THE HECK ARE YOU DRAGGING ME?!

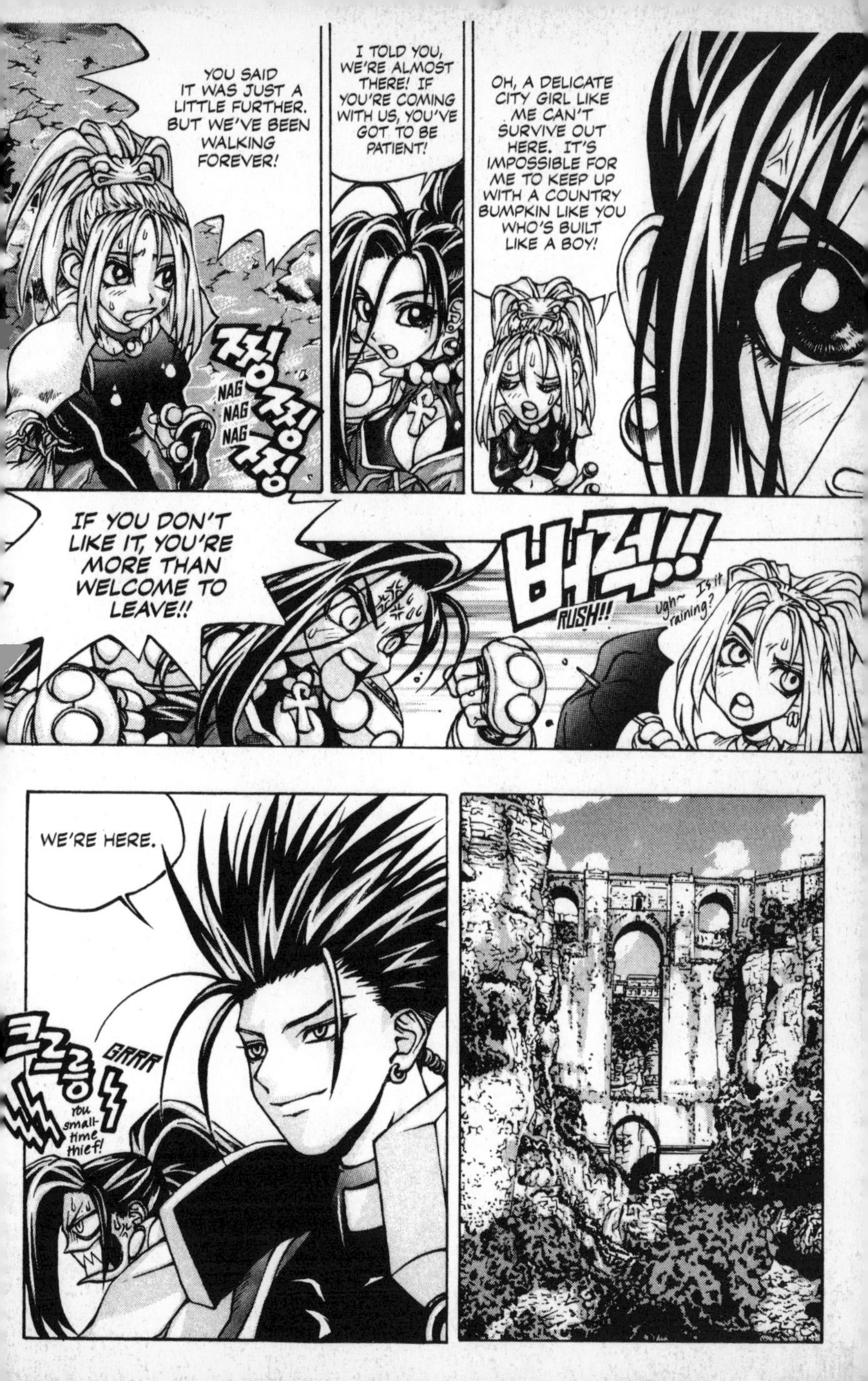
YOU SAID IT WAS JUST A LITTLE FURTHER. BUT WE'VE BEEN WALKING FOREVER!
징징징
NAG NAG NAG
I TOLD YOU, WE'RE ALMOST THERE! IF YOU'RE COMING WITH US, YOU'VE GOT TO BE PATIENT!
OH, A DELICATE CITY GIRL LIKE ME CAN'T SURVIVE OUT HERE. IT'S IMPOSSIBLE FOR ME TO KEEP UP WITH A COUNTRY BUMPKIN LIKE YOU WHO'S BUILT LIKE A BOY!
IF YOU DON'T LIKE IT, YOU'RE MORE THAN WELCOME TO LEAVE!!
버럭!!
RUSH!!
ugh~ Is it raining?
WE'RE HERE.
크르릉
GRRR
you small-time thief!

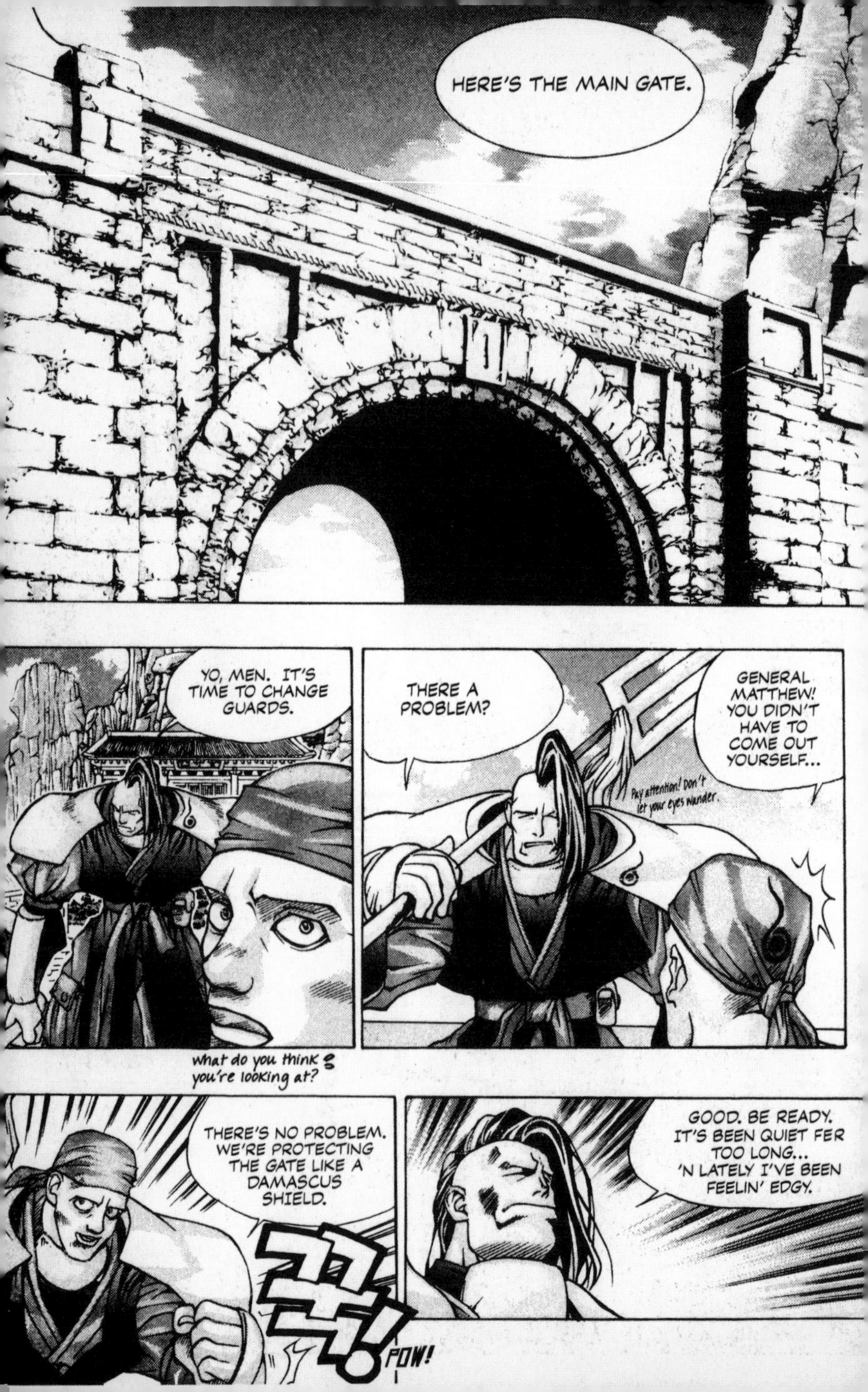
HERE'S THE MAIN GATE.
YO, MEN. IT'S TIME TO CHANGE GUARDS.
what do you think you're looking at?
THERE A PROBLEM?
GENERAL MATTHEW! YOU DIDN'T HAVE TO COME OUT YOURSELF...
Pay attention! Don't let your eyes wander.
THERE'S NO PROBLEM. WE'RE PROTECTING THE GATE LIKE A DAMASCUS SHIELD.
POW!
GOOD. BE READY. IT'S BEEN QUIET FER TOO LONG... 'N LATELY I'VE BEEN FEELIN' EDGY.

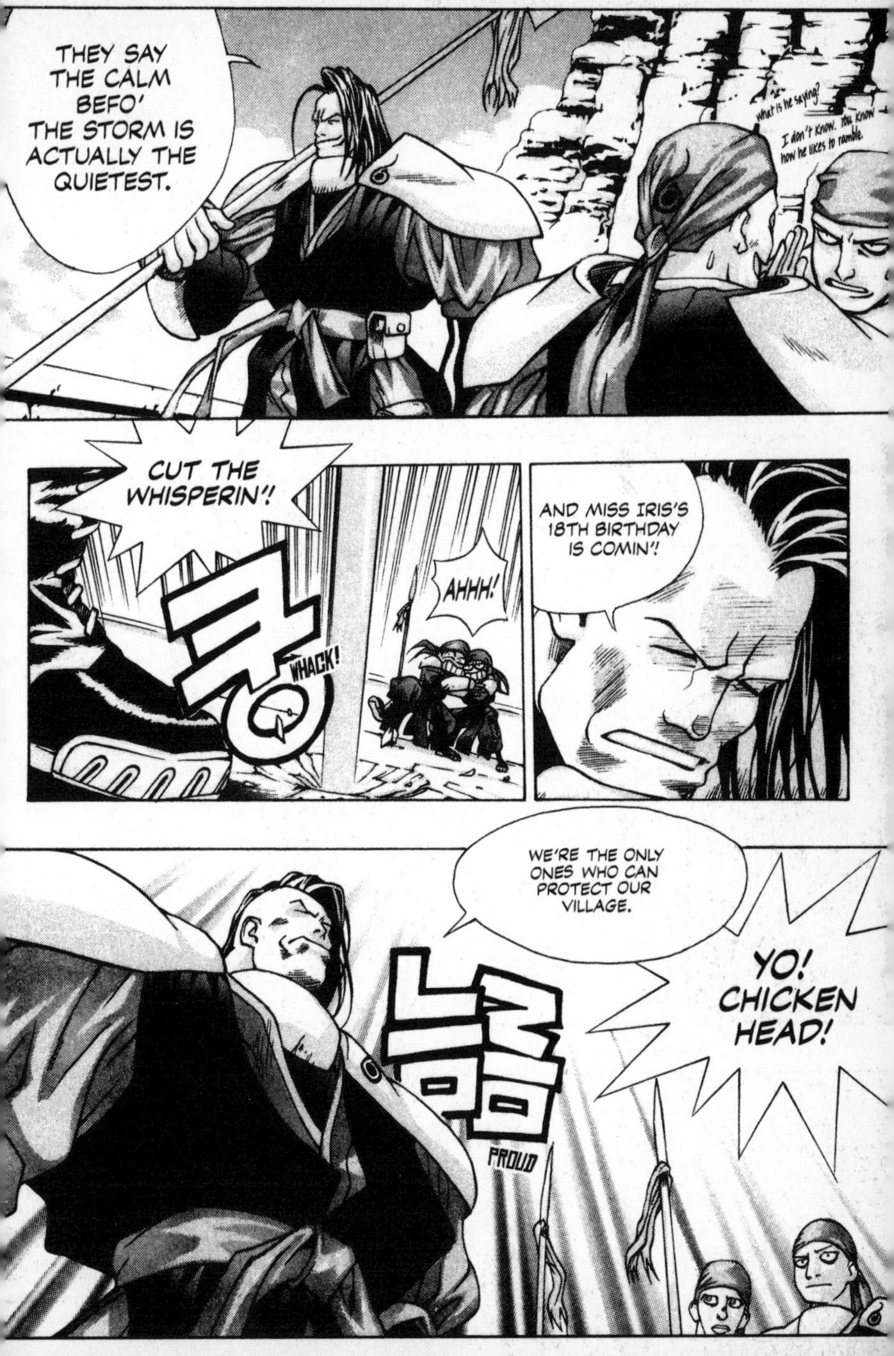
THEY SAY THE CALM BEFO' THE STORM IS ACTUALLY THE QUIETEST.
What is he saying?
I don't know. You know how he likes to ramble.
CUT THE WHISPERIN'!
WHACK!
AHHH!
AND MISS IRIS'S 18TH BIRTHDAY IS COMIN'!
WE'RE THE ONLY ONES WHO CAN PROTECT OUR VILLAGE.
PROUD
YO! CHICKEN HEAD!

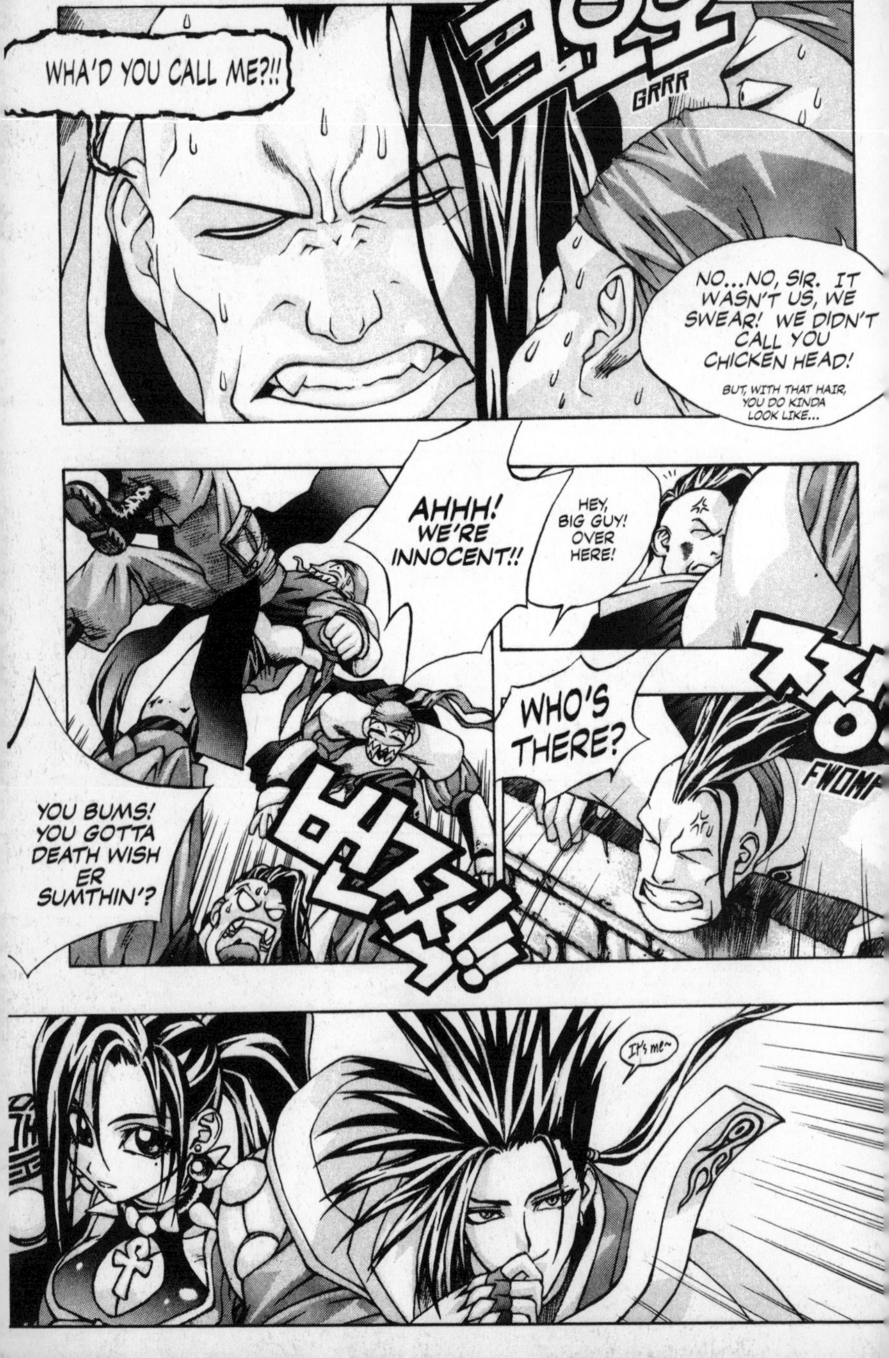
WHA'D YOU CALL ME?!!
그으으
GRRR
NO...NO, SIR. IT WASN'T US, WE SWEAR! WE DIDN'T CALL YOU CHICKEN HEAD!
BUT, WITH THAT HAIR, YOU DO KINDA LOOK LIKE...
AHHH! WE'RE INNOCENT!!
HEY, BIG GUY! OVER HERE!
YOU BUMS! YOU GOTTA DEATH WISH ER SUMTHIN'?
WHO'S THERE?
FWOMP
It's me~

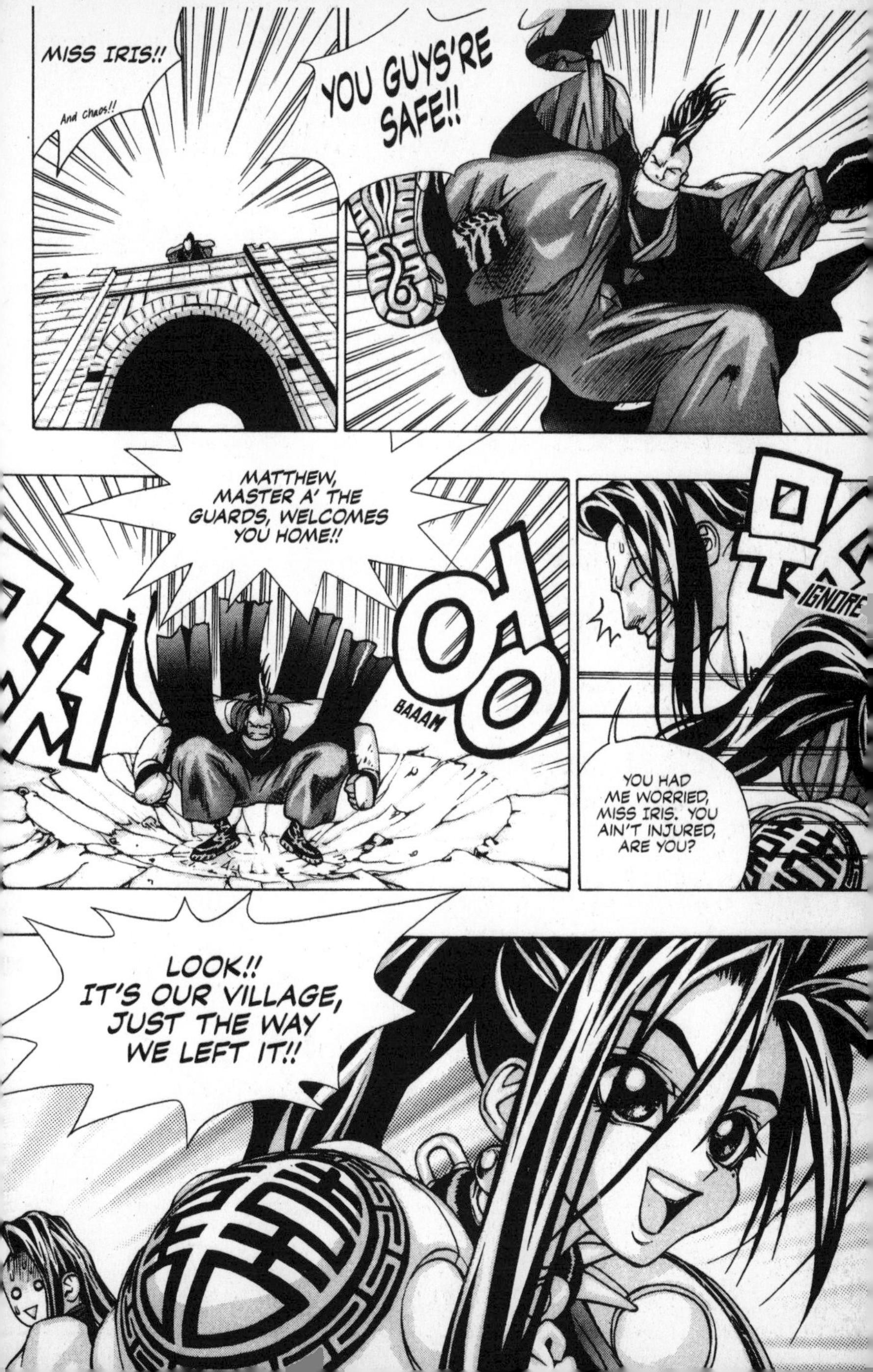
MISS IRIS!!
And chaos!!
YOU GUYS'RE SAFE!!
MATTHEW, MASTER A' THE GUARDS, WELCOMES YOU HOME!!
BAAAM
IGNORE
YOU HAD ME WORRIED, MISS IRIS. YOU AIN'T INJURED, ARE YOU?
LOOK!! IT'S OUR VILLAGE, JUST THE WAY WE LEFT IT!!

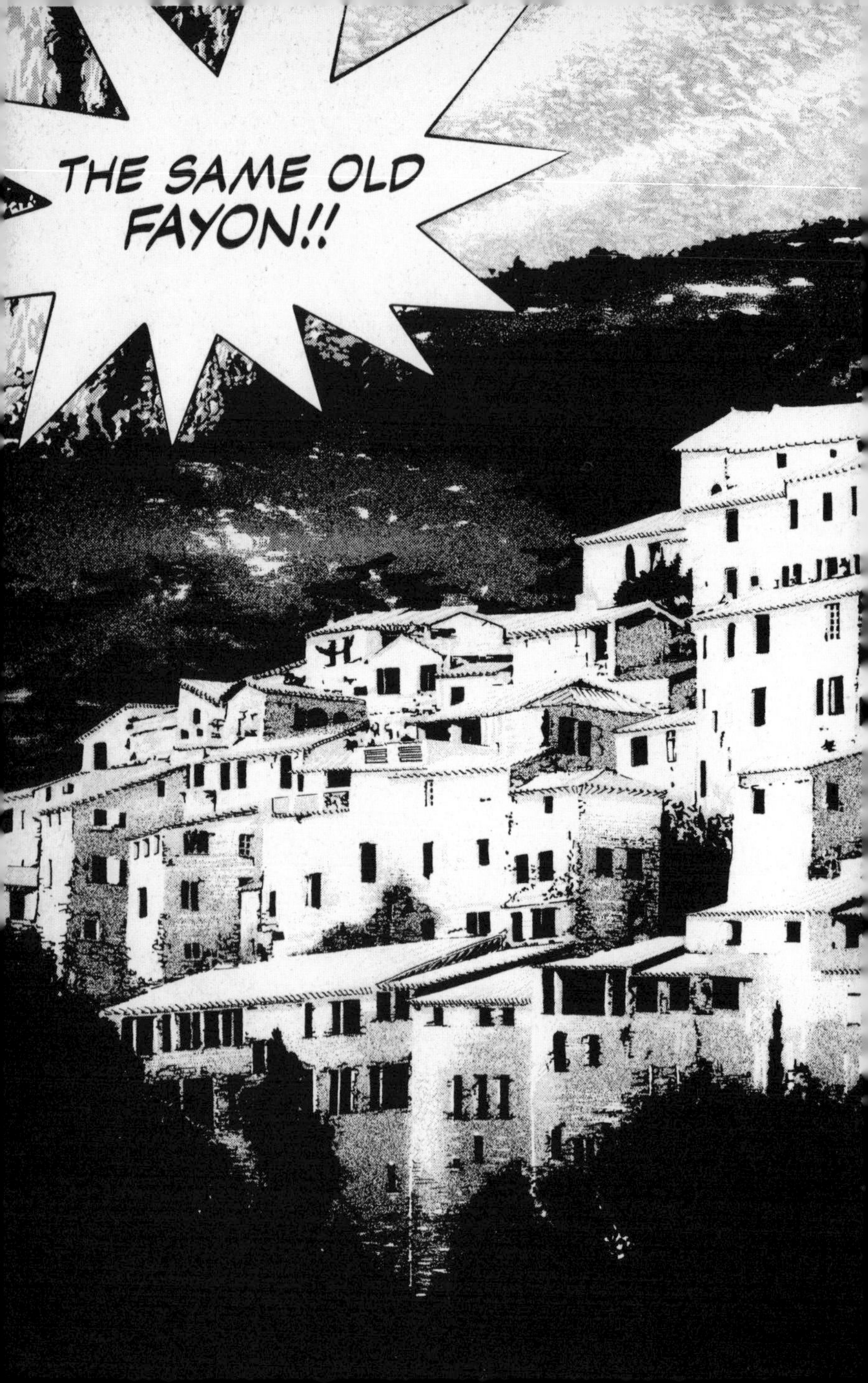
THE SAME OLD FAYON!!

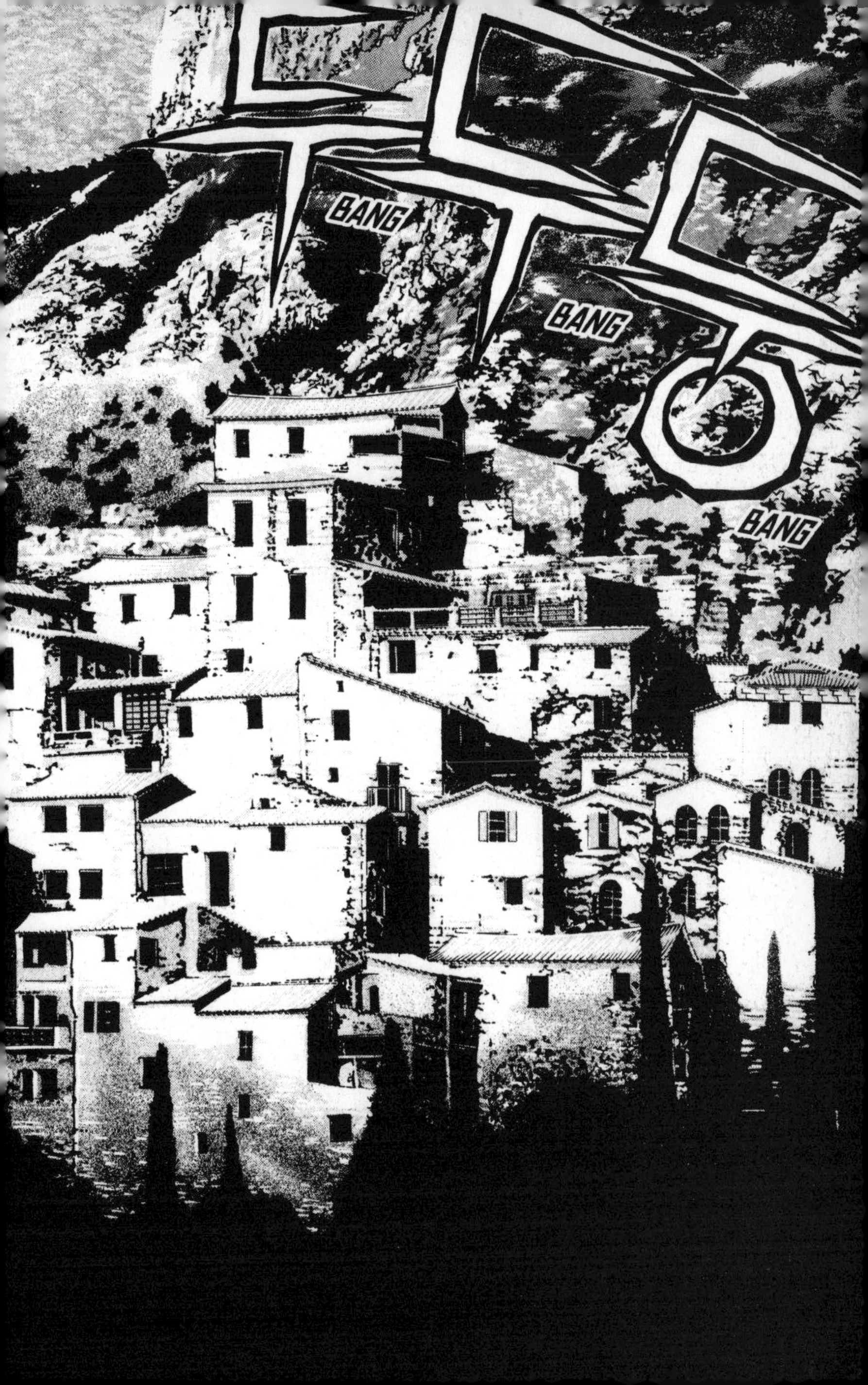
BANG
BANG
BANG

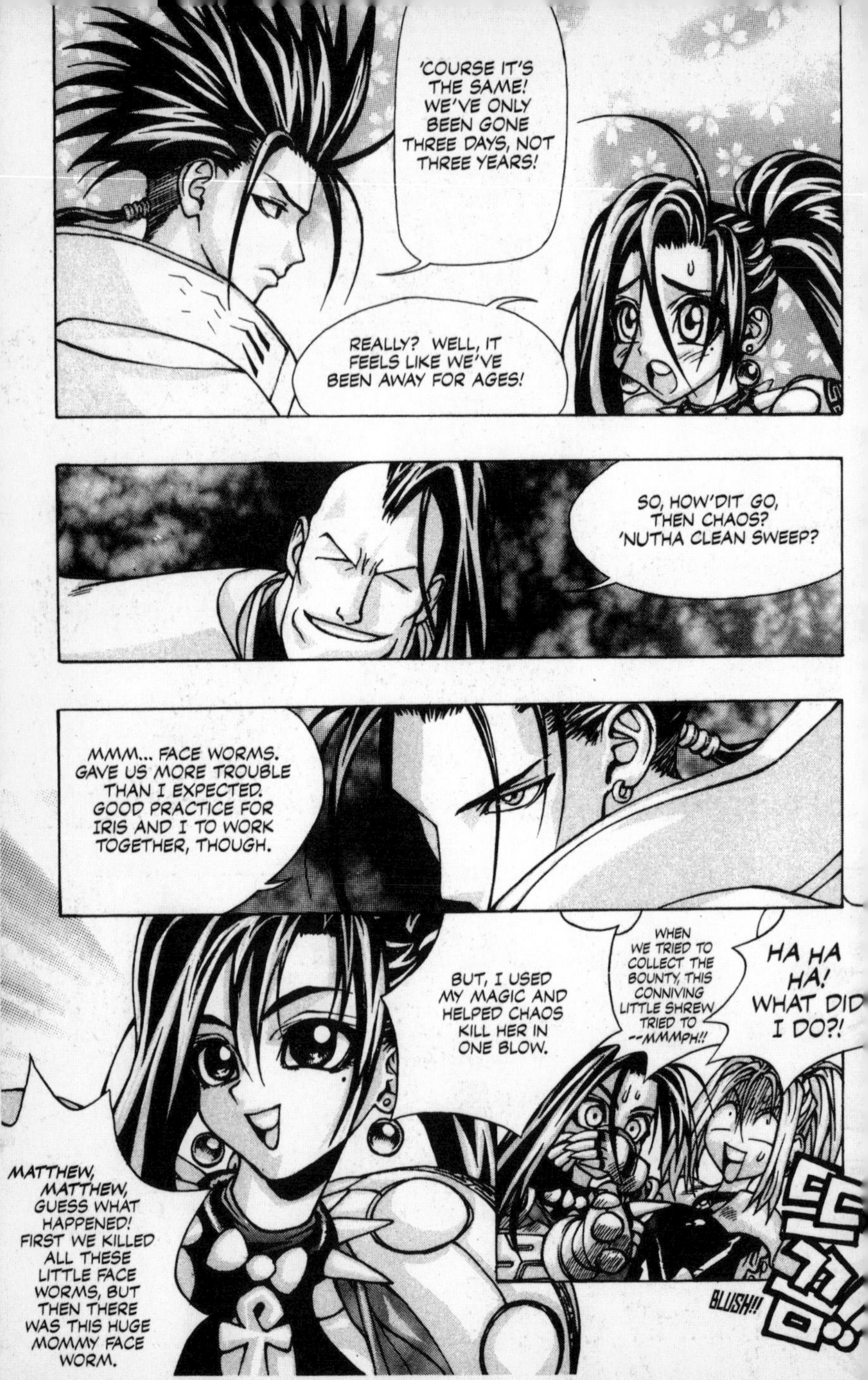
'COURSE IT'S THE SAME! WE'VE ONLY BEEN GONE THREE DAYS, NOT THREE YEARS!
REALLY? WELL, IT FEELS LIKE WE'VE BEEN AWAY FOR AGES!
SO, HOW'DIT GO, THEN CHAOS? 'NUTHA CLEAN SWEEP?
MMM... FACE WORMS. GAVE US MORE TROUBLE THAN I EXPECTED. GOOD PRACTICE FOR IRIS AND I TO WORK TOGETHER, THOUGH.
MATTHEW, MATTHEW, GUESS WHAT HAPPENED! FIRST WE KILLED ALL THESE LITTLE FACE WORMS, BUT THEN THERE WAS THIS HUGE MOMMY FACE WORM.
BUT, I USED MY MAGIC AND HELPED CHAOS KILL HER IN ONE BLOW.
WHEN WE TRIED TO COLLECT THE BOUNTY, THIS CONNIVING LITTLE SHREW TRIED TO --MMMPH!!
HA HA HA! WHAT DID I DO?!
BLUSH!!

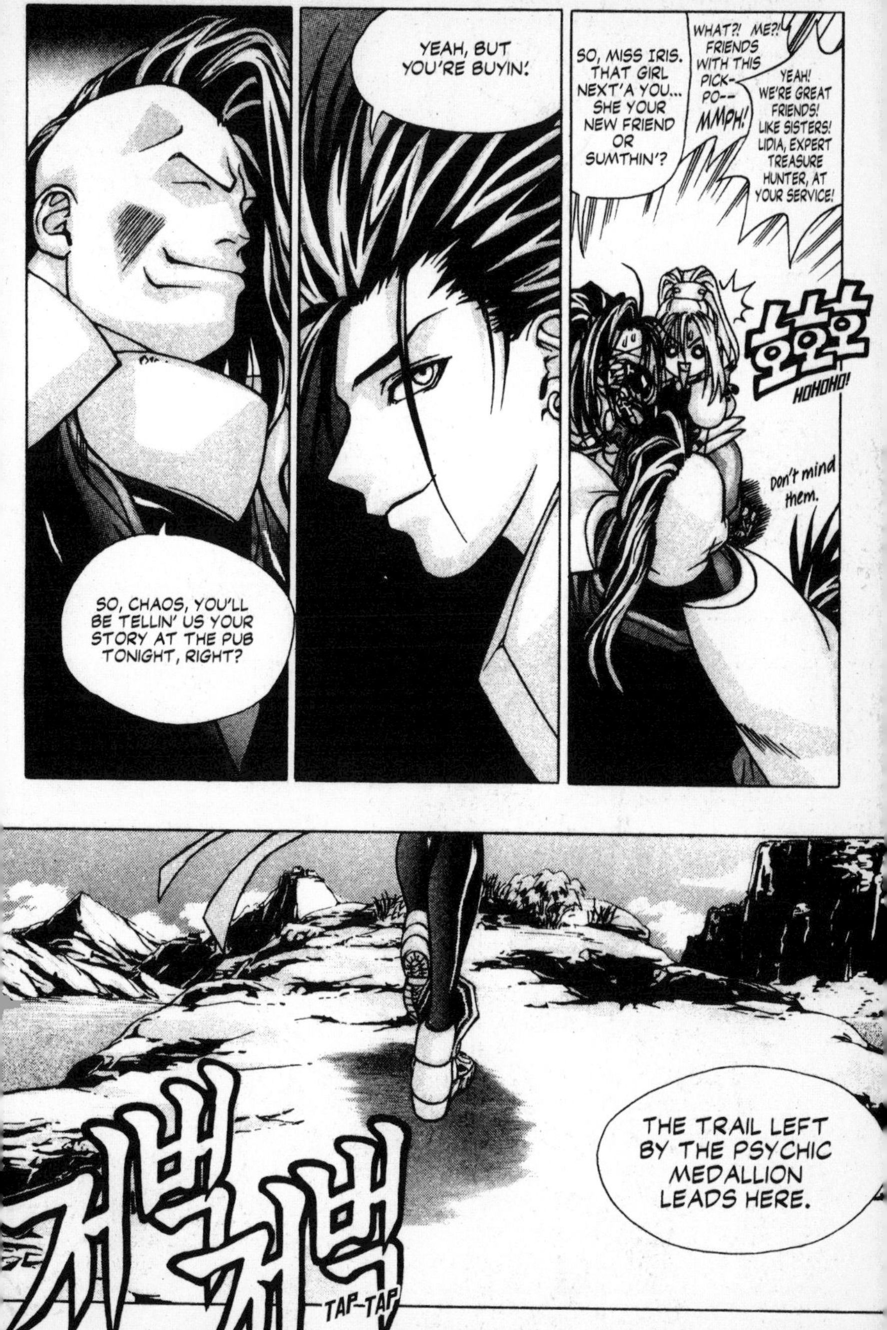
SO, CHAOS, YOU'LL BE TELLIN' US YOUR STORY AT THE PUB TONIGHT, RIGHT?
YEAH, BUT YOU'RE BUYIN'.
SO, MISS IRIS. THAT GIRL NEXT'A YOU... SHE YOUR NEW FRIEND OR SUMTHIN'?
WHAT?! ME?! FRIENDS WITH THIS PICK-PO-- MMPH!
YEAH! WE'RE GREAT FRIENDS! LIKE SISTERS! LIDIA, EXPERT TREASURE HUNTER, AT YOUR SERVICE!
호오호
HOHOHO!
Don't mind them.
저벅저벅
TAP-TAP
THE TRAIL LEFT BY THE PSYCHIC MEDALLION LEADS HERE.

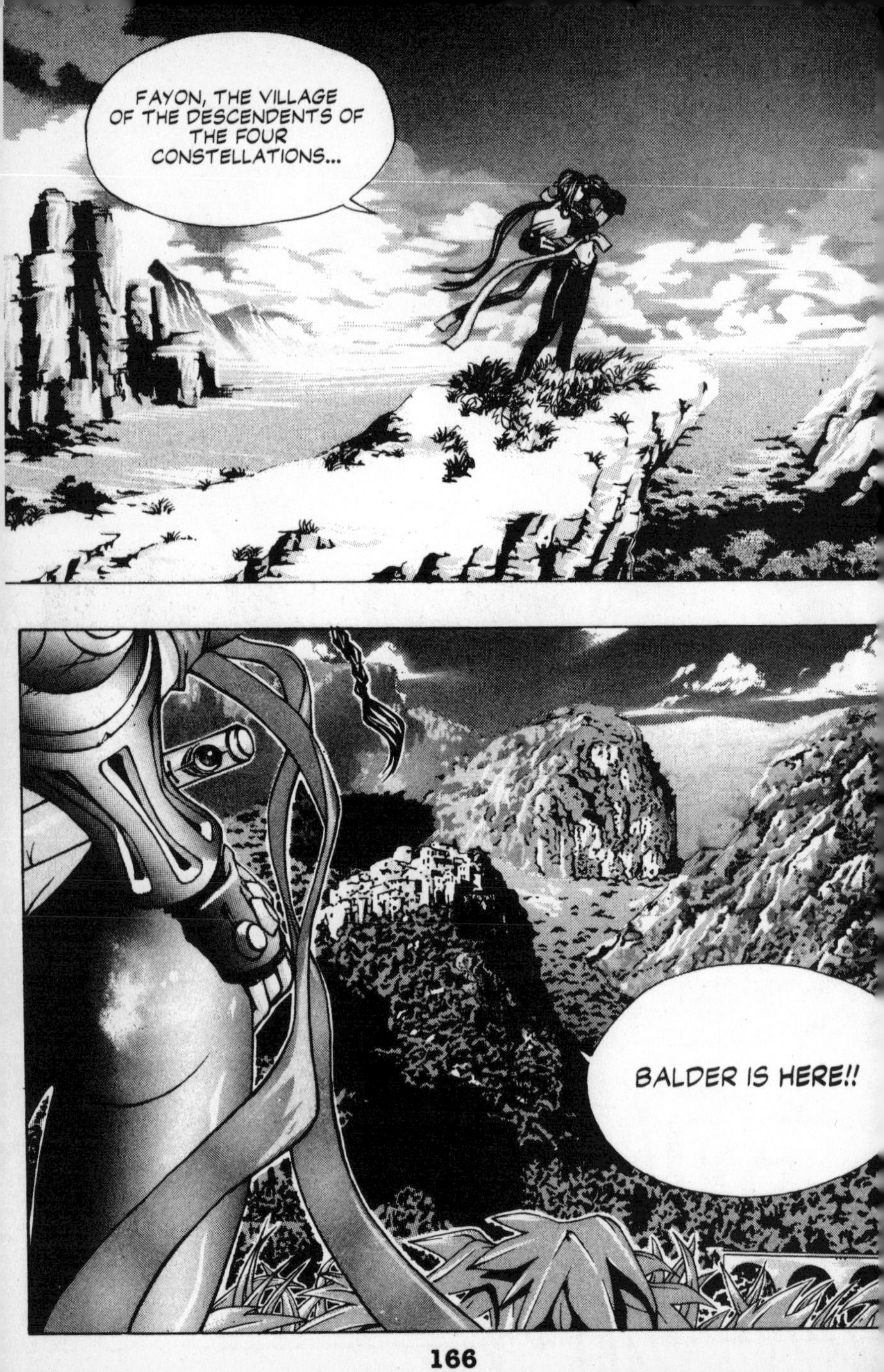
FAYON, THE VILLAGE OF THE DESCENDENTS OF THE FOUR CONSTELLATIONS...
BALDER IS HERE!!

RAGNARÖK

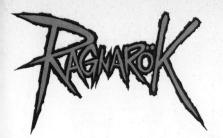

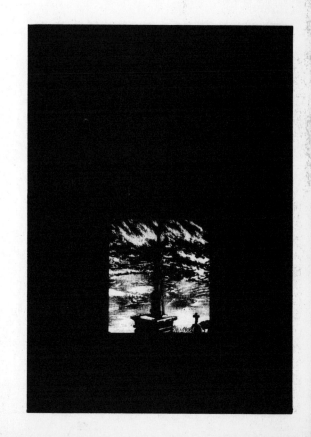

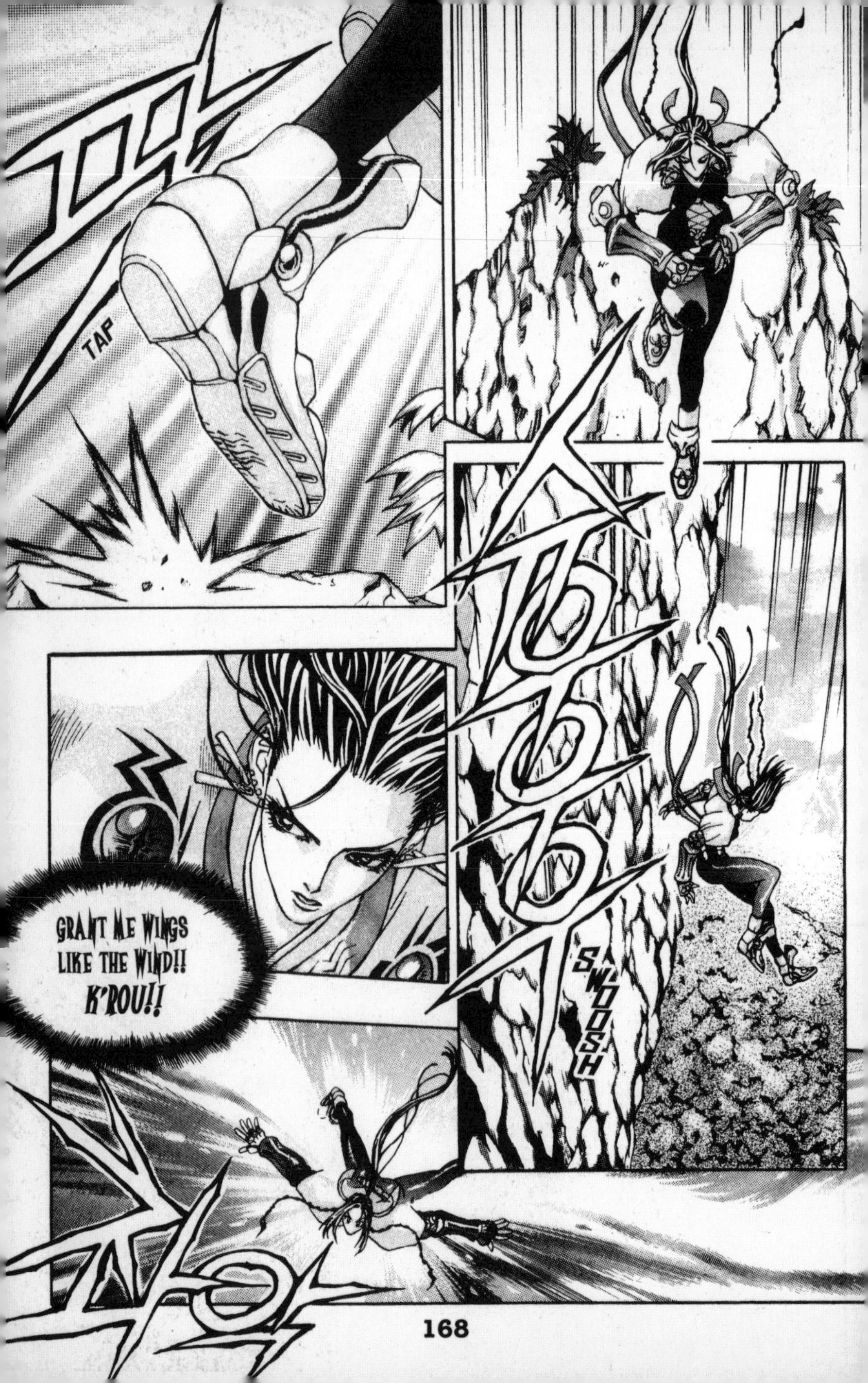
TAP
GRANT ME WINGS LIKE THE WIND!! K'ROU!!
SWOOSH

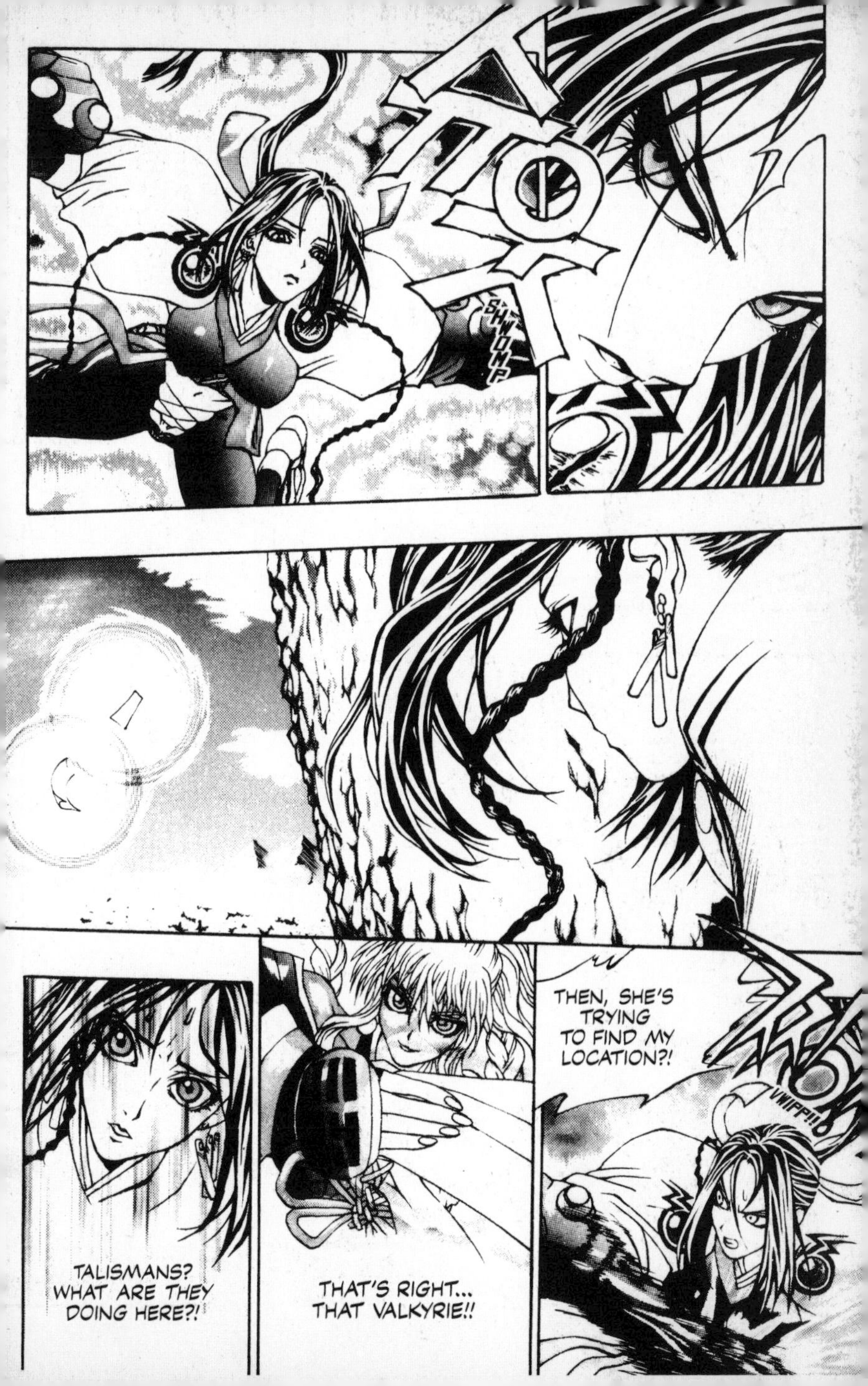
SHWOMP
TALISMANS? WHAT ARE THEY DOING HERE?!
THAT'S RIGHT... THAT VALKYRIE!!
THEN, SHE'S TRYING TO FIND MY LOCATION?!
VWIPP!!

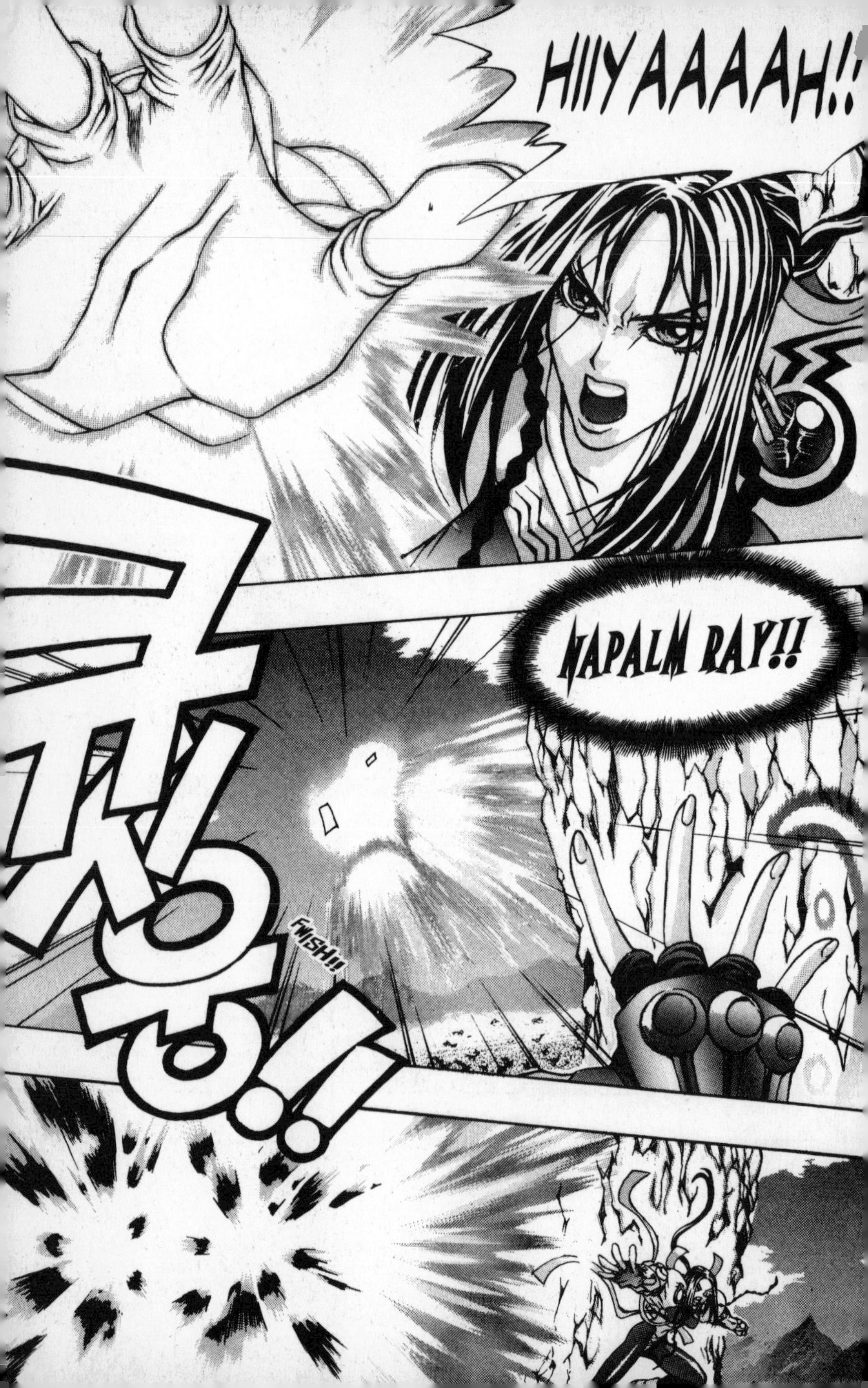
HIIYAAAAH!!
NAPALM RAY!!
FWISH!!

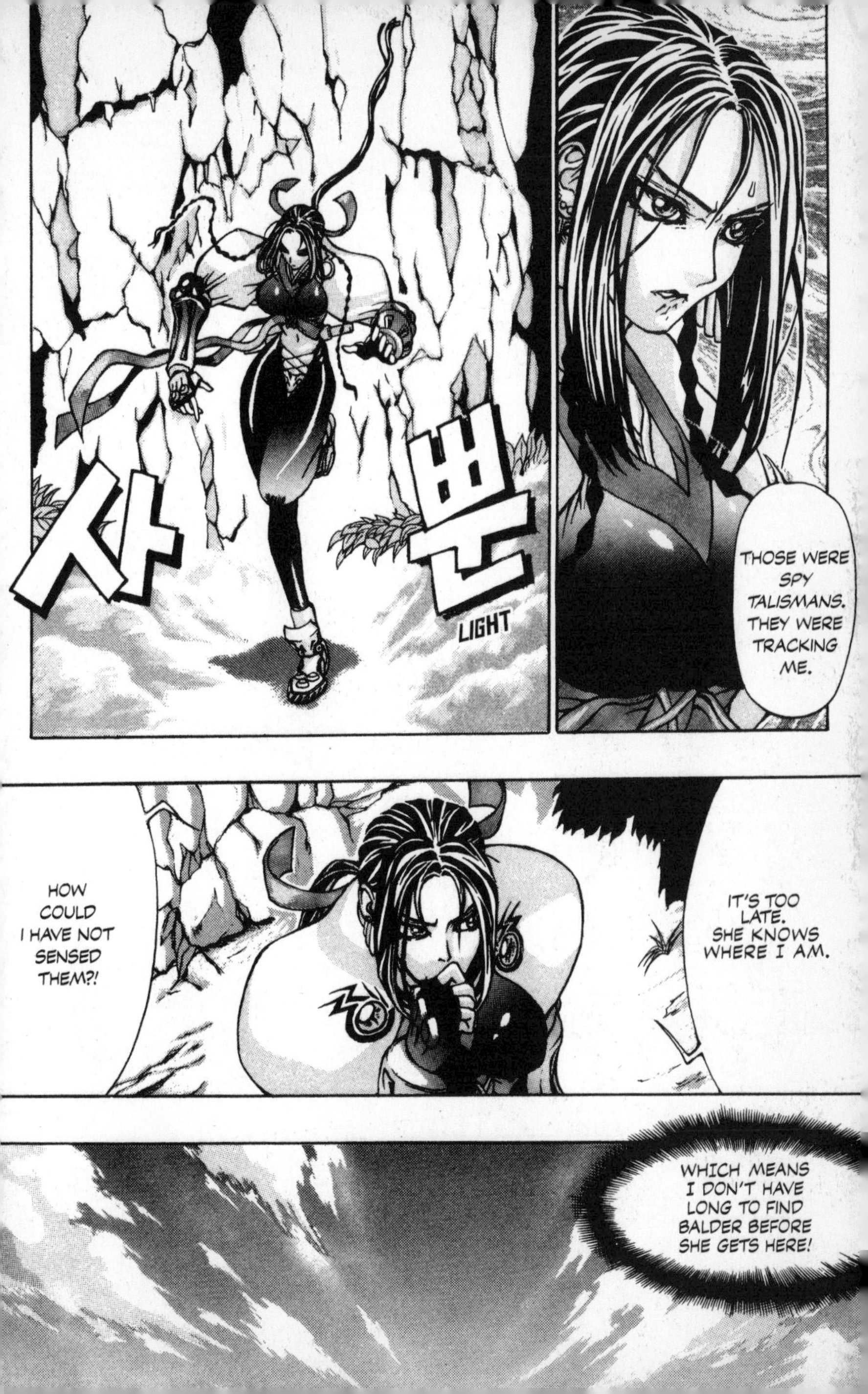
LIGHT
THOSE WERE SPY TALISMANS. THEY WERE TRACKING ME.
HOW COULD I HAVE NOT SENSED THEM?!
IT'S TOO LATE. SHE KNOWS WHERE I AM.
WHICH MEANS I DON'T HAVE LONG TO FIND BALDER BEFORE SHE GETS HERE!

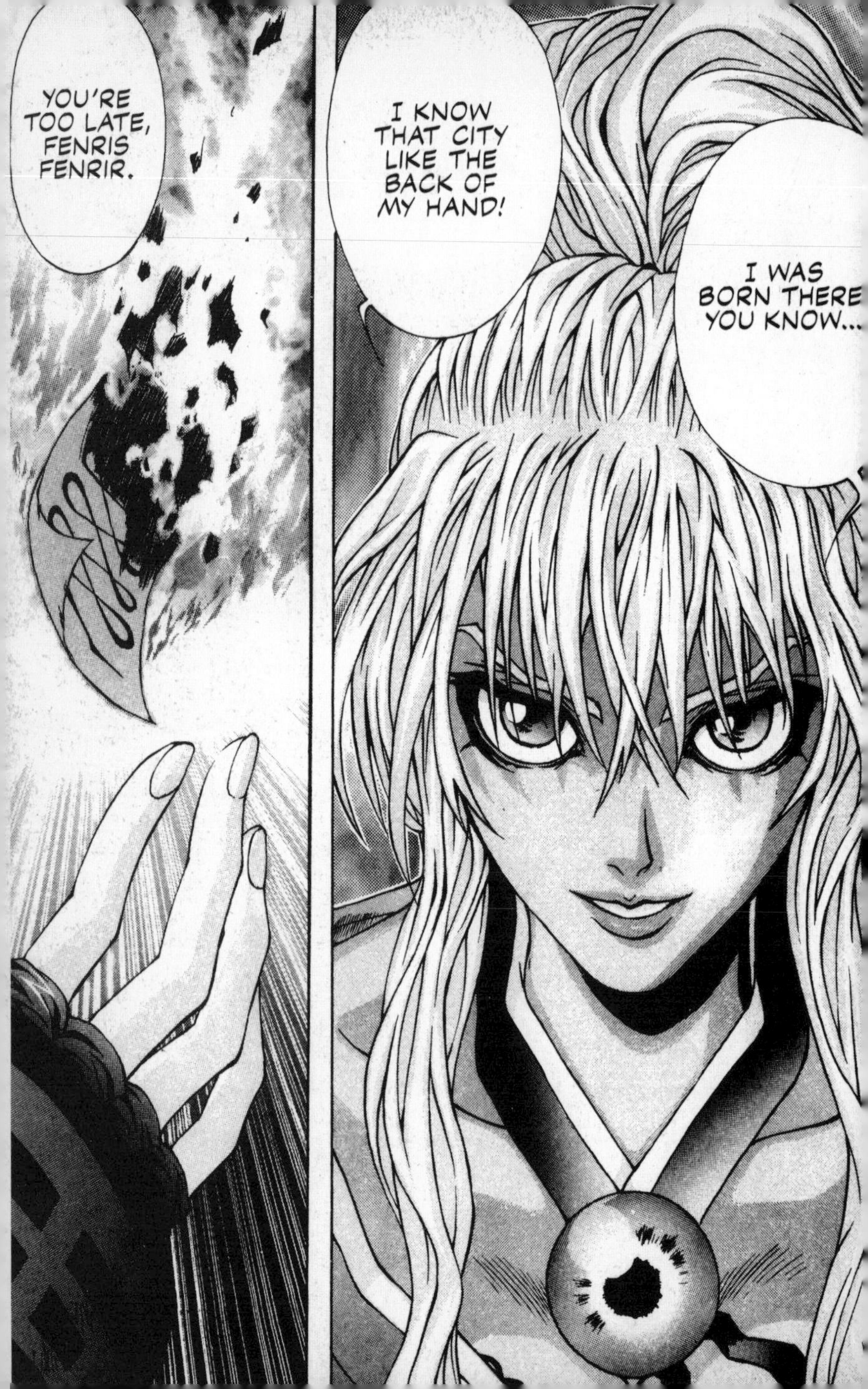
YOU'RE TOO LATE, FENRIS FENRIR.
I KNOW THAT CITY LIKE THE BACK OF MY HAND!
I WAS BORN THERE YOU KNOW...

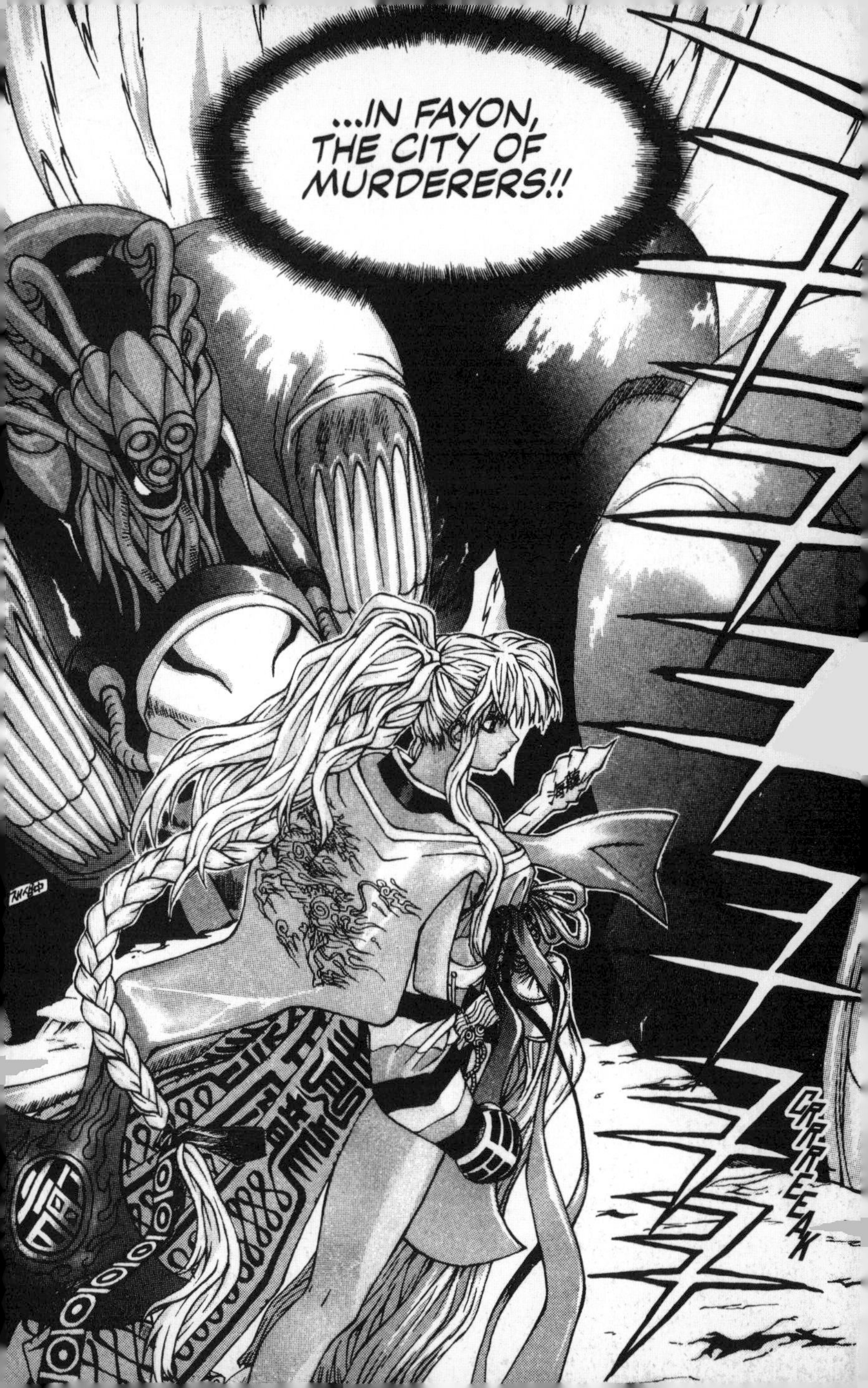
...IN FAYON, THE CITY OF MURDERERS!!
CRRREEAK

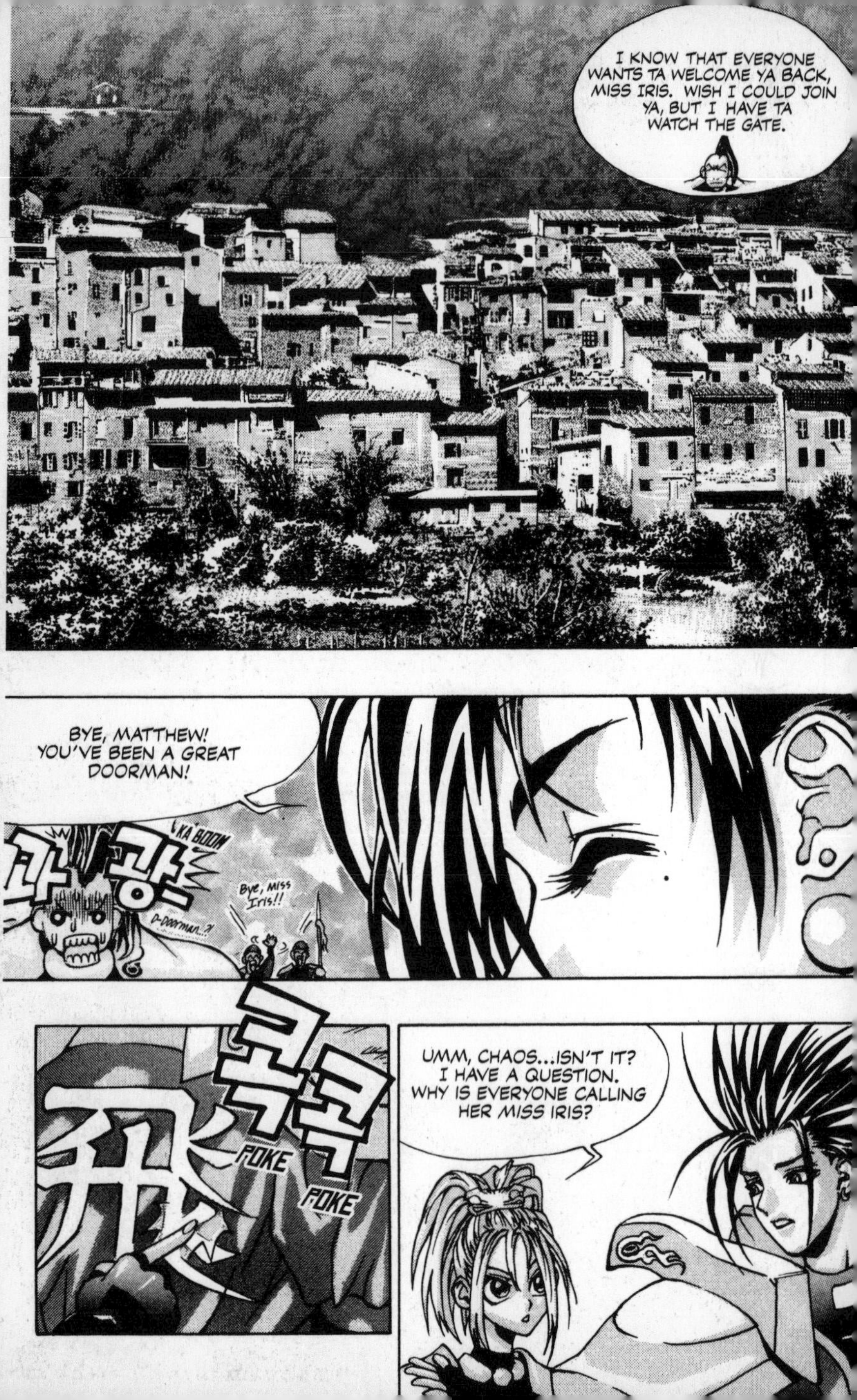
I KNOW THAT EVERYONE WANTS TA WELCOME YA BACK, MISS IRIS. WISH I COULD JOIN YA, BUT I HAVE TA WATCH THE GATE.
BYE, MATTHEW! YOU'VE BEEN A GREAT DOORMAN!
KA BOOM
D-Doorman...?!
Bye, Miss Iris!!
POKE
POKE
UMM, CHAOS...ISN'T IT? I HAVE A QUESTION. WHY IS EVERYONE CALLING HER MISS IRIS?

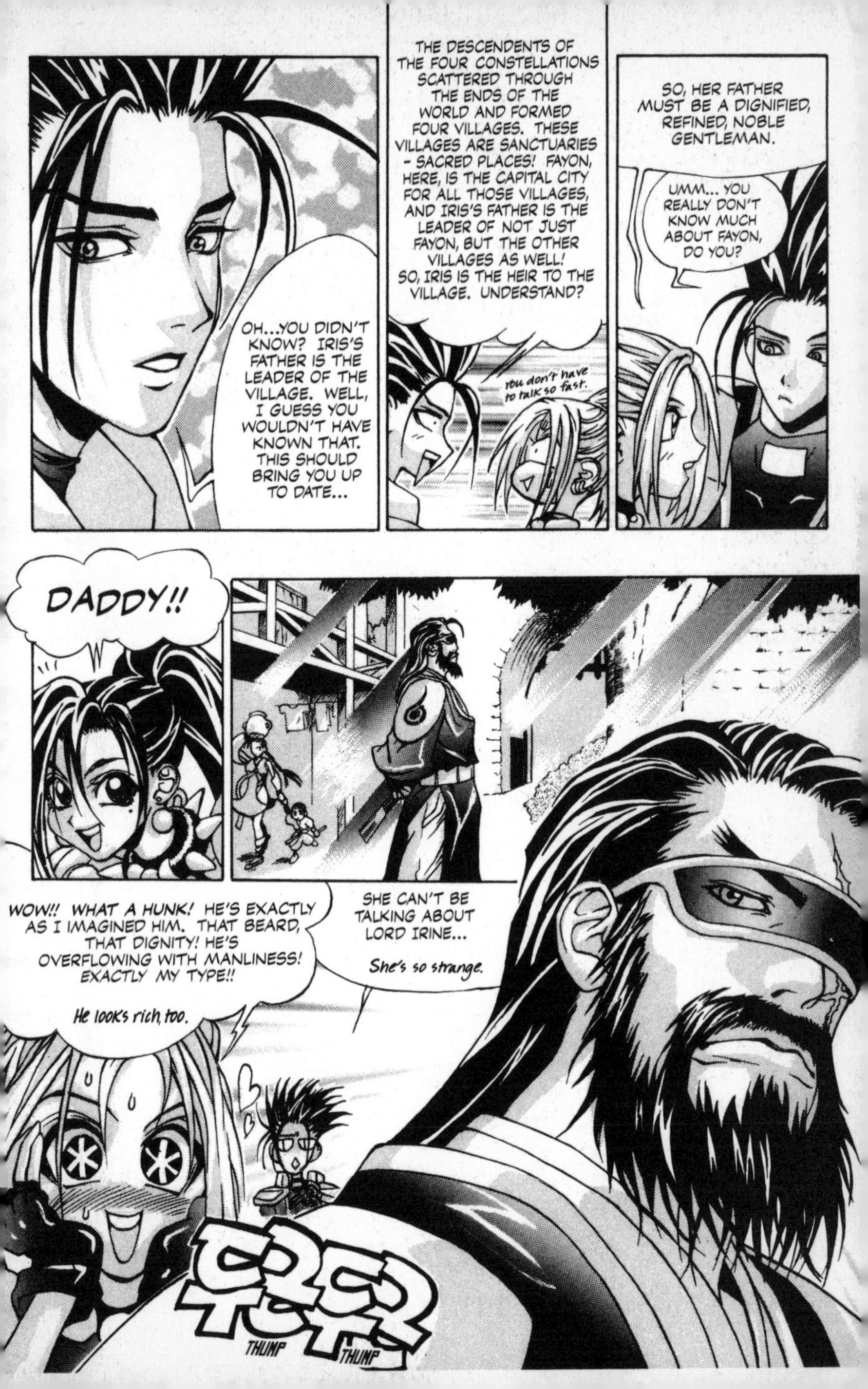
OH...YOU DIDN'T KNOW? IRIS'S FATHER IS THE LEADER OF THE VILLAGE. WELL, I GUESS YOU WOULDN'T HAVE KNOWN THAT. THIS SHOULD BRING YOU UP TO DATE...
THE DESCENDENTS OF THE FOUR CONSTELLATIONS SCATTERED THROUGH THE ENDS OF THE WORLD AND FORMED FOUR VILLAGES. THESE VILLAGES ARE SANCTUARIES - SACRED PLACES! FAYON, HERE, IS THE CAPITAL CITY FOR ALL THOSE VILLAGES, AND IRIS'S FATHER IS THE LEADER OF NOT JUST FAYON, BUT THE OTHER VILLAGES AS WELL! SO, IRIS IS THE HEIR TO THE VILLAGE. UNDERSTAND?
You don't have to talk so fast.
SO, HER FATHER MUST BE A DIGNIFIED, REFINED, NOBLE GENTLEMAN.
UMM... YOU REALLY DON'T KNOW MUCH ABOUT FAYON, DO YOU?
DADDY!!
WOW!! WHAT A HUNK! HE'S EXACTLY AS I IMAGINED HIM. THAT BEARD, THAT DIGNITY! HE'S OVERFLOWING WITH MANLINESS! EXACTLY MY TYPE!!
He looks rich, too.
SHE CAN'T BE TALKING ABOUT LORD IRINE...
She's so strange.
THUMP THUMP

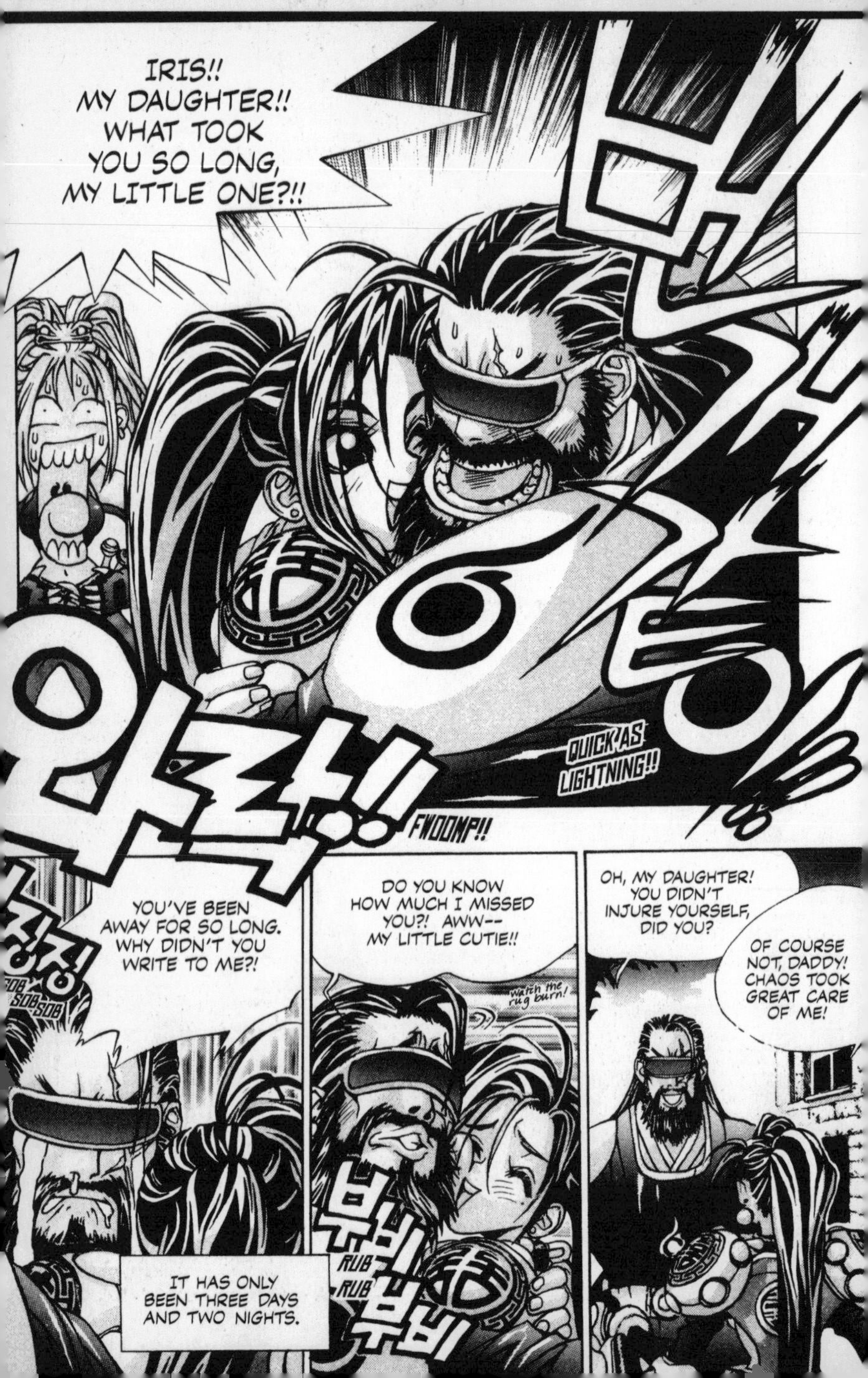
IRIS!! MY DAUGHTER!! WHAT TOOK YOU SO LONG, MY LITTLE ONE?!!
QUICK AS LIGHTNING!!
FWOOMP!!
YOU'VE BEEN AWAY FOR SO LONG. WHY DIDN'T YOU WRITE TO ME?!
SOB SOB SOB
IT HAS ONLY BEEN THREE DAYS AND TWO NIGHTS.
DO YOU KNOW HOW MUCH I MISSED YOU?! AWW-- MY LITTLE CUTIE!!
watch the rug burn!
RUB RUB
OH, MY DAUGHTER! YOU DIDN'T INJURE YOURSELF, DID YOU?
OF COURSE NOT, DADDY! CHAOS TOOK GREAT CARE OF ME!

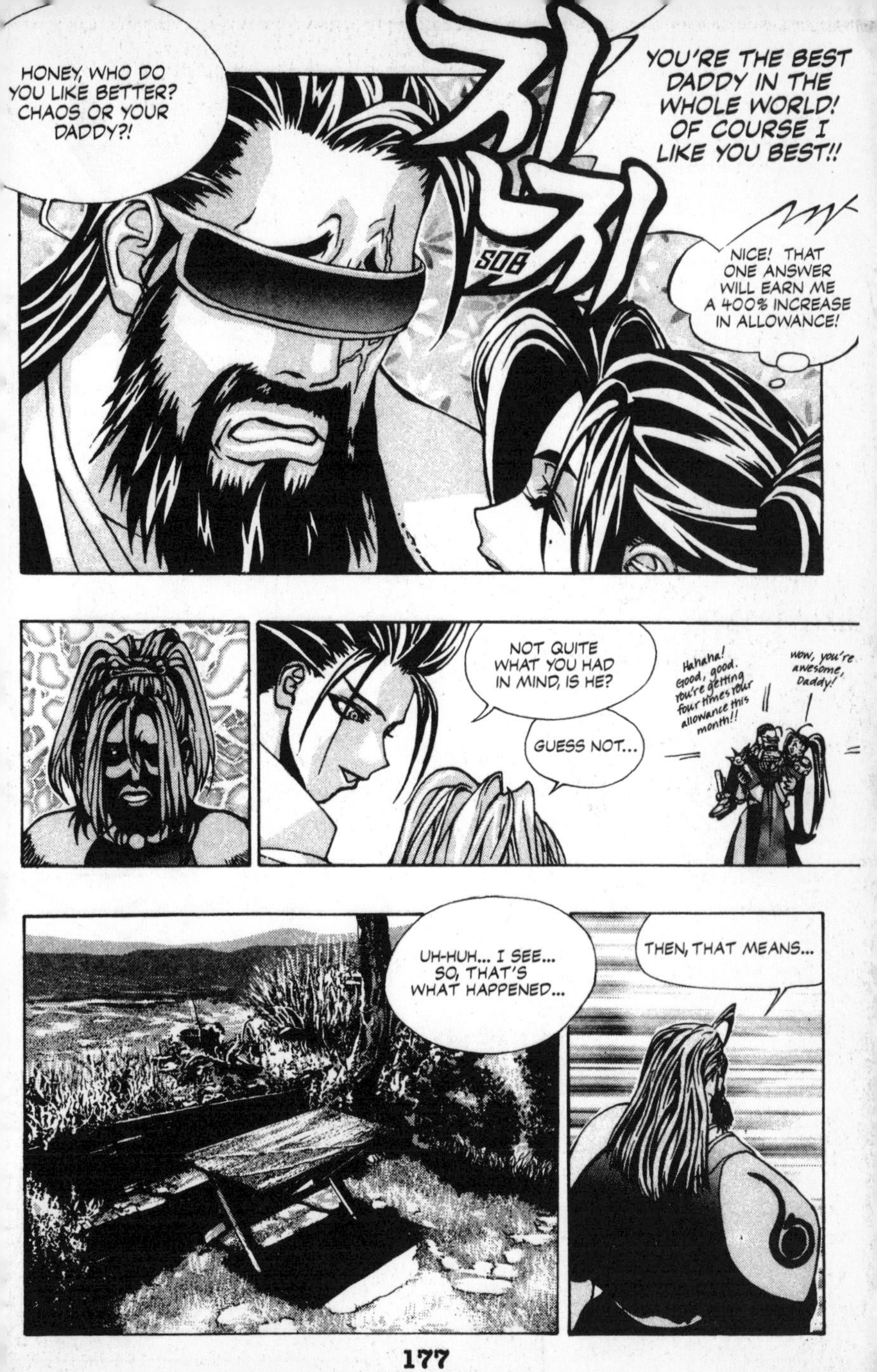
HONEY, WHO DO YOU LIKE BETTER? CHAOS OR YOUR DADDY?!
SOB
YOU'RE THE BEST DADDY IN THE WHOLE WORLD! OF COURSE I LIKE YOU BEST!!
NICE! THAT ONE ANSWER WILL EARN ME A 400% INCREASE IN ALLOWANCE!
NOT QUITE WHAT YOU HAD IN MIND, IS HE?
GUESS NOT...
Hahaha! Good, good. You're getting four times your allowance this month!!
Wow, you're awesome, Daddy!
UH-HUH... I SEE... SO, THAT'S WHAT HAPPENED...
THEN, THAT MEANS...

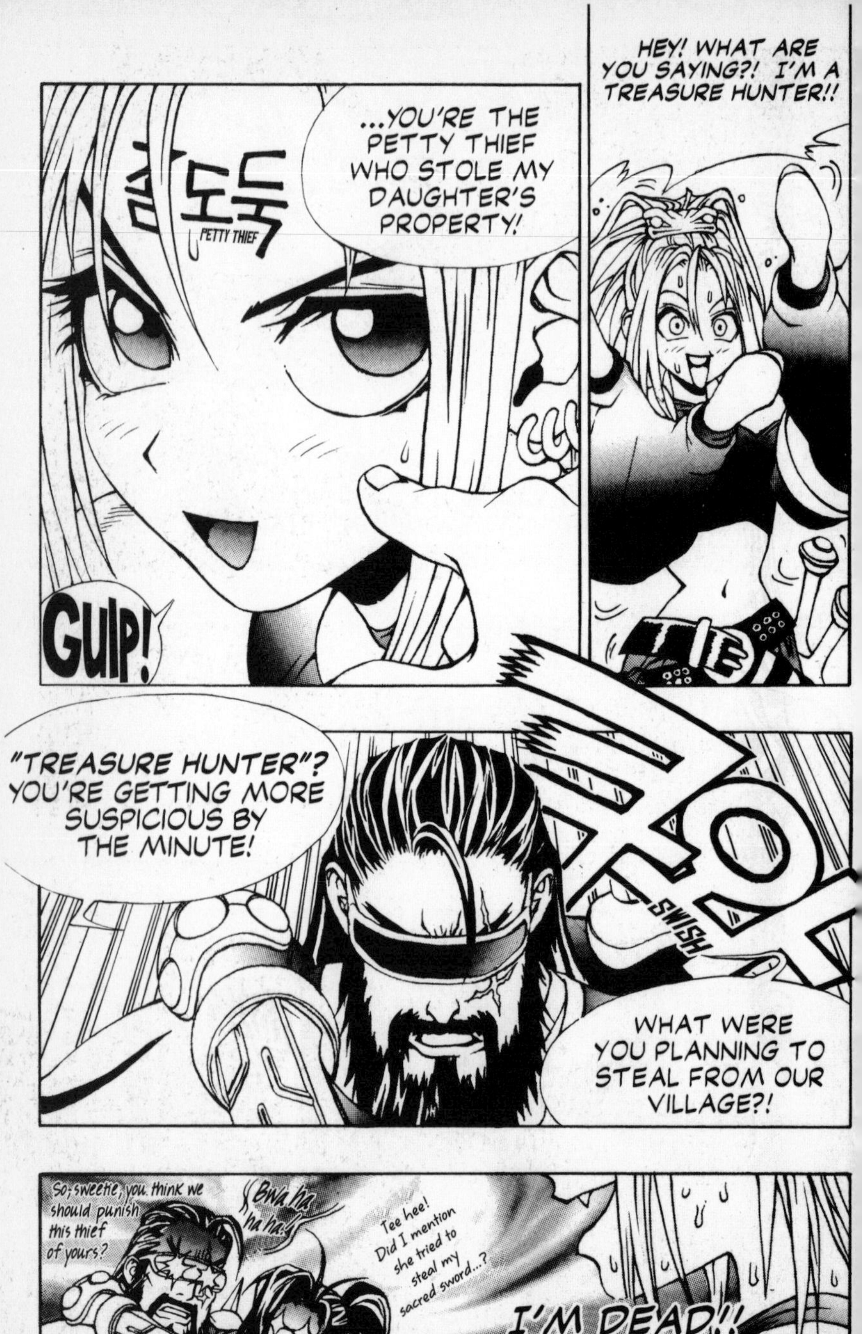

도둑
PETTY THIEF
...YOU'RE THE PETTY THIEF WHO STOLE MY DAUGHTER'S PROPERTY!
GULP!
HEY! WHAT ARE YOU SAYING?! I'M A TREASURE HUNTER!!
"TREASURE HUNTER"? YOU'RE GETTING MORE SUSPICIOUS BY THE MINUTE!
SWISH
WHAT WERE YOU PLANNING TO STEAL FROM OUR VILLAGE?!
So, sweetie, you think we should punish this thief of yours?
Bwa ha ha ha...
Tee hee! Did I mention she tried to steal my sacred sword...?
I'M DEAD!!

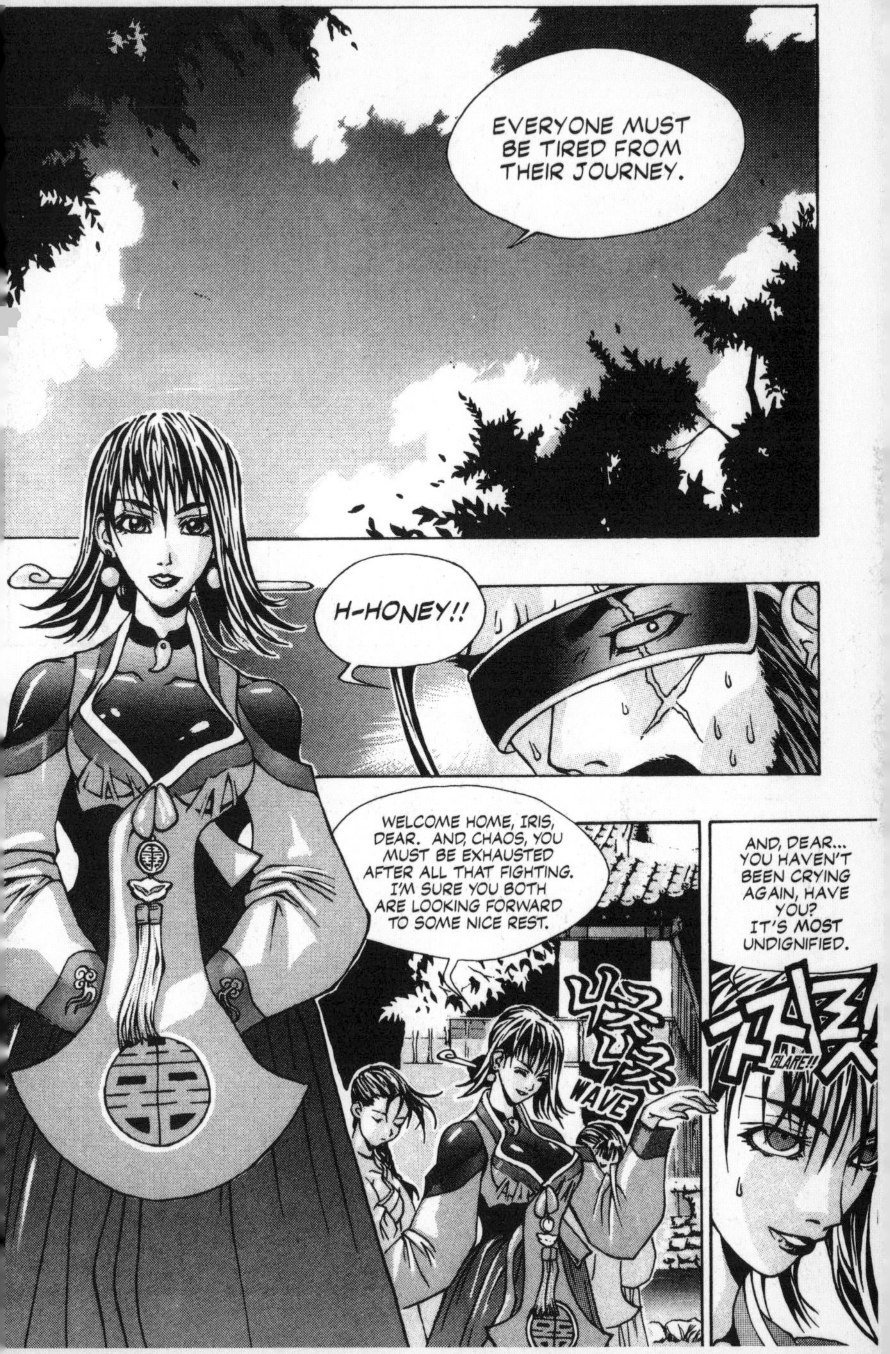
EVERYONE MUST BE TIRED FROM THEIR JOURNEY.
H-HONEY!!
WELCOME HOME, IRIS, DEAR. AND, CHAOS, YOU MUST BE EXHAUSTED AFTER ALL THAT FIGHTING. I'M SURE YOU BOTH ARE LOOKING FORWARD TO SOME NICE REST.
WAVE
AND, DEAR... YOU HAVEN'T BEEN CRYING AGAIN, HAVE YOU? IT'S MOST UNDIGNIFIED.
GLARE!!

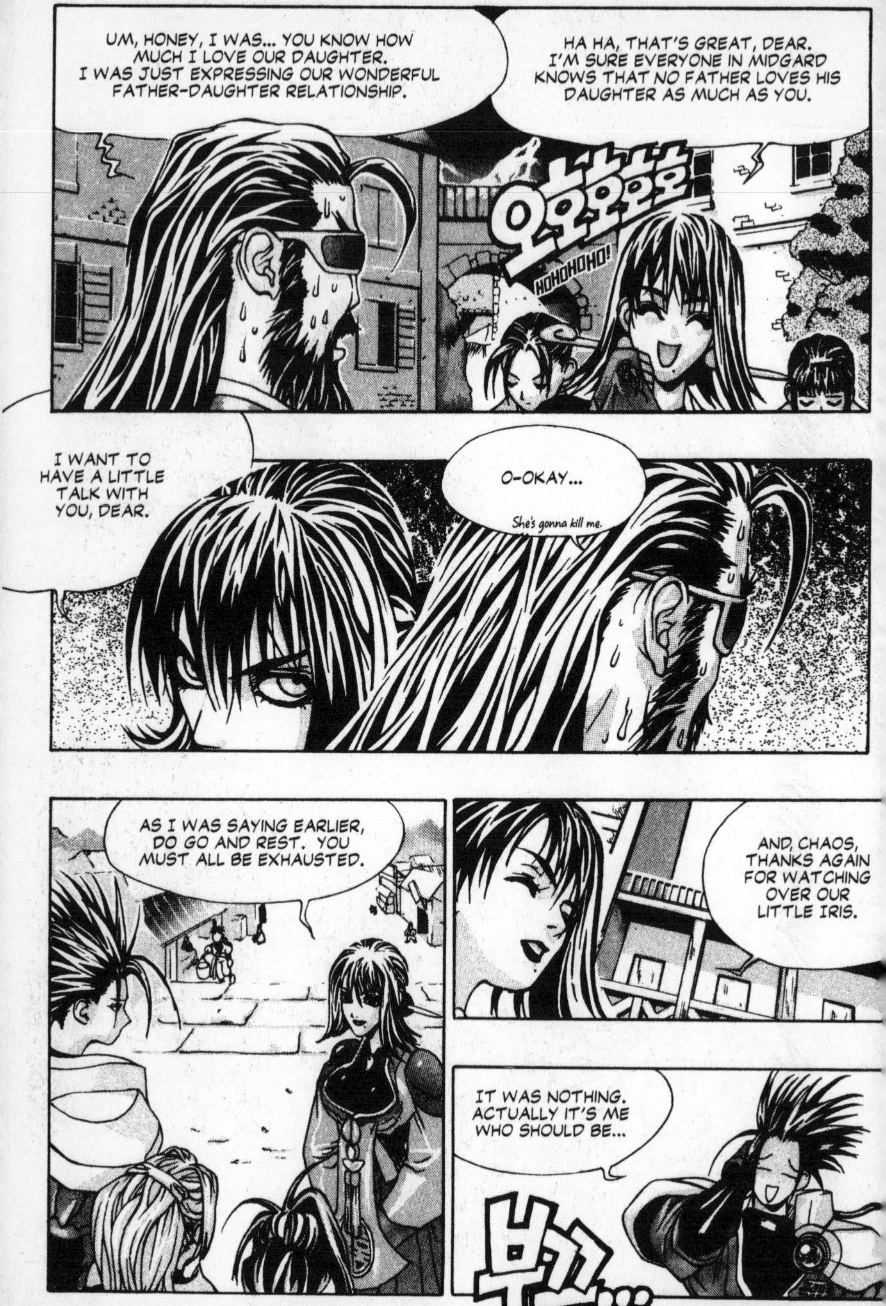
UM, HONEY, I WAS... YOU KNOW HOW MUCH I LOVE OUR DAUGHTER. I WAS JUST EXPRESSING OUR WONDERFUL FATHER-DAUGHTER RELATIONSHIP.
HA HA, THAT'S GREAT, DEAR. I'M SURE EVERYONE IN MIDGARD KNOWS THAT NO FATHER LOVES HIS DAUGHTER AS MUCH AS YOU.
오호호호호
HOHOHOHO!
I WANT TO HAVE A LITTLE TALK WITH YOU, DEAR.
O-OKAY...
She's gonna kill me.
AS I WAS SAYING EARLIER, DO GO AND REST. YOU MUST ALL BE EXHAUSTED.
AND, CHAOS, THANKS AGAIN FOR WATCHING OVER OUR LITTLE IRIS.
IT WAS NOTHING. ACTUALLY IT'S ME WHO SHOULD BE...
부끄...
BLUSH...

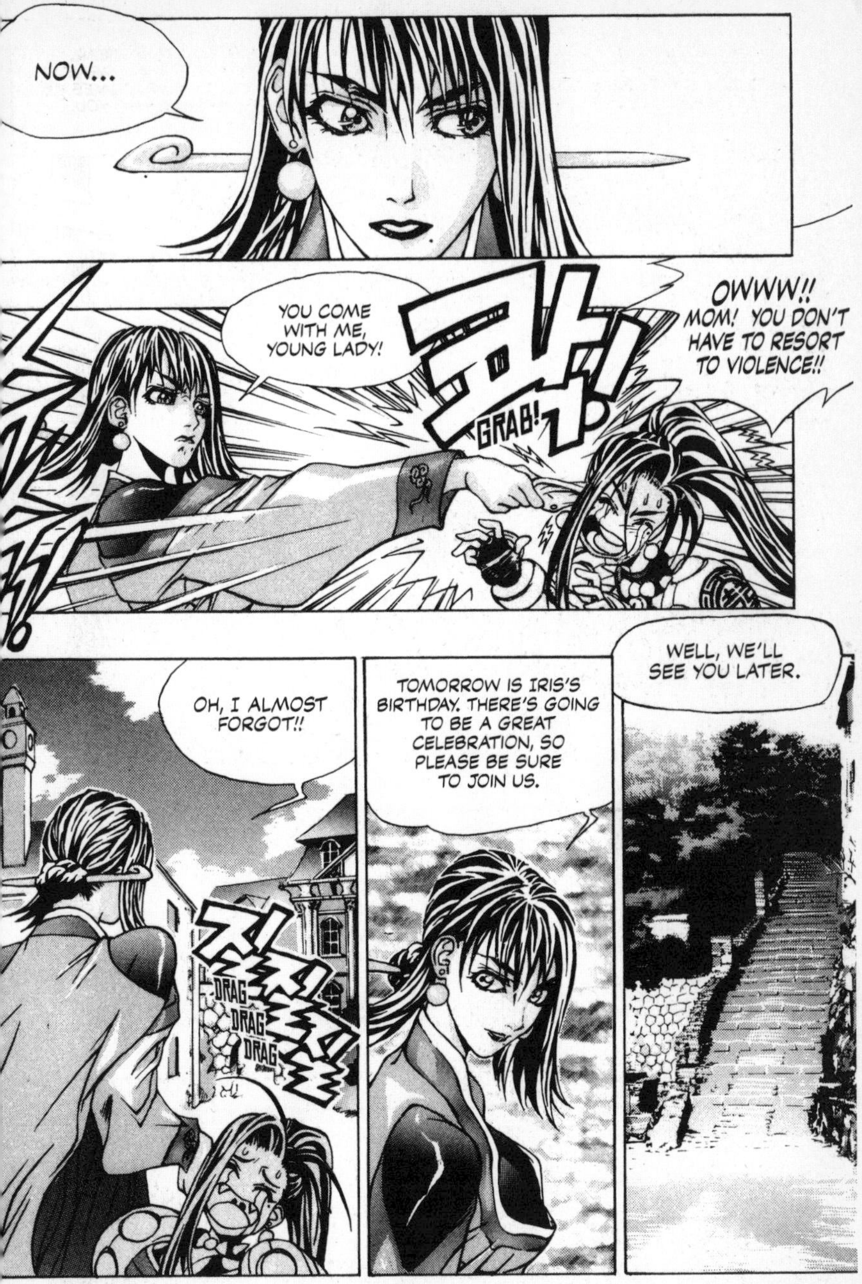
NOW...
YOU COME WITH ME, YOUNG LADY!
GRAB!
OWWW!! MOM! YOU DON'T HAVE TO RESORT TO VIOLENCE!!
OH, I ALMOST FORGOT!!
DRAG DRAG DRAG
TOMORROW IS IRIS'S BIRTHDAY. THERE'S GOING TO BE A GREAT CELEBRATION, SO PLEASE BE SURE TO JOIN US.
WELL, WE'LL SEE YOU LATER.

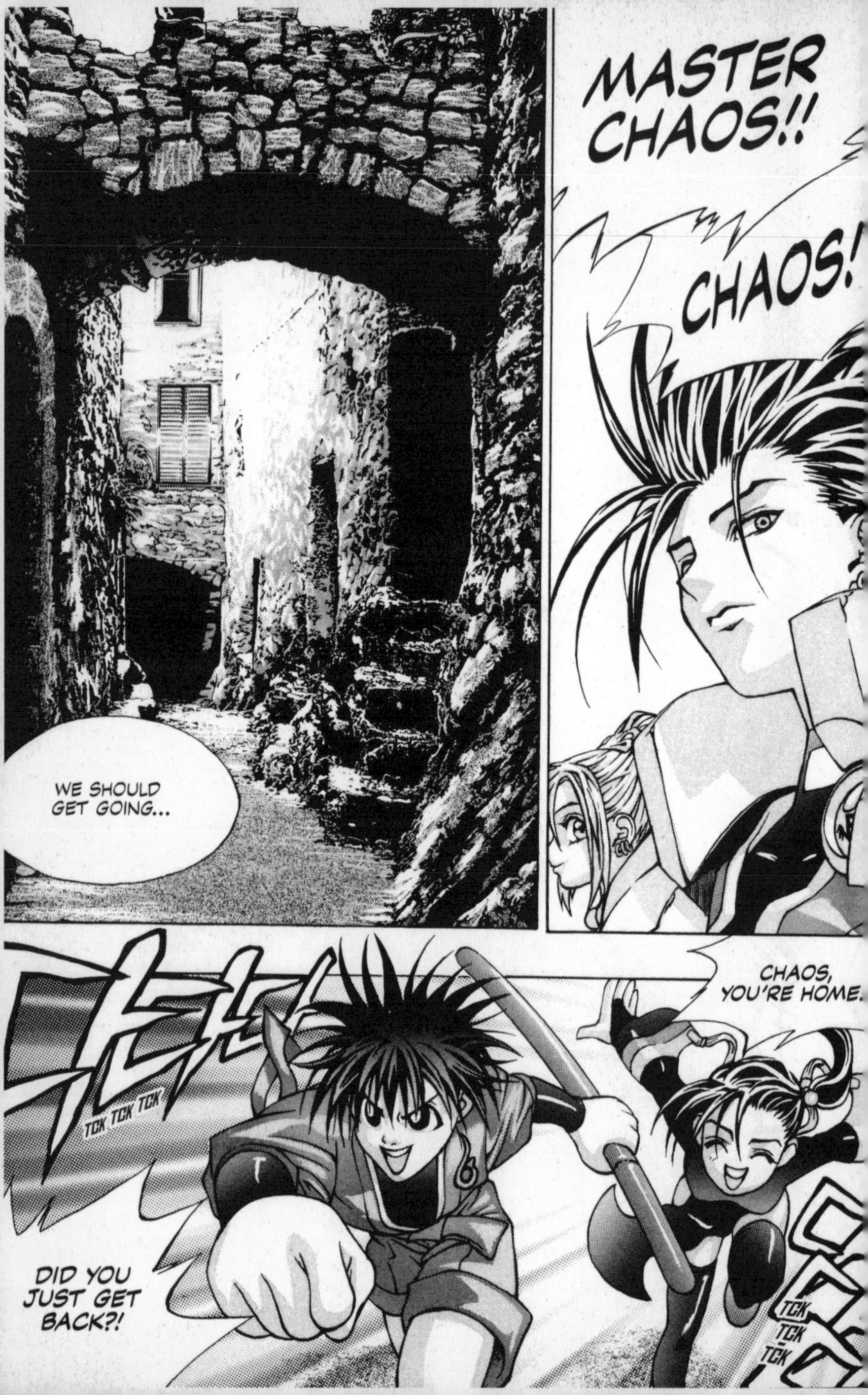
WE SHOULD GET GOING...
MASTER CHAOS!!
CHAOS!
TCK TCK TCK
DID YOU JUST GET BACK?!
CHAOS, YOU'RE HOME.
TCK TCK TCK

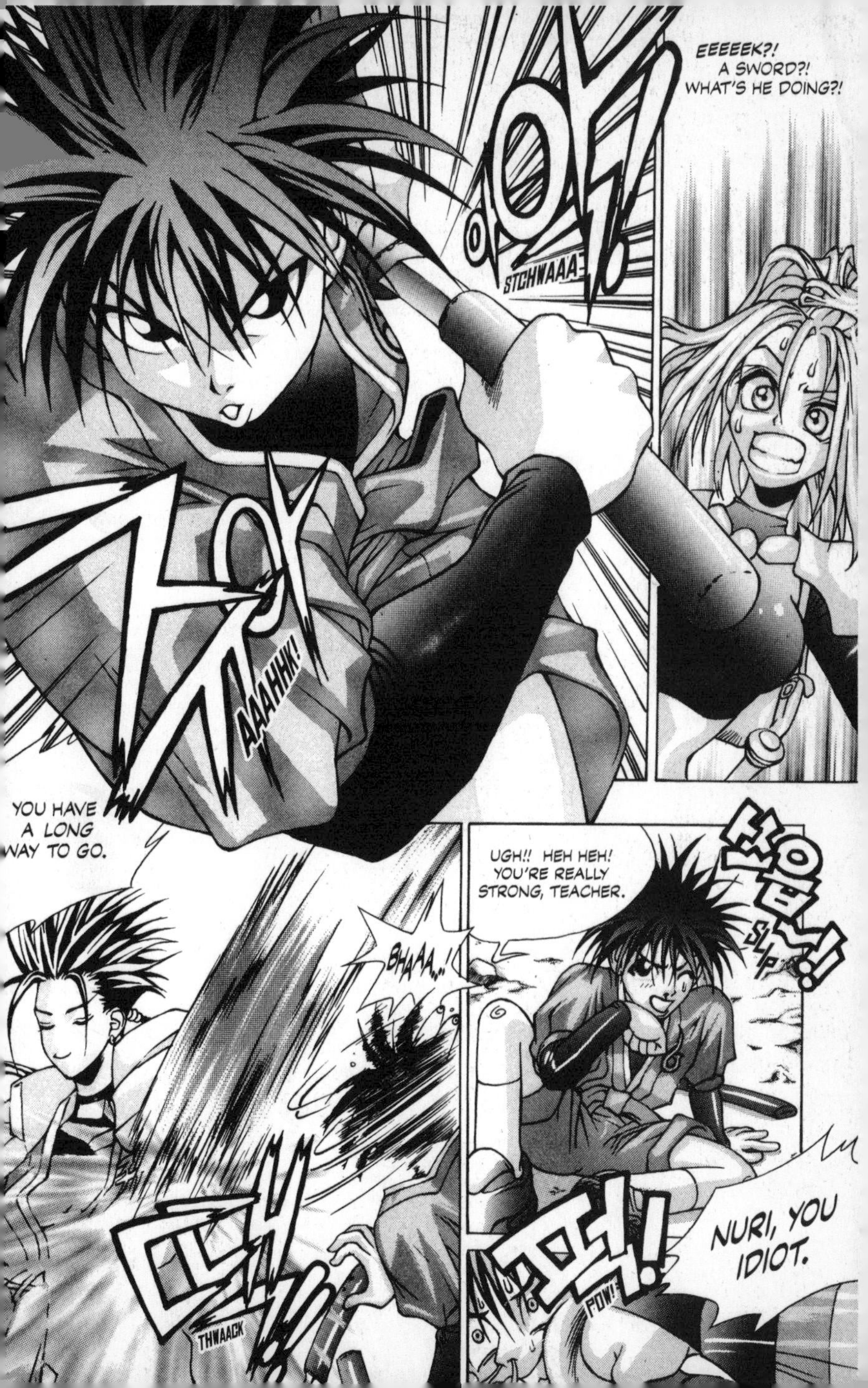
STCHWAAA!
AAAHHK!
EEEEEK?! A SWORD?! WHAT'S HE DOING?!
YOU HAVE A LONG WAY TO GO.
BHAAA..!
THWAACK
UGH!! HEH HEH! YOU'RE REALLY STRONG, TEACHER.
SLIP
POW!
NURI, YOU IDIOT.

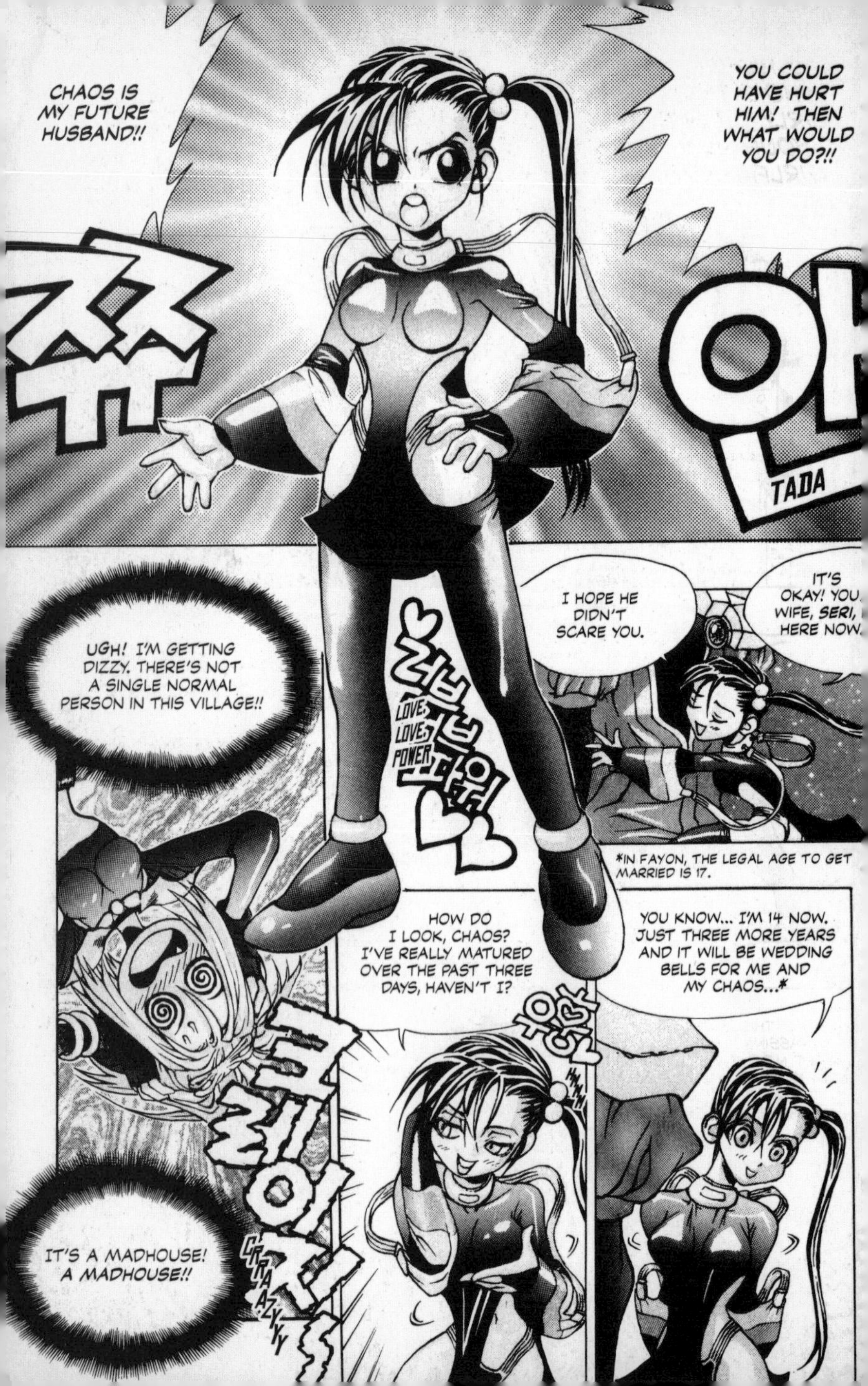
CHAOS IS MY FUTURE HUSBAND!!
YOU COULD HAVE HURT HIM! THEN WHAT WOULD YOU DO?!!
TADA
UGH! I'M GETTING DIZZY. THERE'S NOT A SINGLE NORMAL PERSON IN THIS VILLAGE!!
IT'S A MADHOUSE! A MADHOUSE!!
CRRAAZYYY
LOVE, LOVE, POWER
I HOPE HE DIDN'T SCARE YOU.
IT'S OKAY! YOU. WIFE, SERI, HERE NOW.
*IN FAYON, THE LEGAL AGE TO GET MARRIED IS 17.
HOW DO I LOOK, CHAOS? I'VE REALLY MATURED OVER THE PAST THREE DAYS, HAVEN'T I?
YOU KNOW... I'M 14 NOW. JUST THREE MORE YEARS AND IT WILL BE WEDDING BELLS FOR ME AND MY CHAOS...*

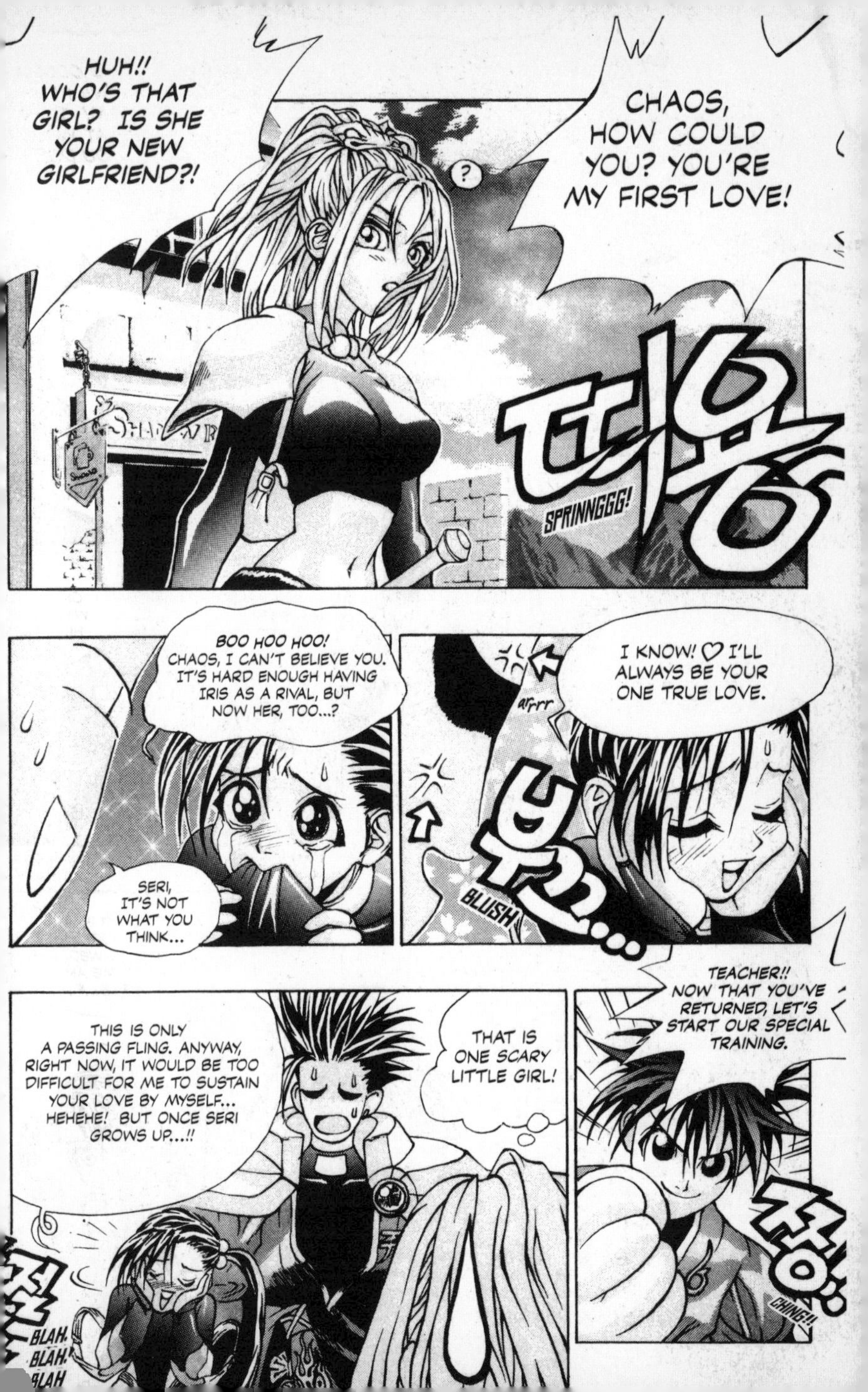
HUH!! WHO'S THAT GIRL? IS SHE YOUR NEW GIRLFRIEND?!
?
CHAOS, HOW COULD YOU? YOU'RE MY FIRST LOVE!
SPRINNGGG!
BOO HOO HOO! CHAOS, I CAN'T BELIEVE YOU. IT'S HARD ENOUGH HAVING IRIS AS A RIVAL, BUT NOW HER, TOO...?
SERI, IT'S NOT WHAT YOU THINK...
I KNOW! ♡ I'LL ALWAYS BE YOUR ONE TRUE LOVE.
arrrr
BLUSH
THIS IS ONLY A PASSING FLING. ANYWAY, RIGHT NOW, IT WOULD BE TOO DIFFICULT FOR ME TO SUSTAIN YOUR LOVE BY MYSELF... HEHEHE! BUT ONCE SERI GROWS UP...!!
THAT IS ONE SCARY LITTLE GIRL!
BLAH. BLAH. BLAH
TEACHER!! NOW THAT YOU'VE RETURNED, LET'S START OUR SPECIAL TRAINING.
CHING!!

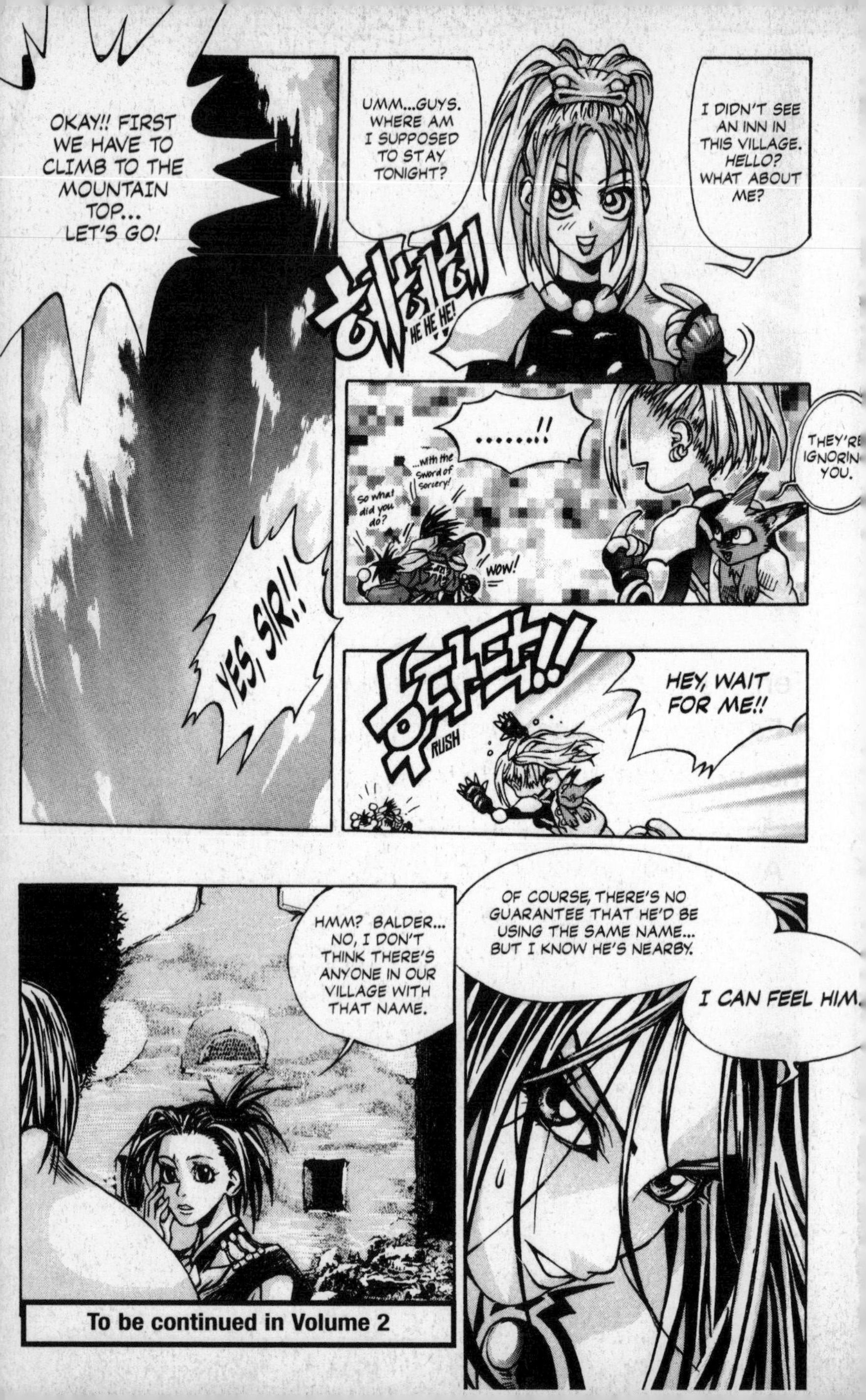

OKAY!! FIRST WE HAVE TO CLIMB TO THE MOUNTAIN TOP... LET'S GO!
YES, SIR!!
UMM...GUYS. WHERE AM I SUPPOSED TO STAY TONIGHT?
히히히
HE HE HE!
I DIDN'T SEE AN INN IN THIS VILLAGE. HELLO? WHAT ABOUT ME?
So what did you do?
...with the Sword of Sorcery!
WOW!
.......!!
THEY'RE IGNORING YOU.
후다닥!!
RUSH
HEY, WAIT FOR ME!!
HMM? BALDER... NO, I DON'T THINK THERE'S ANYONE IN OUR VILLAGE WITH THAT NAME.
To be continued in Volume 2
OF COURSE, THERE'S NO GUARANTEE THAT HE'D BE USING THE SAME NAME... BUT I KNOW HE'S NEARBY.
I CAN FEEL HIM.

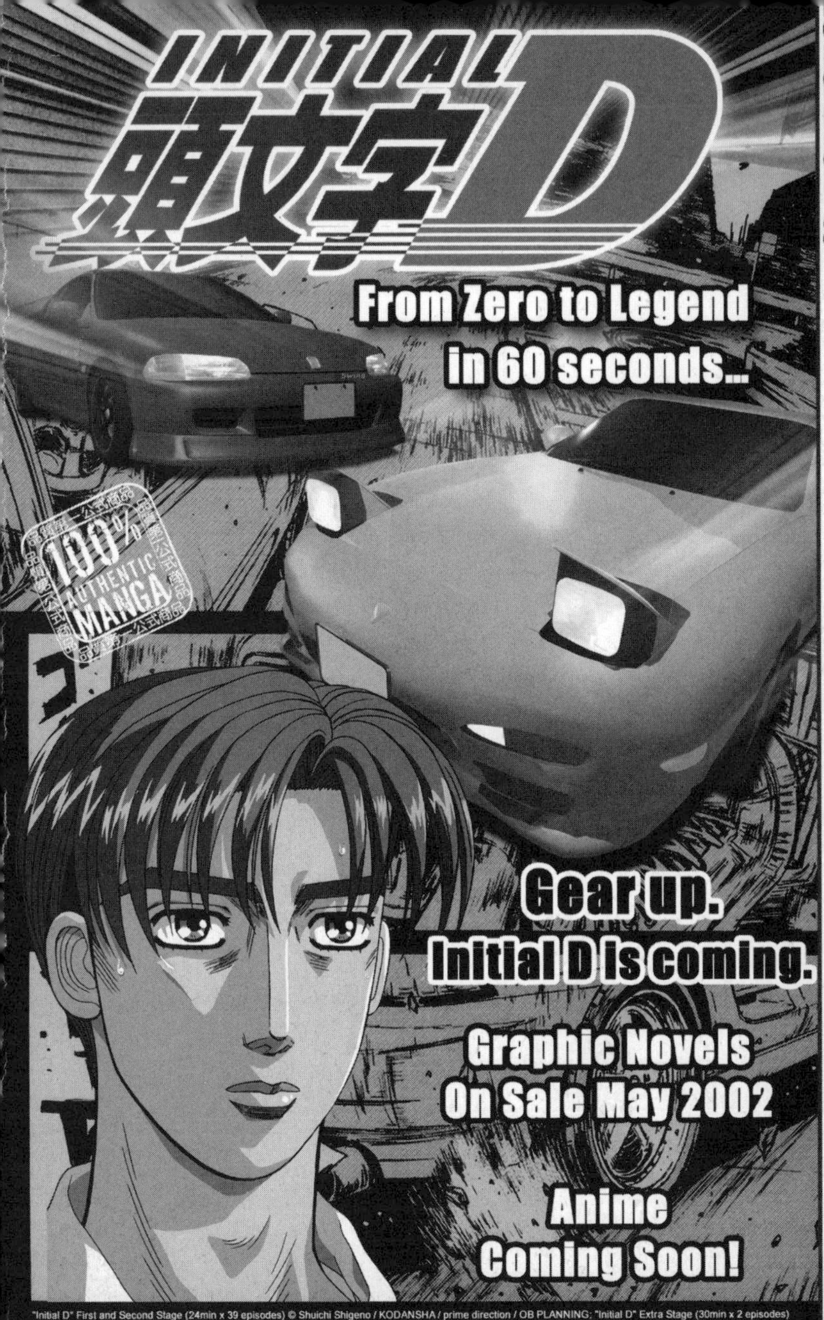
INITIAL
頭文字D
From Zero to Legend
in 60 seconds...
100% AUTHENTIC MANGA
Gear up.
Initial D is coming.
Graphic Novels
On Sale May 2002
Anime
Coming Soon!

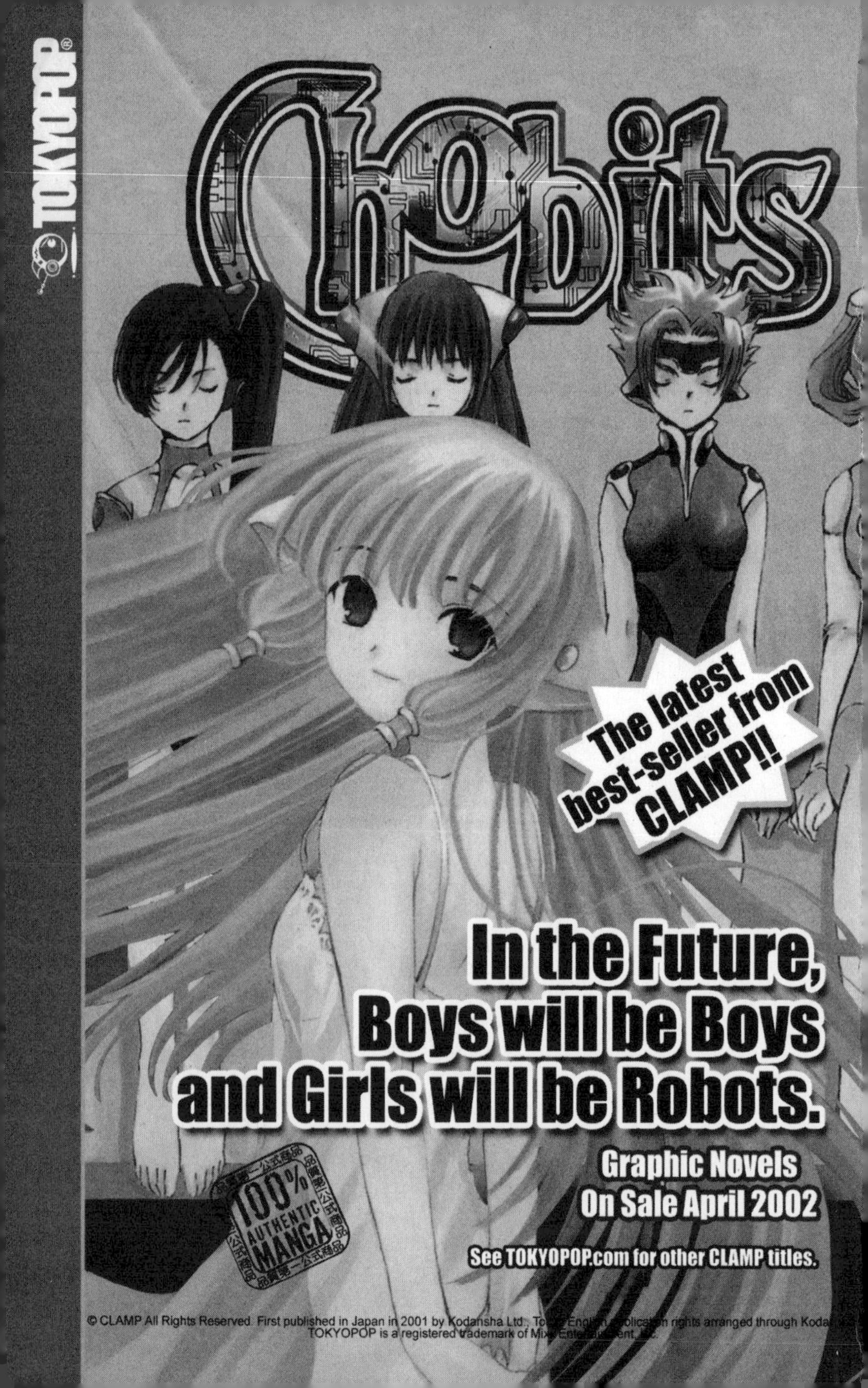
TOKYOPOP
Chobits
The latest best-seller from CLAMP!!
In the Future, Boys will be Boys and Girls will be Robots.
Graphic Novels On Sale April 2002
100% AUTHENTIC MANGA
See TOKYOPOP.com for other CLAMP titles.
© CLAMP All Rights Reserved. First published in Japan in 2001 by Kodansha Ltd.,
TOKYOPOP is a registered trademark of